2/1/23

Muslim Religious Authority in Central Eurasia

Brill's Inner Asian Library

Edited by

Michael R. Drompp
Devin DeWeese
Mark C. Elliott

VOLUME 43

The titles published in this series are listed at *brill.com/bial*

Muslim Religious Authority in Central Eurasia

Edited by

Ron Sela
Paolo Sartori
Devin DeWeese

BRILL

LEIDEN | BOSTON

Cover illustration: Grave marker in the cemetery at the shrine complex of Shopan Ata, Mangghïstau oblïsï, western Kazakhstan (2010, Devin DeWeese)

Library of Congress Cataloging-in-Publication Data

Names: Sela, Ron, editor. | Sartori, Paolo, 1975- editor. | DeWeese, Devin A., 1956- editor.
Title: Muslim religious authority in Central Eurasia / edited by Ron Sela, Paolo Sartori, Devin DeWeese.
Description: Leiden ; Boston : Brill, 2023. | Series: Brill's Inner Asian library, 1566-7162 ; vol. 43 | Includes index.
Identifiers: LCCN 2022044610 (print) | LCCN 2022044611 (ebook) | ISBN 9789004510111 (hardback) | ISBN 9789004527096 (ebook)
Subjects: LCSH: Islam—Asia, Central—History. | Authority—Religious aspects—Islam.
Classification: LCC BP63.A34 M837 2023 (print) | LCC BP63.A34 (ebook) | DDC 297.0958—dc23/ENG/20220928
LC record available at https://lccn.loc.gov/2022044610
LC ebook record available at https://lccn.loc.gov/2022044611

Typeface for the Latin, Greek, and Cyrillic scripts: "Brill". See and download: brill.com/brill-typeface.

ISSN 1566-7162
ISBN 978-90-04-51011-1 (hardback)
ISBN 978-90-04-52709-6 (e-book)

This book is printed on acid-free paper and produced in a sustainable manner.

Contents

PART 3
Authority Embodied: Lives and Histories of Holy Persons and Lineages

PART 4
Authority Mobilized: Religious Institutions and Frameworks for Contestation

Acknowledgments

This volume is the product of an international workshop on authority in Islam in Muslim Eurasia, convened at Indiana University Bloomington in March 2017. The workshop constituted a part of the Indiana University's Islamic Studies Program's initiative on the 'Fragmentation of Religious Authority in Islam,' an initiative that closely examines one of the most fiercely contested phenomena among Muslims in both Muslim-minority and Muslim-majority societies. Additional international workshops on this theme, with a regional focus on South Asia and Sub-Saharan Africa, were since convened at Indiana University's India Gateway Office in New Delhi in January, 2019, and the university's Gateway Office in Berlin in October, 2019.

The 2017 Bloomington workshop benefitted from the participation of many scholars. We wish to thank the presenters and discussants whose contributions and remarks were not included in this volume but whose input is very much reflected in its contents. They include: Ulan Bigozhin, Noor Borbieva, Alfrid Bustanov, Ian Campbell, Jamal J. Elias, Seema Golestaneh, Marianne Kamp, Paul Losensky, Patrick Michelson, Leone Musgrave, James Pickett, Nazif Shahrani, Gulnaz Sibgatullina, and Jennifer Webster. We are especially grateful to Robert Crouch, Assistant Director of Indiana University's Islamic Studies Program, for his invaluable organizational, logistical, and editorial skills.

We wish to acknowledge the financial support of multiple agencies and institutions. At Indiana University, the project received grants from the university's New Frontiers in the Arts and Humanities Program, the College of Arts and Humanities Institute, the Office of the Vice President for International Affairs, the Inner Asian and Uralic National Resource Center, the Russian and East European Institute, the Hamilton Lugar School of Global and International Studies, and the Institute for European Studies. We also wish to acknowledge our valued partnership with the Austrian Science Fund (FWF) START Program Y704 – Seeing Like an Archive that assisted in bringing several scholars from Europe and Russia to Bloomington.

Figures

Notes on Contributors

Sergey Abashin
is Professor of Anthropology at the European University at Saint-Petersburg (Russia). His main research topics include imperial and Soviet transformations in Central Asia, and post-Soviet migrations. He has published two monographs (in Russian): *Nationalisms in Central Asia: in search of identity* (St. Petersburg: Aleteiia, 2007), and *Soviet kishlak: between colonialism and modernization* (Moscow: NLO, 2015), as well as articles about Central Asian Islamic studies: "The Logic of Islamic Practice: A Religious Conflict in Central Asia," *Central Asian Survey*, 25/3 (2006), pp. 267–286; "A Prayer for Rain: Practicing being Soviet and Muslim," *Journal of Islamic Studies*, 25/2 (2014), pp. 178–200.

Ulfat (Ulfatbek) Abdurasulov
(Ph.D. 2009, History Institute, Tashkent) is a Research Fellow at the Austrian Academy of Sciences. His research focuses on the history of Islamic Central Asia, the history of the Russian protectorates in Central Asia, early modern diplomatic history, as well as the history of early modern record-keeping and knowledge production in Central Eurasia. Dr. Abdurasulov's publications appeared in academic journals, such as *Der Islam*, *Ab Imperio*, *Islamic Law and Society*, *Itinerario*, and *JESHO*. Together with Paolo Sartori, he co-authored the monograph *Seeking Justice at the Court of the Khans of Khiva (19th–Early 20th Centuries)* (Leiden: Brill, 2020).

Bakhtiyar Babajanov
is Senior Researcher at the Institute of Oriental Studies of the Uzbek Academy of Sciences, Tashkent. He is the author of *Kokandskoe Khanstvo: politika, vlast', religiia* (Kyoto-Tashkent, 2010) and *Epigrafika v arkhitekturnom landshafte Khivy: Mechety, pogrebal'nye kompleksy, medrese, dvortsy, vorota* (Vienna: Austrian Academy of Sciences, 2020).

Devin DeWeese
is Professor Emeritus of Central Eurasian Studies at Indiana University. His research has focused on issues of Islamization in Central and Inner Asia, the social and political roles of Sufi communities, and Sufi literature and hagiography in Persian and Chaghatay Turkic. He is the author of *Islamization and Native Religion in the Golden Horde* (1994) and (with Ashirbek Muminov) of *Islamization and Sacred Lineages in Central Asia*, vol. I: *Opening the Way for Islam: The Ishaq Bab Narrative, 14th–19th Centuries* (2013). His most recent article

is "Encountering Saints in the Hallowed Ground of a Regional Landscape: The 'Description of Khwārazm' and the Experience of Pilgrimage in 19th-Century Central Asia," in *Saintly Spheres and Islamic Landscapes*, ed. Daphna Ephrat, Ethel Sara Wolper, and Paulo G. Pinto (Leiden, 2021).

Allen Frank
is an independent scholar in Takoma Park Maryland, USA. His focus of interest is the Islamic history of Russia and Central Asia. His recent publications include *Kazakh Muslims in the Red Army, 1939–1945* (Leiden: Brill, 2022), *Gulag Miracles: Sufis and Stalinist Repression in Kazakhstan* (Vienna: Austrian Academy of Sciences, 2019), Saduaqas Ghïlmani, *Biographies of the Islamic Scholars of Our Times* I–II, (Istanbul: IRCICA, 2018) (co-editor with Ashirbek Muminov and Aytzhan Nurmanova).

Benjamin Gatling
is Associate Professor in the English Department and Director of the Folklore Program at George Mason University. His research interests include oral narrative, performance, the ethnography of communication, and Persianate oral traditions. He is the author of *Expressions of Sufi Culture in Tajikistan* (University of Wisconsin Press, 2018).

Agnès Kefeli
is Clinical Full Professor of Religious Studies at Arizona State University and the author of *Becoming Muslim in Imperial Russia*, which received the 2015 Reginald Zelnik Book Prize of the Association for Slavic, East European, and Eurasian Studies. She is especially interested in conversion, popular contestation of official identities, production of religious knowledge, collective memory, and women's activities in the religious sphere, in the past as well as in the present. Her work draws on fieldwork observations, Russian-language archival documents, and Turkic literature, which has played and still plays an important role in the Islamization and re-Islamization of Eurasia and Central Asia. To support her current research on various forms of Tatar enchantment in Soviet and Post-Soviet Eurasia, she was awarded a National Humanities Center Fellowship (Benjamin N. Duke Fellowship of the Research Triangle Foundation) and several summer fellowships from the Slavic and Eastern European Center of the University of Illinois in Urbana Champaign. Her latest articles include: "Noah's Ark Landed in the Ural Mountains: Ethnic and Ecological Apocalypse in Tatarstan," published by *Russian Review*, and "Varieties of Tatar Esotericism in Post-Soviet Russia," which will be published by the same journal.

Paolo Sartori
is Senior Research Associate at the Austrian Academy of Sciences, where he also serves as the Chairman of the Committee for the Study of Islam in Central Eurasia (1552–2000s). He has two main fields of interest in his current research: the social and intellectual history of Muslim communities living under Tsarist and Soviet rule; and practices of record-keeping and knowledge production in the Muslim world in the early modern and modern period. He is the author of *Visions of Justice: Sharia and Cultural Change in Russian Central Asia* (Leiden: Brill, 2016), *Eksperimenty imperii: Adat, shariat i proizvodstvo znanii v Kazakhskoi stepi* (Moscow: NLO 2019), with Pavel Shabley, and *Seeking Justice at the Court of the Khans of Khiva (19th–Early 20th Centuries)* (Leiden: Brill 2020), with Ulfat Abdurasulov. He also serves as the Editor-in-Chief of the *Journal of the Economic and Social History of the Orient* and the *Journal of Central Asian History* (Brill).

Wendell Schwab
is an academic adviser in the Bellasario College of Communications at the Pennsylvania State University. He writes about Islam, media, and nationalism in Kazakhstan. His publications have appeared in *Central Asian Affairs*, *Central Asian Survey*, and *Contemporary Islam*.

Ron Sela
is Associate Professor of Central Asian history in the Department of Central Eurasian Studies at Indiana University Bloomington, where he also serves as Director of the Sinor Research Institute for Inner Asian Studies. He has been studying Central Asian history and historiography, and self-representation in Muslim literary traditions. Sela is the author of *The Legendary Biographies of Tamerlane: Islam and Heroic Apocrypha in Central Asia* (Cambridge University Press, 2011).

Pavel Shabley
is Associate Professor at the Kostanay branch of Chelyabinsk State University, Kazakhstan. His major research interest is the history of Islam in the Kazakh Steppe and the study of the Orenburg Mohammedan Spiritual Assembly. His recent publications include "Semia Iaushevikh i ee okruzhenie," *Acta Slavica Iaponica*, 38 (2017), pp. 23–50; with Paolo Sartori, *Eksperimenty imperii: Adat, shariat i proizvodstvo znanii v Kazakhskoi stepi* (Moscow: NLO, 2019).

Shamil Shikhaliev

Ph.D. in History, is Senior Research Fellow at the Institute of Oriental Studies, Moscow, and Research Fellow at the University of Amsterdam. He specializes in Sufism, Islamic law, networks of Islamic education and Islamic written culture in Russia. He is co-author of *The History of the Life and Work of Ali Kayayev and Sayfulla-kadi Bashlarov: Documents and Materials* (with Amir R. Navruzov, in Russian); *Fiqh and Muslim Customary Law in Russian Daghestan: Sources and Studies* (with Vladimir O. Bobrovnikov and Magomed G. Shekhmagomedov, in Russian); "Downward Mobility and Spiritual Life: The Development of Sufism in the Context of Migrations in Daghestan, 1940s–2000s," in *Migration, De-Stalinisation, Privatisation and the New Muslim Congregations in the Soviet Realm (1950s–2000s)*, eds. Stephane A. Dudoignon and Christian Noack (Klaus Schwarz Verlag: Berlin, 2014); "Muslim Reformism in Daghestan (1900–1930)," *Gosudarstvo, religiia, tserkov' v Rossii i za rubezhom* 35/3 (2017).

William A. Wood

(Ph.D. 1999, Indiana University) is Professor of Islamic and Russian History at Point Loma Nazarene University in San Diego, California. His doctoral dissertation explored the relationship of the Sariq Turkmens of Merv with the Khanate of Khiva in the early nineteenth century. His publications include *A Collection of Tarkhan Yarlïqs from the Khanate of Khiva* (Indiana University, 2005), and the entry on "Khorezm and the Khanate of Khiva" in the *Oxford Research Encyclopedia of Asian History* (Oxford University Press, 2019). His current research involves the activity of British missionaries in Central and South Asia in the 19th and early 20th centuries.

Introduction

Ron Sela, Paolo Sartori, and Devin DeWeese

Religious authority – namely, the recognized capacity of an individual or a group or an institution to sanction the undertaking of religious acts, both private and public – affects many Muslims (and non-Muslims) in their everyday lives as well as in exceptional circumstances.[1] Whether derived from culturally accepted traditions, from legal and bureaucratic norms, from charismatic or successful individuals, or from unique personal or communal experiences, religious authority has an enormous impact on the behavior of Muslims everywhere.[2] Whether invested in centralized institutions or in diffuse and highly localized phenomena, religious authority may be understood as an arena of contestation that inevitably overlaps with issues of broad political and social consequence, but reaches into intimate personal spaces as well, and the many spheres of human experience in which religious authority may be activated are matched by a diversity of ways of asserting it and appealing to it. Whether concentrated in a few centers of authority or highly decentralized, or even seemingly fragmented, religious authority serves as a paradigmatic lens through which to examine the full range of religious activity among Muslims, past and present.

Recently, there seems to be a general perception of a growing fragmentation and decentralization of religious authority in the Muslim world. No particular locale or community appears to be unaffected by the phenomenon. Internet sites, videos, "social" media, TV programs, ad-hoc establishments, itinerant carriers of religious messages, everyone and anyone now seems to be able to cast himself or herself as an authority-wielding Muslim. While a longer arc of decentralization might be traced for authority in the Muslim world, developments in the last two centuries seem, to some, to have hastened the process considerably.

---

1 We are, of course, conscious that "authority" should not be conceptualized solely in terms of power relations and should be understood also "in contradistinction to both coercion by force and persuasion through arguments;" see Hannah Arendt, "What is Authority?" in *Between Past and Future* (New York: Viking Press, 1961), p. 93.

2 To understand more fully what we mean by 'authority' in Islam, consult Devin DeWeese, "Authority," in *Key Themes for the Study of Islam*, ed. Jamal J. Elias (Oxford: Oneworld, 2010), 26–52. For an excellent, but very different understanding of religious authority in Islam see Asma Afsaruddin's entry in the *Encyclopaedia of Islam*, 3rd edition (ed. K. Fleet, G. Krämer, D. Matringe, J. Nawas, and E. Rowson): "Authority, religious."

 | DOI:10.1163/9789004527096_002

In this context, it seems that the "crisis" of the scholars of Islam (*ʿulamāʾ*) has been given the most attention, particularly when the state constrains the scope of their functions and controls their juridical output. Intensifying appeals from the scholars, judges, imams, and leaders of official religious boards and organizations who are widely regarded as the guardians, transmitters and interpreters of religious knowledge, doctrine, and law to regulate Islam (and, in essence, to reclaim their increasingly diminishing power) seem to fall on deaf ears. The *ʿulamā*'s anxiety over the fragmentation of religious authority is particularly noticeable in their characterization of the trend in terms of *fawḍā* – namely, chaos or anarchy.[3]

Attempts to counter this phenomenon have been many, and the reaction by *ʿulamāʾ* all over the world to – what amounts to, practically – the defiance of their authority serves to exemplify how potent this issue has become.[4] The so-called 2005 Amman Message (*Risālat Ammān*), for example, was a reaction to widespread "disobedience" concerning Muslim identity and the treatment of non-Muslims. One of the main issues of concern was the lack of control over who could issue legal opinions (*fatwā*s) and what such opinions should entail.[5] Calls to regulate *fatwā*s have been growing in conjunction with what mainstream officials consider *al-fatāwa al-shādhdha* (*shādhdha* ranges in meaning from isolated, uncommon, irregular or odd to even deviant or abnormal).[6]

At the heart of this current debate stands what some scholars have termed a 'Crisis of Authority,' stemming from Muslims' reactions to constructions of 'modernity' and to the West, to the advent of new modes of knowledge transmission, including vernacularism, print culture, new media, and new and more immediate opportunities and challenges, in a process that has been going on for approximately two centuries.[7] Other scholars have stressed processes of

---

3 See in this regard, Michael Slackman's June 11, 2007, article in the *New York Times*: "A fatwa free-for-all in the Islamic world."

4 See interviews and sermons by Mehmet Görmez, head of Turkey's Presidency of Religious Affairs (*Diyanet İşleri Başkanlığı*); Ahmed el-Tayeb, Grand Imam of al-Azhar in Cairo; Muhammad Taqi Usmani, mufti and shikhul Islam of Pakistan and Chairman of the International Shariah Standard Council in Bahrain; Kyai al-Hajj Ali Musthafa Ya'qub, grand imam of the Istiqal mosque in Jakarta; Syed Ahmed Bukhari, Shahi Imam of the Jama Masjid in Delhi, among others.

5 Meetings along the Amman model continue until today, for example, in the gatherings of the Islamic Fiqh Academy (IFA), boasting a membership from 40 countries, from Brunei to Burkina Faso.

6 This was also the title of an influential 2010 book by the noted Egyptian theologian Yusuf al-Qaradawi.

7 See, for example, Francis Robinson, "Crisis of Authority: Crisis of Islam?," *Journal of the Royal Asiatic Society*, Series 3, 19/3 (2009), pp. 339–54.

secularization, through the same period, as generating the perceived fragmentation (and loss) of authority among the *ʿulamāʾ*. These assessments, however, offer only a partial view of the causes of the perceived fragmentation of authority in Islam. Indeed, the very notion of "fragmentation" in contemporary Islam originates from a discourse that takes states' monopolies over the definition and exercise of religious authority as a given. It also posits the multiplicity, plurality, and diversity of religious authority as manifestations of (potential) opposition to the state. However, the pluralism of religious authority was not just a reaction to modernizing trends and authoritarian states, for the diversity of religious authority predates, in fact, modernizing currents. Indeed, religious authority, as experienced by many, if not most Muslim practitioners, rests only *partially* in the hands of state officials, and the reach of 'modernity' has been far from uniform. As for secularization, the supposed "fragmentation" that has sapped the authority of the *ʿulamāʾ* has been due as much to avowedly religious programs of claiming or seeking authority as to the forces of irreligion, however much those religious programs have themselves been affected by developments ascribed to modernity or secularism. Moreover, we would emphasize that Muslims tend to view authority in flexible terms, and as extending beyond the legal sphere – e.g., a dream, an omen, advice from a teacher or a respected member of the family, a blessing bestowed during a visit to a sacred tomb, etc. It is therefore our conviction that historicizing the manifestations and the many embodiments of religious authority should yield a better framework for understanding its significance in Islam, its developments, and its trajectories.

The aim of the present volume, indeed, is not to contribute to any particular definition of "authority," or to insist on any directionality in the historical development of religious authority. Rather than any theoretical intervention, our aim is to contribute to *historicizing* the question of religious authority, by beginning to stack up historical case studies about the exercise, negotiation, or institutionalization of authority, and to do so for a part of the Muslim world – the post-Soviet space of Central Eurasia – that so far has been largely left out of scholarly explorations into issues of religious authority.[8]

8 The literature on Islam in the Soviet and post-Soviet space has paid little attention to issues of religious authority. Not surprisingly, Mark Saroyan was ahead of his time in terms of a thoughtful approach to the subject; see his "Authority and Community in Soviet Islam," in *Accounting for Fundamentalisms: The Dynamic Character of Movements*, ed. Martin E. Marty and R. Scott Appleby (Chicago: University of Chicago Press, 1994; *The Fundamentalism Project*, Vol. 4), 513–530. More recently, relevant issues are explored in the contributions to *Islamic Authority and the Russian Language: Studies on Texts from European Russia, the North Caucasus, and West Siberia*, ed. Alfrid K. Bustanov and Michael Kemper (Amsterdam:

In seeking to address religious authority as a chiefly practical rather than theoretical problem, we are acknowledging that "authority" itself is for the most part alien to the internal discourse of many religious traditions; the sources themselves typically consider "authority" only tangentially, whether through a simple, tacit assumption that a certain individual or institution possesses authority, or through the attachment of some sort of 'insignia' or pedigree of authority that remains outside the issue at hand. As for addressing the question of Muslim religious authority in Central Eurasia, in addition to filling a gap in scholarly discourse on religious authority, by adding Central Eurasian perspectives on and contexts for questions of religious authority, we also seek to address an additional sort of blank space, in still-prevailing perspectives on Islam in that region. After the fall of the USSR, that is, it was often assumed – by many Muslims in the region, by most 'students' of or propagandists against Islam in the region, and by most of those in the West who took an interest in the Muslims of the USSR – that Muslim religious authority necessarily lay *outside* the Soviet and newly post-Soviet space. Most observers, and many of the observed, were led, by familiar but simplistic narratives about Islam, to look beyond Soviet borders for *real* Muslim religious authority, the sources of which were presumed to lie in the Middle East, in the Arab world, in the places where Islam began – *not* in the far-flung places to which it spread, and in which it was often presumed to have been adulterated or vitiated by local contaminants or influences. The religion of Islam might be encountered, in some more or less attenuated form, according to this narrative, in China, or India, or Africa, but one would not look for the religious *authority* of Islam in those places, and one would certainly not look for an authoritative engagement with Islam in a region where governmental and societal forces had been arrayed *against* Islam for several generations.

That narrative, of course, is misleading, biased, and profoundly flawed, and the best way to build an effective counternarrative is by appealing to historical experience. To begin with, the narrative is premised on a Sovietological approach to Islam – an approach, that is, predicated upon the assumption that Soviet atheism and its attendant policies of forced secularization triumphed over Muslim-ness, thereby impoverishing the Islamic sphere of Central Eurasia by constraining its sources of authority. Not only is this narrative empirically

---

Uitgeverij Pegasus, 2012). A recent volume framed more broadly – *L'autorité religieuse et ses limites en terres d'islam: Approches historiques et anthropologiques*, ed. Nathalie Clayer, Alexandre Papas, and Benoît Fliche (Leiden: Brill, 2013) – includes one paper on Central Asia (focused on the 16th century), and none on other parts of what would become the Soviet space. Central Eurasia is entirely unrepresented in *Speaking for Islam: Religious Authorities in Muslim Societies*, ed. Gudrun Krämer and Sabine Schmidtke (Leiden: Brill, 2006).

unsubstantiated, but, with a remarkably ironic twist, it also tends to take at face value what was produced by Soviet sociologists of religion and propagandists alike. At the same time, the narrative is, after all, at heart a deeply 'fundamentalist' narrative, in insisting that religious authority remains rooted in its place of origin, in its foundational scriptural sources, and in its 'original' sacred language and its historical or contemporary speakers; and just as fundamentalist narratives in many religious contexts seek to ignore or deny the historical lived experience of religion in favor of 'returning' to an original core, this narrative ignores the long history of Muslims re-rooting Islam in their own regions and in their own writings and in their own languages.

For the region focused on here, the post-Soviet space of Central Eurasia, the narrative is also misleading in ignoring the growing body of studies showing how Muslim religious practice not only survived throughout Soviet rule, but often thrived, in its own way. Muslims adapted, dynamically, to shifts in Soviet policy and in public mores, developing new and sometimes distinctive permutations of the negotiations of religion and power between their communities and their representatives, on the one hand, and the state structures and practices that exercised control over those communities, on the other (whether those state structures and practices had any roots in Muslim tradition or not). We can now understand, 30 years after the fall of Soviet power, that the experience of Muslims in the USSR in some ways continued patterns of adaptation and negotiation known from Muslim history in the lands that became the USSR, and known from Muslim history elsewhere as well; we can also now understand that the long history of Muslims locating religious authority locally in the various regions that came under Soviet rule in fact continued through the Soviet era into post-Soviet times. Since, in any case, Muslims in the post-Soviet world have themselves been groping toward a new understanding of the parameters of their engagement with religious authority (however much it may be encoded in terms of returning to or restoring a past), it is time to add the voices of Soviet Muslims, and their predecessors and successors, to broader inquiries about religious authority in the Muslim world. The present volume thus seeks not only to acknowledge the history and ongoing reality of negotiating Muslim religious authority within the former Soviet space before, during, and after the seven decades of Soviet rule, but to offer specific case studies of those negotiations.

The question of religious authority offers a particularly useful vantage point from which to 'introduce' Central Eurasian Muslim voices to the wider field of Islamic studies, in part because of the distinctive juncture at which that region finds itself in the aftermath of the Soviet collapse, but also because of the problematic legacy of scholarship on the region. What has been termed the "Sovietological" literature on Islam in the USSR offered a host of tropes and rubrics for framing the subject, along with multiple sets of shopworn dichotomies for analyzing it (Islam vs. Soviet, Islam vs. nationality, official vs. unofficial Islam, conservative vs. progressive Islam, etc.). Such literature staked out a series of tendentious and counterproductive stances that hampered real understanding, insisting that the Soviet and post-Soviet space is sui generis, or asking only about "policy" toward Muslim religiosity (forgetting that even the best-laid policies generate both evasion and unforeseen consequences), or assuming that Muslim experience in this space is best understood as some sort of "encounter" between an abstracted and rarified "Islam" and the chimera of "modernity." Those features can still be found in scholarship, but have been critiqued and duly left behind in the present volume, with confidence that framing our questions in terms of Muslim religious authority in this context will yield answers that are not only more illuminating, but are also more relevant to the specific regions under consideration, and more firmly rooted in broader historical patterns that are visible with an expanded perspective.

The latter point is worth emphasizing here, insofar as the volume is also premised on the assumption that examples of negotiating or debating religious authority drawn from a given historical period may be revealing and instructive beyond the confines of that period, and indeed that overly-concretized historical periodization is more often the enemy than the friend of historical understanding. We reject, that is, the notion that historical examples drawn from early 19th-century Central Asia, for instance, are irrelevant to an understanding of developments and processes during the Tsarist, Soviet, and post-Soviet periods, simply because of a postulated rupture in historical continuity occasioned by the Russian conquest, or by the October Revolution. The question of religious authority must necessarily be addressed as the product of historically-specific developmental processes affecting Muslims in Central Eurasia, processes that feature both recognizable continuities and distinct ruptures over time.[9] The continuities and ruptures, in turn, that yield the

9 Aspects of ruptures and continuities in Muslim culture during the Soviet period have been variously discussed in Paolo Sartori, "Of Saints, Shrines, and Tractors: Untangling the Meaning of Islam in Soviet Central Asia," *Journal of Islamic Studies*, 30 (2019), pp. 367–405; Paolo Sartori and Bakhtiyar Babajanov, "Being Soviet, Muslim, Modernist and Fundamentalist in 1950s Central Asia," *Journal of the Economic and Social History of the Orient*, 62/1 (2019), pp. 108–165; James Pickett and Matthew Melvin-Koushki, "Mobilizing Magic: Occultism in Central Asia and the Continuity of High Persianate Culture under Russian Rule," *Studia Islamica*, 111/2 (2016), pp. 231–284; James Pickett, *Polymaths of Islam: Power and Networks of Knowledge in Central Asia* (Ithaca and London, Cornell University Press, 2020), pp. 248–256; Eren Tasar, "Institutions: A Lens on Soviet Islam" [Book Discussion on *Soviet and Muslim: The Institutionalization of Islam in Central Asia* by Eren Tasar], *Central Asian Affairs*, 7 (2020), pp. 370–375.

particular configurations of religious authority in a given time and place in the region – setting the stage, of course, for the observance and acceptance of a given configuration of authority, but also for its contestation – have been shaped by the interaction of Muslim and non-Muslim frameworks for knowing and acting in religious terms with Muslim and non-Muslim patterns of governance and social administration.

Both the Soviet and Tsarist regimes, for instance – without here taking stock of further shifts in policy and practice within both these eras, or of the longer perspective that might include Chinggisid regimes among both the non-Muslim and Muslim governing systems that affected Muslim religiosity in Central Eurasia – acted upon their Muslim subjects, who 'acted back' upon their regimes, sometimes actively embracing governmental initiatives or finding in them a way out of onerous social strictures imposed by Muslim-ness, sometimes allowing, consciously or not, their frameworks of Muslim religious knowledge and action to be shaped by the practice and rhetoric of governmental institutions, sometimes resisting or evading governmental practice and rhetoric, sometimes compartmentalizing their responses, in thought and action, based on a myriad of personal, familial, regional, or 'national' considerations that nonetheless resulted in 'religious' calculations, and sometimes exhibiting a feigned or very real obliviousness to the very idea that their Muslim way of life might somehow be at odds with their government's policies and practices.[10] The constantly rewoven fabric of religiosity in Muslim Central Eurasia thus reveals differential appropriations from the Tsarist and Soviet dispensations, turning certain formerly alien perspectives into wholly 'indigenized' outlooks, and turning some formerly commonplace Muslim frameworks of knowledge into seemingly alien and archaic, or merely arcane, semantic fields that have lost meaning for many; the *differential* character of such appropriations, however, ensures that very little is entirely lost or left behind from the stock of societal resources that can be drawn upon in facing the next challenge to religious meaning and belonging.

But in this regard, too, it is important to note that presumed demarcations of historical patterns are often misleading. The Central Asian khanates that were conquered by Tsarist Russia in the 19th century were not secular states, much less atheistic, but they nevertheless claimed a monopoly on authority, in the person of the *khān* or *amīr*; the claim of such rulers, and the state apparatus they led, to wield power, and authority, over religious classes of various sorts, whether jurists or Sufis, was not uncontested, but posed challenges to

10 For the Tsarist context, see Paolo Sartori, *Visions of Justice: Sharīʿa and Cultural Change in Russian Central Asia* (Leiden: Brill, 2016); for the Soviet era, see Jeff Eden, *God Save the USSR: Soviet Muslims and the Second World War* (Oxford: Oxford University Press, 2021).

religious life not entirely unlike the challenges posed by the Soviet regime.[11] The point is that for various questions about life outside or beneath or above the state and its officials and bureaucracies, including especially religious life and religious discourse, failing to look beyond the chronological borders defined by the advent or demise of a particular state regime deprives the historian of potentially useful examples and patterns through which to better understand the period that is her central focus; denying or ignoring or misreading continuities through multiple historical periods defined in terms of the life of a particular state regime amounts to as much of a historical fallacy as would denying or ignoring the changes brought in many spheres by some state regimes.

This is ultimately why historicizing the question of religious authority, examining particular cases of its discussion or negotiation or implementation, and considering those cases together without prejudging what should be segregated solely on the basis of a state-centered chronology can illuminate phenomena and patterns that might go undetected and unnoticed through more conventional approaches to dividing up the past. Rather than making a specific argument about Muslim religious authority in Central Eurasia, then, or advocating any specific conceptual approach to the study of Muslim authority, this volume aims to begin that stacking-up of case studies, assembling new explorations that address quite different aspects of the question of religious authority among Muslims in Central Eurasia, but share a commitment to rigorously historicize manifestations of and engagements with religious authority; and given the damage that Sovietology has caused (and is still causing) to the historiography of religion in Muslim Central Eurasia, the volume must also aim, through the assembled studies, to correct a host of egregiously erroneous arguments and assumptions that still clutter the popular and scholarly literature on Islam in the Soviet and post-Soviet worlds, comprising the recent history of Central Eurasia.

Although the full spectrum of the responses of Soviet Muslims, as Muslims, to the Soviet system has only recently become a serious object of study, we

11 See, for example, Bakhtiiar Babadzhanov, *Kokandskoe khanstvo: Vlast', politika, religiia* (Tokyo/Tashkent: NIHU Program Islamic Area Studies Center at the University of Tokyo [TIAS]/Institut Vostokovedeniia Akademii Nauk Respubliki Uzbekistan, 2010); Andreas Wilde, *What Is Beyond the River? Power, Authority and Social Order in Eighteenth and Nineteenth-Century Transoxania* (Vienna: Verlag der Osterreichischen Akademie der Wissenschaften, 2016); Ulfat Abdurasulov, "Ot Arabshakhidov k Kungradam: Dinamika i politicheskii landshaft Khorezma v period pravleniia dvukh dinastii," *O'zbekiston tarixi* (February 2013), pp. 17–32.

believe it will be better understood with attention to the question of authority.[12] What are the sources of authority that have underlain, or currently underlie, the intellectual, ritual, and social enactments of Muslim-ness in the Soviet, and pre-Soviet, and post-Soviet spaces under consideration here? Are currently-invoked sources of authority different from those invoked in the past? If so, are they different because of global currents or developments that transcend Muslim historical experience ("modernity," "nationalism," etc.), because of the distinctive political and cultural context of Russian and Soviet rule, or because of some other reasons, perhaps not yet clearly recognized? If they are not substantially different, do they reflect continuities through the Soviet era, 'restorations' or revivals of authoritative power lost or submerged under Russian or Soviet domination, or something else? How do different groups, with different visions of Muslim-ness, contest or negotiate different sources of authority? Where, and in what form, do those sources of authority reside nowadays, and in the past, and what sort of networks, or hierarchies, are detectable among them? How does adaptation to new technologies of communication or self-expression affect sources of authority, the hierarchies among them, and the interaction between Muslims and the state, between Muslims and non-Muslims, or between different visions of Islam?

These are some of the questions that underlie the studies prepared for this volume. In keeping with the thematic focus on religious authority and the broader goal of assembling case studies that historicize religiosity in Central Eurasia, we have purposefully avoided a strictly chronological or regional grouping of the contributions, placing them instead in four thematic sections. This necessarily means that not all regions of the former Soviet space (which in any case shared different groupings among themselves in different historical periods), and not all of the three broad chronological parameters that are 'covered' here (framed in a tendentious and misleading shorthand as pre-Soviet, Soviet, and post-Soviet) are represented under each thematic section; but this volume is only a beginning, and we hope and expect that further case studies will fill out the matrix of time, region, and approach.

Accordingly, the first chapter stands alone in critically addressing theoretical and methodological issues in the analysis of religious life in the Soviet and post-Soviet eras, and seeks to highlight what was problematical in the study of Islam in the USSR as it developed before, and well after, the fall of the Soviet

12 Here, again, "religious" authority is meant, with the caveat that what is "religious" bleeds into and stains a host of other modes and loci of authority as defined in scholarship uninterested in religion (or convinced that it is necessarily a shrinking semantic field), including "political," "cultural," and "ethical."

state; it reflects a recognition that considerations of religious authority in Central Eurasia are still inevitably in conversation, to a greater or lesser extent, with the "Sovietological" literature noted above, and attempts to outline not only how, but also why, so much of it was wrong-headed, while also suggesting ways to take religion more seriously as part of the Soviet experience.

The next three chapters (which do happen to address the post-Soviet contexts of Tatarstan, Tajikistan, and Kazakhstan) comprise Part 2, framed in terms of "Authority Enunciated," since each chapter addresses the revival of public religious discourse in Muslim Central Eurasia, following its sometimes submerged character during the Soviet era. Agnès Kefeli explores the vigorous discourse in post-Soviet Tatarstan about multiple ways of connecting to the authority of the Prophet Muḥammad; Benjamin Gatling addresses the role of Tajik 'hagiographical' narratives about the eponym of the Ḥanafī juridical school in renegotiating Muslim-ness and in nation-building; and Wendell Schwab considers dimensions of the religious authority built by a broadcast- and social-media celebrity in Kazakhstan. All three chapters in this section explore how that revived religious discourse addresses new issues, in new ways, but still in the framework of historically transmitted discursive patterns and conventions; they also show how religious discourse in itself returned to the public sphere as a phenomenon of social, economic, and even political importance.

The four chapters in Part 3, "Authority Embodied," address a common theme in the manifestation of religious authority in the Muslim world, namely the perceived sacrality of individuals, often together with their families and descendants, as embodiments of sacred authority. In this case, religious authority stems less from what these individuals, or their proxies, say or do, than from who and what they are. Historically this phenomenon reminds us that the scriptural focus of some contemporary Muslim movements – which themselves often inevitably project religious authority onto men or women deemed holy for more than their scriptural prowess – has never been the only story in the Muslim world, and that persons whose lives are seen as models, or indeed embodiments, of Islam have been accorded remarkably strong degrees of authority in their communities, sometimes inherited over centuries. Within this rubric, William Wood examines the religious authority wielded by sons and disciples of a prominent Sufi shaykh among the Turkmens in the mid-19th century; Ulfat Abdurasulov explores the mediational role of another set of hereditary Sufi shaykhs and other holy men in 19th- and early 20th-century Khorezm, highlighting the key role of the Khivan khans in 'endorsing' the holiness of the figures whose mediation they employed; Allen Frank discusses the religious authority embodied in the hereditary lineage of a Tatar Sufi shaykh active in southern Kazakhstan in the 19th and early 20th centuries, whose descendants were revered in the region during the Soviet and post-Soviet eras; and Sergey Abashin traces the exercise, and transfer, of authority within a hereditary lineage of shrine-keepers in late-Tsarist and Soviet Tajikistan, whose authority likewise spanned the Soviet and post-Soviet eras.

Part 4, "Authority Mobilized," includes three chapters that explore religious authority in another commonly encountered framework: religious institutions, which not only may link religious communities with the larger state-framework in which they live (as in each case explored here), but also provide a context for the contained and moderated contestation of religious authority, in both ways serving as a potential venue for the activization and mobilization of religious authority for particular social or economic or political goals. In this final section, Pavel Shabley dissects the competing voices active in interpreting the *sharīʿa* for Tsarist-era Kazakhs, addressing the interactions of the imperial bureaucracy and the Orenburg Muslim Spiritual Assembly, based in Ufa, in the context of the Kazakh steppe in the late-Tsarist era; Shamil Shikhaliev offers a broad survey of Muslim discourse in Soviet-era Daghestan, highlighting the institutions and the issues debated both within them and outside them, tracing the intensification of anti-Sufi rhetoric in some circles, and revealing the frequent blindness of officials to ongoing patterns of Muslim religious discussion and debate; and finally, Paolo Sartori and Bakhtiyar Babajanov bring to light a set of remarkable letters addressed by Soviet Uzbeks, from the 1960s, '70s, and '80s, to the official religious board headquartered in Tashkent, underscoring both the letter-writers' recognition of the Soviet mufti's authority, and their suspicions about the propriety of the religious board's shifting message. The chapters in this section also deal with the proliferation of religious authority in the context of an avowedly secular state, one that claimed a monopoly on authority; we find that in this regard, the secular, and avowedly antireligious state was not as disruptive to discourses of authority as we might suppose – and indeed, as *was* supposed in most discussions of Islam in the Soviet Union.

The chapters will speak for themselves, we believe, and together they lead us not in a chronological march or a series of regional tours, but in a thematic progression from shaping and reshaping the authority of religious discourse, through cases of individuals and families regarded as imbued with religious authority by dint of charisma, piety, or heredity, to the institutions established in order to both regulate and disseminate religious authority for eminently practical purposes. Together they underscore the value of combining historical and anthropological approaches, and of recognizing that historical patterns may help us understand contemporary developments, and vice-versa.[13] There is naturally more to say about questions of religious authority in this vast arena of Muslim Central Eurasia, but it is hoped that the present contributions will suggest both the hermeneutic utility, and the historical appropriateness, of turning to this sort of analytical framework in seeking to understand the past and present of Islam in Eurasia.

We believe the assembled studies have much to offer to the field of Islamic studies, and not merely to the niche – sometimes not even framed in terms of Islamic studies – that has dealt with the Muslims of Central Eurasia. More ambitiously, the volume is intended to re-situate Islamic religious authority in the regions explored, and not merely to provide material and examples from the former Soviet space to the field of Islamic studies, but also to remind that wider field that when it comes to grappling with the question of religious authority, and more broadly, to simply living Muslim lives, there is no 'peripheral' Muslim region, and there are no 'peripheral' Muslims.

Bibliography

Abdurasulov, Ulfat. "Ot Arabshakhidov k Kungradam: Dinamika i politicheskii landshaft Khorezma v period pravleniia dvukh dinastii." *O'zbekiston tarixi* (February 2013), pp. 17–32.

Afsaruddin, Asma. "Authority, religious." *Encyclopaedia of Islam*, 3rd edition, ed. K. Fleet, G. Krämer, D. Matringe, J. Nawas, and E. Rowson, Leiden: Brill, 2020.

Arendt, Hannah. "What is Authority?" In *Between Past and Future* (New York: Viking Press, 1961).

Babadzhanov, Bakhtiiar. *Kokandskoe khanstvo: Vlast', politika, religiia*. Tokyo/Tashkent: NIHU Program Islamic Area Studies Center at the University of Tokyo [TIAS]/ Institut Vostokovedeniia Akademii Nauk Respubliki Uzbekistan, 2010.

Bustanov, Alfrid K., and Michael Kemper, eds. *Islamic Authority and the Russian Language: Studies on Texts from European Russia, the North Caucasus, and West Siberia*. Amsterdam: Uitgeverij Pegasus, 2012.

Clayer, Nathalie, Alexandre Papas, and Benoît Fliche, eds. *L'autorité religieuse et ses limites en terres d'islam: Approches historiques et anthropologiques*. Leiden: Brill, 2013.

13 Given the disciplinary variety reflected in the chapters, as well as the variety of languages and scripts underlying them, we have left it to each author to choose the transliteration scheme, and the reference style, most appropriate to his or her subject, without insisting on one standardized system or style as 'normative.'

DeWeese, Devin. "Authority." In *Key Themes for the Study of Islam*, ed. Jamal J. Elias (Oxford: Oneworld, 2010), pp. 26–52.

Eden, Jeff. *God Save the USSR: Soviet Muslims and the Second World War*. Oxford: Oxford University Press, 2021.

Krämer, Gudrun, and Sabine Schmidtke, eds. *Speaking for Islam: Religious Authorities in Muslim Societies*. Leiden: Brill, 2006.

Pickett, James. *Polymaths of Islam: Power and Networks of Knowledge in Central Asia*. Ithaca and London: Cornell University Press, 2020.

Pickett, James, and Matthew Melvin-Koushki. "Mobilizing Magic: Occultism in Central Asia and the Continuity of High Persianate Culture under Russian Rule." *Studia Islamica*, 111/2 (2016), pp. 231–284.

Robinson, Francis. "Crisis of Authority: Crisis of Islam?" *Journal of the Royal Asiatic Society*, Series 3, 19/3 (2009), pp. 339–354.

Saroyan, Mark. "Authority and Community in Soviet Islam." In *Accounting for Fundamentalisms: The Dynamic Character of Movements*, ed. Martin E. Marty and R. Scott Appleby (Chicago: University of Chicago Press, 1994; *The Fundamentalism Project*, Vol. 4), pp. 513–530.

Sartori, Paolo. "Of Saints, Shrines, and Tractors: Untangling the Meaning of Islam in Soviet Central Asia." *Journal of Islamic Studies*, 30 (2019), pp. 367–405.

Sartori, Paolo. *Visions of Justice: Sharīʿa and Cultural Change in Russian Central Asia*. Leiden: Brill, 2016.

Sartori, Paolo, and Bakhtiyar Babajanov. "Being Soviet, Muslim, Modernist, and Fundamentalist in 1950s Central Asia." *Journal of the Economic and Social History of the Orient*, 62/1 (2019), pp. 108–165.

Tasar, Eren. "Institutions: A Lens on Soviet Islam" [Book Discussion *Soviet and Muslim: The Institutionalization of Islam in Central Asia* by Eren Tasar]. *Central Asian Affairs*, 7 (2020), pp. 370–375.

Wilde, Andreas. *What Is Beyond the River? Power, Authority and Social Order in Eighteenth and Nineteenth-Century Transoxania*. 3 vols. Vienna: Verlag der Osterreichischen Akademie der Wissenschaften, 2016.

PART 1

Analytical Frameworks and Approaches

The Soviet Union in Islamic Studies

Some Reflections on Envisioning the USSR as a Religious Space

Devin DeWeese

The chapter that follows attempts to assess the lingering impact of Sovietological approaches to Islam upon the study of Islam in the Soviet and post-Soviet worlds, and particularly upon the question of religious authority in those worlds.[1] It is a considerably shortened and restructured adaptation of a keynote address presented at a conference (entitled "The Languages of Soviet Islam: Ideologies, Networks, and Practices") in St. Petersburg in April 2016, which was itself a distillation of a broader critique of scholarship on Islam in the Soviet (and pre-Soviet and post-Soviet) space; that critique began in earnest, for me, just a decade after the dissolution of the USSR, in a review essay on Yaacov Ro'i's book, *Islam in the Soviet Union*, in which prodigious archival material was put to use in a rickety analytical framework that I argued should have been abandoned even in Soviet times, but in any case should have at least been refined, if not wholly jettisoned, ten years after the end of the USSR.[2] Within a few years of that review essay's publication (and quite unrelated to its arguments, which seemed to draw little notice for many years), a series of contributions by younger scholars began to appear, suggesting that the field might be getting its act together; though most retained, in my view, some notable 'survivals' of the Sovietological past, they marked, together, an important step forward, both in terms of the collection of data and in terms of analysis and interpretation.

In the decade that followed those initial steps in the right direction, a growing number of similar works appeared in print, alongside a steady flow of publications that largely continued in the Sovietological style, suggesting that the longstanding missteps of Sovietological scholarship could not yet be

1 Research for this chapter, and for several of my publications referred to in it, was supported in part by a grant from the Carnegie Corporation of New York; the statements made and views expressed are solely the responsibility of the author. I am grateful also for the help of Andrew B. Stone, then a doctoral student at the University of Washington in Seattle, who worked for a year as my research assistant.

2 Devin DeWeese, "Islam and the Legacy of Sovietology: A Review Essay on Yaacov Ro'i's *Islam in the Soviet Union*," *Journal of Islamic Studies*, 13/3 (2002), pp. 298–330.

 | DOI:10.1163/9789004527096_003

fully consigned to the dustbin of academic history;[3] I occasionally pointed out some lingering problems, chiefly in reviews and other minor venues, but for the 2016 conference, I outlined a broader range of the flawed narratives and interpretative pitfalls that had developed in Sovietological scholarship from the 1970s on, and to some extent still plague the study of Islam in the Soviet and post-Soviet worlds, comprising in all 15 'fields of error.' This litany of misconceptions and misguided approaches provided, I argued, a framework for a more thorough critique of both past and current literature dealing with Islam in Central Asia, or in other parts of the former Soviet Union. Each topic has both historical and contemporary dimensions, and many overlap somewhat with one another, but together they both frame, or characterize, the salient stances, assumptions, and habits of the Sovietological approach to Islam, and signal the broad outlines, at least, of the arguments that can undermine those same stances, assumptions, and habits.

In the aftermath of the conference, held less than a year later, at which most of the chapters in this volume were presented, I re-ordered the 15 points and condensed the discussion in order to better address the question of religious authority in 'Central Eurasian' Islam. I have grouped the 15 points into three uneven categories. The first includes those with salient historical dimensions that speak to what I regard as the urgent need to shed the persistent dividing line imposed, in scholarly training and in scholarly audiences, between 'historical' and 'contemporary' studies, and to recognize – in practical terms, beyond lip-service and platitudes – the impossibility of understanding the present without improving our engagement with the past; for many of these, I and others have been able to advance challenges and critiques in recent years, and I will mostly summarize or refer to arguments made elsewhere. The second category will also be quickly summarized; though not yet critiqued or even problematized, the points included in it mostly speak to, or emerged from, the interests of policy analysts, and need not detain us here.

The third category, however, will be given more attention, insofar as the 'fields of error' included in it are all rooted in inadequate, or simply unhelpful, ways of thinking about religion, and could be easily cleared away – and indeed, might never have come to dominate the Sovietological or 'post-Sovietological' literature – if more historians and social scientists were better-versed in the conceptual and analytical contributions of the field of religious studies; the misconceptions, or unhelpful assumptions, considered here, after all,

3 For a fresh and thorough critical review of the historiography of Soviet Islam, see now Eren Tasar, "*Mantra*: A Review Essay on Islam in Soviet Central Asia," *Journal of the Economic and Social History of the Orient*, 63 (2020), pp. 389–433.

fundamentally shape our understanding of the very context in which diverse claimants to 'religious' authority contend. We will thus consider these issues in somewhat greater depth, and then step back to suggest how more fruitful ways of thinking about religious life might point to some unexpected ways to approach the Soviet Union, and the post-Soviet space, as distinctive religious environments worthy of attention by students of religion.

1 The Litany of Misconceptions: 15 'Fields of Error' in the Legacies of Sovietological Scholarship on Islam

1.1 *Historically-Rooted Misconceptions*

1) The notion of **'light' and inconsequential or defective Islamization** among the formerly nomadic peoples of Central Asia (above all the Qazaqs and Qïrghïz, but including even the Türkmens, and at least some Uzbeks): In some cases *all* of Central Asian Islam, and indeed all of 'Soviet Islam,' is declared to be defective, and not even 'really' Islamic, with two analytical subsets: either it was always thus, with Islam never really 'taking root' in the region (a ludicrous historical proposition, to be sure, but one that passes for serious historical background in much of the literature), or the Soviet experience 'corrupted' Islam in the region, and made it light, inconsequential, or defective. I have sought to undercut this notion, with regard to Islam among nomadic peoples in Central and Inner Asia, beginning with my study of Islamization in the Golden Horde,[4] which was focused less on countering such claims by saying "No, Islam *was* strong" among the nomads, than on asking for a more meaningful and sensible approach to what 'Islamization' might mean, and how we might detect it historically. Nevertheless, neither my arguments nor those of others have made much of a difference in the 'post-Sovietological' literature.

As for the version of this fallacy that blames the Soviet experience for weakening Islam, this has been maintained not only by Western post-Sovietologists, but by some in the post-Soviet space who use it to criticize and, as they intend, to reform Islam among their fellows, and of course by external Salafists and Islamists. Both versions of the fallacy, in any case, are closely linked with the second of these 'fields of error.'

4 *Islamization and Native Religion in the Golden Horde: Baba Tükles and Conversion to Islam in Historical and Epic Tradition* (University Park: Pennsylvania State University Press, 1994); and see my "Islamization in the Mongol Empire," in *The Cambridge History of Inner Asia: The Chinggisid Age*, ed. Nicola Di Cosmo, Allen J. Frank, and Peter B. Golden (Cambridge: Cambridge University Press, 2009), pp. 120–134.

2) The broad acquiescence, in Sovietological literature, in the **analytical fragmentation** of the religious lives of Central Asian Muslims, adopted by Soviet, nationalist, and fundamentalist circles, into narrowly construed 'Islamic' elements, on the one hand, and 'folk' or 'popular' or 'everyday' elements, usually classed as '**survivals**' of pre-Islamic religions, on the other (with 'women's religion,' especially, relegated to the latter category): This fragmentation continues in post-Soviet times, with appeals to presumed 'national' pre-Islamic traditions (some are rooted in 19th-century evolutionary models of religion, e.g., shamanism or animism; others are rooted in constructions of regional religious history, e.g., Zoroastrianism; and others are more recent concoctions, e.g., Tengrism). The net result of such analytical fragmentation is to ignore, or miss, the coherence of religious life, and its meaningfulness *as* religious life, to those who engage in activities relegated by the analysts to different 'origins;' it also obscures, or ignores, the more revealing historical process whereby phenomena with possible origins in pre- or non-Islamic contexts were Islamized and made part of Muslim practice, and typically entails an ahistorical leap across centuries of Muslim tradition, to locate the 'origins' of a certain rite, or a certain 'belief,' in a more distant past.

This analytical strategy, with its concomitant privileging of presumed primordial cultural features portrayed as underlying the 'superficial' superstructure of 'ideology' with which religion is identified, overlaps strongly with the issues discussed below in connection with the neglect of approaches and conceptual frameworks rooted in the field of religious studies; but it also has important historical dimensions – both in terms of the 'ahistorical' approach to the past it often entails, and in terms of the need for debunking specific cases of alleged 'survivals' through historical research – and belongs among the historically-based issues that have drawn some critical attention.[5]

3) A pattern of remarkable **misinterpretations of the roles of Sufi communities** in Tsarist, Soviet, and post-Soviet times – but especially in the Soviet

---

5 See my "Survival Strategies: Reflections on the Notion of Religious 'Survivals' in Soviet Ethnographic Studies of Muslim Religious Life in Central Asia," in *Exploring the Edge of Empire: Soviet Era Anthropology in the Caucasus and Central Asia*, ed. Florian Mühlfried and Sergey Sokolovskiy (Münster: Lit Verlag, 2011; Halle Studies in the Anthropology of Eurasia, vol. 25), pp. 35–58; see also my "Shamanization in Central Asia," *Journal of the Economic and Social History of the Orient*, 57 (2014), pp. 326–363, and "Dog Saints and Dog Shrines in Kubravī Tradition: Notes on a Hagiographical Motif from Khwārazm," in *Miracle et karāma: Hagiographies médiévales comparées*, 2, ed. Denise Aigle (Turnhout, Belgium: Brepols, 2000; Bibliothèque de l'école des hautes études, sciences religieuses, vol. 109), pp. 459–497, as well as my comments in a review of *Shamanism and Islam: Sufism, Healing Rituals and Spirits in the Muslim World*, ed. Thierry Zarcone and Angela Hobart (London/New York: I.B. Tauris, 2013), in *International Journal of Turkish Studies*, 22/1–2 (Fall 2016), pp. 200–206.

era: Beginning with Alexandre Bennigsen, a small but surprisingly vocal group of Western scholars claimed that Sufism was the key to keeping Muslim religiosity alive in the USSR, and that Sufism manifested itself chiefly in the form of clandestine but potentially militant opposition to Soviet authority. I have elsewhere addressed the problems with the Bennigsen approach at length, as well as some of the re-thinking I believe is needed, suggesting that 'Sufism' took multiple social forms even before the Soviet era, and that expectations about what 'Sufism' should look like led Sovietologists to miss many of its manifestations.[6]

4) The inordinate attention to, and uncritical assessment of, the 'reformist' elements of the late 19th and early 20th centuries, the so-called **Jadidists**: Interpreted in isolation from the study of earlier reformist impulses and of broader trends in religious history in the world of 'Russian Islam,' the figures identified as or linked with the Jadidists, through seriously skewed misjudgments of their orientation and historical appeal, were typically portrayed as popular and 'modernizing' forces opposed by obscurantist clerics; in fact it can be argued that these reformist impulses had much in common with puritanical and exclusivist approaches to Islam,[7] and in many respects cleared the way for the heightened appeal, in some circles, of such rigorist approaches. Yet not only Sovietologists, but more serious historians of imperial Russia as well, have tapped into *jadīdist* rhetoric and lumped all "pre-modern" religion into one 'opposing' category; they have then turned to the 'modernists' who speak a familiar language, in familiar media, and effectively suspended their critical judgment in assuming that the claims of the reformists were not polemical rhetoric requiring contextualization and fair assessment, but were simply and straightforwardly accurate characterizations of their society's shortcomings.

6 "Re-Envisioning the History of Sufi Communities in Central Asia: Continuity and Adaptation in Sources and Social Frameworks, 16th–20th Centuries," in *Sufism in Central Asia: New Perspectives on Sufi Traditions, 15th–21st Centuries*, ed. Devin DeWeese and Jo-Ann Gross (Leiden: Brill, 2018), pp. 21–74. See also the insightful comments of Eren Tasar in "Sufism on the Soviet Stage: Holy People and Places in Central Asia's Socio-Political Landscape after World War II," in the same volume, pp. 256–283, as well as the comments of Sergei Abashin in "Sufizm v Srednei Azii: Tochka zreniia ètnografa," *Vestnik Evrazii* (*Acta Eurasica*), 2001, No. 4, pp. 117–141.

7 For a discussion of the differences and commonalities between 'modernist' and 'purist' Salafism, see Henri Lauzière, "The Construction of *Salafiyya*: Reconsidering Salafism from the Perspective of Conceptual History," *International Journal of Middle East Studies*, 42 (2010), pp. 369–389; and see also Lauzière's *The Making of Salafism: Islamic Reform in the Twentieth Century* (New York: Columbia University Press, 2016), esp. chapters 3 and 4.

I have recently discussed what I see as some of the many problems with 'Jadidocentric' scholarship,[8] though the pioneering work with regard to this critique began over twenty years ago.[9] However, interest in, and admiration of, the Jadidists, as well as an exaggeration of their appeal and impact, continue to rest not only on the religious misjudgment noted above, but on lapses of historical interpretation as well, including a privileging of print media that guarantees the exclusion of alternative perspectives reflected in handwritten materials, and an uncritical acceptance of the inexorability (and, as is often openly expressed, the preferability) of a particular set of historical phenomena and adaptations labeled (with obvious partiality) 'modernity.' What has not yet been thoroughly problematized or explored, however, is the way in which the Jadidist narrative shaped Sovietological understandings of the character of Islam in the Soviet Union, and thereby shaped even the current 'normative' views of Islam in the post-Soviet space.

5) An ongoing difficulty in coming to terms with 'official Islam,' i.e., the **institutional framework** established for Muslim communities during the Soviet era: The range of oversimplifications and mischaracterizations arising from discussions of the official Muslim religious boards is quite breathtaking, and is perhaps on a level close to the range of blunders with regard to Sufism. Sovietological scholarship insisted that the organs of 'official Islam' were entirely co-opted by the state, that their officials had 'sold out' any semblance of sincerity (an essential requirement for religiosity in the Sovietological model), and that the official religious boards had no 'popular' support (a claim that should have been put to rest already by the turmoil in several of the religious boards in very late Soviet times, which showed that these structures, and their personnel, *did* matter to many Muslims). At the same time, Sovietological scholarship avoided nuance in assessing the loyalties of 'official' religious personnel, and overlooked internal differences in the boards, whether between center and periphery, between regions, or between 'national' groups; it also

8 "It was a Dark and Stagnant Night ('til the Jadids Brought the Light): Clichés, Biases, and False Dichotomies in the Intellectual History of Central Asia," *Journal of the Economic and Social History of the Orient*, 59/1–2 (2016), pp. 37–92.

9 Above all in the work of Allen J. Frank; see especially his *Islamic Historiography and 'Bulghar' Identity among the Tatars and Bashkirs of Russia* (Leiden: Brill, 1998), and his *Muslim Religious Institutions in Imperial Russia: The Islamic World of Novouzensk District and the Kazakh Inner Horde, 1780–1910* (Leiden: Brill, 2001). See also the overview of Jeff Eden, Paolo Sartori, and Devin DeWeese, "Moving Beyond Modernism: Rethinking Cultural Change in Muslim Eurasia (19th–20th Centuries)," *Journal of the Social and Economic History of the Orient*, 59/1–2 (2016), pp. 1–36.

ignored shifts in religious and juridical orientation within the boards, and the often quite permeable 'boundaries' between 'official' and 'unofficial' religious personnel and institutions.

Challenges to these shortcomings have come from a wide range of other scholars;[10] above all, the way was paved for a better understanding of the internal workings of the boards, and the networks of connections borne by their personnel, by better access to archival materials in post-Soviet times. Considerable advances were evident in Ro'i's *Islam in the Soviet Union* (2000), despite its general analytical dependence upon Sovietological perspectives, but more recently a richly detailed picture of the boards as religious institutions has been advanced in studies of their personnel,[11] of their *fatwās*,[12] of

10 Already in 1991, I took issue with some of these questionable assumptions and mischaracterizations in a paper, entitled "The Changing Face of 'Official Islam' in the Soviet Union," presented at the American Academy of Religion's annual meeting, held in Kansas City little more than a month before the dissolution of the Soviet Union.

11 See, for instance, S.A. Dudoignon, "From Revival to Mutation: The Religious Personnel of Islam in Tajikistan, from de-Stalinization to Independence (1955–91)," *Central Asian Survey*, 30 (2011), pp. 53–80; Bakhtiyar Babadjanov, "Debates over Islam in Contemporary Uzbekistan: A View from Within," in *Devout Societies vs. Impious States? Transmitting Islamic Learning in Russia, Central Asia and China, through the Twentieth Century* (Proceedings of an International Colloquium Held in the Carré des Sciences, French Ministry of Research, Paris, November 12–13, 2001), ed. Stéphane Dudoignon (Berlin: Schwarz, 2004), pp. 39–60; idem, "*Ulama*-Orientalists: *Madrasa* Graduates at the Soviet Institute of Oriental Studies," in *Reassessing Orientalism: Interlocking Orientologies during the Cold War*, ed. Michael Kemper and Artemy M. Kalinovsky (London/New York: Routledge, 2015), pp. 84–119; and see the publication of the remarkable biographical dictionary compiled by a leading figure in the religious hierarchy of Soviet Kazakhstan, Saduaqas Ghïlmani, *Zamanïmïzda bolghan ghŭlamalardïng ömïr tarikhtarï/Biographies of the Islamic Scholars of Our Times*, ed. Ashirbek Muminov, Allen J. Frank, and Aitzhan Nurmatova (Istanbul: Research Centre for Islamic History, Art and Culture [IRCICA], 2018), vol. I (Arabic script Kazakh text), vol. II (English translation).

12 E.g., Michael Kemper and Shamil Shikhaliev, "Administrative Islam: Two Soviet Fatwas from the North Caucasus," in *Islamic Authority and the Russian Language: Studies on Texts from European Russia, the North Caucasus, and West Siberia*, ed. Michael Kemper and Alfrid K. Bustanov (Amsterdam: Pegasus, 2012), pp. 55–102; Bakhtiyar Babajanov and Sharifjon Islamov, "*Sharīʿa* for the Bolsheviks? *Fatvās* on Land Reform in Early Soviet Central Asia," in *Islam, Society and States Across the Qazaq Steppe (18th–Early 20th Centuries)*, ed. Niccolò Pianciola and Paolo Sartori (Vienna: Verlag der Österreichischen Akademie der Wissenschaften, 2013), pp. 233–265; Jeff Eden, "A Soviet Jihad against Hitler: Ishan Babakhan Calls Central Asian Muslims to War," *Journal of the Economic and Social History of the Orient*, 59 (2016), pp. 237–264; Paolo Sartori and Bakhtiyar Babajanov, "Being Soviet, Muslim, Modernist, and Fundamentalist in 1950s Central Asia," *Journal of the Economic and Social History of the Orient*, 62/1 (2019), pp. 108–163.

their institutions,[13] and in the remarkable synthesis of archival material and nuanced analysis in the work of Eren Tasar.[14]

6) Dependence upon the mantra of **'Islam vs. nationalism'** as an analytical strategy, ubiquitous in the Sovietological literature, and curiously revived in post-Soviet times: This dependence underlay framing the key question to ask about Central Asians, or Muslims in general, in the Soviet era as whether Islam or nationalism was more important; the usual conclusion was that nationalism prevailed.[15] This was, in all likelihood the most frequently repeated 'problematical' claim, or assumption, about Islam in the Soviet era: it usually involved, first, separating 'religion' from 'national' feeling, and, second, arguing or claiming that 'religion' was on the wane, while nationalism was the wave of the present, and, presumably, the future.

Broadly speaking, the entire Sovietological and post-Sovietological enterprise, in addressing the issue of 'religion vs. nationalism,' as it was framed, ignored religiously-framed notions of communal identity that dominated in earlier times, but also persisted, with remarkable adaptivity, into the Soviet era; it posed false, or at least unilluminating, alternatives, rather than textured and intermingling layers, in analyzing communal identities; and it assumed an 'evolutionary' developmental sequence, with religious identities prior to the more 'modern' national ones. One might suggest that this sequence has clearly been laid to rest by the recent spread of Islamist agendas, but the preeminence (and, often, superiority) of national and ethnic sentiment over religious feeling is still a cherished assumption of most specialists on the Soviet and post-Soviet eras.

In that regard, it is noteworthy that the most recent twist in this cherished assumption is to privilege national identities over Islamic identity (again, the

---

13 Eren Tasar, "The Official Madrasas of Soviet Uzbekistan," *Journal of the Economic and Social History of the Orient*, 59/1–2 (2016), pp. 265–302.

14 Eren Tasar, *Soviet and Muslim: The Institutionalization of Islam in Central Asia* (Oxford: Oxford University Press, 2017).

15 Oddly enough, on this front, Bennigsen was somewhat of an outlier; though he stressed, and studied, the emergence of nationalism (and the impact of 'national' consciousness on communism), he sought to argue a stronger role for 'religion,' as he framed it, in supporting – actually or potentially – hostility toward the Soviet state on the part of Soviet Muslim citizens. His arguments were based on an understanding of 'religion' as an ideological system with an underlying institutional framework, and on an understanding of 'Islam' as a universal focus of religious attachment; his writings suggest that he did not envision 'Islam' as something deeply embedded in the historical and cultural consciousness of Soviet Muslims. It was, rather, a belief system with some accompanying rituals, and one could measure fidelity to religion, as opposed to fidelity to the Soviet system, by the extent of 'belief' and of the performance of the 'basic' rituals.

possibility of multiple kinds of Muslim identity is typically not countenanced) by insisting that Islam became, in Soviet times, merely a component of national identity and culture, i.e., just a part or subset of an identity that is fundamentally 'national' in essence. This, of course, was the claim of Adeeb Khalid in *Islam After Communism* (2007), but it is shared by many, if not most, observers of post-Soviet Islam. It is as if these observers took the famous *ḥadīth*, affirming that "Love of country is part of faith" (*ḥubb al-waṭan min al-īmān*) and, implicitly declaring that the Prophet Muḥammad got it wrong, turned it backwards, to read that "Faith is part of love of country."

Such assumptions naturally rest on the developed theories of nationalism that inevitably privilege the constructed world of 'modernity' as providing the conditions in which nationalism emerges. Without entering into debate here with those theorists, or with their admirers among students of Soviet and post-Soviet Muslim 'nationalities,' we may suggest that what both camps miss – the theorists and the 'applied' students of Soviet Muslim nationalism – is the still largely unstudied role of earlier – but again, ongoing – patterns of placing Islam at the center of communal identity, whether through stories of Islamization that serve as communal legends of origin, through the sacralization of communal space through shrines, or through various articulations of communal kinship rooted in ancestral saints.[16] That these patterns might be labeled 'traditional' and hence 'pre-modern' – despite their adaptability and their circulation in 'modern' times – should not deter us from considering their impact in the Soviet era, and in the here-and-now;[17] but they most assuredly

---

16 For communal legends of origin, see, for example, my *Islamization and Native Religion*, and Frank, *Islamic Historiography*; for shrines, see Allen J. Frank, "Islamic Shrine Catalogues and Communal Geography in the Volga-Ural region: 1788–1917," *Journal of Islamic Studies*, 7 (1996), pp. 265–286, and my "Encountering Saints in the Hallowed Ground of a Regional Landscape: The 'Description of Khwārazm' and the Experience of Pilgrimage in 19th-Century Central Asia," in *Saintly Spheres and Islamic Landscapes*, ed. Daphna Ephrat, Ethel Sara Wolper, and Paulo G. Pinto (Leiden: Brill, 2021), pp. 183–218; for ancestral saints, see the studies of the *khoja* phenomenon and the Türkmen *öwlät* cited below; and for still other 'pre-modern' modes of framing communal identity, see Allen J. Frank, "Turkmen Literacy and Turkmen Identity before the Soviets: the *Ravnaq al-Islām* in its Literary and Social Context," *Journal of the Economic and Social History of the Orient*, 63 (2020), pp. 286–315.

17 Through the end of the Soviet era, it was common to hear Central Asian Turks (outside educated elite circles) refer to the language they spoke using not the terms for their national languages as defined through Soviet language policy, but instead their particular equivalent of the Uzbek *musulmanchä*, i.e., the Muslim language, implicitly contrasted with non-Muslim Russian; though hardly an overt or conscious challenge to linguistic nationalism, such usage should remind us of the ongoing tendency, in the 'age of nationalism,' to frame aspects of cultural identity in religious terms. Similarly, the oft-cited

do not enter into the 'theories' of national sentiment developed by specialists armed with – as must be acknowledged – a shallower historical perspective. I hope to address this issue in more depth at a later time.

1.2 *Misconceptions Rooted in Policy- and Threat-Analysis*

7) The ongoing predominance of **the 'threat assessment' approach and the hunt for militancy**: As noted in connection with Sufism, Western Sovietologists were keenly interested in currents of Muslim religiosity in the Soviet Union that (1) could be found to be significant and strong (ironically countering the narrative of the diminution of religiosity), and (2) could be taken as likely to lead to political and even militant opposition to the Soviet state. The habit of looking for political activity and militant opposition has continued into the post-Soviet era, even as the eagerness to find such militancy has shifted toward labeling it as a problem and as a terrorist threat, with only occasional recognition of post-Soviet manipulations of fears of such threats. There is a strong strain of scholarship on 'Islam in the post-Soviet space,' as a result, that is only interested in assessing the threat – in that space, or beyond it – and judges the importance of religious currents on that basis: if a phenomenon seems to pose a threat of terrorism, then it is worth tracking and studying; if not, who cares?[18]

This approach naturally begs the question of causality and likely trajectories for turning religion into a motivation for political or military activity; one would think that analysts concerned about failures to 'connect the dots' might take a broader view of how to identify religious currents worthy of study. More broadly, however, this approach stands in the way of building foundations for the serious understanding of religious phenomena across a wide spectrum of social, economic, political, and, yes, religious aspirations; and in any case, the treatment of religion, and of Islam, in works explicitly cast as policy analyses and threat-assessments is routinely among the worst to be found in all

---

self-evaluation among 'secular' Soviet Muslims – "we are atheists, but that doesn't mean we don't believe in God!" – should remind us that like other 'religious'-isms, "atheism" too could become a communal label signaling group solidarity rather than adherence to an 'essential' belief.

18 This is not the place to address the history of the funding mechanisms that still link government agencies, and government-connected NGOs, think-tanks, and foundations, with 'threat-assessment'-style 'research,' chiefly by political scientists, but the impact of this particular model of circular academic codependence on the literature in the field (especially by political scientists) should not be overlooked; for a relevant, and foundational, study, see Artemy M. Kalinovsky, "Encouraging Resistance: Paul Henze, the Bennigsen School, and the Crisis of Détente," in *Reassessing Orientalism: Interlocking Orientologies during the Cold War*, ed. Michael Kemper and Artemy M. Kalinovsky (London/New York: Routledge, 2015), pp. 211–232.

of the literature inspired by, or repetitive of, Sovietological approaches and conclusions.[19]

8) The analysis of Central Asia, and Islam there, with respect to **the Turkish or Iranian model**: This 'field of error' was quite prevalent in the immediate aftermath of the Soviet Union's dissolution, through the 1990s, though it has receded considerably more recently; it was rooted in a widespread neglect, among students of Soviet and contemporary Central Asia, of the region's distinctive political and cultural history and religious profile, and in a crude logic of ethnic determinism that encouraged assumptions that new Turkic or Iranian nations would naturally mimic the choices of the one Turkish or Iranian state (this is the one misconception noted here that is decidedly not "Sovietological" in origin – though it was occasionally heard in analyses from the Soviet era as well – insofar as it played down even the political and cultural impact of the Soviet experience). This tendency was not limited to the vacuous articles on "which way will Central Asia go" (i.e., will the 'stans take Iran or Turkey as a model in dealing with Islam), but has a historical dimension as well, involving projections of Turkish Islam, especially, into Central Asia, past and present.

9) The **misinterpretation of extremist agendas**, and of the broader framework of exclusivist and 'fundamentalist' approaches to Islam, as 'traditional'

---

19 For a recent example, the discussion of Islam in Turkmenistan included in Annette Bohr, "Turkmenistan: Power, Politics and Petro-Authoritarianism" (London: Russia and Eurasia Programme of Chatham House/Royal Institute of International Affairs, 2016), pp. 49–53, is a treasure-trove of ludicrous characterizations and baseless claims, reflecting many of the 'fields of error' noted here. In addition to the expected juxtapositions of Sufis vs. *ʿulamā*, and of the *sharīʿa* vs. *adat* (the latter, we are told, "had been passed down for many centuries" [p. 51], evidently unlike the ever-fresh *sharīʿa*) and the reversion, in full Sovietological mode, to mosque-counts, *madrasa*-counts, clergy-counts, and *ḥājjī*-counts, we find some specific iterations of the misconceptions outlined above, including the trope of light Islamization ("Islamic doctrine had never taken root as firmly in Turkmenistan as it had in other Muslim areas, including the older, sedentary territories of Central Asia" [p. 51]) and the emphasis upon nomadic Islam as substandard ("The Turkmen, like other nomadic peoples, preferred to pray in private rather than visit a mosque," and "A mobile lifestyle necessarily favoured a non-scriptural, popular version of Islam while naturally curtailing the presence of professional clergy" [p. 51]), as well as analytical fragmentation ("Islam in Turkmenistan," we are told, "is an unusual blend of Sufi mysticism, orthodox (Sunni) Islam, and shamanistic and Zoroastrian practices. The cult of ancestors is still observed, and reverence for members of the four holy tribes (the *owlat*) remains strong" [p. 49; in fact, six groups are usually counted as the *öwlät*]); elsewhere, the author's risible distinction between "folk Islam" and "orthodox Islam" (using, inexplicably, the Persian phrases "*Islam-i halq*" and "*Islam-i kitab*," respectively) itself reflects the kind of inadequate 'parsing' of Islam discussed below, but evokes another point in asking whether "folk Islam" is a national or religious phenomenon [p. 50].

or as relics of the 'medieval' past, ignoring what some have argued is the essentially modern character of fundamentalisms, and ignoring also the joint assault on traditional patterns of religious life in the Soviet and post-Soviet worlds by the Soviet state and, often, its successor governments, by the official Soviet religious directorates and their heirs, by Soviet-trained nationalists, and by home-grown and foreign Islamists eager to shape religious discourse in the post-Soviet world, and willing to exploit the insecurity of many Muslims in that world regarding the 'quality' of their knowledge and practice of Islam: This, to be sure, is a problem of Islamic studies more broadly, at present,[20] but is of particular importance for the post-Soviet world; it is closely related to the next point.

10) A set of wrong-headed assumptions about **the impact of Soviet ideology and Soviet-style 'modernization:'** This is a feature, in fact, of post-Sovietology more than of the earlier phase in the development of the field; we often read, that is, that the attraction that Islamist ideology or Salafist modes of religiosity hold for some post-Soviet Muslims stems from the failure of Soviet or Marxist ideology, or from the failure of the Soviet system to fully 'modernize' the lives and thought of Soviet Muslims. Soviet ideology, in this view, was undermined by the collapse of the Soviet Union and left a hole in the minds, and lives, of Muslims who were thus vulnerable to a 'competing' ideology to fill the void.

Such narratives, however, once again overlook the similarities between the intellectual formations to which 'reformist' and 'puritanical' religion tends to appeal, and those for which Soviet ideology, and Soviet 'modernity,' in fact offered superb preparation. Though this pattern may change, much

---

20 The misinterpretation of Islamist or Salafist religiosity is perhaps most clearly evident in the bewildering prescriptive rhetoric, in the popular media but often in broader 'scholarship' as well, insisting that the Islamic world is sorely in need of a Reformation such as occurred in Christendom 500 years ago; the prescription is obviously tinged with tropes of Muslim 'backwardness' and 'medieval' obscurantism, and on its face should be offensive to Catholics, but it overlooks the obvious parallels between Protestant critiques of Catholicism and Wahhābī and later Salafist critiques of *taqlīd*-bound, saint-centered Islam. The movements from which today's Muslim extremist agendas have emerged *were* the Protestant Reformation's equivalents in Muslim history. To be sure, the religious and intellectual links between the Reformation and rigid scriptural literalism have long been overlooked, in the context of European history as well, in favor of the narrative claiming that the expansion of literacy entailed by Protestant religiosity led to the Enlightenment and 'modern' liberal democracy (rather than to 'fundamentalism' and intolerance); the publication date of a key challenge to that narrative may remind us of its tenacity: see James Simpson, *Burning to Read: English Fundamentalism and its Reformation Opponents* (Cambridge, Massachusetts: Belknap Press of Harvard University Press, 2007).

of the sociological and ethnographic scholarship on post-Soviet Islam suggests that the appeal of Islamist or Salafist or "Wahhabi" rhetoric about purifying Islam, and oneself, is strongest precisely among the most 'Sovietized' of Soviet Muslims; those who remained closer, that is, to the 'traditional' modes of religiosity now attacked by Salafist groups have been as a rule less attracted by such rhetoric, and less inclined to see shrine-centered practices or healing traditions or amulet-collecting and so forth as contrary to Islamic rectitude.[21] On the intellectual level, the analysis of religion offered by Soviet ideology, which distinguished 'real' from 'folk' Islam and saw in the latter a pre-Islamic or 'national' aberration, likewise prepared those Soviet Muslims who drank most deeply from the Marxist-Leninist well to find the Salafist distinctions quite sound and acceptable. The combination of Soviet ideological and intellectual training (through the educational system) and a social and political environment in which former Soviet Muslim citizens have been encouraged to 'recover' something in their heritage or culture that the Soviet system had taken away from them provides an ideal foundation for 'returning' to Islam, and for choosing the version of Islam most in accord with the ways in which Soviet training taught Sovietized Muslims to think about Islam, and about religion.

Those pervasive Soviet understandings of what religion is are quite clearly paralleled in many Islamist agendas, which differ, to be sure, with regard to where religion should *belong*, but which ironically reinforce predispositions shaped by the Soviet system regarding what religion should *be*. It is thus, arguably, not the *failure* of Soviet ideology that has fostered radicalization in the post-Soviet Muslim world, but its success.

11) Faulty assumptions about the overall **'directionality' of religious developments** assumed to characterize the Soviet era: A final problematical assumption of the Soviet era that spilled over into post-Soviet times has to do with the insistence that what the Soviet era oversaw, and promoted, was a gradually accelerating diminution of religiosity among Soviet Muslims. This naturally fit into broader narratives of 'secularization' as an accompaniment of 'modernization,' beyond the Soviet world.[22] Already in the classic *Islam in*

21 See, for example, Wendell Schwab, "Traditions and Texts: How Two Young Women Learned to Interpret the Qur'an and Hadiths in Kazakhstan," *Contemporary Islam*, 6 (2012), pp. 173–197.

22 For a recent critical examination of the stock narrative of secularization leading to nationalism (as a replacement for religiosity) outside the Soviet context, see Geneviève Zubrzycki, *Beheading the Saint: Nationalism, Religion, and Secularism in Quebec* (Chicago: University of Chicago Press, 2016).

the Soviet Union, published in English in 1967, Bennigsen and Lemercier-Quelquejay wrote:

> What remains of the Muslim religion after some fifty years of administrative, police and 'scientific' measures designed to encompass its disappearance? On the surface, very little. The five 'pillars of the faith' … incumbent on all believers are no longer observed regularly.[23]

We will return, below, to the faulty metric for religiosity evoked in this assessment, but it is immediately noteworthy that so much scholarship on "Islam in the Soviet Union" concluded that religiosity had waned so thoroughly during the Soviet period, and that it had no 'public' dimension because of Soviet restrictions, and yet simultaneously argued that its most important role might nevertheless be to foster anti-Soviet sentiments among a population that was potentially hostile toward Soviet rule on multiple grounds.

In Soviet and often in post-Soviet times, the 'decline in religiosity' has been argued on the basis of the typical tools of Sovietology: mosque counts, madrasa counts, numbers of those who performed their prayers ('openly,' in the counted mosques), counts of antireligious lectures, and so forth. Such unilluminating markers and measures, constantly highlighted in Sovietological literature, were never suitable as accurate indicators of Muslim religious life. All these effects were real, to be sure, but they hardly give a realistic idea of the character of Muslim religious life, and to ignore (or deny the existence of) extensive religious practice in the late Soviet era (whether as a result of repression or 'modernization' and its presumed effects on religiosity) is to miss the ways in which the Soviet experience maintained, or heightened, a basic receptivity to religious dialogue (including that of Islamist groups), and to miss the ways the Soviet experience shaped the debate that ensued in post-Soviet times about the character and meaning of Islam (and Islamism). There can be little doubt that Soviet policy intended for Islam to disappear, but confusing policy with results is the business of politicians, not historians or analysts;[24] the further irony is that Islam disappeared only from the sight of those who used the wrong tools to search for it, and who defined it in such a way as to keep it out of sight. This issue will be discussed in more depth in the following section.

---

23 Alexandre Bennigsen and Chantal Lemercier-Quelquejay, *Islam in the Soviet Union* (New York: Praeger, 1967), p. 178.

24 Muslims are all but invisible in the recent study of Victoria Smolkin, *A Sacred Space is Never Empty: A History of Soviet Atheism* (Princeton, New Jersey: Princeton University Press, 2018), which nevertheless outlines well the failures of the Soviet project of promoting atheism, and of Soviet policies on religion in general.

1.3 *Misconceptions Rooted in Flawed Approaches to Religion*

12) The adoption, in Soviet, Sovietological, and post-Sovietological scholarship, of **narrow and unfruitful definitions and 'measures' of religiosity** that privilege standards of an essentialized 'Islam' over longstanding patterns of actual religious thought, practice, and attachment: In most discussions of Soviet and post-Soviet Islam, religious life – insofar as it could be seen through the veils of Soviet isolation – was measured not against religious life in the region on the eve of the establishment of Soviet power, or of the Russian conquest, but against an abstract and essentialized vision of what "Islam" was assumed to be, based on scriptural norms and idealized notions of the obligations of Muslim religious observance. This approach ironically turned visions of Islam that we would class as "Salafist" and, with appropriate caveats, "fundamentalist," into the norm against which actual religious life would be measured, first by Soviet writers, but eventually by Western scholars who knew to be skeptical of Soviet assessments in some contexts, but dropped their skepticism when dealing with 'academic' Soviet writing on Islam.

These unhelpful measures of religiosity include essentially meaningless standards of literacy or religious knowledge and specialization; they were rehearsed quite often in the Soviet era, but they have taken on new life in the post-Soviet age, as previously impossible research methods have become practicable, including survey research. Even partisans of surveys will acknowledge that the results are only as good as the questions employed; consider the following account, from a survey published in 1994:

> ... respondents were asked, 'Do you consider yourself a believer?' Those who answered yes were then asked, 'What faith do you profess?' ... The proportion expressing faith in Islam was higher among the Kyrgyz (81%) than among the Uzbeks (52%) and Kazakhs (49%). The high incidence of believers among the Kyrgyz is somewhat surprising since they (and the Kazakhs) often describe themselves as the 'least Islamic and most European' of the Central Asian peoples.... almost a third of the Uzbek believers and two-thirds of the Kazakh believers could not correctly translate the sentence 'There is no God other than Allah and Mohammed is his prophet' from the Arabic. Furthermore, about two-fifths of the Uzbek believers and three-quarters of the Kazakh believers said that they do not pray.[25]

---

25 Richard B. Dobson, "Islam in Central Asia: Findings from National Surveys," *Central Asia Monitor*, 1994, No. 2, pp. 18–19.

As we see, not only ignorance or neglect of specific ritual obligations, but ignorance of Arabic as well, was taken as a sign of defective Islam; religiosity was defined in terms of faith and the performance of religious rites, in a way that Salafists would find comforting. The demand to translate the *shahāda* is of particular irony, overlooking what the *shahāda* is and does from a Muslim standpoint. But such measures extended, in Soviet times, to both official and 'unofficial' clergy: many of both classes were decried for their ignorance of the Qur'ān, or of Arabic, or for illiteracy in general. Yet it is sobering to consider how thoroughly such meaningless measures were absorbed and perpetuated by analysts attempting to assess Soviet and post-Soviet Islam:

> Very few people in Central Asia possess more than a basic awareness that they are Muslim ... On a more practical level, few people speak Arabic, and even fewer can read it. The five pillars of Islam and rituals for prayer are known only in fragments, if at all. Even self-proclaimed 'believing Muslims' often lack the most fundamental knowledge: one third of this number could not translate the *Shahada* from Arabic.... The type of Islamic revival or renaissance that occurred after the disintegration of the Soviet Union must be judged, therefore, with such considerations in mind.[26]

As for ritual observance, another survey explored the question of whether subjects performed their "required" religious rites always, or only sometimes.[27] One wonders if it never occurred to those who formulated such questions that the answers might be considerably skewed precisely among the sort of people they might otherwise, given a moment's reflection, regard as particularly pious or devoted – that is, the sort of people who, sincerely or insincerely, gave voice to the virtue and propriety of humility and self-abasement, expressing one's imperfect, inadequate, undeserving character, or were indeed genuinely conscious of a certain incompatibility between religiosity and outright boasting. Perhaps the majority of respondents, who claimed to be observant 'sometimes'

---

26 Petra Steinberger, "'Fundamentalism' in Central Asia: Reasons, Reality, and Prospects," in *Central Asia: Aspects of Transition*, ed. Tom Everett-Heath (New York: RoutledgeCurzon, 2003), p. 224. Elsewhere, in the midst of quite muddled speculation about the implications of Central Asians' low level of "Islamic knowledge," Steinberger first doubts that someone lacking even "minimal knowledge of the Koran" could actually *be* an Islamist, but concludes that it might be plausible to argue that "a rapid rediscovery of the Koran could prevent Central Asians from being manipulated by extremists" (p. 244, n. 66); evidently, if Central Asians would only learn the fundamental sacred texts better, they would be immune to fundamentalism.

27 Richard Rose, "How Muslims View Democracy: Evidence from Central Asia," *Journal of Democracy*, 13/4 (October 2002), pp. 102–111.

(let us leave aside for now the problems entailed by referring to "required" practices and so forth), were merely being humble, or were simply acknowledging that their religious performance was lower than their religious aspiration, or were just modestly giving voice to some quite human self-doubt; perhaps some of these were not just reminded of their imperfection by the posing of the question during the survey, but were given to greater introspection and self-accounting by deep religious feeling (of course, awareness of religiously motivated or religiously framed humility or self-doubt may be especially difficult to come by among those trained to detect signs of ethnic, national, or sectarian 'pride'). Perhaps those (18% of the total) who were sure that they 'always' observed what was required of them should be dismissed either as liars or as obscenely prideful, and in either case counted as the *least* religious group within the sample.

Perhaps more instructive than the problematical wording of such questions, however, is simply what was counted, i.e., the kinds of 'religious' behavior that the surveys sought to quantify: belief, observance of the five pillars of Islam, and occasionally observance of various prohibitions, with alcohol consumption invariably stressed, but an arguably more pervasive historical marker of Muslim identity – the avoidance of pork – rarely mentioned. Let us briefly consider the kinds of things omitted from such surveys, ostensibly focused on 'religiosity.'[28]

28 It is worth noting here that Soviet antireligious literature often included survey data that – whatever we might argue about the implications of the aims underlying the collection of the data, the accuracy and honesty of their reporting, or the very context of antireligious workers asking about religious activity – were based on better questions than those that dominated Western literature from early post-Soviet times. In some of the very latest examples of antireligious literature, for instance, we find, instead of questions about 'belief' and translating Arabic, age-based data on participation in fasting, circumcision, and Muslim marriage and funeral rites (K.A. Azhybekova, *Molodezh' i problemy psikhologii religii i ateizma v usloviiakh sovremennoi NTR* [Frunze: Ilim, 1989], p. 131), and, alongside questions about performance of ritual prayers, questions about going to holy places, familial observance of *Qurbān-bayrām*, and views on circumcision and Muslim wedding rites and funerals (O.I. Pal'vanova, *Osobennosti ateisticheskogo vospitaniia zhenshchin v sovremennykh usloviiakh* [Ashkhabad: Ylym, 1988], pp. 51–53); in the latter case, the results, not surprisingly, are analyzed in terms of 'pre-Islamic' or Islamic origins (p. 59), but elsewhere we find information on falling numbers of sheep sacrificed during *kurban-ait* (through the 1970s, in this case) juxtaposed with an account of the *imam* of a mosque in Pavlodar openly encouraging observance of the feast (in 1979), and reminding his listeners that it was not necessary to know Arabic to be a faithful Muslim, and that those unable to sacrifice a sheep could nonetheless still cut meat into pieces for guests (K. Shulembaev, *Obraz zhizni, religiia, ateizm (Obshchee i osobennoe v obraze zhizni i religioznykh verovaniiakh kazakhov i voprosy ateisticheskogo vospitaniia)* [Alma-Ata: Kazakhstan, 1988], pp. 134–135). Even late-Soviet antireligious activists brought their own misconceptions to their work, to be sure, and using such data still presents substantial

As noted, the surveys often ask about prayer; but a key issue linked with prayer that is typically ignored is the notion of ritual purity, and the structuring of space and time so as to facilitate the maintenance and restoration of purity through specific ablutions and broader cleanliness standards; purity, indeed, has been a key component of Muslim identity, with non-Muslims recognized as impure. These issues are left unaddressed in the 'religion surveys.'

Similarly, issues of dress and comportment and the *adab* of speech and conduct are nowhere recognized as 'religious' matters to be measured or asked about. Patterns of dress of course changed significantly in the world of Soviet Islam, though various adaptations of older patterns, generally cast as reflective of 'national' customs of dress, in fact expressed mores rooted in religious principles and *adab* (headcoverings, maintaining modesty, etc.). It is worth noting, further, with regard to comportment, that ways of behavior and principles of conduct and the very forms of ordinary human actions remain part of the Muslim inheritance, even when not recognized by those who observe them, simply as the way things are to be done, or as the way Uzbeks or Qazaqs do things (I have in mind, for example, modes of greeting, showing deference, performing quite mundane actions, and simple physical bearing). For a time in the early post-Soviet period, my university town, Bloomington, was often the place to witness young Central Asians, even the most ostensibly 'secularized,' after long isolation from the rest of the Muslim world, encountering non-Central Asians who inexplicably behaved like Uzbeks or Qazaqs, and realizing that what they had assumed was Uzbek behavior was part of a "Muslim way" that was also manifested in the behavior of Pakistanis and Moroccans.

The point is not that the unconscious Muslim-ness of their conduct is more important than their conscious description of their conduct as 'the Qazaq way' or 'Uzbek etiquette,' and so forth; the point is that at a fundamental level of everyday life and ordinary activity, beyond matters of belief or unbelief, practice and piety or laxness and secularism, the very physicality of ordinary mannerisms is imbued with a recognizable Muslim component that (1) links the individual with a broader world, the Islamic world, (2) sets him apart not just from non-Qazaqs, for example, but from non-Muslims, and (3) offers a potential 'entry point' for the choice of deepening and interiorizing a rationale for such 'Muslim' behavior, whether in traditional terms (through the aim to recover or reconnect with a religious past as part of one's true heritage or identity), or in modern/reformist terms (through appeals by rigorists to bring conduct into closer accord with ideal models, and to instruct oneself in the foundations of such behavior in the Qur'ān and *ḥadīth*s).

---

problems of analysis and interpretation, but the problems are quite different from those raised by the vapid questions noted above from Western literature.

In the same vein, Sovietologists and post-Sovietologists would say, for example, that familial relations are a 'national' or ethnic matter, and might be influenced somewhat by 'religious' requirements – or, more likely, they will note that 'religious' concerns enter in as a focus for generational conflict between parents and children, for instance – but are not in and of themselves 'religious.' This is precisely what is meant by speaking of the need to expand our understanding of what is religious, and it is not merely to exalt a preferred category of analysis: family relations are 'religious' because the patterns that dominate in them have been shaped by religious models for generations (whether or not they were somehow explicitly prescribed, or can be linked with a positive injunction in some scriptural source: this is not the issue, and is not what makes them religious; rather, whatever their origin, they have been fitted into a religious framework by association with the Prophet's example, the ways of the ancestors, etc.).

The range of manifestations of Muslim religiosity that were almost never measured, or much discussed, in Sovietological literature is much wider, however; it includes a host of phenomena that can all be detached from 'religion' only through the narrowest and most historically-uninformed definition of 'religion.' Yet much discussion of Islam in the post-Soviet world still proceeds on the basis of surveys, and other research modes, that are framed without addressing these phenomena, and in fact without any awareness of them. What kind of picture of religiosity, in Soviet or post-Soviet times, can such measures yield? We will return shortly to some specific examples of what was missed, and is often still being missed, through the application of such faulty measures, and definitions, of religious life.

13) A *series* of **inadequate and misleading ways of "parsing" Islam**, involving the creation of largely arbitrary categories into which aspects of Muslim religiosity are divided: Most of these involve the creation of simple binary oppositions, and all of them parallel the inadequate measures of religiosity outlined above. Within the sphere of 'religion,' Sovietological scholarship treated us to a host of these pairs: 'official' vs. 'unofficial' religion or Islam, orthodoxy vs. heterodoxy, bookish vs. unlearned religion, elite vs. popular, legalist vs. Sufi, learned vs. folk, high vs. low, and 'modern' vs. 'pre-modern' versions of religion. The specific content of each of these binary oppositions might vary from writer to writer, but the usefulness of framing religious phenomena in this way was rarely questioned.[29]

---

29 See the perceptive, and well-grounded, comments on both the content and the framing of one of these oppositional categories in Rebecca Gould, "The Modernity of Premodern Islam in Contemporary Daghestan," *Contemporary Islam*, 5 (2011), pp. 161–183.

Perhaps the quintessentially 'Sovietological' binary opposition, of course, was the division of official vs. unofficial (or 'parallel') Islam, a distinction that in principle makes some sense in legal and administrative terms, but inevitably entailed a misguided mapping of legal status onto modes of religiosity, styles of religious practice, and types of religious specialists; this conflation of legal/administrative categories with modes of religiosity was then often projected into the past, but it caused the most mischief in accounts of Islam in the Soviet era.[30]

We can readily think of other oversimplified contrasts: conservative vs. liberal, traditional vs. modernist, political vs. quietist, militant vs. non-threatening, and so forth. Consider, for instance, the use of such terms, with regard to Muslims in the Soviet world, as 'liberal,' 'moderate,' 'conservative,' or 'radical;' while these terms may have a more-or-less recognized meaning and referential power in political science, such terms can occasion considerable mischief when applied to religious currents, to religiously-informed political and social agendas, and to social groups. We often hear, that is, characterizations of various Muslim peoples in parts of the Soviet and post-Soviet space as a predominantly 'moderate' Islamic population; but what in the world does 'moderate' mean in such a context? Leaving aside their frequent rehearsal in the 'threat-assessment' framework of 'policy analysis' noted briefly above, such terms warrant discussion and problematization if they are to be retained, but in most instances they would best be abandoned.

It is also worth noting that some phenomena could move around, from one pole, among our binary oppositions, to the other; the transformation of Sufism, after all, from a militant threat to a mainstay of peaceful and 'national' Islam and back to at least some sort of threat, in post-Soviet times, is a case in point.

The distinction made between 'folk' and 'real' Islam, or 'everyday' vs. 'formal' Islam, is equally harmful. The notion of '*bytovoi Islam*,' after all, sets up a distinction that inevitably casts the 'everyday' version as inferior to the 'real' or 'formal' version, and also makes a distinction in terms of context and

---

30 Not surprisingly, post-Soviet legal categories have followed their Soviet models in being based upon, and further reinforcing, simplistically dichotomous framings of religious attachment and affiliation; whether defined in terms of "traditional" religions vs. "new" varieties, of "indigenous" vs. "alien" traditions, or of faiths "historically implanted" in national soil vs. those counted, in effect, as noxious 'ideological' weeds or invasive species, post-Soviet nations have adopted legal categorizations for 'permitted' religious activities that are even less rooted in informed assessments of the diverse modes and measures of human religiosity than was the Soviet-era framework (derived mostly from Orthodox Christianity) for declaring some religious practice and affiliation tolerable and permitted, and others forbidden (less informed, that is, from the standpoint of both 'ideology' and social profile, but often based on 'bad history' as well).

functionality; just as we might use our 'everyday' china for ordinary meals, while reserving our best settings for formal occasions, or just as we wear our 'everyday' clothes more regularly than we put on our best, the 'ordinary' version of Islam is taken to be less valuable, even if it is more comfortable, than the formal version that is kept in reserve. The metaphor ends with the latter point, of course: those who deploy 'everyday Islam' are typically assumed *not* to be holding the real, formal, more valuable version in reserve.

Another additional noteworthy feature of this analytical mischief is the recurrent theme of religion becoming 'just' life-cycle rites; we are often told, that is, of the distinction between 'high' Islam and 'folk' Islam, with life-cycle rites relegated to the latter, and we are likewise told in some cases that a given community (perhaps nomadic, or implicitly ignorant, or in some cases all Soviet Muslims) has forgotten or abandoned learned Islam, and adheres *only* to the life-cycle rites of 'folk Islam.'[31] But consider the implication here: when 'religion' has to do with ideas about God and the afterlife, and with the performance of prayers and so forth, it is both important and authentic; but when 'religion' affects 'only' such minor events in a person's life as birth, marriage, and death, it is readily dismissed as insignificant and somehow aberrant.

The larger problem here, of course, is that such an attitude forestalls coming to terms with the ways in which the most intimately experienced aspects of religiosity might interact with and shape, or be shaped by, other aspects of religiosity that post-Sovietological researchers might find more significant; once again, it is the central, if often misguided, concerns of such researchers that suffer the most, in terms of understanding, from their short-sighted and profoundly unimaginative approaches.

We may also consider, however, the broader reach of such binary oppositions, to govern, and segregate, religion itself. The literature on 'Islam in the Soviet Union,' that is, 'contributed' to scholarship on religion not only a series of binary oppositions within the world counted as 'religious,' but a larger binary opposition between 'religion' and other phenomena regarded as standing outside religion. From 'religion vs. nationalism' and 'religion vs. secularism' or 'religion vs. modernity,' all writ broadly, to 'Islamic vs. Soviet' or 'Muslim vs. Marxist' in a somewhat narrower framework, these simplistic binary oppositions were rarely argued, but were simply assumed as the starting points

31 For early challenges to such analytical mischief regarding life-cycle rites and the honoring of ancestors among Soviet and post-Soviet Muslims, see Bruce G. Privratsky, *Muslim Turkistan: Kazak Religion and Collective Memory* (Richmond, Surrey: Curzon Press, 2001), and, for a different part of Central Asia, I. Bellér-Hann, "'Making the Oil Fragrant': Dealings with the Supernatural among the Uyghurs in Xinjiang," *Asian Ethnicity*, 2/1 (2001), pp. 9–23.

for discussion, in 'Sovietological' scholarship, with 'religion' understood and defined in the most constricted terms; often the definition of religion, if ever made explicitly, guaranteed that many things would stand outside it, and the ensuing analysis of the various binary oppositions was offered as proof of the basic correctness of the definition.

We might object here that narrow, limited, and constricted understandings of religion are simply the result of, and a measure of, the success of modernity and of the secularization it brings. It is incumbent upon scholars, however, not merely to accept and assume the prejudices current in their time, and not merely to speak a single language, as it were, but to be able to suspend, or transcend, commonly accepted assumptions and interpretations, and to master the discourse of multiple communities; more broadly, it is increasingly being recognized that 'religion vs. the secular' is itself an overdrawn dichotomy in real life, one that is seldom helpful if we seek to grasp the very concrete and 'messy' manifestations of religiosity in the 'modern' world.[32]

Nevertheless, uncritical – and simply uninformed – assumptions about what should be considered 'religious' and what should not continue to yield a host of unhelpful distinctions (e.g., religion vs. politics, religion vs. nationalism, religion vs. culture, etc.) and a wide-ranging pattern of clouded thinking in studies of Islam in the post-Soviet world. These assumptions rest on an essentially circular argument requiring 'definitional' mischief: 'religion' and religiosity and 'religious' motivations, etc., are defined in extremely narrow terms that exclude nearly everything having any connection to normal life in the world from what can be considered 'religious' (i.e., religion is praying, performing rites mentioned in some sacred text, or otherwise conforming to the essentialized 'pedagogical minimum' of being a Muslim); the circle is then completed by declaring that most Soviet Muslims were, or are, not 'religious' in this way, and religion is thus found to have only a narrow impact.

This tendency extends even to considerations of the 'threat' supposedly posed by radical Islamists with political aspirations couched in rhetoric deemed 'religious;' such overtly Islamic political goals, including for instance the establishment of an 'Islamic state,' are then made the standard for 'religious' influence on politics, most 'post-Soviet Muslims' are declared not to want such a thing, and so their political aspirations are declared to be

32 For two recent works that may be read as arguments for recognizing the pervasive 'intrusions,' into the modern and the secular, of a more broadly-envisioned religiosity, in both intellectual and physical terms, see Jason Ā. Josephson-Storm, *The Myth of Disenchantment: Magic, Modernity, and the Birth of the Human Sciences* (Chicago: University of Chicago Press, 2017), and Robert A. Orsi, *History and Presence* (Cambridge, Massachusetts: The Belknap Press of Harvard University Press, 2016).

untouched by Islam. In this way, for instance, political organizing – an obviously problematical proposition, after all – was taken as the measure for a 'religious' impact on society and politics, but religiously informed notions of social and individual justice are excluded. The point is that religious identity has been shaped in the past and continues to be shaped by experiences and forces well beyond the rather narrow range of activities typically classed as 'religious;' and in the end, if there is indeed a correlation between an 'Islamic identity' and support for 'political Islam,' does it not become even more important to envision, and understand, multiple varieties of Islamic identity and their historical development?

Finally, on another front, but still among the simplistic binary oppositions that prevail in this field, it is worth noting that even the basic juxtaposition of 'Islamic' vs. 'Soviet' is beginning to break down, through work recognizing that Soviet Muslims could aspire to be good Soviet citizens and good Muslims at one and the same time.[33]

14) The discourse of religion as **morality**: This is a relative newcomer to the language of scholarship on Soviet and post-Soviet Islam; it was virtually unheard of in the Soviet era, and in some ways marked a step forward in post-Soviet considerations of Islam in Central Asia, but I believe it too holds some potential for mischief, and, more broadly, for muddying the waters instead of bringing clarity. I have in mind here the recent spate of sociological and ethnographic studies that foreground issues of 'morality' when discussing issues that would once have been framed within the general rubric of 'Islam in the Soviet Union.' There was not much discussion of 'morality' in the Sovietological literature, aside from the occasional acknowledgment that members of the official religious establishments (who else could be heard, after all?) sometimes affirmed the confluence, of sorts, between socialist morality and Muslim moral principles. More recently, however, discussions of 'Islam in a particular post-Soviet space' have often put issues of morality, moral aspirations, and the

33 This is the argument of Eren Tasar's *Soviet and Muslim*, but see also his "Islamically Informed Soviet Patriotism in Postwar Kyrgyzstan," *Cahiers du monde russe*, 52/2–3 (2011), pp. 387–404. Now see also Jeff Eden, *God Save the USSR: Soviet Muslims and the Second World War* (Oxford: Oxford University Press, 2021); in different ways, both Tasar and Eden show how Soviet Muslims managed to negotiate an unquestionably religious space for themselves – within an environment only partly shaped by Soviet ideology, policy, and law hostile to Islam, and to religion in general – not through open or clandestine opposition to the Soviet regime, but through learning, as solid Soviet citizens, how to read both the ideals and realities of Soviet rule and then how to use those ideals and realities for aims they could argue, or simply assume, were fully compatible with the Soviet experiment.

construction of moral selves at the forefront, to the point that other aspects of religiosity recede into the background or disappear altogether.

To some extent this trend must be taken as a positive development, insofar as acknowledging that religiously-informed moral development should be part of what we mean by 'Islam in the post-Soviet world,' or anywhere, for that matter, marks a step forward from looking for 'Islam' only in the threatening, the militant, or the overtly political. Yet at the same time, there is a danger in 'renaming' religion as morality. Sometimes this may be done in line with various theoretical constructions, or simply because some academics are uncomfortable with 'religion' in the first place and find 'morality' a more soothing, less intellectually threatening concept. But this renaming may also tend to crowd out the many other facets of religiosity that cannot be reduced to morality, and it risks, once again, privileging the versions of Islam that downplay or reject those other facets and 'sell' their brand of religion as a means of personal moral cultivation.[34]

In other words, this academic trend risks privileging the scripturalist, reformist, and puritanical versions of Islam, by foregrounding individual moral development, and individual moral responsibility, along with the various directions in which these concerns may lead; this approach may thus contribute to another unhelpful bifurcation of 'Islam' into its 'moral' components, deemed positive, and its ritual, thaumaturgical, therapeutic, aesthetic, and social components, relegated to secondary importance and perhaps framed as harmful. Scholarship highlighting 'morality' as the key 'field' in which religion operates may subtly privilege rigorist and scripturalist versions of Islam and their call for moral purification; though they can also be punctilious with regard to standards of 'bodily purity,' for instance, these standards are cast in a 'moral' framework of observing divine injunctions. But should this sort of understanding dominate our sense of what 'religion' is, at the expense of less self-conscious habits also rooted in the Qurʾān, *ḥadīth*, or *adab*? By privileging such views, the growing scholarship on 'morality' risks suggesting that Islam

34 It also risks overlooking the important sphere of religious expression that seeks cultivation and personal development not chiefly in terms of morality and ethics, but in terms of material success and skill in negotiating the social worlds of politics or work and business (motives which our knee-jerk, Protestant-based notions of religion, if not overcome or at least suspended, might immediately define – unhelpfully – as 'worldly' or even 'cynical' and hence 'non-religious'); for a discussion of the latter, see Alfrid K. Bustanov, "Beyond the Ethnic Traditions: Shamil' Aliautdinov's Muslim Guide to Success," in *Islamic Authority and the Russian Language: Studies on Texts from European Russia, the North Caucasus, and West Siberia*, ed. Alfrid K. Bustanov and Michael Kemper (Amsterdam: Pegasus, 2012), pp. 143–164.

is about personal ethical behavior, but not about personal hygiene, dress, or comportment (much less about personal or social experiences at a shrine, and so forth).

15) The **neglect of a series of manifestations of Muslim religiosity in the Soviet era:** This 'field of error' covers a host of phenomena and developments, some neglected because of inadequate sources – though a lack of imagination regarding what sort of sources to explore was a defining shortcoming of Sovietological scholarship on Islam – and others neglected because of misguided assumptions about where religiosity was manifested and how it might be measured (as considered above). We are, to be sure, gradually learning the extent of what we did not know that we did not know about 'Islam in the Soviet Union,' through increased access to archival material, to private collections of manuscripts, papers, and memorabilia, and, here and there, to the living memories of Muslims and others who lived through substantial portions of the Soviet era.[35] The body of 'new sources' of the post-Soviet era will no doubt continue to expand; but the flaws of Sovietology cannot be explained solely in terms of problems with access to sources.

It is certainly true that the Soviet era posed major difficulties in terms of sources to explore for evidence of Muslim religiosity; the scarcity of 'direct' sources, however, might have spurred a search for other kinds of materials to be explored for such evidence, and such a search could have gone hand in hand with an expanded grasp of the forms religious expression might take, but neither ever happened in the world of Sovietology. When long ago I began teaching a course called, initially, "Islam in the Soviet Union," I used to remind students that, beyond the press reports and anti-religious literature relied upon by the Sovietologists – whose method was largely to attempt to read between the lines of official publications of various sorts – there were other kinds of materials that could be used to try to better understand Muslim religious life in the USSR. I usually stressed ethnographic literature and the insights to be gained from 'epic' and folkloric materials, replete with elements of Muslim religiosity that were often overlooked, but I also stressed the basic, but largely untapped, value of the historical record, and historical sources on Islam in the various regions of Soviet Islam, both as a baseline for measuring the impact of Soviet policies, and above all simply as a storehouse of

---

35 See, for example, Alfrid K. Bustanov, "Muslim Literature in the Atheist State: Zainap Maksudova between Soviet Modernity and Tradition," *Journal of Islamic Manuscripts*, 9 (2018), pp. 1–31; idem, "Against Leviathan: On the Ethics of Islamic Poetry in Soviet Russia," in *The Piety of Learning: Islamic Studies in Honor of Stephan Reichmuth*, ed. Michael Kemper and Ralf Elger (Leiden: Brill, 2017), pp. 199–224.

information needed to understand the 'shape' of Muslim religiosity in those areas, offering a grounded perspective that could help make sense of, or point out the improbability of, the claims and representations of Bennigsen and others.

Ironically, some neglected developments were directly connected with the emergence of extremist groups in Central Asia, but were completely missed by most outside observers, whose Sovietological training left them unaware of the context and substance of significant developments, and who focused their attention instead on issues of lesser consequence. Studies of the religious fault-lines that emerged already in Soviet times – fault lines that had little to do with the standard Sovietological 'parsing' of 'official' vs. 'unofficial' Islam, and more to do with longstanding divides in Muslim juridical interpretation – began to appear already in the first decade of the 21st century,[36] as did extensive publications of texts illuminating the debates that unfolded between upholders of longstanding Central Asian ways of being Muslim, on the one hand, and Salafi-inspired opponents, and 'reformers,' of indigenous, or indigenized, models of Islam, on the other;[37] that the debates occurred both outside the official religious boards and within them – with the latter developments ironically strengthening the appeal of Salafi-style versions of Muslim religiosity – underscores the vitality of religious discourse, and disagreements, in the Soviet environment.

---

36 See, for example, Bakhtiyar Babadjanov and Muzaffar Kamilov, "Muhammadjan Hindustani (1892–1989) and the Beginning of the 'Great Schism' among the Muslims of Uzbekistan," in *Islam in Politics in Russia and Central Asia*, ed. Stephane Dudoignon and Komatsu Hisao (London: Kegan Paul, 2001), pp. 195–220; Babadjanov, "Debates over Islam in Contemporary Uzbekistan;" Ashirbek Muminov, "Fundamentalist Challenges to Local Islamic Traditions in Soviet and Post-Soviet Central Asia," *Empire, Islam, and Politics in Central Eurasia*, ed. Uyama Tomohiko (Sapporo: Slavic Research Center, Hokkaido University, 2007), pp. 249–261; M. Olimov and S Shokhumorov, "Islamskie intellektualy v Tsentral'noi Azii XX v.: Zhizn' i bor'ba Mavlavi Khindustoni (1892–1989)," *Vostok* (*Afro-aziatskie obshchestva: Istoriia i sovremennost'*), 2003, No. 6, pp. 33–47; Tasar, "The Offical Madrasas;" Sartori and Babajanov, "Being Soviet, Muslim, Modernist, and Fundamentalist;" and the invaluable contributions to the volume *Islamic Education in the Soviet Union and its Successor States*, ed. Michael Kemper, Raoul Motika, and Stefan Reichmuth (London/New York: Routledge, 2010).

37 See B.M. Babadzhanov, A.K. Muminov, and A. fon Kiugel'gen, *Disputy musul'manskikh religioznykh avtoritetov v Tsentral'noi Azii v XX veke* (Almaty: Daik-Press, 2007), and the series prepared by Allen J. Frank, *Uzbek Islamic Debates: Texts, Translations, and Commentary* (with Jahangir Mamatov; Springfield, Virginia: Dunwoody Press, 2006), *Popular Islamic Literature in Kazakhstan: An Annotated Bibliography* (Hyattsville, Maryland: Dunwoody Press, 2007), and *Tatar Islamic Texts* (Hyattsville, Maryland: Dunwoody Press, 2008).

More broadly, these studies should remind us that if we look only at developments of the post-Soviet era, and attempt to understand either the broader 'resurgence' of Islamic religious life (broadly conceived), or the narrower appeal of Islamist groups, solely as consequences of the demise of the Soviet state and its antireligious policies, we will have missed much of the spadework and fertilization of earlier decades that prepared the ground, often in ironic ways, for the growth of Islamist movements, and we will have ignored the structure of continuities and discontinuities in Muslim thought, stretching back much further than the Soviet era, into which the current debates about what "Islam" should mean must rightfully be situated.

On the other hand, a wider range of religious developments in the Soviet era, and religious continuities with still earlier periods, were completely invisible to outside observers during Soviet times, and have been neglected or ignored in post-Soviet times as well. For example, economic issues were, naturally, central to the Soviet Marxist project; but we rarely find any discussion of the impact of Soviet policies on the religious aspects of economic life, aside from accounts of the seizure of *waqf*-property and 'religious' buildings, and their transformation into other uses, or of the scale of donations made to the official religious boards. These issues are of clear importance, but the penetration of religion into economic life goes much deeper. Unaware of the multiple ways in which labor and economic life were sacralized in pre-Soviet Muslim society,[38] for instance, Sovietologists rarely discussed the social, and religious, impact of the decoupling of religion and work that occurred through the Sovietization of economic life; but by the same token, they also missed the continuation and adaptation of the religious aspects of traditional occupations in spheres that had been re-shaped by the Soviet transformations of economic life.[39]

---

38 See the study of Jeanine Elif Dağyeli, *'Gott liebt das Handwerk:' Moral, Identität und religiöse Legitimierung in der mittelasiatischen Handwerks-risāla* (Wiesbaden: Reichert Verlag, 2011), and her "La construction des identités collectives d'après les chartes des corps de métier (risāla) en Asie centrale," *Cahiers d'Asie Centrale*, 19–20 (2011), pp. 73–84.

39 See, for example, the account of an auto mechanics' guild in Khorezm in the 1950s, in G.P. Snesarev, "Traditsiia muzhskikh soiuzov v ee pozdneishem variante u narodov Srednei Azii," in *Polevye issledovaniia Khorezmskoi èkspeditsii v 1958–1961 gg.*, II: *Pamiatniki srednevekovogo vremeni; Ètnograficheskie raboty* (Moscow: Izd-vo AN SSSR, 1963; = *Materialy Khorezmskoi èkspeditsii*, vyp. 7), pp. 155–205; and for a saint's shrine at a hydroelectric station (in Russian, *gidro-èlektricheskaia stantsiia*, with the acronym GÈS), known as "*GÈS äulie*," see *Qazïnalï ongtüstik*, t. 22 (Almaty: Nŭrlï Älem, 2011), pp. 165–166 (I am indebted to Allen Frank for this reference).

Similarly, the ongoing vitality of shrine traditions, and the maintenance of shrine facilities – sometimes with the acquiescence of officials, sometimes despite their efforts, and in both cases effectively 'subversive' of official policy – was largely ignored by most outside observers in Soviet times, and this habit continued long into the post-Soviet era; the key economic roles played by shrines, and the impact (and evasion) of Soviet strictures upon them, were rarely subjects of interest to students of Soviet or post-Soviet Islam, and the same is true of the much more basic centrality of shrines for Muslim burial rites and their importance for families and larger communities. To his credit, Bennigsen did pay attention, if in historically uninformed ways, to 'Sufi shrines,' which he sought to link with Sufi orders, and in which he saw centers of organizational resistance to Soviet power; most Sovietological assessments of shrine culture, however, in both Soviet and post-Soviet times, proceeded from the assumption that shrines were at best a concession to 'popular religion,' or at worse belonged wholly to the world of 'folk Islam' (or 'pre-Islamic' Islam!) rather than to real Islam, consciously or unconsciously channeling the Salafist-style critiques of shrine visitation.

With shrine-centered religious practice thus framed as outside the bounds of Islam, most post-Sovietological writers paid little attention to exploring shrines as religious spaces and as the setting for religious rites, or even as focal points of religious contention between upholders and critics of the legitimacy of the visitation of saints' shrines. As a result, shrines remained largely invisible in discussions of post-Soviet Islam through the 1990s, and although attention to shrines has increased substantially in the past 15 years, they rarely figure in most 'policy analysis' frameworks (unless as evidence of the tainted character of Islam in post-Soviet environments).[40]

The ritual, social, and economic aspects of shrine culture are naturally instructive with regard to the landscapes of Soviet and post-Soviet Islam, but shrines also served as sites where the lore of saints was 'packaged' and transmitted, and where both local communities and pilgrim communities from other regions sought, and experienced, different kinds of religious authority. Yet studying Soviet-era adaptations of hagiographical narratives was not in the repertoire of Sovietological training. The Soviet world seems not to have yielded the specific sorts of 20th-century adaptations of shrine- and saint-lore,

40 Such inattention to, or misconstruing of, shrine traditions contrasts sharply with the nuanced and historically grounded discussion of shrines in R.D. McChesney, *Central Asia: Foundations of Change* (Princeton, New Jersey: The Darwin Press, 1996), pp. 71–115, and in McChesney's *Four Central Asian Shrines: A Socio-Political History of Architecture* (Leiden: Brill, 2021).

and of actual hagiographical texts, explored by Rian Thum in another part of Central Asia,[41] but hagiographical tales circulating among Soviet citizens, and employed by them to do everything from explaining communal origins to negotiating social or familial tensions, were amply documented by Soviet ethnographers[42] – who, to be sure, insisted on paying attention not to their adaptation from earlier versions or to their use, but to their presumed status as repositories of hoary 'traditions' that predated Islamization, in the familiar cant reflecting the notion of religious 'survivals.'

Until recently students of Soviet Islam have mostly ignored this rich narrative material, however, missing a body of locally-rooted lore that is connected to historical narrative patterns, to be sure, but speaks to the ways in which Soviet Muslims made sense of and coped with the pressures of Soviet life.[43] Indeed, the vitality and dynamism of particular modes of hagiographical narratives – stories of miraculous deliverance from repression, of supernaturally supercharged Soviet machinery, or of the dire punishments that awaited the officials who bulldozed a saint's shrine – and their use in a subtly subversive rhetoric that challenged, if not overtly opposing or resisting, Soviet power are showcased in the materials from Soviet Kazakhstan recently assembled and analyzed by Allen Frank.[44]

Also noteworthy among the manifestations of religiosity missed in Soviet times, and still largely ignored today in post-Sovietological literature, is the set of communally-enacted rituals, often rooted in Sufi practice but long ago adapted in other social settings, that came to be labeled as something other than Muslim rituals, as I have explored elsewhere.[45] Likewise, the Soviet

41 Rian Thum, *The Sacred Routes of Uyghur History* (Cambridge, Massachusetts: Harvard University Press, 2014).

42 See, for instance, G.P. Snesarev, *Khorezmskie legendy kak istochnik po istorii religioznykh kul'tov Srednei Azii* (Moscow: Nauka, 1983).

43 See now the study of Paolo Sartori, "Of saints, shrines, and tractors: Untangling the meaning of Islam in Soviet Central Asia," *Journal of Islamic Studies*, 30 (2019), pp. 367–405.

44 Allen J. Frank, *Gulag Miracles: Sufis and Stalinist Repression in Kazakhstan* (Vienna: Austrian Academy of Sciences Press, 2019; Veröffentlichungen zur Iranistik, Nr. 84; Studies and Texts on Central Asia, Band 2).

45 See my "Shamanization," and "Re-envisioning the History of Sufi Communities," as well as my foreword to *Sobranie fetv po obosnovaniiu zikra dzhakhr i sama'*, ed. B.M. Babadzhanov and S.A. Mukhammadaminov (Almaty: Daik-Press, 2008), pp. 9–15. Material on similar rituals can be mined from the rich contributions to *Allah's Kolkhozes: Migration, De-Stalinisation, Privatisation and the New Muslim Congregations in the Soviet Realm (1950s–2000s)*, ed. Stéphane Dudoignon and Christian Noack (Berlin: Klaus Schwarz Verlag, 2014); see also Sergei Abashin, "A Prayer for Rain: Practising Being Soviet and Muslim," *Journal of Islamic Studies*, 25/2 (2014), pp. 178–200, and with reference both to ritual and to Islamically-infused framings of kinship, Sergei Abashin, *Sovetskii kishlak:*

era saw the overt suppression of the prestige, and documentary legacies, of Muslim sacred lineages, whether *khoja* groups or 'holy tribes,' defined through religiously-rooted genealogical traditions; but it also saw the maintenance of the lore of these communities, and the dramatic resurfacing, and reformulation, of such familial 'domestications' of sacrality, often linked to shrine traditions and accompanied by old and new iterations of their genealogical 'charters,' are among the most remarkable features of Muslim religiosity in the post-Soviet era.[46]

Yet the intimate connection between Islam and kinship structures has also remained off the radar of much of the literature on Islam in the post-Soviet world, despite the clear social, economic, and even political importance of these religiously-defined groups, and despite the key links between the sacralization of kinship and the sacralization of the nation. Just as we seldom encounter, in Sovietological literature, allusions, even, to the phenomenon of 'holy families' as embodiments of Islamic identity, we likewise find little about healing practices that involve 'religion' in the most intimate aspects of ordinary life, or about the ubiquitous amulets and charms that are likewise tangible embodiments, and symbols, of religiosity; similarly, discussions of 'religious education' typically ignored the countless practical examples and 'instructional' venues that shape religious performance and identity, evidently because they stand outside the formal framework of a 'religious' school.

All these developments are gradually being brought to light, however; they include not simply the continuation, or 'revival,' of old patterns, but adaptive responses to official policies, and dynamic new variations on older patterns,

---

Mezhdu kolonializmom i modernizatsiei (Moscow: Novoe Literaturnoe Obozrenie, 2015), esp. pp. 498–546.

46 For an overview of the *khoja* phenomenon, see my foreword to *Islamizatsiia i sakral'nye rodoslovnye v Tsentral'noi Azii: Nasledie Iskhak Baba v narrativnoi i genealogicheskoi traditsiiakh*, Tom 2: *Genealogicheskie gramoty i sakral'nye semeistva XIX–XXI vekov: nasab-nama i gruppy khodzhei, sviazannykh s sakral'nym skazaniem ob Iskhak Babe / Islamization and Sacred Lineages in Central Asia: The Legacy of Ishaq Bab in Narrative and Genealogical Traditions*, Vol. 2: *Genealogical Charters and Sacred Families: Nasab-namas and Khoja Groups linked to the Ishaq Bab Narrative, 19th–21st Centuries*, ed. Ashirbek Muminov, Anke von Kügelgen, Devin DeWeese, Michael Kemper (Almaty: Daik-Press, 2008), pp. 6–33; see also S.N. Abashin, "Potomki sviatykh v sovremennoi Srednei Azii," *Ètnograficheskoe obozrenie*, 2001, No. 4, pp. 62–82, and Ulan Bigozhin, "Shrine, State, and Sacred Lineage in Post-Soviet Kazakhstan," Ph.D. dissertation, Indiana University, 2017. The classic Soviet-era study of the Türkmen holy tribes is S.M. Demidov, *Turkmenskie ovliady* (Ashkhabad: Ylym, 1976); the holy tribes received no attention in Adrienne Lynn Edgar, *Tribal Nation: The Making of Soviet Turkmenistan* (Princeton, New Jersey: Princeton University Press, 2004).

such as the emergence of Russian as a 'language of Islam,'[47] or the 'nationalized' refractions of shrine culture in the *Ata zholï* movement (now banned) in Kazakhstan.[48] In time, with increasing attention and an effort to understand them against the backdrop of historical patterns that do not always fall neatly within the temporal markers of Tsarist or Soviet history, their study will enrich, and transform, our understanding of Muslim religious life in the Soviet era, and facilitate the inclusion of Muslim voices in our understanding of the broader historical experience of the USSR.[49]

2 Religion 101

The problematical features outlined here need to be individually addressed and analyzed, both in terms of critiquing them and in terms of building an alternative narrative. Yet it is also possible to distill something further from this list, in terms of identifying the overarching problems that have yielded such deficiencies in the field. As indicated above, the final four of the 15 'fields of error,' and indeed quite a few of the rest, at least in part, can be subsumed into a broader patter of resistance, among those who have written about Soviet and post-Soviet Islam, to thinking about 'religion' using the conceptual tools and analytical frameworks developed in the field of religious studies over the past century.[50]

Most specialists, that is, who have written about some aspect of Islam in the Soviet and post-Soviet world have discussed religious life uncritically, without giving the terminology they employ, or the conceptual frameworks they

47 See the contributions to *Islamic Authority and the Russian Language: Studies on Texts from European Russia, the North Caucasus, and West Siberia*, ed. Alfrid K. Bustanov and Michael Kemper (Amsterdam: Uitgeverij Pegasus, 2012), as well as Alfrid K. Bustanov, "The Language of Moderate Salafism in Eastern Tatarstan," *Islam and Christian-Muslim Relations*, 28/2 (2017), pp. 183–201.

48 See Aitzhan Nurmanova, "Pilgrimages to Mazars in Contemporary Kazakhstan: The Processes of Revivalism and Innovation," in *Mazar: Studies on Islamic Sacred Sites in Central Eurasia*, ed. Sugawara Jun and Rahile Dawut (Tokyo: Tokyo University of Foreign Studies, 2016), pp. 63–72; and the earlier study of Pawel Jessa, "Aq jol Soul Healers: Religious Pluralism and a Contemporary Muslim Movement in Kazakhstan," *Central Asian Survey*, 25/3 (2006), pp. 359–371.

49 On this goal, see Paolo Sartori, "Towards a History of the Muslims' Soviet Union: A View from Central Asia," *Die Welt des Islams*, 50 (2010), pp. 315–334.

50 This is not, of course, the only field in which such resistance may be lamented; see the comments about the study of Islamic origins in Aaron W. Hughes, "Religion without Religion: Integrating Islamic Origins into Religious Studies," *Journal of the American Academy of Religion*, 85/4 (2017), pp. 867–888 [pp. 880–881].

assume, the considered and thoughtful treatment they would naturally devote, in their respective disciplines, to various levels of professional jargon. Rather, they have seemed to assume that religion itself, as a category, and the terminology of religion and religious life, have self-evident and universally accepted meanings; they have applied what appear to be "common-sense" understandings of what religion is and of how it should be discussed, without problematizing the terminology or the conceptual frameworks it presupposes. This resistance to engaging critically with religious studies is strongest, it seems, among political scientists, less so among anthropologists, with sociologists somewhere in the middle (hampered by their ruthlessly presentist perspective), though unfortunately many historians likewise resist thinking more broadly, or deeply, about 'religion.'

The discussion of religion by such 'resisters' tends to reflect the ordinary, and contemporary Western, expectations about what religion is and where it is found and how it 'acts,' without further reflection, and without being informed by, or utilizing the tools of, the more specialized inquiry of religious studies.[51] In Europe and the U.S., some of those unfruitful ways of thinking about religion are rooted, indeed, in cherished assumptions about our 'civil religion' that are not unlike many of the restrictions on religious life in the former USSR, e.g., the insistence that religion be a personal matter, that it be first and foremost a matter of belief, and indeed 'private' belief, that it should be restricted in its impact, as much as possible, to particular times (one day a week) and places (a church, a mosque), and that it should have little or nothing to do with work and economic activity, with education, with public, civic, and governmental affairs, or with the larger world of culture and society. It should be obvious, of course, that approaching religious life from this perspective leaves one grossly ill-equipped to understand the functioning of religion through most of human history, and still today, among 'religious' people; but in case it is not obvious, scholarship on religion has moved steadily away from many of the common

51 Those Western expectations, shaped by post-Reformation and post-Enlightenment critiques of religion and (whether pro- or anti-religion) broadly reflecting Protestant Christian conceptualizations of religion, have been called out as particularly problematical with regard to understanding Muslim experience (see, for example, Carl W. Ernst, *Following Muhammad: Rethinking Islam in the Contemporary World* [Chapel Hill: University of North Carolina Press, 2003]), but they continue to inform the basic assumptions underlying discussions of Islam in the Soviet and post-Soviet environments, shaping many of those 15 'fields of error.'

assumptions that stand in the way of a better and more fruitful understanding of religiosity.[52]

Scholarship on religion has moved away, that is, from essentialist understandings of particular traditions that focus on laying out the 'basic doctrines' and 'essential duties' of a given religious system, usually based on the 'foundational' texts discussed under the rubric of 'scripture;' it has moved away from an exclusive focus on 'belief' and toward an enhanced, deepened exploration of ritual systems and performative paradigms; and it has moved toward considering religion as a category of belonging and participation and community, stressing the social and communal aspects of religious life and religious affiliation, and recognizing that belonging to a religiously-defined community is often as central a part of religious life, and religious meaning, as is 'belief' in particular doctrines or the practice of particular rites.

Within this triad of religious 'basics,' however – belief/doctrine/worldview/ knowledge, ritual/practice/action, and community/fellowship/sociability (i.e., affiliation with a group that understands itself *as* a group *because* of its religious orientation) – belief alone takes center stage in most ordinary contemporary Western understandings of religion; and the tendency to foreground belief is further entrenched in the subject of Soviet Islam, insofar as the Soviet state defined religion primarily in terms of belief, and identified those of its citizens deemed particularly in need of 'reform' or education as "believers." Such a definition had much to do with the shortcomings of Soviet antireligious policies among Muslims, but all too often scholarship on Islam in the Soviet and post-Soviet worlds has followed Soviet policy into the analytical dead-end of emphasizing belief, and believers, as the key categories for framing religiosity.

To reduce religion, however, to a yes-or-no question, to the acceptance or rejection of an intellectual proposition, is immediately recognizable as an inadequate way of approaching or understanding the ways in which religion has manifested itself, or been experienced, in most of human history. To begin

---

52 This is not to say that the movement is yet complete; for a concise and insightful discussion of the place of Islam in religious studies, and of the notion of 'religion' in Islam – highlighting commonalities between Muslim and Western conceptions of 'religion,' the diversity of Muslim 'religiosity,' and disjunctures that render commonplace understandings of 'religion' a poor framework for approaching Islam – see Ahmet T. Karamustafa, "Islamic *Dīn* as an Alternative to Western Models of 'Religion,'" in *Religion, Theory, Critique: Classic and Contemporary Approaches and Methodologies*, ed. Richard King (New York: Columbia University Press, 2017), pp. 163–171.

with, defining religious activity in terms of 'belief' immediately imposes an 'either/or' dichotomy that is belied by the lives and activities of those who actually participate in religious traditions, and by an appreciation of the grey areas of religious life, of multiple layers of commitment, and of varied understandings of religious obligations and expectations. In some circles, to equate religion with belief and with intellectual propositions also relegates religious adherents to the world of the gullible, the irrational, or the uneducated; 'believers' are viewed as holding untenable ideas, rather than as making their experience meaningful, and indeed building selves and 'writing' or rewriting lives, by using the wider range of tools provided by religious life – wider, that is, than simply doctrine and belief.

Moreover, approaching religious 'belief' as an internal mental process, i.e., a positive and conscious agreement with a particular idea or assertion (or with a set of such assertions) immediately relegates, for example, an unconsciously internalized set of assumptions and outlooks that affect the way individuals perceive the world, that shape their entire experience of it, and that comprises, in effect, their 'religious' worldview, to a category outside 'belief' and hence, from this limited perspective, outside 'religion.' In addition, focusing on 'belief,' and on adherents of a religious system as its 'believers,' elevates this purely internal, mental act to the level of the definitive marker of commitment and devotion to a particular religious tradition, and implicitly downgrades those who participate in their religious tradition with their words and their bodies, or who seek social ties that may or may not be dependent upon shared 'belief.'

For all the reasons outlined here, finally, an emphasis on 'belief' as the defining feature of religiosity is fundamentally out of step with the particular religious system we are concerned with here; whether by characterizing Islam as more concerned with orthopraxy than orthodoxy, or by pointing out the key social markers of *īmān* (for which 'faith' or 'belief' are only approximate renderings), we should know that reducing Islam to 'belief' alone is entirely unhelpful for the purpose of understanding Muslim religiosity. This, of course, should not be surprising; the emphasis upon 'belief' as the key to religion naturally stems from Protestant-style (and Enlightenment-approved) critiques of 'empty ritual,' deemed less significant (and less efficacious for salvation, in the Protestant context) than the inner belief of the heart, and contemporary morality is especially critical of those who just 'go through the motions' without believing (arguably more critical than of those who believe without practicing, who are merely hypocrites, or fallen). Scholarship on religion *began* by applying approaches to religiosity rooted in Protestant sensibilities to other religious traditions, but it has largely abandoned such biases in the course of expanding our understanding of religious life.

One additional contribution of scholarship on religion has been to distinguish not only multiple modes of religiosity, but multiple modes of religious discourse, ranging from the doctrinal and exegetical to the mythic, and including moral, aesthetic, therapeutic, and mystical modes as well; indeed, 'discourse' itself is a misnomer, insofar as non-verbal symbolic and iconographic communication enhances the richness of most religious traditions, Islam included. None of the products of Sovietological scholarship, however, has ever addressed even the most basic issues surrounding these multiple 'languages' of religion, or grappled with how 'religiosity' should be understood, or how it might be assessed.

Let us consider further some of the implications of the ways we talk about religion, and especially of the metaphors we assume, even if we seldom make them explicit, in our discussions of religiosity. One especially rich and instructive exploration, with particular relevance for the Soviet and post-Soviet world, appears in an article from 2001 by Tony Stewart, a specialist on South Asian Islam and Hindu-Muslim relations;[53] his discussion resonates particularly with our consideration of the notion of religious 'survivals' and of the binary oppositions posed in Sovietological literature, but offers broader reminders about the assumptions hidden in uncritical discourse about religion.

Stewart's article makes important points about the insights to be gained by exploring religious encounters through linguistic boundaries and bridges, but includes a discussion of the notion of religious 'syncretism' that every student of Islam in the Soviet and post-Soviet worlds should read; he challenges the usefulness of the notion of 'syncretism' and outlines four basic metaphorical frameworks used to signal the 'impurity' of phenomena deemed 'syncretic.' The first is the language of borrowing and influence, the former derived from economics, the latter from astrology and hydraulics. In the first case, as Stewart notes, those on the 'borrowing' side are implicitly "not sufficiently creative or independent to think for themselves" and "must take prefabricated ideas or rituals from somewhere else," inevitably using the 'borrowed' items "improperly, that is, *not* as they were 'meant to be used.'"[54] The language of 'influence,'

53 Tony Stewart, "In Search of Equivalence: Conceiving the Muslim-Hindu Encounter through Translation Theory," *History of Religions*, 40/3 (2001), pp. 260–287; reprinted in *India's Islamic Traditions, 711–1750*, ed. Richard M. Eaton (New Delhi: Oxford University Press, 2003), pp. 364–392. Stewart acknowledges the role, in shaping his analysis, of George Lakoff and Mark Johnson, *Metaphors We Live By* (Chicago: University of Chicago Press, 1980).

54 Stewart, "In Search of Equivalence," p. 271.

meanwhile, drains volition from the interaction, "making one group dependent, passively receptive, and therefore of less value than the source."[55]

Stewart's second category is drawn, as he notes, from woodworking: it is the metaphor of "veneer" and "overlay," which is particularly insidious because it offers "the appearance of accounting for historical change."[56] Yet

> ... veneers are generally thin layers of fragile ornamental wood or other material bonded to a foundation that is coarse and sturdy. Subject to delamination, the veneer is easily damaged or destroyed, that is, it is impermanent, while the permanent base continues to function as it always had, perpetrating a not-so-subtle political commentary by the choice of metaphor.[57]

Third, Stewart suggests that "alchemy" is the most widely-used metaphor of syncretism, in part because the chemical reactions posited thereby are generally understood as dangerous; as he writes, "such daring processes create new entities that often have little or no use, and can in fact be fatal to those who come into contact with them, as religious reformers are quick to point out."[58] More common than this reactive model, however, is what Stewart refers to as the "mixture" model, "a colloidal suspension of two ultimately irreconcilable liquids that will inevitably separate." In either case, Stewart concludes, "the parts retain their unique identities, implying that their essences are unchanged and their concoction [is] little more than a momentary juxtaposition."[59]

Stewart's fourth metaphorical model comes from biology, imagining syncretism as entailing the offspring of two 'parents' with whom the offspring is not identical; if a trait in the offspring can be linked with one particular parent, then that parent is shown to be dominant, but if a true blend is achieved, the offspring is a hybrid that either cannot reproduce (for being sterile) or cannot 'breed true,' and thus "disaggregate in one or two generations."[60] All these models, Stewart concludes – with equal relevance for the full range of binary oppositions noted above from the Sovietological literature – "presuppose essentialized, dehistoricized, monolithic entities that interact in ways that cannot be described directly, only metaphorically ..."[61]

55 Stewart, "In Search of Equivalence," p. 271.
56 Stewart, "In Search of Equivalence," p. 271.
57 Stewart, "In Search of Equivalence," pp. 271–272.
58 Stewart, "In Search of Equivalence," p. 272.
59 Stewart, "In Search of Equivalence," p. 272.
60 Stewart, "In Search of Equivalence," p. 272.
61 Stewart, "In Search of Equivalence," p. 273.

At nearly the same time as Stewart's article appeared, a specialist on Chinese religion, Robert Campany, offered another set of such metaphors, partly overlapping with Stewart's.[62] Campany notes our tendencies to speak of religion as a living organism (as when we speak of Islam "growing," "flourishing," being "transplanted," or having "roots," as "absorbing" outside elements, or, of special importance for our purposes, as "surviving"), as a personified agent (as when we speak of Islam "teaching" certain things, or "offering" something to would-be converts), as a marketable commodity (as when we refer to the "appeal" of Islam), or as a military unit (as when we insist that Islam "advanced" or "conquered" an area or was deeply "entrenched"). He also discusses the metaphorical language that refers to religions as substances (which spread, flow, or diffuse), as buildings (with foundations, structures, and levels), as containers within which people and various paraphernalia are stored or belong, or, somewhat more diffusely, as things that people bear, carry, and sometimes offer to others. The point is not simply that we should not use such language, but that we should be self-conscious and cautious when we are inclined to. How much problematical writing about "Islam in the Soviet Union" could have been improved simply by keeping such caution in mind?

More broadly, indeed, if we could have required those who produced the existing literature about Islam in Central Asia or the Soviet world to read a bit more deeply in ways of thinking about religion – or if prevailing standards of scholarship in this field demanded at least this minimum of thoughtfulness – then we might not read the repeated discussions of 'believers' or the meaningless measures of religiosity; we would not be told quite so often that someone, or some group, was not 'religious' because some obligations were ignored or imperfectly observed; we would not be reminded that something could not be 'religious' because it was economic, political, social, cultural, etc.; and we might have been spared many of the iterations of the 15 fields of error outlined above.

3 Suggestions for Re-Envisioning the Field of Soviet and Post-Soviet Islam

With these basic considerations about approaches to religious life in mind, alongside that litany of 15 flawed narratives embedded in the literature for a half-century, what can we conclude – or at least suggest – about how to

62 Robert Ford Campany, "On the Very Idea of Religions (In the Modern West and in Early Medieval China)," *History of Religions*, 42/4 (2003), pp. 287–319 [pp. 294–299].

conceptualize the Soviet and post-Soviet 'fields' in which contestations of religious authority have been and are being negotiated? It is one thing to take note of how previous scholarship overlooked or misconstrued interesting, and important, continuities and adaptations in religiosity that were underway in the Soviet era, and a wider range of permutations unfolding now, in multiple post-Soviet spaces; taking note of them should help us avoid similar mistakes in the future, but filling in or correcting the developments that were missed or misconstrued is also important for improving our understanding of the Soviet system as a whole, and of the contemporary post-Soviet present. From another perspective, however, missing or misconstruing those developments, or exploring them *only* as idiosyncratic aberrations rooted in a defunct system and its supposedly diminishing legacies, keeps them 'out of sight' for the wider world of Islamic studies, or religious studies, fields that might draw important insights from them.

The potential benefits of such insights point to the need to put the study of Islam in the Soviet Union in closer dialogue with Islamic studies, and religious studies, and to turn from our instinct to consider how 'Islam' and Muslims fared under the Soviet regime and its post-Soviet modulations, toward considering the USSR as a distinctive religious space that was, among other things, home to quite diverse Muslim communities, and to many local and regional 'vernaculars' of Islam. To this end, I would suggest some possible benefits of shifting our perspective in this way.

(1) Our models of 'Soviet atheism' may stand in the way of recognizing how the USSR served, in effect, as a kind of harbor for religious vernaculars; on the model of other imperial structures in which certain kinds of diversity could flourish as long as political loyalty was maintained, we might begin to see the preservation, or even cultivation, of local varieties of Islam as one of the key features of the Soviet era. It may be suggested, that is, that what the Soviet Union maintained, ironically, for 70-odd years during the 20th century – a time marked in the rest of the world by seemingly unidirectional cultural and economic changes presaging 'globalization' and a weeding-out of local particularism, in religion as in other spheres – was a space in which local and regional vernaculars of Muslim religiosity could endure and develop, in some measure 'preserved' and ironically safeguarded from the trends, and efforts, toward a 'global standardization' of Islam in some quarters.

In particular, reversing our perspective, and framing our inquiry in terms of the place of the Soviet Union in Islamic history – rather than simply maintaining our questions about the place of Islam in the Soviet Union – may help to remind us – as no amount of thinking or writing about 'Islam in the Soviet Union' has seemed to do during the past 50 years – that what we imagine when we speak of 'Islam' is best understood – or perhaps, indeed, can *only* be understood – in specific, particular, and above all *local* contexts, and that thinking about 'Islam' in the abstract – or, to put it another way, thinking about 'Islam' *as a 'global' phenomenon* – inevitably muddies the waters, fogs the glass, and disconnects us from real sources, and real people.

Instead of assuming, that is, that 'Islam' is a pre-determined category of analysis, or that 'Muslims' are a recognizable social group, with said category or group occupying a space (conceptual or physical) within a political and social entity defined as 'the Soviet Union,' can we imagine 'Islam' in a way that allows us to see the religious, social, and even political principles we associate with Islamic thought and history having a hand in shaping the Soviet Union and making it what it became, and can we imagine Muslims in a way that allows us to see them, or some of them, not just being acted upon by 'the Soviet system,' but as having a hand in forging that system? This will be difficult if we understand the shaping and forging of the Soviet world as entirely the work of policy and state action from the top down, but it is increasingly being recognized that the evasions of and partial compliance with – if less often open resistance to – policy and state action on the part of ordinary Soviet citizens also shaped Soviet society, and that alignments and convergences and negotiations between Soviet policies and Soviet Muslim citizens that run counter to our established narratives of Soviet vs. Muslim were likewise important in the formation and functioning of Soviet society.

More important, perhaps, can we derive these better, or more instructive, imaginings about Islam and Muslims by studying the experience of Muslims who happened to be Soviets, and privileging it as indeed the valid experience of Muslims, rather than qualifying it as merely the experience of *Soviet* Muslims? Instead of proceeding from an assumption, rooted in Cold War-era divisions, that Muslims in the Soviet world were necessarily aberrant, or necessarily 'oppressed,' can we at least allow that Muslims in the Soviet world *were* Muslims? To put it another way, what can the experience of Muslims – however we define this category – who happened to be Soviet citizens reveal to us about what it is to be Muslim, and about 'Islam'? Can studying the experience of Muslim Soviets help us to de-globalize our understanding of 'Islam' or of 'religion,' and restore local and regional communities – with or without 'states,' and with or without 'national' or ethnic markers – to center stage?

It is in fact precisely because I am uncomfortable with the implications of the various qualifiers typically attached to the term 'Islam' when referring to local manifestations (instead of latching onto 'global' abstracts), whether 'vernacular' or 'local' or 'popular' or 'everyday' or 'unofficial' or 'parallel' (the latter three especially frequent in the Soviet context) that I think the Soviet world can be instructive, by way of reminding us that 'Islam' is everywhere and always experienced, and therefore *created*, locally.

(2) Another possible implication of that shift in perspective is suggested in part by the multiple religious vernaculars 'sheltered' or developed in the Soviet context, but is somewhat ironic, again, in view of our assumptions about the Soviet Union as an anti-religious state. Just as revisionist historians of the Soviet era, reminding us to focus on the actual consequences of Soviet rule rather than the policies, and their ideological underpinnings, that were enacted, often quite imperfectly, under Soviet rule, have argued the ironic contribution of the Soviet Union to forming and favoring national structures and divisions,[63] we might ask if the Soviet Union should be regarded not just as an 'affirmative action empire,' but in some significant ways also as an 'ecumenical empire.' In this regard it is no doubt significant that in several parts of the post-Soviet world – one thinks of the Volga-Ural region and 'European Russia' more broadly, but also specifically of Kazakhstan – the rhetoric of what we might call the "Friendship of the Faiths" has succeeded to the place once occupied by the rhetoric of the "Friendship of the Peoples" as part of official policy (one that fosters particular historical reconstructions, as well). This shift obviously reflects the late-Soviet demise of antireligious propaganda, and the collapse of the USSR itself, but just as post-Soviet nationalism has been shaped by notions of nationality developed in the Soviet era, so too do post-Soviet governments' rhetoric and policies regarding religion bear the imprint not only of specific Soviet policies, but of the wider Soviet-era discourse about religion.

(3) The irony of religious ecumenism as a legacy of the anti-religious Soviet state is matched, moreover, by the irony of an anti-religious state effectively heightening the role of religion in its successor states (parallel, perhaps, to those unintended nation-building consequences). Indeed, we might argue that the officially atheist and irreligious Soviet state left two broad legacies in religious terms, beyond the questionable 'reduction' in religiosity often imputed to it, in the political structures that succeeded it: first, in a few cases, it left a legacy of religiously-shaped conflict (however much the religious component was downplayed or denied), whether between Muslims (Azeris) and Christians (Armenians) in the Transcaucasus, or between Sunni Tajiks and Ismāʿīlīs; and

63 E.g., Yuri Slezkine, "The USSR as a Communal Apartment, or How a Socialist State Promoted Ethnic Particularism," *Slavic Review*, 53 (1994), pp. 414–452; Terry Martin, *The Affirmative Action Empire: Nations and Nationalism in the Soviet Union, 1923–1939* (Ithaca, New York: Cornell University Press, 2003); Francine Hirsch, *Empire of Nations: Ethnographic Knowledge and the Making of the Soviet Union* (Ithaca, New York: Cornell University Press, 2005).

second, in several cases, it left a legacy of foregrounding 'religious policy' as a key marker of proper governance.

In Central Asia, that is, the Soviet legacy in religious terms has been to raise the profile of religion as an arena in which the state must be involved or stake a position. In post-Soviet Kazakhstan, for instance (and to a lesser extent, in Kyrgyzstan), the government points to religious 'ecumenism' as a marker of legitimacy and moderation, replacing the rhetoric of "Friendship of the Peoples" with, as noted, the rhetoric of "Friendship of the Faiths," and thereby putting religion front and center as a concern of the nation. In Uzbekistan and Tajikistan, and to some extent in Kazakhstan, post-Soviet governments have made efforts, often clumsy, to define an acceptable, state-sanctioned version of Islam, likewise acknowledging the centrality of religion in the public life of the nation. In Turkmenistan, finally, religion, broadly understood, was *the* key arena in which the first post-Soviet (and final Soviet) leader tried to carve out a distinctive personal, and national, identity; Türkmenbashi's *Ruh-nama* may seem to be a one-off aberration, but it may also be seen as a natural extension of the kind of local or regional vernacular of Muslim religiosity, in this case refracted in 'epic' terms, that the Soviet era in fact sheltered and perhaps fostered.[64]

All these phenomena have drawn some attention within the framework of nationalism, as efforts to define specific, and acceptable, national versions of Islam, which are then understood (in the west, at least, and in "post-Sovietology") as "the Uzbek way" or "the Kazakh way" or "the Turkmen way," as if religion were not involved; in this narrative, nationalism, as the key 'outcome' of the Soviet era, combined with legacies of Soviet policy and politics, in terms of defining an officially tolerable range of religious practice, yields the post-Soviet Central Asian governments' positions regarding Islam. Yet we can also look at these positionings, to assert a distinctive 'national' or – let us suggest, local – version of Islam, as the ironic elevation of religion to the public sphere that marks another Soviet contribution that is no less significant (and no less ironic) than the Soviet contribution to forging nations.

---

64 See the discussion of Amieke Bouma, "Turkmenistan: Epics in Place of Historiography," *Jahrbücher für Geschichte Osteuropas*, 59/4 (2011), pp. 559–583. Türkmenbashi famously sought to shape his cult while still alive, but similar, if perhaps less extreme, developments may be seen in Uzbekistan – with the siting of the burial place of Islam Karimov, likewise the transitional leader from Soviet to post-Soviet times, and its emergence as a shrine in Samarqand – and in Kazakhstan, with the sacralization of a 'national,' but wholly Soviet, figure; on the latter, see Elena Larina, "'Kunaev – on sviatoi': Novaia pamiat' o sovetskom vozhde," in *Islam v Rossii i Evrazii XVI–XXI vv.* (*pamiati Dmitriia Iur'evicha Arapova*), ed. T.V. Kotiukova (St. Petersburg: Aleteiia, 2021), pp. 640–652.

The Soviet experiment, that is, left in its wake a social and even political space in which religion held not the lower profile or invisibility advocated in Soviet policy, but a more prominent profile, and indeed a central position; whether this higher profile should be understood as the ironic legacy of the intensity or narrow targeting of antireligious efforts, inversely heightening the role of religion by taking it so seriously, may be debated, but it is nevertheless clear that the post-Soviet governments have all felt obliged to be, or to pretend to be, respectful of Islam, to make it part of their nation-building projects, and even to invoke it in various public arenas – including some known from much earlier times, such as the political theater of the leader performing *ziyārat* to key saints' shrines.

These demonstrations, or manipulations, have been undertaken, to be sure, alongside severe restrictions on religious life, as defined in narrow terms, and severe oppression of those who engage in particular activities counted as 'religious' by the post-Soviet governments; such policies, and their 'definitional' underpinnings are also part of the Soviet legacy, and they, like their Soviet precedents, have had very real effects and have harmed particular individuals and groups. They also continue the Soviet pattern of unintended consequences, rooted in the profound misunderstandings of religious life carried over from Soviet to post-Soviet institutions. Yet they are not the entire story, as the other faces of post-Soviet Islam make clear; once again, however, specialists have focused on the restrictions and repressive measures as the only continuities from Soviet policy, and are missing other developments that may be more significant, and may have more lasting consequences.

From this perspective, then, we may understand that the Soviet Union not only provided a space for the development of vernacular Islams; it also provided a space for Islam to develop in dialogue with other religious traditions, in a kind of Soviet ecumenism that continues in some quarters down to the present. This, in turn, compels us to take seriously the question of the 'religious' character of the Soviet Union – or, more properly, the place of the Soviet Union in the history of religions, and not simply as a state 'opposed' to religion, but as a state that was home to a remarkable diversity of religious communities, and above all as a state that fostered distinctive developments in religious phenomena.

We may find further evidence of the 'sheltering' and cementing of religious identities – again, not static ones, but adaptive ones – in the Soviet context in the ironic valorization implied by the 'internal' vs. 'external' labels applied to religious currents in several post-Soviet spaces: when post-Soviet states seek or affirm a 'national' version of Islam and decry religious influence from outside the respective countries as alien and harmful – much as the Russian government distinguishes between home-grown Christian groups and those whose importation from abroad is targeted for halting – they implicitly mark religious currents rooted in native soil as valuable and legitimate, in this case in direct opposition to the rhetoric of the Soviet era, in which all religions were artificially imposed, and in which Islam, in particular, was a religion brought from outside the borders of the future USSR.

(4) These specific considerations all suggest a broader challenge to our habits of thinking about 'religion in the Soviet Union,' one that must begin by acknowledging the vibrancy and dynamism of the religious scene in the Soviet Union, and of the USSR as a religious space. Our usual thinking, that is, about religious communities merely being acted upon by the Soviet system, being oppressed by it, and enduring to emerge, battered but still alive, after its passing may be understood as a legacy of the political concerns of the Cold War, but it still serves as a basic analytical framework for thinking about various religious currents and communities, including those linked with Islam. As an alternative it may be helpful to suggest that the Soviet Union was in fact the scene of dynamic and creative religious developments – some known from their legacies, in the post-Soviet space, and others known from the Soviet era itself – that render the USSR a prime, but long-neglected, subject for scholarship rooted in the field of religious studies, and Islamic studies. It will nevertheless be important, as that neglect is lifted, to approach the subject free of assumptions that became deeply entrenched in the Soviet era.

No one would study, or attempt to narrate, the religious history of any part or period of the Roman empire within a framework that stressed the 'official' emperor-cult, or the persecution of Christians, or the crushing of Judean statehood as the sole significant factor in defining or assessing religious life in the world ruled from Rome. And yet parallel focuses and assumptions continue to dominate the way we think of religion in the USSR, and even in its successor states: we overemphasize state policy and state institutions, often without even trying to look beyond 'official' frameworks of state action and state-based 'information' sources; and we assume an oppositional stance between the state and virtually any and all manifestations of religiosity – because the state was, after all, officially antireligious – whether those manifestations were framed in terms of religious groups suffering persecution by the state, or in terms of religion as a phenomenon supposedly subsumed into 'national' aspirations suppressed by the state. Moving beyond these limited, and limiting, perspectives on Soviet religion will facilitate a better and more balanced understanding of the many ways in which religiosity could manifest itself, even in an imperial system with an official, and explicit, stance on modes and focuses of religious expression.

Once we look beyond, that is, what Sovietology taught us to think of with regard to the inevitable, essential, and insurmountable opposition between "Islam" and religiosity, on one side, and "Soviet atheism" on the other, we can begin to appreciate what should have been obvious in the first place, and what is now, in any case, beginning to draw some attention, as noted, namely that it was quite possible – and, indeed, more the norm than the exception – for Muslims in the Soviet Union to consider themselves both good Muslims and good Soviet citizens, at the same time. This suggests, in turn, that Soviet identity itself was not something we can understand in essentialized opposition to ideas or lifeways we assume must be incompatible with it; rather, it too was subject to being infused with religious meaning, whether that religious meaning involved what we regard as formalized state-sponsored 'ritual' activity (as in the ritual reiteration of Lenin's tomb in the central squares of the satellite capital cities of Soviet union republics), or what we regard as personal 'secular' responses to official ideology (as in young people's dreams of Lenin offering guidance in their life choices),[65] or what we regard as 'religiously' framed passive resistance to aspects of Soviet life (as in the genre of stories, noted above, about 'magical' retribution for officials involved in bulldozing shrines), or what we must recognize as religious validation of Soviet patriotism. If Soviet identity could be so heavily infused with religiosity of a sort, alongside its officially anti-religious stance, then it should not be difficult to accept that Muslim religiosity could not only coexist with it, but could reinforce it.

This recognition has particularly important implications with regard to expanding the source base, as noted above, for the study of Soviet and post-Soviet Islam: once we begin to consider the USSR as a distinctive religious space – and to consider Muslims as inhabitants of that space, rather than somehow standing outside of it (whether for being Muslim and hence automatically isolated from Soviet-ness, or for not being Muslim in the right way) – and once we expand our understanding of what being 'religious' may encompass, we can begin to come to terms with the Soviet Union as a significant 'generator' of religious texts, materials that are all the more valuable for originating and circulating beneath the surface of state-sanctioned, and state-censored, print media.

65 For discussions of Soviet Marxism-Leninism as a religious system, see Nina Tumarkin, *Lenin Lives! The Lenin Cult in Soviet Russia* (Cambridge, Massachusetts: Harvard University Press, 1983); Christel Lane, *The Rites of Rulers: Ritual in Industrial Society – The Soviet Case* (Cambridge: Cambridge University Press, 1981); and James Thrower, *Marxism-Leninism as the Civil Religion of Soviet Society* (Lewiston, New York/Queenston, Ontario/Lampeter, Wales, UK: The Edwin Mellen Press, 1992; Studies in Religion and Society, Vol. 30).

From the standpoint of such sources as well, I would argue, as noted, that the study of Soviet and post-Soviet Islam needs to be re-situated in the framework of Islamic studies; but at the same time, I believe the study of Islam in the Soviet era has something to offer toward a better understanding of the Soviet experience more broadly. In particular, we might be led toward a more nuanced conception of how, and when, the officially atheist Soviet state oversaw a profoundly 'religious' country; acknowledging this will require us to keep in check our knee-jerk reactions about what 'religion' is, but it will help us, I believe, to continue extracting our understanding of the Soviet experience from the ideological legacies of the 20th century, and framing it in actual human, historical terms.

Bibliography

Abashin, S.N. "Potomki sviatykh v sovremennoi Srednei Azii." *Ètnograficheskoe obozrenie*, 2001, No. 4, pp. 62–82.

Abashin, Sergei. "A Prayer for Rain: Practising Being Soviet and Muslim." *Journal of Islamic Studies*, 25/2 (2014), pp. 178–200.

Abashin, Sergei. *Sovetskii kishlak: Mezhdu kolonializmom i modernizatsiei.* Moscow: Novoe literaturnoe obozrenie, 2015.

Abashin, Sergei. "Sufizm v Srednei Azii: Tochka zreniia ètnografa." *Vestnik Evrazii* (*Acta Eurasica*), 2001, No. 4, pp. 117–141.

Azhybekova, K.A. *Molodezh' i problemy psikhologii religii i ateizma v usloviiakh sovremennoi NTR*. Frunze: Ilim, 1989.

Babadjanov, Bakhtiyar. "Debates over Islam in Contemporary Uzbekistan: A View from Within." In *Devout Societies vs. Impious States? Transmitting Islamic Learning in Russia, Central Asia and China, through the Twentieth Century* (Proceedings of an International Colloquium Held in the Carré des Sciences, French Ministry of Research, Paris, November 12–13, 2001), ed. Stéphane Dudoignon (Berlin: Schwarz, 2004), pp. 39–60.

Babadjanov, Bakhtiyar. "Ulama-Orientalists: Madrasa Graduates at the Soviet Institute of Oriental Studies." In *Reassessing Orientalism: Interlocking Orientologies during the Cold War*, ed. Michael Kemper and Artemy M. Kalinovsky (London/New York: Routledge, 2015), pp. 84–119.

Babadjanov, Bakhtiyar, and Muzaffar Kamilov. "Muhammadjan Hindustani (1892–1989) and the Beginning of the 'Great Schism' among the Muslims of Uzbekistan." In *Islam in Politics in Russia and Central Asia*, ed. Stéphane Dudoignon and Komatsu Hisao (London: Kegan Paul, 2001), pp. 195–220.

Babajanov, Bakhtiyar, and Sharifjon Islamov. "Sharī'a for the Bolsheviks? Fatvās on Land Reform in Early Soviet Central Asia." In *Islam, Society and States Across the Qazaq Steppe (18th–Early 20th Centuries)*, ed. Niccolò Pianciola and Paolo Sartori (Vienna: Verlag der Österreichischen Akademie der Wissenschaften, 2013), pp. 233–265.

Babadzhanov, B.M., A.K. Muminov, and A. fon Kiugel'gen. *Disputy musul'manskikh religioznykh avtoritetov v Tsentral'noi Azii v XX veke*. Almaty: Daik-Press, 2007.

Bellér-Hann, I. "'Making the Oil Fragrant': Dealings with the Supernatural among the Uyghurs in Xinjiang." *Asian Ethnicity*, 2/1 (2001), pp. 9–23.

Bennigsen, Alexandre, and Chantal Lemercier-Quelquejay. *Islam in the Soviet Union*. New York: Praeger, 1967.

Bigozhin, Ulan. "Shrine, State, and Sacred Lineage in Post-Soviet Kazakhstan." Ph.D. dissertation, Indiana University, 2017.

Bohr, Annette. "Turkmenistan: Power, Politics and Petro-Authoritarianism." London: Russia and Eurasia Programme of Chatham House/Royal Institute of International Affairs, 2016.

Bouma, Amieke. "Turkmenistan: Epics in Place of Historiography." *Jahrbücher für Geschichte Osteuropas*, 59/4 (2011), pp. 559–583.

Bustanov, Alfrid K. "Against Leviathan: On the Ethics of Islamic Poetry in Soviet Russia." In *The Piety of Learning: Islamic Studies in Honor of Stephan Reichmuth*, ed. Michael Kemper and Ralf Elger (Leiden: Brill, 2017), pp. 199–224.

Bustanov, Alfrid K. "Beyond the Ethnic Traditions: Shamil' Aliautdinov's Muslim Guide to Success." In *Islamic Authority and the Russian Language: Studies on Texts from European Russia, the North Caucasus, and West Siberia*, ed. Alfrid K. Bustanov and Michael Kemper (Amsterdam: Pegasus, 2012), pp. 143–164.

Bustanov, Alfrid K. "The Language of Moderate Salafism in Eastern Tatarstan." *Islam and Christian-Muslim Relations*, 28/2 (2017), pp. 183–201.

Bustanov, Alfrid K. "Muslim Literature in the Atheist State: Zainap Maksudova between Soviet Modernity and Tradition." *Journal of Islamic Manuscripts*, 9 (2018), pp. 1–31.

Bustanov, Alfrid K., and Michael Kemper, eds. *Islamic Authority and the Russian Language: Studies on Texts from European Russia, the North Caucasus, and West Siberia*. Amsterdam: Uitgeverij Pegasus, 2012.

Campany, Robert Ford. "On the Very Idea of Religions (In the Modern West and in Early Medieval China)." *History of Religions*, 42/4 (2003), pp. 287–319.

Dağyeli, Jeanine Elif. "La construction des identités collectives d'après les chartes des corps de métier (risāla) en Asie centrale." *Cahiers d'Asie Centrale*, 19–20 (2011), pp. 73–84.

Dağyeli, Jeanine Elif. *'Gott liebt das Handwerk:' Moral, Identität und religiöse Legitimierung in der mittelasiatischen Handwerks-risāla*. Wiesbaden: Reichert Verlag, 2011.

Demidov, S.M. *Turkmenskie ovliady*. Ashkhabad: Ylym, 1976.

DeWeese, Devin. "Dog Saints and Dog Shrines in Kubravī Tradition: Notes on a Hagiographical Motif from Khwārazm." In *Miracle et karāma: Hagiographies médiévales comparées*, 2, ed. Denise Aigle (Turnhout, Belgium: Brepols, 2000; Bibliothèque de l'école des hautes études, sciences religieuses, vol. 109), pp. 459–497.

DeWeese, Devin. "Encountering Saints in the Hallowed Ground of a Regional Landscape: The 'Description of Khwārazm' and the Experience of Pilgrimage in 19th-Century Central Asia." In *Saintly Spheres and Islamic Landscapes*, ed. Daphna Ephrat, Ethel Sara Wolper, and Paulo G. Pinto (Leiden: Brill, 2021), pp. 183–218.

DeWeese, Devin. Foreword to *Islamizatsiia i sakral'nye rodoslovnye v Tsentral'noi Azii: Nasledie Iskhak Baba v narrativnoi i genealogicheskoi traditsiiakh*, Tom 2: *Genealogicheskie gramoty i sakral'nye semeistva XIX-XXI vekov: nasab-nama i gruppy khodzhei, sviazannykh s sakral'nym skazaniem ob Iskhak Babe / Islamization and Sacred Lineages in Central Asia: The Legacy of Ishaq Bab in Narrative and Genealogical Traditions*, Vol. 2: *Genealogical Charters and Sacred Families: Nasab-namas and Khoja Groups linked to the Ishaq Bab Narrative, 19th–21st Centuries*, ed. Ashirbek Muminov, Anke von Kügelgen, Devin DeWeese, Michael Kemper (Almaty: Daik-Press, 2008), pp. 6–33.

DeWeese, Devin. Foreword to *Sobranie fetv po obosnovaniiu zikra dzhakhr i sama'*, ed. B.M. Babadzhanov and S.A. Mukhammadaminov (Almaty: Daik-Press, 2008), pp. 9–15.

DeWeese, Devin. "Islam and the Legacy of Sovietology: A Review Essay on Yaacov Ro'i's Islam in the Soviet Union." *Journal of Islamic Studies*, 13/3 (2002), pp. 298–330.

DeWeese, Devin. *Islamization and Native Religion in the Golden Horde: Baba Tükles and Conversion to Islam in Historical and Epic Tradition*. University Park: Pennsylvania State University Press, 1994.

DeWeese, Devin. "Islamization in the Mongol Empire." In *The Cambridge History of Inner Asia: The Chinggisid Age*, ed. Nicola Di Cosmo, Allen J. Frank, and Peter B. Golden (Cambridge: Cambridge University Press, 2009), pp. 120–134.

DeWeese, Devin. "It was a Dark and Stagnant Night ('til the Jadids Brought the Light): Clichés, Biases, and False Dichotomies in the Intellectual History of Central Asia." *Journal of the Economic and Social History of the Orient*, 59/1–2 (2016), pp. 37–92.

DeWeese, Devin. "Re-Envisioning the History of Sufi Communities in Central Asia: Continuity and Adaptation in Sources and Social Frameworks, 16th–20th Centuries." In *Sufism in Central Asia: New Perspectives on Sufi Traditions, 15th–21st Centuries*, ed. Devin DeWeese and Jo-Ann Gross (Leiden: Brill, 2018), pp. 21–74.

DeWeese, Devin. Review of Shamanism and Islam: Sufism, Healing Rituals and Spirits in the Muslim World, ed. Thierry Zarcone and Angela Hobart (London/New York: I.B. Tauris, 2013). *International Journal of Turkish Studies*, 22/1–2 (Fall 2016), pp. 200–206.

DeWeese, Devin. "Shamanization in Central Asia." *Journal of the Economic and Social History of the Orient*, 57 (2014), pp. 326–363.

DeWeese, Devin. "Survival Strategies: Reflections on the Notion of Religious 'Survivals' in Soviet Ethnographic Studies of Muslim Religious Life in Central Asia." In *Exploring the Edge of Empire: Soviet Era Anthropology in the Caucasus and Central Asia*, ed. Florian Mühlfried and Sergey Sokolovskiy (Münster: Lit Verlag, 2011; Halle Studies in the Anthropology of Eurasia, vol. 25), pp. 35–58.

Dobson, Richard B. "Islam in Central Asia: Findings from National Surveys." *Central Asia Monitor*, 1994, No. 2, pp. 18–19.

Dudoignon, S.A. "From Revival to Mutation: The Religious Personnel of Islam in Tajikistan, from de-Stalinization to Independence (1955–91)." *Central Asian Survey*, 30 (2011), pp. 53–80.

Dudoignon, Stéphane and Christian Noack, eds. *Allah's Kolkhozes: Migration, De-Stalinisation, Privatisation and the New Muslim Congregations in the Soviet Realm (1950s–2000s)*. Berlin: Klaus Schwarz Verlag, 2014.

Eden, Jeff. *God Save the USSR: Soviet Muslims and the Second World War*. Oxford: Oxford University Press, 2021.

Eden, Jeff. "A Soviet Jihad against Hitler: Ishan Babakhan Calls Central Asian Muslims to War." *Journal of the Economic and Social History of the Orient*, 59 (2016), pp. 237–264.

Eden, Jeff, Paolo Sartori, and Devin DeWeese. "Moving Beyond Modernism: Rethinking Cultural Change in Muslim Eurasia (19th–20th Centuries)." *Journal of the Social and Economic History of the Orient*, 59/1–2 (2016), pp. 1–36.

Edgar, Adrienne Lynn. *Tribal Nation: The Making of Soviet Turkmenistan*. Princeton, New Jersey: Princeton University Press, 2004.

Ernst, Carl W. *Following Muhammad: Rethinking Islam in the Contemporary World*. Chapel Hill: University of North Carolina Press, 2003.

Frank, Allen J. *Gulag Miracles: Sufis and Stalinist Repression in Kazakhstan*. Vienna: Austrian Academy of Sciences Press, 2019 (Veröffentlichungen zur Iranistik, Nr. 84; Studies and Texts on Central Asia, Band 2).

Frank, Allen J. *Islamic Historiography and 'Bulghar' Identity among the Tatars and Bashkirs of Russia*. Leiden: Brill, 1998.

Frank, Allen J. "Islamic Shrine Catalogues and Communal Geography in the Volga-Ural Region: 1788–1917." *Journal of Islamic Studies*, 7 (1996), pp. 265–286.

Frank, Allen J. *Muslim Religious Institutions in Imperial Russia: The Islamic World of Novouzensk District and the Kazakh Inner Horde, 1780–1910*. Leiden: Brill, 2001.

Frank, Allen J. *Popular Islamic Literature in Kazakhstan: An Annotated Bibliography*. Hyattsville, Maryland: Dunwoody Press, 2007.

Frank, Allen J. *Tatar Islamic Texts*. Hyattsville, Maryland: Dunwoody Press, 2008.

Frank, Allen J. "Turkmen Literacy and Turkmen Identity before the Soviets: the Ravnaq al-Islām in its Literary and Social Context." *Journal of the Economic and Social History of the Orient*, 63 (2020), pp. 286–315.

Frank, Allen J., with Jahangir Mamatov. *Uzbek Islamic Debates: Texts, Translations, and Commentary*. Springfield, Virginia: Dunwoody Press, 2006.

"*GÈS* äulie." *Qazïnalï ongtüstïk*, t. 22 (Almaty: Nŭrlï Älem, 2011), pp. 165–166.

Ghïlmani, Saduaqas. *Zamanïmïzda bolghan ghŭlamalardïng ömïr tarikhtarï/ Biographies of the Islamic Scholars of Our Times*, ed. Ashirbek Muminov, Allen J. Frank, and Aitzhan Nurmatova. Istanbul: Research Centre for Islamic History, Art and Culture [IRCICA], 2018.

Gould, Rebecca. "The Modernity of Premodern Islam in Contemporary Daghestan." *Contemporary Islam*, 5 (2011), pp. 161–183.

Hirsch, Francine. *Empire of Nations: Ethnographic Knowledge and the Making of the Soviet Union*. Ithaca, New York: Cornell University Press, 2005.

Hughes, Aaron W. "Religion without Religion: Integrating Islamic Origins into Religious Studies." *Journal of the American Academy of Religion*, 85/4 (2017), pp. 867–888.

Jessa, Pawel. "Aq jol Soul Healers: Religious Pluralism and a Contemporary Muslim Movement in Kazakhstan." *Central Asian Survey*, 25/3 (2006), pp. 359–371.

Josephson-Storm, Jason Ā. *The Myth of Disenchantment: Magic, Modernity, and the Birth of the Human Sciences*. Chicago: University of Chicago Press, 2017.

Kalinovsky, Artemy M. "Encouraging Resistance: Paul Henze, the Bennigsen School, and the Crisis of Détente." In *Reassessing Orientalism: Interlocking Orientologies during the Cold War*, ed. Michael Kemper and Artemy M. Kalinovsky (London/New York: Routledge, 2015), pp. 211–232.

Karamustafa, Ahmet T. "Islamic *Dīn* as an Alternative to Western Models of 'Religion'." In *Religion, Theory, Critique: Classic and Contemporary Approaches and Methodologies*, ed. Richard King (New York: Columbia University Press, 2017), pp. 163–171.

Kemper, Michael, and Shamil Shikhaliev. "Administrative Islam: Two Soviet Fatwas from the North Caucasus." In *Islamic Authority and the Russian Language: Studies on Texts from European Russia, the North Caucasus, and West Siberia*, ed. Michael Kemper and Alfrid K. Bustanov (Amsterdam: Pegasus, 2012), pp. 55–102.

Kemper, Michael, Raoul Motika, and Stefan Reichmuth, eds. *Islamic Education in the Soviet Union and its Successor States*. London/New York: Routledge, 2010.

Lakoff, George, and Mark Johnson. *Metaphors We Live By*. Chicago: University of Chicago Press, 1980.

Lane, Christel. *The Rites of Rulers: Ritual in Industrial Society – The Soviet Case*. Cambridge: Cambridge University Press, 1981.

Larina, Elena. "'Kunaev – on sviatoi': Novaia pamiat' o sovetskom vozhde." In *Islam v Rossii i Evrazii XVI–XXI vv. (pamiati Dmitriia Iur'evicha Arapova)*, ed. T.V. Kotiukova (St. Petersburg: Aleteiia, 2021), pp. 640–652.

Lauzière, Henri. "The Construction of Salafiyya: Reconsidering Salafism from the Perspective of Conceptual History." *International Journal of Middle East Studies*, 42 (2010), pp. 369–389.

Lauzière, Henri. *The Making of Salafism: Islamic Reform in the Twentieth Century*. New York: Columbia University Press, 2016.

Martin, Terry. *The Affirmative Action Empire: Nations and Nationalism in the Soviet Union, 1923–1939*. Ithaca, New York: Cornell University Press, 2003.

McChesney, R.D. *Central Asia: Foundations of Change*. Princeton, New Jersey: The Darwin Press, 1996.

McChesney, R.D. *Four Central Asian Shrines: A Socio-Political History of Architecture*. Leiden: Brill, 2021.

Muminov, Ashirbek. "Fundamentalist Challenges to Local Islamic Traditions in Soviet and Post-Soviet Central Asia." In *Empire, Islam, and Politics in Central Eurasia*, ed. Uyama Tomohiko (Sapporo: Slavic Research Center, Hokkaido University, 2007), pp. 249–261.

Nurmanova, Aitzhan. "Pilgrimages to Mazars in Contemporary Kazakhstan: The Processes of Revivalism and Innovation." In *Mazar: Studies on Islamic Sacred Sites in Central Eurasia*, ed. Sugawara Jun and Rahile Dawut (Tokyo: Tokyo University of Foreign Studies, 2016), pp. 63–72.

Olimov, M., and S. Shokhumorov. "Islamskie intellektualy v Tsentral'noi Azii XX v.: Zhizn' i bor'ba Mavlavi Khindustoni (1892–1989)." *Vostok* (*Afro-aziatskie obshchestva: Istoriia i sovremennost'*), 2003, No. 6, pp. 33–47.

Orsi, Robert A. *History and Presence*. Cambridge, Massachusetts: The Belknap Press of Harvard University Press, 2016.

Pal'vanova, O.I. *Osobennosti ateisticheskogo vospitaniia zhenshchin v sovremennykh usloviiakh*. Ashkhabad: Ylym, 1988.

Privratsky, Bruce G. *Muslim Turkistan: Kazak Religion and Collective Memory*. Richmond, Surrey: Curzon Press, 2001.

Rose, Richard. "How Muslims View Democracy: Evidence from Central Asia." *Journal of Democracy*, 13/4 (October 2002), pp. 102–111.

Sartori, Paolo. "Of Saints, Shrines, and Tractors: Untangling the Meaning of Islam in Soviet Central Asia." *Journal of Islamic Studies*, 30 (2019), pp. 367–405.

Sartori, Paolo. "Towards a History of the Muslims' Soviet Union: A View from Central Asia." *Die Welt des Islams*, 50 (2010), pp. 315–334.

Sartori, Paolo, and Bakhtiyar Babajanov. "Being Soviet, Muslim, Modernist, and Fundamentalist in 1950s Central Asia." *Journal of the Economic and Social History of the Orient*, 62/1 (2019), pp. 108–163.

Schwab, Wendell. "Traditions and Texts: How Two Young Women Learned to Interpret the Qur'an and Hadiths in Kazakhstan." *Contemporary Islam*, 6 (2012), pp. 173–197.

Shulembaev, K. *Obraz zhizni, religiia, ateizm* (*Obshchee i osobennoe v obraze zhizni i religioznykh verovaniiakh kazakhov i voprosy ateisticheskogo vospitaniia*). Alma-Ata: Kazakhstan, 1988.

Simpson, James. *Burning to Read: English Fundamentalism and its Reformation Opponents*. Cambridge, Massachusetts: Belknap Press of Harvard University Press, 2007.

Slezkine, Yuri. "The USSR as a Communal Apartment, or How a Socialist State Promoted Ethnic Particularism." *Slavic Review*, 53 (1994), pp. 414–452.

Smolkin, Victoria. *A Sacred Space is Never Empty: A History of Soviet Atheism*. Princeton, New Jersey: Princeton University Press, 2018.

Snesarev, G.P. *Khorezmskie legendy kak istochnik po istorii religioznykh kul'tov Srednei Azii*. Moscow: Nauka, 1983.

Snesarev, G.P. "Traditsiia muzhskikh soiuzov v ee pozdneishem variante u narodov Srednei Azii." In *Polevye issledovaniia Khorezmskoi èkspeditsii v 1958–1961 gg.*, II: *Pamiatniki srednevekovogo vremeni; Ètnograficheskie raboty* (Moscow: Izd-vo AN SSSR, 1963; = *Materialy Khorezmskoi èkspeditsii*, vyp. 7), pp. 155–205.

Steinberger, Petra. "'Fundamentalism' in Central Asia: Reasons, Reality, and Prospects." In *Central Asia: Aspects of Transition*, ed. Tom Everett-Heath (New York: RoutledgeCurzon, 2003), pp. 219–243.

Stewart, Tony. "In Search of Equivalence: Conceiving the Muslim-Hindu Encounter through Translation Theory." *History of Religions*, 40/3 (2001), pp. 260–287; reprinted in *India's Islamic Traditions, 711–1750*, ed. Richard M. Eaton (New Delhi: Oxford University Press, 2003), pp. 364–392.

Tasar, Eren. "Islamically Informed Soviet Patriotism in Postwar Kyrgyzstan." *Cahiers du monde russe*, 52/2–3 (2011), pp. 387–404.

Tasar, Eren. "Mantra: A Review Essay on Islam in Soviet Central Asia." *Journal of the Economic and Social History of the Orient*, 63 (2020), pp. 389–433.

Tasar, Eren. "The Official Madrasas of Soviet Uzbekistan." *Journal of the Economic and Social History of the Orient*, 59/1–2 (2016), pp. 265–302.

Tasar, Eren. *Soviet and Muslim: The Institutionalization of Islam in Central Asia*. Oxford: Oxford University Press, 2017.

Tasar, Eren. "Sufism on the Soviet Stage: Holy People and Places in Central Asia's Socio-Political Landscape after World War II." In *Sufism in Central Asia: New Perspectives on Sufi Traditions, 15th–21st Centuries*, ed. Devin DeWeese and Jo-Ann Gross (Leiden: Brill, 2018),pp. 256–283.

Thrower, James. *Marxism-Leninism as the Civil Religion of Soviet Society*. Lewiston, New York/Queenston, Ontario/Lampeter, Wales, UK: The Edwin Mellen Press, 1992 (Studies in Religion and Society, Vol. 30).

Thum, Rian. *The Sacred Routes of Uyghur History*. Cambridge, Massachusetts: Harvard University Press, 2014.

Tumarkin, Nina. *Lenin Lives! The Lenin Cult in Soviet Russia*. Cambridge, Massachusetts: Harvard University Press, 1983.
Zubrzycki, Geneviève. *Beheading the Saint: Nationalism, Religion, and Secularism in Quebec*. Chicago: University of Chicago Press, 2016.

PART 2

Authority Enunciated: The Revival of Religious Discourse in Muslim Eurasia

The Return of Jinn and Angels

Repairing Access to Prophetic Authority in Tatarstan

Agnès Kefeli

After the break-up of the Soviet Union, a number of Volga Tatar intellectuals and imams, who still lived with the memory of the deportation of imams to labor camps and the destruction of mosques and schools in the 1930s, took great pains to reconnect their youth to the eschatological dimension of Islam, previously rejected by the communist regime. One of their tasks was to repair access to Prophetic authority through the reprinting and reworking of older cosmological/eschatological myths in their fictional and non-fictional works. They viewed the persistence of atheism, scientific materialism, non-observance of religious obligations, and mixed marriages as a continued threat to the inherited dominance of Islam as their identity marker. Globalization offered new identity possibilities leading some to explore evangelical Christianity, Hinduism, Buddhism, and other so-called "non-Orthodox" expressions of Islam.

In this context, Tatar Muslim intellectuals, educators, and imams had to contend with these new realities and recreate sacred landscapes or mythical geographies that would speak to the youth and older generations who were still skeptical of official representatives of any religion. In their depiction of the Qurʾanic story and the afterlife, these intellectuals and imams did not emphasize rationality, modernist symbolism, critical analysis of legal sources, or the contextual historicization of scriptures. Instead, they highlighted miracles, myth, and scriptural literalism as sources of authority. Angels, jinn, prophets, and the dead, that is the *ghayb* or unseen, are all integral parts of this world; their stories can serve as a more effective device to promote or police correct behavior in a milieu where Muslims constitute a minority and where Muslims rarely live in all-Muslim neighborhoods or buildings. It is not to say that Islam played no role in the life of Soviet Tatars, but their limited access to Islamic literature, and Soviet public education did produce a rupture in their religious conception of the world. For some Tatar imams and intellectuals, the miraculous as source of ultimate authority could once again mark boundaries between Muslim Tatars and non-Muslim Russians, and most of all convince nominal Muslim Tatars (apostates, hypocrites, and atheists) to join their "true Muslim" brethren (whoever they are).

 | DOI:10.1163/9789004527096_004

Since 1992, Islam has experienced a revival among the Tatars of the middle Volga, the second largest ethnic group in Russia. Foreign Muslim missionaries from Saudi Arabia have promoted Wahhabism or traditionalist Salafism, a literalist reform movement that dates to the eighteenth-century theologian and activist Muḥammad ibn ʿAbd al-Wahhāb (1703–1792).[1] The Saudis have financed the reconstruction of mosques and distributed Wahhabi literature, including calls for holy war against the Western and Israeli "crusaders." Younger Tatar imams who have studied in Saudi Arabia on Saudi fellowships in the Islamic University of Medina and also at Al-Azhar university in Egypt where the Shafii school of law is dominant, came into conflict with the older generation who received their training in Central Asia in Soviet times. Trained in both early Maliki and Shafii jurisprudence, these new imams attacked indigenous local forms of religiosity such as the *mevlud* (the festival commemorating the birthday of the Prophet Muhammad), pilgrimages to holy shrines, veneration of the tombs of Sufi saints, memorials for the dead, and performance of music, dance, and skits on major religious festivals. Many other Tatar imams and intellectuals defended these practices as legitimate expressions of their faith and culture. They attacked their opponents as agents of a foreign spirituality that might lead to Arabicization of the native Tatar ethnos and to civil inter-ethnic strife. New debates about what constitutes "true Islam" and "heterodox" Islam arose, echoing earlier prerevolutionary ones in jadid (modernist) literature, but this time with a very different outcome, a return to the mythical.[2]

It has long been argued that Wahhabi influences entered the former Soviet space after its breakup. New research, however, suggests that such influences entered Central Asia much earlier through the work of Middle Eastern students and broadcasts from Iran, and this new reality applies to Tatarstan as well. Idris Ghalävetdin (Aliautdinov, b. 1963), one of the most active traditionalist Salafi imams in Chally (Naberezhnye Chelny) and founder of the famous Ioldyz madrasa, which closed in 1990s for jihadist activities, was a student of Nurulla Muflikhunov, who had studied at the Mir-i ʿArab Madrasa in

1 Jonathan Brown has helpfully discussed the taxonomy of modern Muslim trends of thought in his "Scripture in the Modern Muslim World: The Qur'an and Hadith," in *Islam in the Modern World*, ed. Jeffrey T. Kenney and Ebrahim Moosa (New York: Routledge, 2014), 13–33.

2 Räfiyq Mökhämmätshin, "Tatar jämghïyäteneng bügenge problemalarï yaqtïlïghïnda 'Iman' märkäzeneng eshchänlege," *Iman Nurï* (*Islam zhurnalï*), 4 (1996), 17–19; Raufa Urazman, "Narodnye i religioznye obriady," *Iman Nurï* (*Islam zhurnalï*), 4 (1996), 48–50; Guzel' Valeeva-Suleimanova, "Musul'manskaia kul'tura i izobrazhenie cheloveka v tatarskom iskusstve," *Iman Nurï* (*Islam zhurnalï*), 4 (1996), 55–61; Valiulla Iakupov, *K prorocheskomu islamu* (Kazan: Iman, 2006), 167–70, 177, 349–50.

Uzbekistan after the second world war. Because of his attacks against Sufi local expressions of Islam, and his call for Muslims to live only with other Muslims, Muflikhunov was already labeled "Wahhabi" by his fellow imams in the 1980s.[3]

The so-called "Wahhabi" authors' attempt to re-Islamize Tatars shares, however, more common ground with their opponents than acknowledged by the Tatar religious administration or the Academic of Science sociologists.[4] Despite being criticized for promoting an Islam foreign to the land of their ancestors, Tatar "Wahhabi" authors draw from the same conduits of authority – popular didactic works, tales of the Prophets, dreams, healing *baraka*, and jadid works – to transform their contemporaries' demythologized worldviews, charter appropriate attitudes and practices, and solidify communal boundaries. Both trends, labeled by Tatar observers as "good" Hanafi versus "bad" Wahhabi, have relied on native pre-revolutionary eschatological works to reintroduce the supramundane in public discourse. They emphasize miracles, parallel worlds, and the *barzakh*, an intermediary realm where the souls of the dead await Judgment Day and where the dead and the living can communicate through visions and dreams. Those dreams serve as a highway between the two worlds. Resurrecting the *ghayb* in literary and popular discourse is one of the ways that imams and intellectuals (no matter what their interpretation of heterodoxy is) have been reshaping Islamic practice, and redrawing communal boundaries between Muslims and Eastern Orthodox Christians, between Tatars and Russians.

---

3 Bakhtiar M. Babadzhanov, Ashirbek K. Muminov, and Anke von Kügelgen, *Disputy musul'manskikh religioznykh avtoritetov v Tsentral'noi Azii v XX veke* [*Disputes between Muslim Religious Authorities in Central Asia in the Twentieth Century*] (Almaty: Daik-Press, 2007), 7–31; Nurulla Muflikhun Arïslani, *Jännät häm jähännäm yullarï* (Chistopol: Mukhämmäd Muflikhun, 2000), 9, 58, 65–66.

4 Alfrid Bustanov and Michael Kemper, eds., *Islamic Authority and the Russian Language: Studies on Texts from European Russia, the North Caucasus and West Siberia* (Amsterdam: Uitgeverij Pegasus, 2012), 16; Marlène Laruelle and Sébastien Peyrouse, eds., *Islam et politique en ex-URSS: Russie d'Europe et Asie Centrale* [*Islam and Politics in the Former USSR: European Russia and Central Asia*] (Paris: L'Harmattan, 2005), 19; Abdugbari Muslimov, "Napravleniia obrazovaniia sovremennykh rossiiskikh imamov: Sravnitel'nyi analiz musul'manskikh uchebnykh zavedenii shafiitskogo, khanbalitskogo i khanafitskogo napravlenii," in *Innovatsii v sisteme islamskogo religioznogo obrazovaniia v Rossii: Materialy Vserossiiskoi nauchno-prakticheskoi konferentsii* (g. Kazan', 14 noiabria 2006 g.) (Kazan: Institut istorii im. Sh. Mardzhani, 2007), 45–49; Wäliulla Yaghqub, *Tatarstanda räsmi bulmaghan islam: Khäräkätlär, aghïmnar, sektalar* (Kazan: "Iman" näshriyatï, 2003); Valiulla Iakupov, "Lzhedzhadidizm," *Zhurnal 'Musul'manskii mir'* (August 2006): 1–39; idem, "Anti-islam (o raskol'nicheskoi sushchnosti vakhkhabitov-reformatorov)," *Zhurnal 'Musul'manskii mir'* (September 2006): 1–43; idem, "Profilaktika ksenofobii Vakhkhabizma," *Zhurnal 'Musul'manskii mir'* (August 2007): 15–20.

Not everyone though welcomes such return to Islamic practice. Partisans of Euro-Islam such as Rafael Khakimov (b. 1947), a former politician and current academician, and Rashat Safin, a prominent national intellectual, have promoted the idea of Euro-Islam as a bridge between Europe and Asia, and Christianity and Islam. Euro-Islam, as they define it, is the polar opposite of puritanical Saudi Islam. Modern and secular, Euro-Islam supports the privatization of religion, nationalization of Islam, and preservation of equal opportunities for men and women. Vernacular Tatar, not Arabic, should be the language of Islam. Safin, in particular, warns that a return to Islam, as defined by Wahhabi missionaries, could divide the nation and isolate both atheists and Kriashens (Christian Tatars).[5]

Euro-Islam has met its challengers: the traditionalist Salafis such as Imam Malik Ibrakhim of Chally and the controversial writer Fäwziyä Bäyrämova (b. 1950), sympathetic to the Wahhabi critique of popular Sufi practices, and the late traditionalists, including Imam Valiulla Iakupov (Wäliulla Yaghqub, 1963–2012) and writer Färit Yakhin (b. 1961), who emphasized faithfulness to one school of law (Hanafi madhhab) and participation in Sufi practices. Their works will serve as the main pillars of this inquiry into the imaginal of present-day Tatarstan. Both Imam Ibrakhim, who taught at Ioldyz madrasa with Imam Ghalävetdin, and Bäyrämova,[6] who wrote a book inspired by events that occurred in that madrasa and led to the bombing of apartment buildings in Moscow, are sympathetic to the ideals of Ibn ʿAbd al-Wahhāb and later conservative modernist Salafis (Rashīd Riḍā, Sayyid Quṭb in Egypt, and Sayyid Abū'l-ʿAlā' Mawdūdī in South Asia). They turn to what some more traditionalist ulama could consider as un-Qur'anic sources of authority, science and the paranormal, to explore the *ghayb*. Ibrakhim sees the digital world, science-fiction films, paranormal phenomena, dream experiences, or J.R.R. Tolkien's imaginary world of the *Lord of the Rings*, as evidence that human beings are less concerned about their physical survival (as Darwin claimed) than about accessing supramundane realities through their imagination. Why do millions of individuals spend years learning the language of the elves, a language that is

5 F.M. Sultanov, *Islam i tatarskoe natsional'noe dvizhenie v rossiiskom i mirovom musul'manskom kontekste: Istoriia i sovremennost'* (Kazan: RITS Shkola, 1999), 156–58; Rafael' Khakim, *Kto ty, tatarin?* (Kazan: Biblioteka zhurnala "Panorama-Forum," 2002), 11–34; Rashat Safin, *Tatar yulï: Tatar yazmïshïna geosäyäsi analiz* (Kazan: Tatarstan kitap näshriyatï, 2002), 61–62, 82–87.

6 Fäwziyä Bäyrämova, "Songghï namaz," in *Qïrïq sïrt: Romannar* (Kazan: Tatarstan kitap näshriyatï, 2005), 547–671.

not even spoken in this world and has no practical utility?[7] Bäyrämova, leader of the Tatar nationalist party (*Ittifaq*, "Union"), casts near-death experiences and other paranormal events in a literary, religiously inspired mold that can reach a larger audience of people.[8] For both authors, Islam fulfills the soul's longing for parallel universes. Unlike all other imaginary or physical worlds, the most real one is the *ghayb*, from which all realities originate. This certitude is also shared by another writer Yakhin, who helped popularize many Sufi-inspired stories reprinted by Iakupov's press *Iman*.[9] Both Yakhin's and Iakupov's versions of Islam are more inclusive of popular expressions of piety and eager to preserve them. Even Bäyrämova, who ostentatiously rejects Sufism, still draws from its metaphoric power to restore people's inner and outer spiritual life.

In fact, Ibrakhim's and Bäyrämova's appeal to paranormal experiences and spiritualism inadvertently provides a means toward the reactivation or routinization of some major Sufi concepts, such as the dead soul communicating with the living through dreams or the living soul experiencing the most intimate connection between God and the prophet through the performance of basic (long forgotten) religious duties. But, unlike Yakhin and Iakupov, Ibrakhim and Bäyrämova reject older practices such as the anniversaries of the dead (*taghziya* or *iskä alu*) or the visits to holy sites (*ziyarat*). All four, however, despite their different understanding of what constitutes orthodoxy or heterodoxy, express indigenous interpretations of Islamic identity, against Euro-Islam, and find their way into the children's imaginary through public schools with the official approval of the Tatarstani ministry of education. All four react against the Soviet folklorization of Islam as one of the components of Tatar cultural identity and seek to routinize its practice to repair the broken relationship between God and the Tatar nation. Most important, official educational programs salute Bäyrämova's and Yakhin's books as a new type of novellas that can resurrect the spirit of past medieval literature in their

7 Malik Ibrakhim, *Parallel'nyi mir ili mnogoe no ne vse o dzhinnakh* (Kazan: Idel'-Press, 2004); idem, *Perenesenie i voznesenie Proroka ili kto byl pervym kosmonavtom* (Kazan: Idel'-Press, 2006), 108–09; idem, *Smert': Konets ili nachalo* (Kazan: Idel'-Press, 2007), 49.

8 Fäwziyä Bäyrämova, *Tufannan taralghan tatarlar* (Kazan: "Mägharif" näshriyatï, 2004), 255–257; idem, *Alïplar ilendä* (Kazan: Tatarstan kitap näshriyatï, 2002), 130–133.

9 Färit Yakhin, *Iman* (Kazan: "Iman" näshriyatï, 1995); idem, *Tatar shighriyätendä: Dini mistika häm mifologiia* (Kazan: Tatar däwlät gumanitar universitetï näshriyatï, 2000); Färit Yakhin, ed., *Töshlek: Töshlärne yurau kitabï* (Kazan: "Rannur" näshriyatï, 1997).

weaving fiction and religion together, and as a way to reconnect the youth with its Islamic identity and make Islam part of its everyday life.[10]

1 Jinn and Angels

The main challenge for post-Soviet Muslim intellectuals was to re-mythologize the world. Ghabdelkhak Samatov (b. 1930), who has served as an imam in Kazan since 1981, quotes one of his readers saying "In newspapers you write a lot about Qur'anic verses and angels, but you fail to say much about the jinn. Do they really exist?"[11] Indeed, before the revolution of 1917 and during Soviet rule, the spirit world and the jinn in particular came to be relegated to the realm of children's fantasy. Jinn and other spirits were folklorized in Ghabdulla Tuqay's children poetry, and later personified in Soviet Tatar ballet. The pre-revolutionary novelist Fatikh Ämirkhan made fun of jinn exorcists,[12] and the theologian Rizaetdin Fäkhretdin mocked the practice of striking a sick person to release the spirit responsible for the disease.[13] In his advice books, the qadi recommended that mothers avoid going to the healer for medical advice; instead, they should take sickly children to the hospital. Outside Eurasia, many Islamic modernists also dismissed the world of the jinn as irrational superstition.[14]

For the traditionalist Salafi Ibrakhim, the jinn exist and form a fourth dimension of reality; more importantly, one cannot be a Muslim if one doubts their existence. Muslim modernists of the past, he claims, placed too much emphasis on reason in their interpretation of scriptures, calling for an

---

10 Alsu Shämsutova, *Fäwziyä Bäyrämova prozasï* (Kazan: n.p., 2005), 2, 9, 31, 33, 35, 48; D.F. Zahidullina and A.M. Zakirjanov, *Tatar ädäbiyatï: Teoriia, tarikh* (Kazan: Mägharif, 2006), 280–82; Y.M. Jälilova, "Fäwziyä Bäyrämova prozasïn mäktäptä öyränü üzenchälege," in *Aktual'nye problemy sovremennoi tatarskoi filologii*, ed. I.F. Zaripova *et al.* (Ufa: Bashkirskii gosudarstvennyi universitet, 2016), 439–43; *Khäzerge tatar ädäbiyatï* (Kazan: Mägharif näshriyatï, 2008), 251–273, 365–386.

11 Ghabdelkhak Samatov, *Shärighat': Wäghaz, khökem, fätwa, jawap-sawap, kingäshlär* (Kazan: Idel-Press, 2006), 201; Valiulla Iakupov, *Imamy goroda Kazani* (Kazan: Iman, 2008), 53.

12 Fatikh Ämirkhan, "Fätkhulla khäzrät," in *Majaralar dönyasïnda: Povest'lar häm khikäyälär* (Kazan: Tatarstan kitap näshriyatï, 1990), 151–52.

13 Rizaetdin Fäkhretdin, *Tärbiyäle ana* (Kazan: tip. imper. Universiteta, 1898), 7; idem, *Tärbiyäle khatïn* (Kazan: tip. imper. Universiteta, 1899), 29; idem, "Tärjemäi khälem (Ufa, September 1905)," in *Rizaetdin Fäkhretdin: Fänni-biografik jïyïntïq* (Kazan: "Rukhiyät" näshriyatï, 1999), 23–26.

14 Amira El-Zein, *Islam, Arabs, and the Intelligent World of the Jinn* (Syracuse: Syracuse University Press, 2009), ix.

allegorical reading of the texts; in fact, revelation can explain itself without the use of reason. As proofs of the jinn's existence, Ibrakhim quotes not only the Qur'an and multiple hadiths, but also turns to Western spiritualist literature – even at the risk of contradicting himself. Such interest in the paranormal is not new in Islam or Russia. Egypt has been the center of Islamic spiritualist literature in the twentieth century despite attacks of a number of ulama who view spiritualism as non-Qur'anic, and in the Soviet Union, the occult served as a dissident platform to contest the regime's authoritarianism and positivistic attitude toward nature.[15]

Quoting the Egyptian modernist Salafis Muḥammad Rashīd Riḍā and Sayyid Quṭb, Ibrakhim argues that besides our reality, there are many more parallel universes, including those of animals, plants, angels, and jinn. While the animal and plant kingdoms are visible to the eye (albeit poorly understood), the realms of the angels and jinn are veiled from sight (*janna* in Arabic) and cannot be apprehended through reason. The world of the jinn is larger than the planet Earth. According to the Prophet Muhammad, for every human being made of clay there are nine jinn made of smokeless fire. God has assigned everyone a pair of jinn and a pair of angels. He has created jinn, like humans, to praise Him, and jinn, like humans, have the choice to follow His path or go astray. According to the Qur'an and hadith literature, some have converted to Judaism and Christianity, and others to Islam after listening to the Qur'an. They eat, drink, marry, have children, and will face God's judgment. After death, both jinn and humans will occupy hell or paradise. According to Ibrakhim, who here follows Sayyid Quṭb, denying the existence of jinn in the name of rationality goes against the Qur'an and the *sunna*. Science demonstrates that microbes, electricity, magnetism or electrons, although unseen, do exist. The famous Egyptian modernist, Muḥammad Rashīd Riḍā even hypothesized that microbes could be jinn. Every day, humanity discovers new animal species. This does not mean that these species never existed before. Finally, besides revelation, paranormal activity – UFOs, near-death experiences, cursed mummies, shaking tables, and haunted houses – reveals the presence of another world inhabited by spirits. What remains to be done is to give these spirits their proper names.[16]

---

15 Jane Idleman Smith and Yvonne Yazbeck Haddad, *The Islamic Understanding of Death and Resurrection* (Albany: State University of New York Press, 1981), 111–26; Bernice Glatzer Rosenthal, ed., *The Occult in Russian and Soviet Culture* (Ithaca: Cornell University Press, 1997), 1–32; Dan Burton and David Grandy, *Magic, Mystery, and Science: The Occult in Western Civilization* (Bloomington: Indiana University Press, 2004), 127–48.

16 Ibrakhim, *Parallel'nyi mir*, 5, 8–9, 11, 13–14, 16–21, 41–42, 109–10.

Ibrakhim insists that neither reason nor superstitious folk tales can prove the existence of the jinn, but the scriptures can.[17] One sura of the Qur'an is called *Al-Jinn*, and various hadiths portray the Prophet as an exorcist. One time he liberated a child from the hold of a jinn, and another time he killed a jinn who kept him from concentrating on his prayers. Other hadiths mention that a jinn saw the prophet Muhammad, joined Islam, and then converted other jinn. Quoting the fourteenth-century Hanbali Taqī al-Dīn Aḥmad ibn Taymiyya and the Qur'an, Ibrakhim points out that most Jews and Christians believe in the existence of jinn, albeit not the right way. Jews hold that Allah married a jinn who gave Him daughters, and that the jinn are female spirits (Qur'an, 37:158). As for Christians, they view jinn as creatures of fire and mistakenly identify Satan as a fallen angel, while the Qur'an states that Satan was a jinn made of fire and not an angel made of light. Past Islamic exegesis was less certain than Ibrakhim. The famous ninth-century Baghdad historian and theologian Abū Ja'far Muḥammad ibn Jarīr al-Ṭabarī, for instance, maintained a certain ambiguity regarding the nature of Iblis, since some Qur'anic verses implied that Satan was a fallen angel (7:12; 38:76) and others, that he was a jinn (18:50).[18] In Ibrakhim's worldview, there is no more ambiguity: Iblis was a jinn, a fact that deepens theological differences between Islam and Christianity. Ibrakhim even claims, against dominant Islamic scholarship, that there were jinn prophets, not recognized by Christians. Christians also believe that Allah is the God of light and Satan the God of Darkness, which makes them polytheistic.

Because Jews and Christians failed to write down God's revelation immediately, they came to misinterpret scriptures. For Ibrakhim, the way that they view the jinn (when they acknowledge their existence) is no different from polytheistic Arabs, Greeks, Romans, and Hindus, who knew of their existence and adored them as deities and spirits. Satanic jinn are known for entering their idols and have been responsible for their so-called miracles. Ibrakhim cites examples from Catholic or Protestant churches, but cautiously not from the Russian Church despite its veneration of miraculous icons. In Chile, the Virgin Mary came to life and left the chapel to protect the city of Concepcion against Indians in 1600; in Spain, Jesus came alive on the crucifix of Limpias in 1919; and in Great Britain, serpents and dogs, unclean animals in Islam, escaped from churches. All this was the work of evil jinn who can also be found in isolated places, markets where people of false faiths trade goods, toilets, homes

17 Ibrakhim, *Parallel'nyi mir*, 24–27, 39.

18 Ṭabarī, *The History of al-Ṭabarī, Vol. 1: General Introduction and From the Creation to the Flood*, trans. Franz Rosenthal (Albany: State University of New York Press, 1989), 249–57; Burton and Grandy, *Magic, Mystery, and Science*, 145.

of unbelievers (Jews, Christians, atheists), or the homes of those Muslims who neglect their prayers and religious obligations. Jinn enter places where genders mix or where people sing and play music (rock and metal). They especially favor sites where people circumambulate sacred graves, as pilgrims rub their faces with dirt and ask the dead for a blessing. Women (as well as nonbelievers) are more likely to be bewitched by jinn than men or Muslim believers. Most important, jinn harm those who give children non-Muslim names. Adam and Eve, like Jews and Christians today, gave their first offspring names that Iblis suggested to them, and not God's names. The result was that they were born monstrous and died shortly.[19]

Modern medicine cannot cure jinn possession because physicians deny the phenomenon entirely or because they consider it a physiological imbalance to be treated by drugs. For Ibrakhim, however, only prayer can cure jinn possession. In this perspective, the Prophet's healing hadiths, discounted by many modernists, retain their full authority. Borrowing from a contemporary Egyptian sheikh Waḥīd ʿAbd al-Salām Bālī, Ibrakhim advises would-be exorcists to place the possessed person in a perfect Islamic space – a space free from images, talismans, amulets, musical instruments, and perfumes – so that angels may lend their aid. If the patient is female, her body should be entirely covered, except for her eyes and hands, and her husband (or other male relative) should accompany her. All prayers should be recited in Arabic directly from the Qur'an. If the patient loses consciousness, the exorcist should ask for the jinn's name and religion; non-Muslim jinn must convert to Islam, which renders them harmless.[20]

Ibrakhim, a strong proponent of Prophetic medicine, mentions other methods of healing, also supported by Islamic authorities in Saudi Arabia.[21] One remedy is to strike the body to chase the jinn away (as the Prophet did); only the jinn suffers, not the patient. Another is for the sick person to recite prayers over a basin of water and drink from it three days in a row. Listening to the Qur'an continuously with the help of audiotapes or writing prayers in ink, washing them, and drinking them can also hasten the cure. Although Ibrakhim recommends the presence of a specialist to perform the necessary prayers, his book can also serve as a self-help to evict evil jinn.[22] On the Internet, one

19 Ibrakhim, *Parallel'nyi mir*, 30–36, 60–63, 70, 116, 130, 141, 151, 160, 241, 247, 269–72, 274, 293–94, 402.

20 Ibrakhim, *Parallel'nyi mir*, 346–47, 350–51, 353–54.

21 Wahid Abd al-Salam Bali, *How to Protect Yourself from Jinn and Shaytan* (London: Al-Firdous, 2009); Remke Kruk, "Harry Potter in the Gulf: Contemporary Islam and the Occult," *British Journal of Middle Eastern Studies* 32, no. 1 (May 2005): 47–73.

22 Ibrakhim, *Parallel'nyi mir*, 38, 299, 346–47, 350–51, 353–54, 361, 368.

of his readers thanked him for giving her the means to avert the evil eye. In February 2008, at the Kazan kremlin mosque of Qol Sharif, Imam Ramil Yunïsov (b. 1969), who was also trained in Saudi Arabia, quoted the same prescriptions to cure diseases caused by jinn, and the young women who sat near me during his weekly lessons rushed to him and grabbed many of the prayer sheets that he had copied in ink. One pedagogical guide for Kazan public schools even saluted these national modes of healing as an important aspect of Tatar cultural history, now clinically recognized as a form of psychotherapy.[23]

Ibrakhim's portrayal of Iblis and the jinn stands in sharp contrast with that of Yakhin who advocates a return to the Turkic books of the past and rarely quotes modern or foreign authors. A poet, novelist, literary critic, journalist, and literature teacher, Yakhin relies almost exclusively on the tales of the prophets and Sufi accounts that constituted the bulk of popular knowledge of Islam and inspired the works of famous Eurasian and Central Asian poets. While Ibrakhim's references are quite eclectic – English-language spiritualist literature, Salafists from the Middle East or South Asia, famous Russian novelists, personal Bashkir or Tatar acquaintances, and hadiths – Yakhin refers exclusively to Turkic sources of Central Asian, Anatolian, and Volga origins: Khoja Ahmad Yasawi, Sulayman Baqïrghanï, Nasir al-Din al-Rabghuzi, Sufi Allahyar, and Ahmet Bican. Yakhin's goal is to restore this literature as an integral part of the Tatars' spiritual heritage despite previous efforts of jadid writers and communists to sideline it. The famous modernist theologian Fäkhretdin, whom Yakhin quotes abundantly, had indeed blamed these traditional Turkic writers for their fanciful details, aberrant cosmology, reliance on so-called Isra'iliyyat (reports narrated from Jewish sources), and dubious hadiths, but did not call for their incineration. Jadid publishing houses continued printing them until the 1920s. After their ban, many of their cosmological and eschatological themes though survived in the *munajat* (sung prayers) whose main reciters were (but not exclusively) female. For Yakhin and other intellectuals, these abïstays were the keepers of an endangered Islam, which shaped their people's imagination for centuries, in a godless Russian milieu. In his native village, schoolteachers repeated that there was no god, but the abïstays performed rain prayers and other rites to secure God's blessings, and defying modern scientific expectations, the rain poured into the fields. For Yakhin and his publisher Iakupov, this thaumaturgical tradition could bring even more blessings if young Tatars

23 R.Kh. Shäymärdanov and Ä.N. Khujiäkhmätov, *Tatar milli pedagogikasï* (Kazan: "Mägharif" näshriyatï, 2007), 45–46; Valiulla Iakupov, *Imamy goroda Kazani*, 27–28; Ramil Yunïsov, interview by author, Qol Sharif (Kazan, 15 February 2008).

embraced Islam in its Turkic form as it developed since their ancestors' conversion to Islam in the tenth century.[24]

Yakhin provides a more elaborate reconstruction of the jinn's early history and Iblis's origins. While Ibrakhim follows Ibn Taymiyya and his student Ibn Kathīr in portraying Iblis exclusively as a Satanic jinn, Yakhin draws on Turkic Sufi sources to fashion a more complex picture of his origins. According to Yakhin, there was a time when Iblis's nature was originally undefined: neither a jinn nor an angel, he was known not as Iblis but as Azazil (ʿAzāzīl). As a reward for his piety, God raised Azazil to live among the angels in the first level of heaven. Later, God even sent Azazil to earth to persuade the rebellious jinn to return to the right path, to little effect. Enraged, God destroyed the rebels with fire, saving only Azazil and those few jinn who had hearkened to his message. Azazil's piety continued to increase, so that God endowed him with the angelic qualities, placed him in the seventh heaven and, finally, allowed him to enter paradise. There Azazil taught the angels, and his status rose even higher. In the meantime, God created Adam to be a better caretaker of the earth than the jinn had been, and ordered Azazil to bow before him, but Azazil, too proud of his own achievements, refused, for he was made of fire and Adam, only of clay. For Yakhin, whose reconstruction of Iblis's origins reflects one of the many ways Sufi interpreters sought to solve the Qurʾan's textual ambiguity, the hypocritical current imams, the so-called Wahhabis or traditionalist Salafis educated in Saudi Arabia, were like Azazil. They claim to teach the Qurʾan and the truth, but in fact, like Azazil and the hypocrites or outward Muslims (*munafiqun*) of Medina, they are arrogant and contemptuous. Yakhin's interpretation also sends a strong message that God placed human beings above the jinn and gave them greater responsibility and accountability for the environment. Tatars should behave better than the jinn who neglected their religious duties and polluted the earth. Quoting the famous nineteenth-century Turkic poet Miftakhetdin Aqmulla, a former disciple of the Naqshbandi Shaykh Zäynulla Räsüli in Troitsk, Yakhin reminds his readers that a person who does not know the rules of his faith is called "Ivan."[25]

Bäyrämova also battles with the *munafiqun*, but they are not Yakhin's "Wahhabis." In fact, they are those among Eurasianist and modernist secularist Tatars who call Wahhabi anyone who eats halal food, dresses the Islamic way,

24 Aisylu-khadzhi Sadekova, *Ideologiia islama i tatarskoe narodnoe tvorchestvo* (Kazan: Iman, 2000/2001), 4, 17–18; Färit Yakhin, *Aq äbilär doghasï* (Kazan: Tatarstan kitap näshriyatï, 2000), 4–7; idem, *Baqïrghan kitabï* (Kazan: Tatarstan kitap näshriyatï, 2000), 2–8.

25 Färit Yakhin, *Iman* (Kazan: "Iman" näshriyatï, 1995), 4–5, 74–76; Ibn Kathir, *Istorii o prorokakh: Ot Adama do Mukhammeda so slov Ibn Kasira* (Moscow-St. Petersburg: "Dilia," 2008), 11.

opposes Darwinism and music, or condemns visits to holy sites. These hypocrites include Tatars who collaborate with the secret police to keep the young from fighting jihad. In her view, the end of times has already arrived. The jinn world is the present world. Tatars have adopted the Russian way of life, married Russians or Kriashens, lost their language and religion, and buried their dead in Russian cemeteries. In Bäyrämova's view, the Kriashens, a painful reminder of the Tatars' "forced" Christianization, are closely associated with the jinn. In one of her novels, the devout mother of a jihadist is unable to protect her husband from the jinn of a mixed Russian-Kriashen woman who worships icons and works as an exorcist. Conversely, Bäyrämova considers jinn exorcism, practiced by Muslim healers, as an ancient, esoteric art worthy of transmission to the next generation. In one story, an elderly female healer strikes a young girl with a black chicken at the bathhouse (*muncha*), a place of purification, to chase out evil jinn while citing the appropriate healing prayers. The girl later became a healer herself, ready at the age of ninety to transmit her numinous knowledge to the story's hero who had experienced prophetic visions of the Last Hour. Curiously, Bäyrämova, who can be critical of Sufism, did not condemn the Sufi supernatural components of her female characters' spirituality, who ascribe healing powers to sacred springs. Nevertheless, Bäyrämova is still faithful to her so-called Wahhabi ideals since her character's effort to heal her own son with sacred spring water fails. Bäyrämova's God does not forgive the son for having married a Kriashen who cares more about her material comfort than her salvation and whose children, ignorant of the rich history of the Turkic world, married Russians.[26]

2 The Prophet Muhammad and His Miracles

Besides blaming modernists for not reading the Qur'an literally and for not accepting all traditions as valid especially those related to his healing skills and miracles, some Tatar imams and intellectuals question the way that modernists have portrayed the Prophet Muhammad. For the traditionalist Salafi Ibrakhim and the Sufi poetry revivalist, Yakhin, the Prophet is an infallible, perfect figure with extraordinary qualities, and not simply a great political and social leader who might have made mistakes in worldly matters or given the

26 Fäwziyä Bäyrämova, *Khaj köndälege* (Chally: Mädäni jomgha, 1999), 71; idem, *Tufannan taralghan tatarlar*, 237, 242, 244–245, 248; idem, "Songghï namaz," 577, 604, 616; idem, *Däwerlär kücheshendä. Publitsistik yazmalar häm shighïrlär* (Almetyevsk: Tatneft', n.d.), 21, 116, 122.

wrong medical advice.[27] In prerevolutionary modernist literature, the Prophet Muhammad was portrayed as a great social leader or a man of his time who cared for the poor, but not as an extraordinary miracle worker. His only miracle was the Qur'an.[28] According to Ibrakhim, modernists' humanization of the Prophet unfairly stripped him from his many miracles and superhuman qualities that were signs of his prophethood.[29]

In one of the very first biographies of the Prophet published in Tatar in the 1990s, the author, Yakhin, drew from Turkic Sufi literature to portray the Prophet Muhammad as a cosmic figure. Muhammad was God's very first creation after Allah created the Intellect, the Pen, the Tablet, and the first letters of the Arabic alphabet.[30] From every letter, the light of God sprang forth, and God created the Soul of the Prophet out of the letter *mim*. Then, from the Prophet's Soul, God created the tree of certainty upon which He hung the Soul in the shape of a peacock. In front of the Soul, God also hung a mirror. As the Prophet's Soul gazed at its own image in the mirror, it was reminded of God and began to perspire. Out of this perspiration emerged the four caliphs. Then the perspiration from different parts of the Prophet's Soul gave rise to the creatures of heaven and earth. From its head, the angels sprang forth; from its face, God's throne, the Pen and the Tablets, the earth, moon, and stars; from its chest, all prophets and martyrs of the faith; from its back, the Al-Aqsa mosque in Jerusalem, the Kaaba of Mecca, and all madrasas; and from its two brows, the *umma*, community of the Prophet. In its peacock form, the Prophet's Soul sang the praises of God for seventy thousand years until God gave it human form. At the time of prayer, the Prophet would stand up and the spirits of all the other Prophets and all nations circumambulated him for a hundred thousand years (Yakhin uses the term *tawaf* which also applies to the circumambulation of the Kaaba during the hajj). Afterwards, God ordered people to perform their prayers following the shape of the Prophet's name, "Ahmed": first, one should stand as the letter *alif* (which symbolizes God's unity), then bow (like the letter *ha*), then prostrate oneself (like the letter *mim*), and finally kneel (like the letter *dal*).

Faithful to Ibn Taymiyya who rejected the Sufi concept of the Muhammedan Light, Ibrakhim, unlike Yakhin, did not portray Muhammad as pre-existent, but still remembered him as an extraordinary miracle worker whose beauty

---

27 Färit Yakhin, *Päyghambärebez Mökhämmäd* (Kazan: "Rannur" näshriyatï, 1999), 4–14.

28 Rizaetdin Fäkhretdin, *Dini wä ijtimaghïy mäs'älälär* (Orenburg: "Waqt" matbughasï, 1914), 41; Ataulla Baiazitov, *Otnoshenie islama k nauke i k inovertsam* (St. Petersburg: tipografiia "Nur," 1906), 7.

29 Ibrakhim, *Perenesenie i voznesenie*, 33.

30 Yakhin, *Iman*, 31–38.

surpassed that of the Prophet Joseph. Many hadiths witnessed that his face radiated like the moon and his forehead like the sun. Most important, God endowed the Prophet with many miracles, among them the Qur'an, the splitting of the moon, the multiplication of water, the bowing of stones and trees before him, the splitting of his chest, his Night Journey from Mecca to Jerusalem (*isrā'*), and his ascent to the Heavens (*miʿrāj*). Angels split his chest four times, emptying it from all evil – when he was four, ten, forty, just before he received God's first revelation, and at the occasion of his journey to the Heavens. Modernists might have questioned the soundness of the hadiths related to these events; yet, according to Ibrakhim, the Prophet's Night Journey and Ascent happened physically and spiritually, and not in a dream. Disputing these proofs would negate Muhammad's prophethood. Furthermore, Ibrakhim insists that none of these events conflicts with reason and science. Einstein's theory of relativity explains the speed by which the Prophet traveled from Mecca to Jerusalem, and as in Star Wars, it is likely that the Prophet used portals to go from one place to another in the blink of an eye. One day, once human beings develop their scientific abilities, they too will travel through space without spaceships.[31]

Ibrakhim is not the only one who uses the paranormal to re-Islamize Tatars. Bäyrämova successfully weaves Islam and the paranormal together, and because of her literary recasting of spiritualist eschatology, she can reach a much larger (and younger) audience than Ibrakhim. Two of her characters had near-death experiences. An elderly woman had a stroke and lay down, facing Mecca. Her soul, like the Prophet's, traveled through Heaven and Hell. She, who knew little Arabic, miraculously recited the Qur'an sitting up and warned in Tatar of the coming of a new flood at the end of the world if people persisted in their evil ways. After awakening from her extraordinary vision, the woman explained that every living being spoke Arabic in the afterlife thanks to the angels who taught them God's language. The other character, a healer, had a similar experience as a child. While climbing a mountain, she fainted, but angels of light with large wings brought her body to the top of the mountain and cleansed it with the lake water, which according to popular lore contained the remnant of Noah's flood. In both cases, the characters' angelic encounters were no different from that of the Prophet when the angels purified his chest or when he ascended to Heaven. Bäyrämova's description of hell and paradise – as well as her cosmology – draws directly from past Sufi-inspired Turkic eschatological literature.[32]

31 Ibrakhim, *Perenesenie i voznesenie*, 8, 25, 27, 29–30, 108–12.

32 Bäyrämova, *Tufannan*, 149–54, 255–57.

That Tatars live as a minority in a Russian-speaking Christian world also explains their strategic emphasis on the miraculous. Shortly after the Christmas holidays, the children's magazine, *Yalqïn*, noted that Muslims, too, have a special night to celebrate, the *Mi'raj*. The article insists that the Ascension of Muhammad was a physical miraculous experience, confirming his status as the greatest of all prophets: while Abraham lives in the seventh heaven, the closest to God, Jesus is only in the second. Significantly, Jesus's name is first spelled as Iisus Khristos (the Russian way) and then Ghaysa Päyghambär (the Tatar way), ensuring that *Yalqïn*'s young bilingual readers make the connection between the two names. A picture by the artist Rusham Shämsetdinov of an unveiled young bearded Prophet Muhammad climbing a ladder to the Heavens also accompanies the text, ignoring the late prohibition of portraying the prophet with his face uncovered, but competing successfully with the nativity imagery of icons, which Tatar children have been exposed to in their daily contact with Russians.[33] Concomitantly, Yakhin, in an interview given in the same issue, warns that prophets should not be venerated as icons or idols, the way that Christians do with Jesus, for what they will be eternally damned.[34] In this particular instance of religious bricolage, the journal brought the *mi'raj* story and its miraculous characteristics forward to compete with the public celebration of Christmas and give children a possible enchanting alternative. Two special nights, Christmas Eve and the Night of the Mi'raj, came together to draw the line between two different identities.

3 The Afterlife

Around the turn of the twenty-first century, Imam Zöfär Takhawi in Chally, regretted that Tatars were no longer exposed to past Arab eschatology. He praised the work of Saudi visitors who knew their faith even though they had secular jobs, and blamed Tatars for having destroyed mosques and schools, deported their own imams, and added Russian suffixes to their last names. He warned them against their impending Christianization if they continued eating pork and drinking alcohol, and if men no longer taught their wives and children to pray. Those responsible for the decline of religion were the Sufis who drank wine and introduced *bida* (innovation). Only by strictly observing all five prayers could nominal Tatars save themselves from hell: repentance

---

33 Khaji Abdulla Dubin, "Mighraj kichäse," *Yalqïn*, 12 (1993), 24–25.

34 Mödärris Aghlämov, "Densezme min, dinsezme?" *Yalqïn*, 12 (1993), 26–27.

after death would not suffice. In short, Tatars were no better than the kafirs of Mecca.[35]

This emphasis on the afterlife and its dire punishments differs from the recent past. Like their counterparts in the rest of the Islamic world, prerevolutionary Tatar modernists tended to deemphasize the physical aspects of the afterlife and stress human responsibility and science. For them, too much emphasis on the afterlife led the Muslim world to neglect the physical needs of this life and precipitated its economic decline.[36] Conversely, the most vocal Tatars of Chally, Ibrakhim, Takhawi, or Bäyrämova,[37] argue that modernity, which their reform-minded ancestors sought so badly, led to ecological problems, climate change, nuclear disasters, brutal wars, moral devastation, AIDS, and alcoholism. For them, there is no need to change the older corpus of interpretation; science confirms or will confirm the truths of Islam. It is just a matter of time. Ibrakhim goes further: parapsychology, spiritualism or occultism can provide immediate scientific proof of the supernatural.

Ibrakhim offers an interesting spiritualist interpretation of Islam that has deep roots in the history of occultism in both Russia, America, and the Middle East. Just as prerevolutionary Russian occultists found in ancient Egyptian cultures the early premises of Christian truths, the imam finds the first glimmerings of Islamic eschatology in Ancient Egyptian, Maya, and Vedic philosophies. Skipping Judeo-Christian eschatology on the pretext that his readers have already familiarized themselves with its many forms, he repeats the findings of Muslim spiritualists from Egypt, who affirm the total reliability of traditional Muslim medieval literature. Contrary to the claims of secular materialists, cameras have caught images of spirits, and the measurement of bodies before and after death indicates that there is a slight change of body weight – evidence that the soul has departed. Citing works of various American aficionados of the paranormal (the psychic Edgar Cayce, the physician Melvine Morse, the cardiologist Michael Sabom, the evangelical geologist Diana Komp, and the psychologist Charles Tart), Ibrakhim concludes that near-death experiences prove the truth of Islamic eschatology: there is an afterlife in the grave and beyond.[38]

---

35 Zöfär Takhawi, *Iman Yulï* (Chally: n.p., n.d.), 3–11, 14–15, 17, 19–20, 30, 34–35.

36 Fäkhretdin, *Dini*, 46; idem, *Jäwami' al-kälim shärkhe* (Orenburg: Parovaia tipo-litografiia Torg. Doma "A.A. Khusainov," 1917), 286–289, 507–508.

37 Fäwziyä Bäyrämova, *Taralïp yatqan tatar ile* (Kazan: "Ayaz" näshriyatï, 2003), 240–81.

38 Ibrakhim, *Smert'*, 10–11, 52–53, 60–66, 98–102.

In modernist literature, the *barzakh* was understood as a barrier between the dead and the living. The early twentieth-century reformer and qadi, Fäkhretdin cautioned believers against putting too much authority into dreams, one of the ways that in traditional Islam the dead communicated with the living, often warning them of the eschatological consequences of poor religious practice.[39] Ibrakhim's book resurrects the image of the *barzakh* as a permeable barrier and as a place of prayer and purification before judgment day. The dead can see angels and jinn for the first time, meet family members who have died (although in the Qur'an, it is stipulated that such meeting would take place in the garden of Eden), and even visit living family members. Most important, the dead require more help than the living: since the deceased cannot act in this world, they need continual support from their living loved ones. The size of the grave widens as the number of *sawab* (awards for good deeds) increases. As examples of good deeds, Ibrakhim cites praying for the dead, performing the hajj or fasts in the name of the deceased, acting charitably, asking God for His forgiveness, or reimbursing any physical or spiritual debts (missed prayer or fasts). Of course, any good action that still bears consequences for the future will also add to the number of *sawab* for the deceased. For instance, if the deceased helped build a mosque, brought people to Islam, educated his progeny in the faith, and gave alms, the actions of the people who benefited from these acts will also turn into *sawab*. In other words, Ibrakhim's *barzakh* is not entirely sealed. There is room for some form of intercession, despite the final warning that God will be the ultimate decider.[40] Ibrakhim, however – like Fäkhretdin, but unlike Yakhin and Iakupov – does not approve of traditional memorial repasts (*taghziya*) held on the third, seventh, fortieth, and fifty-first days, and on the first anniversary after burial, during which family members, friends, and neighbors gather to distribute alms in the name of the deceased and recite *munajat* calling for the Prophet's intercession.[41] Such repasts, whose main goal is to repay the sins of the deceased, are still held in and outside Tatarstan.[42] Tatars in Astrakhan, for example, believe that the fifty-first day is the most important day. This is the time when the dead suffer most – all their

39 Fäkhretdin, *Jäwami'*, 130–133.

40 Ibrakhim, *Smert'*, 28–30, 137–39, 142–143, 184, 195–96.

41 Dmitrii Makarov and Rafik Mukhametshin, "Official and Unofficial Islam," in *Islam in Post-Soviet Russia: Public and Private Faces*, eds. Hilary Pilkington and Galina Yemelianova (London: RoutledgeCurzon, 2003), 127; Fäkhretdin, *Jäwami'*, 163.

42 Shäymärdanov and Khujiäkhmätov, *Tatar milli pedagogikasï*, 71; Färit Yakhin, *Islam dine nigezläre* (Kazan: "Rannur" näshriyatï, 1997), 229; idem, *Päyghambärlär, färeshtälär, akhirät* (Kazan: "Rannur" näshriyatï, 1999), 299–300.

bones separate from each other – and without the assistance of the relatives' prayers, the suffering would be unbearable.[43]

Ibrakhim's discourse about the afterlife is not that different from those who denounced Wahhabi missionaries' attacks on popular expressions of Islam. Cemeteries, for Ibrakhim, are living places, but the imam of Chally cautions that ultimately God will decide whether prayers and deeds of relatives will count as *sawab* or not. As Ibn ʿAbd-al Wahhāb taught, the only guaranteed intercessor for the Muslim community is the Prophet Muhammad, but this does not mean that God will automatically grant the Prophet's intercession. Likewise, seeking the intercession of holy men, Sufi shaykhs, or pious ancestors in lieu of the Prophet is wrong. Ibrakhim condemns visits and circumambulation of sacred tombs, claiming that satanic jinn in human forms stand by them.[44] Praying to the dead and rubbing people's faces with the dirt of sacred graves are also forbidden. Women, in particular, who are more likely than men to be possessed by jinn, should avoid visiting these places with their children. Except for his reference to Satanic jinn, Ibrakhim's stand against sacred places and the Prophet's intercession is not that different from the reformist theologian Fäkhretdin's. The only difference is that Fäkhretdin preferred to concentrate on the life of the living than on the afterlife. Spiritualist literature provided Ibrakhim the means to return to early representations of the afterlife and discuss their modernity through the lens of new scientific or pseudoscientific research, which, in his mind, could best respond to the needs of a secularized audience.

One urgent question remains: who is to be labeled "kafir"? For the prerevolutionary jadid theologian Musa Bigiev (1873?–1949), who remains very popular among Tatar Eurasianists, God extends his mercy to all confessions. This opinion, however, is condemned as heresy by Imam Idris Ghalävetdin, who once taught in Ioldyz, the same madrasa as Ibrakhim.[45] In his short thematic brochures, adorned with bright color pictures on their front cover, Ghalävetdin declares that Muslims are not guaranteed Heaven, and God will

---

43 N.R. Azizova, *Svadebnaia i pokhoronno-pominal'naia obriadnost' Astrakhanskikh tatar (konets XX–nachalo XXI vv.): Istoriko-etnograficheskoe issledovanie* (Astrakhan: izdatel'stvo AOIUU, 2002), 57.

44 Ibrakhim, *Parallel'nyi mir*, 293–94; idem, *Smert'*, 198.

45 Idris Ghalävetdin, *Mäyetlärne ozatu tärtibe* (Chally: "Täwbä" mächete, 1422/2001), 33–35; idem, *Namaznïng qabul bulmyi, ägär....* (Chally: "Täwbä" machete, 1422/2002), 28; idem, *Möselmannar jähännämgä keräme?* (Iar Chally: "Täwbä" mächete, 1423/2003), 4–12; Musa Dzharullakh Bigiev, "Dokazatel'stva bozhestvennogo miloserdiia (Räkhmät ilahiyä borhannarï)," in *Antologiia tatarskoi bogoslovskoi mysli* (Kazan: Tatarskoe knizhnoe izdatel'stvo, 2005), pp. 77–130.

not judge the "people of the book" by their own laws. Kafirs include those who mocked Islam during the Soviet Union, apostatized from the faith, and consider that all religions are the expression of the same truth. Ghalävetdin's list also comprises those who fail to observe all pillars of the faith, decide on their own what is permissible or forbidden to eat, and drink alcohol. Christians who associate God with a human being, Sufis or those who pray to the saints (*awliya*), women who object to their husband's wish to take three more wives, gays, and those who obey their kafir parents will go straight to hell unless they repent. In death, Muslim and Christian tombs should not look alike: Muslims should have no coffins, no flowers, no fence around the grave, no pictures, and no names of the deceased on the tombstone (except for great ulama). Finally, women should not visit cemeteries, and people should not pray or circumambulate any sacred tomb.

Bäyrämova's list of kafirs does not differ from that of Ghalävetdin or Ibrakhim.[46] In her children's novel, there is no appeal for a Tatar who betrayed the Chechen cause; he ended up in hell. Bäyrämova's description of hell and paradise is far from being metaphorical. In hell, the flames are more painful than in this life and deep wells hide snakes and scorpions whose sting can hurt up to forty years. Conversely, magnificent gardens adorn heaven. They host angels, houris, giants, and the elect who remain forever thirty-three years old in a blissful state. In contrast, Yakhin, who also relies on Turkic sources and depicts the afterlife in similar concrete terms, offers a more conciliatory perspective than Bäyrämova and the Tatar traditionalist Salafis.[47] Both Ibrakhim and Yakhin agree that the baptized of any ethnic background and Tatars who have adopted Russian ways are kafirs since they have ascribed divine attributes to their prophet, Jesus. However, the two authors recognize that Tatars and Russians live in the same milieu. Yakhin proposes that while visiting churches or sharing meals with Christians, Muslims recite the *shahada* (witness of faith) to protect themselves. However, unlike the hardliners imam Takhawi and novelist Bäyrämova, Yakhin believes that in the end all Muslims – even those who had gone astray – will enter paradise. Sins can be repaid in this life and in the grave through communal support. For Yakhin, people's sufferings result not from God but from their ancestors who failed to follow God's will during Soviet times. Now children and grandchildren pay for their sins. Yakhin emphasizes communal responsibility more than individual responsibility, hence the importance of visiting sacred places, knowing one's family tree, marrying Tatars, and observing all facets of Muslim life, including the repasts (*taghziya*).

46 Bäyrämova, *Tufannan*, 270–71.

47 Yakhin, *Iman*, 187–97; idem, *Päyghambärlär, färeshtälär, akhirät*, 299–301.

On these days, Yakhin insists, the dead visit their relatives and friends. Their soul rejoices when family members and neighbors read the Qur'an. Happiness then blesses the land, but darkness befalls it when descendants neglect their religious duties. Conversely, for the writer Bäyrämova, individual responsibility comes first. Knowing one's family tree and visiting sacred graves as historical places and reminders of early Turkic settlements or past jihad are equally important, but this national topography has no salvific properties.[48]

The late imam Iakupov shared Yakhin's views.[49] Ancient death rituals constitute one of the ways that people's suffering in the grave can be alleviated. They might include elements from the Tatars' pagan past, but no more than the Meccan hajj. Forbidding these repasts would be the same as not believing in the afterlife. For other imams, these ceremonies might not be mentioned in the Qur'an or the hadiths, but they have a history embedded in Tatar national past. When Ivan the Terrible sought to convert Tatars forcefully to Christianity, these rituals, which involved prayers to God, recitation of *munajat*, and distribution of alms, helped Tatars keep their faith and identity.[50] Other imams try to find a compromise. Jälil Fazlïev (b. 1956), who also emphasizes communal solidarity over personal responsibility, declares that since Abu Hanifa considered unwise to disregard local customs that did not contravene Islamic law, these gatherings may continue, but they should not be declared *faryz* (obligatory). If people cannot afford inviting relatives and neighbors for these elaborate meals, there is no obligation to hold them.[51] When the Institute of History established the Russian Islamic University of Kazan with the support of Saudi money, there used to be posters plastered in its corridors listing *taghziya* as *bida*. Students debated the lawfulness of these repasts in interactive exercises, and called for their rejection, but when teachers asked whether they would be

---

48 Bäyrämova, *Taralïp*, 52–57, 102–108; idem, *Tufannan*, 270.

49 Iakupov, *K prorocheskomu islamu*, 167–169; idem, *Tatarskoe "Bogoiskatel'stvo" i prorocheskii islam* (Kazan: Iman, 2003); idem, "Khanafitskii mazkhab, ego znachenie i aktual'nost'," https://web.archive.org/web/20071113083846/http://www.imancentre.ru/hanafia.htm (accessed May 21, 2019); "Poseshchenie mogil," https://web.archive.org/web/20071113083933/http://imancentre.ru:80/mogil.htm; "Voznagrazhdenie usopshim: Voznagrazhdenie za chtenie Korana pokoinym," https://web.archive.org/web/20071113142126/http://imancentre.ru/usopwim.htm (accessed May 21, 2019); Yakhin, *Iman*, 17, 20–21; idem, *Päyghambärlär, färeshtälär, akhirät*, 299–300.

50 Iskhaq Lutfullin and Islaev Fayzulkhak, *Dzhikhad tatarskogo naroda* (Kazan: Iman, 1998), 50–51.

51 Jälil khäzrät Fazlïev, *Jälil khäzrät däresläre* (Kazan: Mädäni jomgha, 1999), 138–39; idem, *Yöz ber wäghaz* (Kazan: n.p., 2005), 8; idem, "The Prayers We Perform are for the Spirits of the Ancestors," in *Tatar Islamic Texts*, ed. Allen J. Frank (Hyattsville: Dunwoody Press, 2008), 205–09.

attending such gatherings if relatives or neighbors invited them, the students' answer was unanimously affirmative.[52]

Another topic of contention involves pilgrimages to sacred shrines (*ziyarat*). In his work, Iakupov reminds readers that there was a time when Russians forbade Tatars to live in Bolghar and Biliarsk and crosses covered their mosques.[53] Yet, Tatars continued performing the *zikr* at these sacred sites where Tatars accepted Islam. Opposing *ziyarat* would be the same as saying yes to Christianization. Bäyrämova, on the other hand, is not opposed to the visit itself, but considers praying at the graves as *bida*, and holds this – and the *taghziya* – responsible for the decline of Islam. For her, there is no time to intercede for people who have betrayed their faith and there is always the risk of praying to the dead, but, despite her critical view of popular piety, Bäyrämova draws from it constantly to advance her understanding of Islam. In her children's novel, *Nukh Päyghambär köymäse* (The Prophet Noah's Ark), she "Islamizes" the ecological particularities of the Uralic landscape, which have also inspired many ancient alien theorists on the Web, creating a much larger sacred topography that unites Bashkir and Tatar lands. The famous caves of the former Orenburg province, whose mural paintings date back to the Paleolithic era and where archeologists have excavated gigantic bones, become the site of a fantastic descent of angels after a grandfather prays for the well-being of his land and people. In a dreaming state, his grandson identifies the caves and the history of their inhabitants with a Qur'anic story – when the Prophet Hud tried to convert the people of ʿĀd, a nation of giants but God destroyed them for their impiety – and oral Turkic traditions about a giants' cemetery. Once more in Bäyrämova's literary fantasy, dreams and prayers offer a conduit between this world and the other world. It is not clear what makes these caves different from the other sacred and historical places that Tatars visit for their healing properties, which is often an object of scold for Bäyrämova. Yet, Bäyrämova extends the sacredness of the Turkic landscape, well beyond historical times, calling for its mythologization through the reworking of Qur'anic myths. Her Islamization of the topography is not that different from previous medieval attempts of indigenizing Qur'anic stories in Persian and Turkic epics. Despite her attacks on popular expressions of piety, Bäyrämova constantly draws from them to reaffirm Prophetic authority. On the hajj, she imagines that Mount Arafat intercedes for the pilgrims, prostrating itself toward the Kaaba. She hopes that her prayers at the same Mount will illuminate the

52 Damir Said Shagaviev, interview by author, Russian Islamic University, Kazan, 20 May 2008.

53 Iakupov, *K prorocheskomu islamu*, 169–70.

graves of her ancestors, make the earth lighter and the questioning of angels more bearable, and in the end facilitate their entrance into paradise. Of course, she adds cautiously, such prayers can be performed only in Mecca and not in Tatarstani sacred places. The students I interviewed in Muhammadia madrasa in 2008 also shared her opinion: Bolghar and Biliarsk were places of historical significance worthy of a tourist visit, but they were not intercessory places of worship. Nevertheless, this does not stop public school teachers from having schoolchildren circumambulate the small minaret, and elderly women from performing *zikr* in the ruins of Bolghar city, or people from hanging scarves on the trees and circumambulating the sacred stone of Biliarsk.[54]

Despite being often labeled as Wahhabi under the influence of a foreign madhhab incompatible with the multicultural milieu in which Tatars have been living for centuries as a minority, the eschatology of Bäyrämova, Ibrakhim, and Ghalävetdin is not entirely foreign to Tatars. With some embarrassment, teacher and historian Damir Said Shagaviev in the Russian Islamic University remarked to me in 2008 that the famous nineteenth-century reformer Shihabetdin Märjani was not tolerant toward Russians. In fact, Märjani did not consider Eastern Orthodox Russians as the "people of the book" defined in the Qur'an and the *sunna*. He considered eating with Russians and buying meat from them unlawful because of the way they killed the animals, and even declared that marrying their women was strictly forbidden. Conversely, Märjani believed in the intercession of Sufi shaykhs, rejected the notion of *takfir* (declaring Muslims unbelievers), and held that God would forgive all Muslims. In the same line, the vice-rector of the Islamic university, Suleyman Zaripov, who was trained in Bukhara during perestroika and then sent to the University of Riyadh in Saudi Arabia, believed that his people were more tolerant than his Saudi teachers. Tatarstani imams do not refuse to read the Qur'an for the dead who failed to perform their five prayers or pray at the mosque, and non-believers or apostates are not put to death.[55]

---

54 Bäyrämova, *Tufannan*, 187–89, 212–29, 434–35; Bäyrämova, *Däwerlär kücheshendä*, 122; idem, *Khaj köndälege*, 67, 83, 91.

55 Shihabetdin Mardzhani, *Zrelaia mudrost' v raz"iasnenii dogmatov an-Nasafi: Kitab al-Khikma al-baliga al-dzhaniiia fi sharkh al-'akaid al-khanafiia* (Kazan: Tatarskoe knizhnoe izdatel'stvo, 2008), 84–85, 230–46; Fred Hilgemann, *Le Tatarstan: Pays des musulmans de Russie* (Paris: Éditions Autrement, 2007), 111.

4 Conclusion

Religious revivalism and re-enchantment might not be the right terms to describe the current spiritual landscape of post-Soviet Russia. After all, religion or enchantment has never left the Volga region and the Ural Mountains. Processes of Christianization and Islamization continued uninterrupted throughout the Soviet period, and women, after the Great Patriotic war, often served as the main transmitters of these myths.[56] Nevertheless, new political and scientific myths of human empowerment have challenged older cosmological and eschatological myths. Consequently, these older foundational stories had to adapt quickly to reclaim their authority, and they did it through the work of imams who publish their sermons and advice, and writers who cast their religious conceptions of the world in a literary mold accessible to children. Ibrakhim, largely influenced by Egyptian Islamic literature, relies on the writings of nineteenth-century British spiritualists to validate revelatory cosmogony and counteract the effects of secularization and scientific materialism. For him and Bäyrämova to some extent, spiritualism or occultism is one of the ways to provide scientific proof of the extraordinary and reopen communication between parallel worlds. Likewise, if Tatars adopt a modernist reading of the revelation and its exclusive portrayal of the Prophet as a social leader, this would deplete the revelation of its Prophetic and miraculous authority. Concrete imagery of hell and paradise and renewed belief in angels and jinn can better charter attitudes and practices outside the mosque, and shape communal boundaries, often blurred by daily contact with the "other" (Russian, Kriashen, or Tatar "hypocrites" who have adopted secular ways and collaborated with the authority). But it can also fuel political dissidence vis-a-vis the muftiate and the political center, which explains why Bäyrämova, Ghalävetdin, and Ibrakhim are in constant trouble with the justice system, or why Tatarstan has been plagued by unprecedented acts of violence: the murder of Iakupov in 2012 and the burning of Kriashen churches in 2013.[57]

---

56 Agnès Kefeli, *Becoming Muslim in Imperial Russia: Conversion, Apostasy, and Literacy* (Ithaca and London: Cornell University Press, 2014), 255–264.

57 Azatlïq Radiosï, "Qazanda Wäliulla Yaghqub atïp üterelde, möfti Fäiz khastakhanädä," http://www.azatliq.org/content/muslim-mufti-kazan-terror/24649833.html (accessed May 22, 2019); Andrew Roth, "Two Muslim Officials Attacked in Southern Russia," *New York Times*, July 19, 2012, https://www.nytimes.com/2012/07/20/world/europe/two-muslim-officials-attacked-in-tatarstan-russia.html (accessed May 22, 2019); Mairbek Vatchagaev, "Attacks on Churches and Mosques in Russia on the Rise," *Eurasia Daily Monitor*, December 5, 2013, https://jamestown.org/program/attacks-on-churches-and

Jinn and angels can be effective guardians of religious identity. When I lived in Saint-Petersburg, a Tatar friend of mine jokingly said that now that I took her to visit an Orthodox church, her angel had left her for forty days. She had learned this from an elderly aunt whom I witnessed cursing Russians for their ungodliness, spitting on the floor. Another friend of mine, this time in Tatarstan, refused to enter a Kriashen church because there could be jinn inside. In Orenburg, a mother told her daughter not to stay in the home of a relative who had married a Russian, for their house spirit could harm her. Conversely, other Tatar friends gladly visited Kriashen churches with me and expressed their astonishment that Kriashen Tatars spoke their native language, grieving that their own youth spoke Russian in Tatar mosques. Others in mixed Kriashen and Tatar villages prided themselves that they invited each other for Christian and Muslim festivals, which the fourteenth-century Ibn Taymiyya, main inspirer of Wahhabism, had forcefully condemned.

Mixed marriages are a Tatar reality in urban areas that deeply upset some who fear a loss of identity. Likewise, if Tatars satisfy themselves with being nominal Muslim and fail to comprehend the eschatological dimension of Islam as well as its sacred geography, some believe that they will not be able to tap its power and will not survive as a separate nation. This fear is so strong that public school programs recommend students to read the works of Yakhin and Bäyrämova. Their eschatological approach might differ from one another – Bäyrämova's being quite exclusive, and Yakhin more inclusive – but both authors draw from the same Turkic myths of the afterlife. Their two different readings of "kafirness" may favor possible return or stricter adherence to the faith, while Ibrakhim's spiritualist approach may give Qur'anic myths more authority in a milieu that produces competing narratives critical of religion. In the end, stories can be told in a way that leads to either peace or violence: it is up to their audience to decide.

Bibliography

Äghlämov, Mödärris. "Densezme min, dinsezme?" *Yalqïn*, 12 (1993), 26–27.

Ämirkhan, Fatikh. "Fätkhulla khäzrät." In *Majaralar dönyasïnda: Povest'lar häm khikäyälär* (Kazan: Tatarstan kitap näshriyatï, 1990), 151–152.

-mosques-in-russia-on-the-rise-2/ (accessed May 22, 2019); Gleb Postnov, "Podzhogi tserkvei v Tatarstane priznali teraktami," *Nezavisimaia gazeta*, December 2, 2013, http://www.ng.ru/regions/2013-12-02/1_kazan.html (accessed May 22, 2019).

Arïslani, Nurulla Muflikhun. *Jännät häm jähännäm yullarï.* Chistopol: Mukhämmäd Muflikhun, 2000.

Azatlïq Radiosï. "Qazanda Wäliulla Yaghqub atïp üterelde, möfti Fäiz khastakhanädä." Last Modified 19 July 2012, accessed 22 May 2019. http://www.azatliq.org/content/muslim-mufti-kazan-terror/24649833.html.

Azizova, N.R. *Svadebnaia i pokhoronno-pominal'naia obriadnost' Astrakhanskikh tatar (konets XX-nachalo XXI vv.): Istoriko-etnograficheskoe issledovanie.* Astrakhan: izdatel'stvo AOIUU, 2002.

Babadzhanov, Bakhtiar M., Ashirbek K. Muminov, and Anke von Kügelgen. *Disputy musul'manskikh religioznykh avtoritetov v Tsentral'noi Azii v XX veke.* Almaty: Daik-Press, 2007.

Baiazitov, Ataulla. *Otnoshenie islama k nauke i k inovertsam.* St. Petersburg: tipografiia "Nur", 1906.

Bali, Wahid Abd al-Salam. *How to Protect Yourself from Jinn and Shaytan.* London: Al-Firdous, 2009.

Bäyrämova, Fäwziyä. *Alïplar ilendä.* Kazan: Tatarstan kitap näshriyatï, 2002.

Bäyrämova, Fäwziyä. *Däwerlär kücheshendä. Publitsistik yazmalar häm shighïr'lär.* Almetyevsk: Tatneft', n.d.

Bäyrämova, Fäwziyä. *Khaj köndälege.* Chally: Mädäni jomgha, 1999.

Bäyrämova, Fäwziyä. "Songghï namaz." In *Qïrïq sïrt: Romannar* (Kazan: Tatarstan kitap näshriyatï, 2005), 547–671.

Bäyrämova, Fäwziyä. *Taralïp yatqan tatar ile.* Kazan: "Ayaz" näshriyatï, 2003.

Bäyrämova, Fäwziyä. *Tufannan taralghan tatarlar.* Kazan: "Mägharif" näshriyatï, 2004.

Bigiev, Musa Dzharullakh. "Dokazatel'stva bozhestvennogo miloserdiia (Räkhmät ilahiyä borhannarï)." In *Antologiia tatarskoi bogoslovskoi mysli* (Kazan: Tatarskoe knizhnoe izdatel'stvo, 2005), 77–130.

Brown, Jonathan. "Scripture in the Modern Muslim World: The Qur'an and Hadith." In *Islam in the Modern World,* ed. Jeffrey T. Kenney and Ebrahim Moosa (London and New York: Routledge, 2014), 13–33.

Burton, Dan, and David Grandy. *Magic, Mystery, and Science: The Occult in Western Civilization.* Bloomington: Indiana University Press, 2004.

Bustanov, Alfrid, and Michael Kemper, eds. *Islamic Authority and the Russian Language: Studies on Texts from European Russia, the North Caucasus and West Siberia.* Amsterdam: Uitgeverij Pegasus, 2012.

Dubin, Khaji Abdulla. "Mighraj kichäse." *Yalqïn,* 12 (1993), 24–25.

El-Zein, Amira. *Islam, Arabs, and the Intelligent World of the Jinn.* Syracuse, New York: Syracuse University Press, 2009.

Fäkhretdin, Rizaetdin. *Dini wä ijtimaghïy mäs'älälär.* Orenburg: "Waqt" matbughasï, 1914.

Fäkhretdin, Rizaetdin. *Jäwamiʿ al-kälim shärkhe*. Orenburg: Parovaia tipo-litografiia Torg. Doma "A.A. Khusainov", 1917.
Fäkhretdin, Rizaetdin. *Tärbiyäle ana*. Kazan: tip. imper. Universiteta, 1898.
Fäkhretdin, Rizaetdin. *Tärbiyäle khatïn*. Kazan: tip. imper. Universiteta, 1899.
Fäkhretdin, Rizaetdin. "Tärjemäi khälem (Ufa, September 1905)." In *Rizaetdin Fäkhretdin: Fänni-biografik jïyïntïq* (Kazan: "Rukhiyät" näshriyatï, 1999), 23–26.
Fazlïev, Jälil khäzrät. *Jälil khäzrät däresläre*. Kazan: Mädäni jomgha, 1999.
Fazlïev, Jälil khäzrät. *Yöz ber wäghaz*. Kazan: n.p., 2005.
Fazlyev, Jalil. "The Prayers We Perform are for the Spirits of the Ancestors." In *Tatar Islamic Texts*, edited by Allen J. Frank (Hyattsville, Maryland: Dunwoody Press, 2008), 205–209.
Ghalävetdin, Idris. *Mäyetlärne ozatu tärtibe*. Chally: "Täwbä" mächete, 1422/2001.
Ghalävetdin, Idris. *Möselmannar jähännämgä keräme?* Iar Chally: "Täwbä" mächete, 1423/2003.
Ghalävetdin, Idris. *Namaznïng qabul bulmyi, ägär....* Chally: "Täwbä" mächete, 1422/2002.
Hilgemann, Fred. *Le Tatarstan: Pays des musulmans de Russie*. Paris: Éditions Autrement, 2007.
Iakupov, Valiulla. "Anti-islam (o raskol'nicheskoi sushchnosti vakhkhabitov-reformatorov)." *Zhurnal 'Musul'manskii mir'* (September, 2006), 1–43.
Iakupov, Valiulla. *Imamy goroda Kazani*. Kazan: Iman, 1429/2008.
Iakupov, Valiulla. *K prorocheskomu islamu*. Kazan: Iman, 1427/2006.
Iakupov, Valiulla. "Khanafitskii mazkhab, ego znachenie i aktual'nost'." (2004). https://web.archive.org/web/20071113083846/http://www.imancentre.ru/hanafia.htm (accessed 21 May 2019).
Iakupov, Valiulla. "Lzhedzhadidizm." *Zhurnal 'Musul'manskii mir'* (August, 2006), 1–39.
Iakupov, Valiulla. "Profilaktika ksenofobii Vakhkhabizma." *Zhurnal 'Musul'manskii mir'* (August, 2007), 15–20.
Iakupov, Valiulla. *Tatarskoe "Bogoiskatel'stvo" i prorocheskii islam*. Kazan: Iman, 2003.
Ibn Kathīr, Ismāʿīl ibn ʿUmar. *Istorii o prorokakh: Ot Adama do Mukhammeda so slov Ibn Kasira*. Moscow-St. Petersburg: Dilia, 2008.
Ibrakhim, Malik. *Parallel'nyi mir ili mnogoe no ne vse o dzhinnakh*. Kazan: Idel'-Press, 2004.
Ibrakhim, Malik. *Perenesenie i voznesenie Proroka ili kto byl pervym kosmonavtom*. Kazan: Idel'-Press, 2006.
Ibrakhim, Malik. *Smert': Konets ili nachalo*. Kazan: Idel'-Press, 2007.
Jälilova, Y.M. 2016. "Fäwziyä Bäyrämova prozasïn mäktäptä öyränü üzenchälege." In *Aktual'nye problemy sovremennoi tatarskoi filologii*, ed. I.F. Zaripova *et al.* (Ufa: Bashkirskii gosudarstvennyi universitet, 2016), 439–443.

Kefeli, Agnès. *Becoming Muslim in Imperial Russia: Conversion, Apostasy, and Literacy*. Ithaca, New York, and London: Cornell University Press, 2014.

Khakim, Rafael'. *Kto ty, tatarin?* Kazan: Biblioteka zhurnala "Panorama-Forum", 2002.

Khäzerge tatar ädäbiyatï. Kazan: Mägharif näshriyatï, 2008.

Kruk, Remke. "Harry Potter in the Gulf: Contemporary Islam and the Occult." *British Journal of Middle Eastern Studies* 32/1 (2005), 47–73.

Laruelle, Marlène, and Sébastien Peyrouse, eds. *Islam et politique en ex-URSS: Russie d'Europe et Asie Centrale*. Paris: L'Harmattan, 2005.

Lutfullin, Iskhaq, and Fayzulkhak Islaev. *Dzhikhad tatarskogo naroda*. Kazan: Iman, 1998.

Makarov, Dmitrii, and Rafik Mukhametshin. "Official and Unofficial Islam." In *Islam in Post-Soviet Russia: Public and Private Faces*, edited by Hilary Pilkington and Galina Yemelianova, 117–63. London: RoutledgeCurzon, 2003.

Mardzhani, Shihabetdin. *Zrelaia mudrost' v raz"iasnenii dogmatov an-Nasafi: Kitab al-Khikma al-baliga al-dzhaniiia fi sharkh al-'akaid al-khanafiia*. (Kazan: Tatarskoe knizhnoe izdatel'stvo, 2008).

Mökhämmätshin, Räfïyq. "Tatar jämghïyäteneng bügenge problemalarï yaqtïlïghïnda 'Iman' märkäzeneng eshchänlege." *Iman Nurï* (*Islam zhurnalï*), 4 (1996), 17–19.

Muslimov, Abdugbari. "Napravleniia obrazovaniia sovremennykh rossiiskikh imamov: Sravnitel'nyi analiz musul'manskikh uchebnykh zavedenii shafiitskogo, khanbalitskogo i khanafitskogo napravlenii." In *Innovatsii v sisteme islamskogo religioznogo obrazovaniia v Rossii: Materialy Vserossiiskoi nauchno-prakticheskoi konferentsii* (*g. Kazan', 14 noiabria 2006 g.*) (Kazan: Institut istorii im. Sh. Mardzhani, 2007), 45–49.

Pilkington, Hilary, and Galina M. Yemelianova, eds. *Islam in post-Soviet Russia: Public and private faces*. New York: RoutledgeCurzon, 2003.

"Poseshchenie mogil." accessed 21 May 2019. https://web.archive.org/web/20071113083933/http://imancentre.ru:80/mogil.htm.

Postnov, Gleb. 2013. "Podzhogi tserkvei v Tatarstane priznali teraktami." Nezavisimaia gazeta, 2 December 2013. Accessed 21 December 2016. http://www.ng.ru/regions/2013-12-02/1_kazan.html.

Rosenthal, Bernice Glatzer, ed. *The Occult in Russian and Soviet Culture*. Ithaca, New York: Cornell University Press, 1997.

Roth, Andrew. "Two Muslim Officials Attacked in Southern Russia." New York Times, 19 July 2012. Accessed 22 May 2019. http://www.nytimes.com/2012/07/20/world/europe/two-muslim-officials-attacked-in-tatarstan-russia.html.

Sadekova, Aisylu-khadzhi. *Ideologiia islama i tatarskoe narodnoe tvorchestvo*. Kazan: Iman, 2000/2001.

Safin, Rashat. *Tatar yulï: Tatar yazmïshïna geosäyäsi analiz*. Kazan: Tatarstan kitap näshriyatï, 2002.

Samatov, Ghabdelkhak. *Shärighat': Wäghaz, khökem, fätwa, jawap-sawap, kingäshlär.* Kazan: Idel-Press, 2006.

Shämsutova, Alsu. *Fäwziyä Bäyrämova prozasï.* Kazan: n.p., 2005.

Shäymärdanov, R. Kh., and Ä.N. Khujiäkhmätov. *Tatar milli pedagogikasï.* Kazan: "Mägharif" näshriyatï, 2007.

Smith, Jane Idleman, and Yvonne Yazbeck Haddad. *The Islamic Understanding of Death and Resurrection.* Albany: State University of New York Press, 1981.

Sultanov, F.M. *Islam i tatarskoe natsional'noe dvizhenie v rossiiskom i mirovom musul'manskom kontekste: Istoriia i sovremennost'.* Kazan: RITS "Shkola", 1999.

al-Ṭabarī. *The History of al-Ṭabarī.* Vol. 1: *General Introduction and From the Creation to the Flood.* Tr. Franz Rosenthal. Albany: State University of New York Press, 1989.

Takhawi, Zöfär. *Iman Yulï.* Chally: n.p., n.d.

Urazman, Raufa. "Narodnye i religioznye obriady." *Iman Nurï (Islam zhurnalï)*, 4 (1996), 48–50.

Valeeva-Suleimanova, Guzel'. "Musul'manskaia kul'tura i izobrazhenie cheloveka v tatarskom iskusstve." *Iman Nurï (Islam zhurnalï)*, 4 (1996), 55–61.

Vatchagaev, Mairbek. "Attacks on Churches and Mosques in Russia on the Rise." *Eurasia Daily Monitor*, 5 December 2013.

"Voznagrazhdenie usopshim: Voznagrazhdenie za chtenie Korana pokoinym." accessed 21 May 2019. https://web.archive.org/web/20071113142126/http://iman centre.ru/usopwim.htm.

Yaghqub, Wäliulla. *Tatarstanda räsmi bulmaghan islam: Khäräkätlär, aghïmnar, sektalar.* Kazan: "Iman" näshriyatï, 1424/2003.

Yakhin, Färit. *Aq äbilär doghasï.* Kazan: Tatarstan kitap näshriyatï, 2000.

Yakhin, Färit. *Baqïrghan kitabï.* Kazan: Tatarstan kitap näshriyatï, 2000.

Yakhin, Färit. *Iman.* Kazan: "Iman" näshriyatï, 1995.

Yakhin, Färit. *Islam dine nigezläre.* Kazan: "Rannur" näshriyatï, 1997.

Yakhin, Färit. *Päyghambärebez Mökhämmäd.* Kazan: "Rannur" näshriyatï, 1999.

Yakhin, Färit. *Päyghambärlär, färeshtälär, akhirät.* Kazan: "Rannur" näshriyatï, 1999.

Yakhin, Färit. *Tatar shighriyätendä: Dini mistika häm mifologiia.* Kazan: Tatar däwlät gumanitar universitetï näshriyatï, 2000.

Yakhin, Färit, ed. *Töshlek: Töshlärne yurau kitabï.* Kazan: "Rannur" näshriyatï, 1997.

Zahidullina, D.F., and A.M. Zakirjanov. *Tatar ädäbiyatï: Teoriia, tarikh.* Kazan: Mägharif, 2006.

The Authority of Saintly Narrative

Stories about Abūḣanifa in Tajikistan

Benjamin Gatling

In the spring of 2011, I was with three Sufis at their teashop in the distant suburbs of Dushanbe. While we sipped our tea, we talked about a poetry singing event (*ghazalkhonī*) in which we had all participated the night before and the poems that we had found particularly moving. It was something we often did on the days after *ghazalkhonī*: reflect on what we had experienced and recite poems together. I pulled a small chapbook that I had recently purchased out of my bag to share with them.[1] One of the men straightaway grabbed the booklet, turned to the first page, and read the epigraph aloud:

> Anyone who wants to be a companion of God,
> Tell [them] to sit in the presence of the saints.
>
> MAVLAVĪ[2]

"Jununī is such a huge saint," the man said. The other two men sitting at the table with us nodded along. The man took out his mobile phone and typed out the poem on the phone's text editor, saving it for later.

"What do you mean?" I asked. I thought to myself, "What did Jununī have to do with the poem?"

"It's really important that folks understand this verse," the man replied. "If someone really wants to know God, he has to be a Sufi."

When my friend read the two half-lines of poetry, signed, "Mavlavī," he responded in awe to what he saw as evidence of the poet's wisdom – a poet whom the man thought was Mavlavī Jununī (1810–1887), a Tajik mystic highly regarded by the men at the table (Gatling 2013, 2016). In actuality, the poet was a much more famous, internationally known Mavlavī, Mavlavī Rumī, the author of the most well-known mystical treatise in Muslim history, Mavlavī simply being an honorific for any esteemed, learned Muslim. In reading

1 The book was the *Kashf-ul-Asror: gulchini ghazaliët az devoni Shaĭkh Abdurraḣimi Davlat* (Dushanbe: Ḣumo, 2000), edited by Ismoil Atozoda.

2 This chapter follows the Library of Congress's Romanization tables for Tajiki and Russian language texts. Unless otherwise noted, all translations are my own.

 | DOI:10.1163/9789004527096_005

"Mavlavī," my friend did not recognize Rumī as its referent, but rather took it to refer to Jununī, a figure with whom the man and his friends were much more familiar and whose reputation more directly carried over into their daily ritual practices. My intention is not to lampoon the man's ignorance of Persianate literary traditions or wider Muslim history, but rather to emphasize the degree to which local figures of renown and understandings of Islam were central to how the man and the other men seated with him at the teashop conceived of their personal devotional projects. For them and many of the other Sufis with whom I regularly interacted in Tajikistan, special authority existed within localized systems of meaning, and eminent, local figures reigned supreme within their historical imaginations.

One such figure, whom my friends and acquaintances held in particularly high esteem, was Abūh̊anifa (699–767 CE), the eponymous founder of the H̊anafī *mazh̊ab*, known to most Tajiks simply as the Great Imom (Imomi A''zam). Unlike Jununī, Abūh̊anifa did not hail from the territory within the borders of contemporary Tajikistan, yet many pious Tajiks primarily understand his legacy in local terms, as inextricably connected to what it means to be a Muslim in Tajikistan, not exclusively because of the foundational importance of his scholarship in establishing the models of jurisprudence most clerics in Tajikistan follow. Tradition also relates that Abūh̊anifa's father's family lived in the regions around Kabul in Afghanistan, further cementing his place within the pantheon of local Persianate masters to whom many Tajiks look for pious exemplars (e.g. Shamolov 2009, 47–53).[3]

Images of Abūh̊anifa have figured especially large in the state's religious bureaucracy's constructions of the boundaries of sanctioned Muslim religiosity, both in regard to their imaginaries of the Central Asian religious past and in the service of proscribing forms of public Islam they see as anathema to the state's nation-building projects, e.g. alleged forms of Salafism, political Islam, Sufi *tariqat*, Shiʿi practice, and all manner of other euphemistic accusations against streams of Muslim authority outside of their direct control. The Tajik president, Ėmomalī Rah̊mon, even went as far as to declare 2009 to be "The Year of the Great Imom," and in celebration organs of the government sponsored an international symposium, published scholarly and popular texts, and produced television documentaries on the saint's life and contemporary

3 Of course, irrespective of my friend's ignorance of Rumī's poetical oeuvre, Rumī also shares this distinction, having been born in Balkh in Afghanistan, not far from the southern Tajik border.

import (Epkenhans 2017, 190–92). To boot, Rahmon ostensibly penned books about the saint's life with titles like *The Heritage of the Great Imom and the Dialogue of Civilizations* and *The Great Imom's Life Environment and the World of his Thoughts*.[4]

Whereas members of the state's religious bureaucracy and the governing elite have predictably put forward a vision of religious history that runs in tandem with their secularist visions – a sanitized Abūhanifa who supports the foci of state-sanctioned *khutba*, shrine visitation practices, Muslim pedagogy, and more – other groups, some of whom claim genealogy in Sufi *tariqat*, have appropriated state-sponsored narratives to their own distinct devotional ends. Episodes from Abūhanifa's life figured prominently in the narrative traditions of many Tajik Muslims. I frequently encountered clerics, *pirs*, and other Muslims telling stories they learned from state-produced texts and recasting them as tales modeling the virtues of pious comportment or the cultivation of a proper mystical disposition.

In this chapter, I draw on ethnographic fieldwork conducted in Tajikistan between 2010 and 2014 to discuss three narrative contexts in which individuals told the same story from Abūhanifa's life. I attempt to chart the tension between the purposes to which Abūhanifa's life is variously marshaled – the discursive ground through which Tajik Muslims have imbued certain histories with special authority by precluding others. Abūhanifa has become a potent symbol, ready to be inserted into contemporary debates regarding what Central Asian Muslim life properly entails, and diverse images of the saint serve as useful diagnostics for understanding the contours of contemporary public discourse on Muslim life in Tajikistan and a cipher for the complex negotiations about and re-appropriations of the authoritative Muslim past that are inherent to the contemporary political and religious environment. Telling stories about Abūhanifa provides Tajik Muslims an opportunity to claim rhetorical space for their own specific notions of rightful Muslim religiosity. Or, phrased differently, the agentive capacities inherent to saintly narrative allow its tellers to assemble an authoritative, aspirational version of an Islamic future. Abūhanifa rests as a cogent, authoritative vehicle for localizing Muslimness within Tajikistan's sometimes tumultuous religious field.

---

4 Ėmomalī Rahmon. 2009. *Muhiti zindagī va olami andeshahoi Imomi A"zam*. Dushanbe: Sharqi ozod; Ėmomalī Rahmon. 2009. *Merosi Imomi A"zam va guftugūi tamaddunho*. Dushanbe: Sharqi ozod.

1 Abūh̓anifa and Personal Morality

The village *pir* liked to tell stories. He frequently talked about the lives of saints and episodes from Muslim history.[5] In fact, I first came to the *pir's* house not far from Dushanbe expressly to listen to his stories. An acquaintance of mine, the *pir's* cousin, had recommended him to me as someone who could answer the sorts of questions I often asked about Central Asian Muslim history. During our first conversation together, I asked the *pir* about Abūh̓anifa's importance. I thought that the *pir* might be able to help me understand something I had heard earlier in the week during an interview I had conducted with the *imomi khatib* of a mosque in Dushanbe. The *pir* didn't respond directly to my question. Instead, as he often did, I would find out later, he answered my question with a story.

"One time, Abūh̓anifa's father was walking someplace beside a ditch flowing with water," the *pir* said. "Abūh̓anifa's father saw an apple, so he picked it up and took a bite. He immediately felt pangs of guilt because the apple wasn't his. 'I wonder whose apple it is,' he thought. 'I'm going to find out whose it is.' He looked to where the water was coming from and saw an orchard being tended by its owner. When Abūh̓anifa's father asked for the owner's forgiveness, the owner refused. 'I won't accept your apology unless you marry my daughter, who can't walk, see, or hear,' the man said. Abūh̓anifa's father agreed to the man's condition and married the girl. But when he saw her, he realized how beautiful she was. 'Come to me,' he said to her. 'Your father said that you were blind, lame, and deaf.' The girl replied, 'He said I was blind because I've never seen another man besides my father, lame because I've never left my home, and deaf because I've never heard any speech except for God's.' The girl was the Great Imom's mother. Abūh̓anifa was conceived that night and was their only child."

The *pir's* story wasn't that unusual. Similar tales exist widely in sermon illustrations, didactic literature available for purchase on book carts in front of mosques on Fridays, and even occasionally in school curricula.[6] The

5 Abūh̓anifa's sainthood began early, dating at least as far back as Attor's *Tazkirat ul-avliё*, written in the early thirteenth century.

6 Between 2009 and 2011, some high school students took a weekly course entitled, "Ma"rifati Islom" (Knowledge of Islam). Part of the curriculum included instruction about Abūh̓anifa's life, legacy, and the centrality of H̓anafi *mazh̓ab*. For example, see Barnomai Ta"limi Fanni "Ma"rifati Islom" baroi Sinfi 8. Dushanbe: Vazorati Maorifi Jumh̓urii Tojikiston, 6–7. The curriculum's implementation was uneven, and criticisms abounded that the history teachers tasked with its instruction were unfamiliar with the course's religious content. Even after hundreds of teachers were specially trained to teach

documentaries about and dramatizations of Abūhanifa's life broadcast on Tajik television, similarly included this episode from Abūhanifa's life.[7] From the contextualization cues the *pir* provided, it was clear his chief purpose was to stress personal morality. Immediately after he finished telling me about how Abūhanifa's father married the saint's mother, the *pir* shifted to highlight what behaviors are indicative of believers. Among other behaviors, the *pir* emphasized comporting oneself appropriately, refraining from telling lies and deceitfulness, and abstaining from alcohol.

It is not difficult to read the *pir's* comments about morality as a bridge from the "taleworld" to the "storyrealm," to use Katherine Young's (1987) formation. That is, the *pir's* comments directly linked the world of the story to the storytelling situation, the narrative descriptions of Abūhanifa's parents' extreme piety to my much more ambiguous, perhaps even heretical, orientation to the faith. It was not unusual for Sufis to invite me to recite the declaration of faith and convert to Islam during our first interactions together. However, the *pir's* encouragement was more indirect. He didn't ask me to convert. Instead, he referenced how one draws another to faith, "You don't fight; you attract unbelievers with your piety." Then, he brought it back to Abūhanifa, "Abūhanifa said that if you're around unbelievers, you talk them to them pleasantly and slowly, slowly show them your example. It's not about fighting. It's all about fighting with your own passions, temptations, taming them."

Telling the story about Abūhanifa's birth seemed to fulfill a kind of standard impulse for the *pir*, since a key didactic function of stories like the one about Abūhanifa's birth is to cultivate an ideal self in the listener or reader (Ruffle 2011, 5). That seems to be what the *pir* was suggesting. The story about Abūhanifa's father's scrupulous honesty and his mother's radical chastity served as an example intended to induce both believers and unbelievers to greater piety. The utility of the story about Abūhanifa's birth was not limited to simple admonitions toward ritual diligence or an indictment of one's personal morality or lack thereof. More pointedly, the example provided by Abūhanifa's parents also implicitly suggested a stark disconnect between the devotion of most Tajiks and behavior of their Muslim forebears.

---

it, plans were scuttled in 2011. See http://news.tj/en/news/tajikistan/society/20110205/knowledge-islam-removed-curriculum-tajik-schools-2010-2011-school-year.

7 The film, *The Luminary of Instruction* (Charoghi Hidoiat), broadcast in 2009 on the state-owned television station, Safina, as part of the "Year of the Great Imom," opened with an apple floating in a stream, where Abūhanifa's father kneeled to take a drink water.

2 Abūḣanifa and Societal Critique

Most of my Sufi friends and acquaintances deeply respected Ḣojī Mirzo Ibronov (b. 1967), the erstwhile *imomi khatib* of the Ḣiloli Aḣmar congregational mosque in the southern Tajik city of Kūlob, the region of the country where the Tajik president also shored his base of political support. In the minds of many of the Sufis who lived in and around Ḍushanbe, "*Kūlobī*" carried with it a special pejorative sense. Due to the president's patronage of his home region, many of the men with whom I regularly interacted resented what they saw as an influx of rural, uneducated peasants thrust into the political limelight at the expense of the influence of traditional Tajik power centers. Even so, Ḣojī Mirzo still captured their imagination, often it would seem as a pious counterweight to the hegemony of Kūlob in the Tajik popular imagination.

During the years I lived and visited Tajikistan, Ḣojī Mirzo's sermons seemed ubiquitous. Along with other important clerics like Nuriddin Turajonzoda, Ḣojī Mirzo occupied a tenuous middle ground between pious opponents of the government and the official state religious bureaucracy. Trained at the International Islamic University in Islamabad,[8] he lectured with a cultivated scholarly air. An extremely gifted orator with a penchant for poetic ambiguity, he appealed to a broad swath of Tajik society. Many Tajiks, both men and women, shared and listened to the sermons on their mobile phones and social media platforms like vKontakte and Odnoklassniki.[9] I first heard one of Ḣojī Mirzo's sermons on a friend's phone. We listened together over glasses of tea at a rural cafe not unlike the one with which the chapter began. CDs of Ḣojī Mirzo's sermons sold in kiosks all over Tajikistan. Minibus drivers often played them while they drove between towns or within Dushanbe. In 2014, I browsed a few book stalls, hoping to buy a disc for myself. I never saw the discs displayed openly, but when I asked one shopkeeper about them, he smiled and brought out a spindle of discs from underneath the counter, each selling for three *somonī* (then approximately .60 USD). "It has 284 sermons, all of Ḣojī Mirzo's sermons," he said beaming.

Ḣojī Mirzo glossed portions of the story about Abūḣanifa's birth four times during a series of three sermons he gave in 2010 about Abūḣanifa's life and later widely circulated on CDs like the one I bought and the Internet.[10] Ḣojī Mirzo's Abūḣanifa was not altogether different from the *pir's*, and the narrative

8 http://tojnews.org/tj/personality/khochi-mirzo.

9 Marintha Miles (2015, 378–79, 381) interestingly discusses cases where women sought out Ḣojī Mirzo's sermons, specifically ones about *ḣijob*, despite their explicit address to men.

10 The sermons, numbered in the order of their delivery, appeared at numbers 37, 41, and 43 on the disc. Versions of the sermons are also widely available on YouTube. See for example, https://www.youtube.com/watch?v=FGhUR-05bUo.

arc of his story progressed almost identically. He summed up his purpose in telling the story as, "Seek hard to do what's right." Like the *pir*, Ḣojī Mirzo lauded the example Abūḣanifa's father's set with his honesty and his mother with her chastity and admonished his congregants to emulate their examples. Ḣojī Mirzo told the men gathered in the mosque in 2010, "Follow the example of those knowledgeable … model their characteristics."

The key difference between Ḣojī Mirzo's story and the *pir's* was the degree to which Ḣojī Mirzo elaborated on narrative details. Ḣojī Mirzo took the opportunity to offer commentary on almost every action Abūḣanifa's father and mother took. For example, rather than simply saying that Abūḣanifa's father felt pangs of guilt when he ate the apple, Ḣojī Mirzo supplemented the story's basic plot with interpretations on the specific nature of the guilt. He described Abūḣanifa's father determination at finding the apple's owner, saying, "He would have traveled to the ends of the earth to find the owner of the orchard." He further explained the father's ethical scruples as "fear of the day of judgment" and the mother's piety as "pursuit of the honorable." Abūḣanifa's mother was a "sign of" and a "monument" to goodness. Ḣojī Mirzo also told how after Abūḣanifa's father realized the extent of girl's piety, Abūḣanifa's father prayed *namoz* to thank God for his blessing, and, unprompted, the girl recited her *namoz* alongside him.

More significantly, though still an example to emulate, Ḣojī Mirzo's Abūḣanifa carried a wider resonance. Ḣojī Mirzo used the story of Abūḣanifa's birth as a diagnostic for all of the ills of contemporary Tajik society. "Why isn't there another Abūḣanifa today?" Ḣojī Mirzo asked rhetorically. "Because we're perverse and depraved … the perverse and depraved don't bring forth children like Abūḣanifa … now the young only care about money," he said. Several Fridays later, in the second of his sermons about Abūḣanifa's life, he reminded his audience about Abūḣanifa's birth and its mirror-like quality, reflecting the moral depravity of Tajik society writ large. "So, then why aren't we close to God?" he asked. The story of Abūḣanifa's birth provided an easy answer. Ḣojī Mirzo said, "Their wedding wasn't like ours … there weren't lots of guests … no one came and sat for two or three hours … Abūḣanifa didn't command us to take our daughters to the salon … take her to a stranger to put make up on her." Ḣojī Mirzo's Abūḣanifa leveled a critique of Tajik wedding customs – a favorite target of both reform-minded clerics and the Tajik state (e.g. Marat 2008; Roche 2014, 171). Yet still, Ḣojī Mirzo's reasoning seemed distinct from both camps. He did not emphasize the example of the Prophet, as reformists might, nor did he make an economic argument, as members of Tajikistan's parliament did when they enacted prohibitions on excessive wedding expenditures. Instead, Ḣojī Mirzo embraced the misogynistic subtext of the story, interestingly features that the *pir* did not directly engage, and focused his attention on moral depravity at work all around in the Tajik body politick, in contrast to the seclusion Abūḣanifa's mother practiced and the chastity her seclusion supported.

In quick order, Ḣojī Mirzo referenced the ubiquity of divorce, rampant alcoholism, taking advantage those less fortunate, the pursuit of wealth and power, forsaking *ḣijob*, and even state-mandated proscriptions on religious attire. Ḣojī Mirzo noted that Abūḣanifa hailed from a wealthy family and held the ear of the powerful, yet he turned from it all to a life of Muslim scholarship. He abrogated all claims to worldly acclaim and embraced a life of humble learning. Ḣojī Mirzo's story became more than a simple admonition toward personal piety, but a critique of Tajik society, wedding culture, wealth, and amassing worldly power. Indirectly, his claims even offered veiled criticism of state secularism because of how they referenced policies related to female dress and virtue. Perhaps too, Ḣojī Mirzo's raising the virtues of scholarship above other worldly pursuits in narrating the details of Abūḣanifa's life also offers a small glimpse of his careful attention to the intricacies of Muslim history and scholarship.

After the Committee on Religious Affairs (Komitai oid ba korḣoi din) started distributing approved topic lists for Friday sermons beginning in 2011, and eventually began mandating that some clerics read from a state-produced script, Ḣojī Mirzo resigned from his post as *imomi khatib* in Kūlob (Tucker 2016, 5). Rumors circulated among many of the men I knew that Ḣojī Mirzo had not resigned but instead been forcibly removed, a distinction perhaps more semantic than substantive. Though he does not hold an official office or a public platform for teaching, Ḣojī Mirzo continues to shepherd religious Tajiks informally online. Most significantly, he has interacted directly on social media with Tajiks who have joined ISIS in Syria (Tucker 2016, 7–8), calling on them to return home and submit themselves to government authorities. It is precisely this – a loyal citizenry – to which stories about the Great Imom also hold some purchase.

3 Abūḣanifa and Loyal Citizens

In the fall of 2008, Raḣmon proclaimed that 2009 would be "The Year of the Great Imom," ushering in a year of special celebrations of Abūḣanifa's life and legacy and instrumentalizing Abūḣanifa in support of Raḣmon's regime (Thibault 2016, 2).[11] The year culminated in an international symposium held

11 Mariya Omelicheva (2016) has noted how similar forms of instrumentalization exist in both Kazakhstan and Uzbekistan.

in the fall of 2009, allegedly attended by hundreds of academics from as many as fifty countries from around the world, including even the head of Al-Azhar in Egypt, the center of Sunni Muslim scholarship.[12] Specials aired on state television. Banners hung over Dushanbe's streets. Displays dedicated to Abūḣanifa were placed in public buildings. Local celebrations were organized around Tajikistan, echoing the sentiments expressed in Dushanbe. State-sanctioned books, celebrating the jurisconsult's life and his apparent apolitical worldview, filled Tajik bookstalls. Abūḣanifa was named son of the Tajik nation and appropriated as part of the growing body of new national mythology (Epkenhans 2012). He became a kind of proto-citizen of Tajikistan, not just because of his Persianate ancestry, but also more importantly due to his example – as an embodiment of what an honorable citizen of the Tajik state should aspire to be.[13] The Tajik parliament officially recognized the Ḣanafī stream of jurisprudence as the official school of Tajikistan.[14] And, that year elites celebrated the groundbreaking of what promises to be the largest mosque in Central Asia, funded by the largesse of the government of Qatar. In short, governing elites leveraged the full weight of the state's political apparatus to put forward a coherent notion of Abūḣanifa's life in concert with their own visions of Muslim life in contemporary Tajikistan. Kirill Nourzhanov (2015, 80) goes as far as to write that "the Year of the Great Imom" marked, "a symbolic high point in the Islamicization of nationalist discourse."

It is easy to dismiss the state's fetishization of Abūḣanifa and its proclamation of 2009 as the "Year of the Great Imom" as propagandistic and to interpret efforts at promoting the saint's legacy as contrived attempts to provide a veneer of historical legitimacy to policies that on the surface seem opposed to traditional forms of Tajik religiosity. In many ways, they were, especially in that a saint's 1310th birthday does not often warrant acclaim (Olcott 2012, 56). Many of my Sufi friends and acquaintances had become desensitized to the pervasiveness of state propaganda, at least its omnipresence on Dushanbe's streets and broadcast or printed in Tajikistan's state-controlled media outlets. They were frequently dismissive of governing elites' gestures to recognize Muslim history and their appropriation of religious symbolism, including the potential malevolent motives behind the pomp of state ceremonies devoted to

12 http://www.president.tj/en/taxonomy/term/5/19.

13 This is what distinguishes the official statements of the Tajik state from similar discourse put forward in Uzbekistan. The Karimov regime also emphasized that country's Ḣanafī pedigree, yet in Tajikistan the Great Imom's nationality is Tajik. Frequently, Abūḣanifa appears with the sobriquet, "son of the Tajik nation," emphasizing Tajikistan's national difference.

14 http://www.asiaplus.tj/en/news/tajikistan/power/20090305/hanafi-school-recognized-official-religion-tajikistan.

Abūḣanifa. Seeing the president wearing a pilgrim's robe when he visited Saudi Arabia in order to seek financial support for pet development projects or listening to one of his speeches about the weight of Tajik Muslim history evoked little more than guffaws and knowing winks from many of pious friends.

They were skeptical too because 2009's "Year of the Great Imom" was not unprecedented. The Tajik "performance state" had organized jubilee years before with attendant spectacle and publicity (Adams 2010). In 1999, government organs organized commemorations of the country's purported Samanid heritage. 2006 hailed as the "Year of Aryan Civilization." Additionally, the Ministry of Culture had also previously leveraged the state's performative politics to celebrate the lives of other key figures within the constellation of Tajik Muslim history, though they had not in the past dedicated an entire year for celebrations. For example, at the end of the 1990s, festivities surrounded the jubilee year of Mir Saĭid Alii Ḣamadonī (1314–1384), culminating in the renovation of his shrine with the support of the Iranian government. Similarly, a widely publicized academic conference had been dedicated to I͡aqubi Charkhī (1358–1447), a key figure within the history of Naqshbandī Sufism whose grave sits within Dushanbe's municipal boundaries. Less-history inflected, but just as politically prescient, 2013 had been proclaimed "The International Year of Water Cooperation" following a United Nations program.

Though the "Year of the Great Imom" was not unique in the responses it engendered from organs of state or even with respect to their official sponsorship of celebrations regarding Tajik religious history, it nonetheless had a distinct impact on how many Tajik Muslims imagined the saint and his life. Of course, devotion to Abūḣanifa was not patently new. Yet still, for many Tajiks, apart from those with formal *madrasa* training or those invested in the study of *fiqḣ*, the relative importance of Abūḣanifa within the wider scope of Muslim history was inchoate.[15] Stories, like the one about his birth, were familiar to many – it would seem – based on my anecdotal observations between 2010 and 2014. And, some stories even seemed to be more widely known and circulated. Many people I asked could provide a brief gloss of what they often called, "the apple story." However, the larger corpus of Abūḣanifa's biography had not previously existed as neatly organized and packaged for easy

15 However, for many late Soviet-era *ulamo*, disputes over the scope and relative importance of traditional Ḣanafī jurisprudence were profound. For them, the Great Imom's legacy wasn't inchoate, but rather was the very territory in which they staked their claims over Central Asian religiosity. See (Babadjanov and Kamilov 2001; Babadzhanov, Muminov, and K͡ugel'gen 2007, 47–51, 113–16). SADUM, too, sometimes issued fatwas which contravened Central Asian Ḣanafi consensus, drawing the ire of many traditional *ulamo* (Khalid 2007, 111–13).

distribution and consumption – a fact amplified by the severe restrictions on formal Islamic education both in the Soviet period and in recent decades, as well as the virtual proscription of widely-dispersed informal scholarship due to civil war, labor migration, and more recent state efforts at limiting the mechanisms of Muslim knowledge production.[16] The "Year of the Great Imom" changed that. It cemented the scope of the saint's importance in the minds of many. State attention justified the hefty weight of Abūḣanifa's legacy and magnified his importance. The "Year of the Great Imom" seemed to transform an otherwise distributed discursive landscape into a coherent object for debate. Stories about Abūḣanifa may have been familiar before, but now they took on a defined shape, had a center, and a distribution network.

In 2014, I was sitting with a different village *pir*, this one living in a mountain village near Obigarm, northeast of Dushanbe, when he referenced an intricate story about Abūḣanifa's interactions with the caliph in Baghdad. After the *pir* mentioned the story, I asked him where he had learned it. He responded that he had read it in a book and handed me a slim volume produced for the "Year of the Great Imom" from a stack of papers on a shelf in his guestroom. The *pir* had read from state-produced propaganda, but re-appropriated it for a contrasting devotional end, recasting the state-produced text as a tale modeling mystical disposition. Additionally, one might interpret the other *pir's* story about Abūḣanifa's birth or even Ḣojī Mirzo's sermons as implicit re-appropriations of the "Year of the Great Imom," as both seemed to reference the wider attention paid to Abūḣanifa that year. Indeed, all three cases – the *pirs'* stories and Ḣojī Mirzo's sermons – illustrate how the festivities of 2009 may not have determined how pious Tajiks conceived of Abūḣanifa's life and legacy, but they nonetheless framed some of the possibilities of debate (Rasanayagam 2014), even as state projections of the saint's life differed in significant ways from the *imom's* importance in the minds of many. Despite the state's seeming success in aligning their performative politics with the public discourse of Tajikistan's Muslims, governing elites' attempts at shaping

16 See (Olimova 2005; Abramson 2010; Epkenhans 2010; Roche 2013) for more about formal and informal religious education in Tajikistan during the late Soviet period, the civil-war era, and more recently in the first decade of the new millennium. The intensity of state oversight over the formal institutions of Islamic learning quickened beginning in 2010. There remains one institution of Islamic higher learning the Islamic University of Imom Termizī in Dushanbe. By the fall of 2016, the Ministry of Education had shuttered the few remaining *madrasas*. "The Law on Parental Responsibility," passed in 2010, even went as far as forbidding children from attending Friday prayers. Though its application remains uneven, the law provides security services broad authority to regulate religious instruction that exists outside of official frameworks.

interpretation were not nearly as successful as they might have hoped. As the second *pir's* reinterpretation of the story about Abūḣanifa and the caliph illustrates, just because governing elites rendered the debate possible, they could not control on what terms it unfolded.

For many of the men I knew, it was the books about Abūḣanifa's life that had the deepest resonance over the other aspects of the year's celebrations. Books in their materiality exist seemingly independent from the contexts that engender them, if not from their contexts of production, then at least of their reception (Stewart 1993, 22–23). The story of Abūḣanifa's birth, i.e. the apple story, appears in a number of books published or widely circulated that year, each time recounted along with a number of other well-known episodes from Abūḣanifa's life in titles like *Stories from the Times of the Great Imom*, *The Life of Imom Abūḣanifa*, *The Virtues of the Great Imom*.[17] Most of the texts do not include explicit commentary on the anecdotes they include. Instead, they simply begin with a short introduction and follow successively with stories, absent any commentary. As such, one must look to the contextualization provided by the larger constellation of events that occurred during the "Year of the Great Imom," including Ėmomalī Raḣmon's writings and speeches, to gain a clearer picture of the stories' purposes and how governing elites conceived of Abūḣanifa's importance.

Prior to 2009, two facets of Islam had captured the special attention of individuals within the president's think tank (Markazi Tadqiqoti Strategii nazdi Prezidenti Jumḣurii Tojikison): its supposed "innate humanitarian nature" and "patriotism" (Nourzhanov 2015, 79). As such, some argued that the state might find success by leveraging Muslim history and instrumentalize its symbols in support of domestic politics. Tellingly, Raḣmon (2009, 178) clarified his almost identical purposes in celebrating Abūḣanifa's life in a speech to commemorate the saint's jubilee year, "To prevent such undesirable phenomena [the threat of religious extremism], we must use the theory and life experience [sic] of the Great Imam."[18] In earlier speeches, Raḣmon (2006, 197–200) had similarly interpreted the lesson of Abūḣanifa's life as to protect "unity," "stability," and "security," the precise aims of his own domestic religious policies. At other points, Raḣmon presented Abūḣanifa as an enemy of "fanaticism," as an advocate for "harmony" and "tolerance," and as a promoter of "state-systems" and

---

17 Ravshani Ḣamroḣ and Ibroḣimi Naqqosh, *Qissaḣo az Rūzgori Imomi A"zam*. Dushanbe: Safvat, 2008; Muḣammad Amini Ḣusenpur, *Zindagonii Imom Abūḣanifa* (*r*). Dushanbe: Safvat, 2009; *Manoqibi Imomi A"zam*. Dushanbe: Markazi Islomii Jumḣurii Tojikiston, 2009.

18 I have included here the official English-language translation of Raḣmon's remarks.

the Tajik "nation." For Raḣmon and other governing elites, Abūḣanifa's hagiography's greater importance comes in its utility as "nationography" (Paul 2002; Louw 2007, 60).

The ostensible aims of the "Year of the Great Imom" seemed not so much to promote Ḣanafī jurisprudence over the more rigid and politically active schools of Muslim thought commentators feared were gaining traction in the region, but to wield the entire weight of Abūḣanifa's biography in support for the political status quo. Whereas for the *pir*, the story of Abūḣanifa's birth became an object lesson in personal morality, and for Ḣojī Mirzo the story seemed especially oriented toward broader societal critique, in the context of state-sponsored publications during the "Year of the Great Imom" governing elites marshal the same biography – including but not limited to the circumstances surrounding Abūḣanifa's birth – to cultivate and encourage a loyal citizenry. On the surface, this conclusion seems all the more puzzling in that Abūḣanifa likely died while under house arrest for having refused overtures expressed by the Caliph al-Mansur or even possibly due to Abūḣanifa's opposition to the caliph's policies (Yanagihashi 2014). Such dissonance between a history and its use highlights the significance of such reconfigurations of Abūḣanifa's life within the present religious moment.

4 Reconfiguring Abūḣanifa

When I first heard the story about Abūḣanifa's birth from the *pir* that day in village, it did not immediately capture my attention. It was not until I had heard it again recounted almost identically in one of Ḣojī Mirzo's sermons played on a friend's mobile phone and later saw that it figured in the literature produced by the state for the "Year of the Great Imom," that my curiosity was piqued. Both the narrators and the printed texts told an identical story, but for seemingly different and likely even contradictory purposes. The fact that different narrators or editors use the same story about Abūḣanifa's life for different purposes may not on the surface distinguish the uses of saintly narrative in Tajikistan from other Muslim contexts, of which the valorization of pious exemplars and/or constructions of retrospective saintly biography are a part. That is, the significance of the *pir*, Ḣojī Mirzo, and members of the governing elite all telling or distributing the same story about Abūḣanifa's birth does not derive simply from the fact that they use the same story toward different ends or the complementary proposition that a story's meanings are always contextually derived. However, the former still merits special attention because the process of how this happens points toward some of the particularities of the Central Asian context because of how Tajik Muslims invest the saint with differential forms of authority.

Stories about Abūḣanifa originate from the same body of already authoritative texts. While the "Year of the Great Imom" may have organized a heretofore chaotic discursive landscape, state celebrations were not primary to legitimating devotion to the saint. The stories' authority primarily derived from the connections their tellers made between the Tajik present and the sacred past the stories represented (DeWeese 2009, 31). In connecting one's stories to an already authoritative sacred past – that is, marking one's stories as traditional and engaging the rhetoric of tradition – irrespective of their actual contents, one can invest one's stories with an air of unassailable authority and authenticity (Howard 2013; Schmitt 2013). This vernacular authority, not one endowed by the *ulamo* or attested to in scripture, points both to, in Bakhtin's (1984, 143) terms, how Tajikistan's pious Muslims and its governing elite live in a world of other's words and to the salience of the wider reservoir of already authoritative texts of which the story about Abūḣanifa's birth is a part.

However, the various uses to which Abūḣanifa's birth story is positioned suggest that though there may be broad, even collective, consensus over the notions of religious authority the corpus of Abūḣanifa's stories represent, consensus over authority is not necessarily unifying. Paradoxically, a unifying consensus over traditional authority is just as likely to be destabilizing. Members of the governing elite cannot easily dislodge the authority the body of narratives already possesses. If narrators or governing elites cannot outright dismiss the cultural authority of a story about Abūḣanifa's life, then the only recourse they hold is to reconfigure the religious reality to which the stories refer. The apple story and other saintly narratives like it are ripe for reconfiguration.[19]

Hagiographical genres – oral or written, whether recounted conversationally among friends or in front of thousands during a Friday *khutba*, distributed on discs or online, or packaged in chapbook form for propagandistic purposes during state-sponsored celebrations – carry with them a focus on instantiating an ideal among their hearers or readers. At the same time, exactly what is signified, what ideal they index, does not immediately follow. The story operates as a shifting signifier, an empty vehicle ready for reconfiguring. Indeed, reconfiguration seemingly is a broader generic feature of saintly narrative because its purpose is to communicate an ideal and make that ideal the now. So, for Tajik

19 "Interpret(ion)/reinterpret(ion)" might similarly capture the discursive work in which Abūḣanifa's tellers engage, but I have chosen "reconfiguration" in order to avoid confusing what the *pir*, Mirzo, and the governing elite do from the interpretation (*ijtiḣod*) of the *ulamo*.

Muslims Abūhanifa is simply an authoritative sign ready to be deployed,[20] and the meanings communicated through stories about him are contingent, easily shifting between signified ideals that on the surface can be contradictory or seemingly mutually exclusive, as the three versions of the story about Abūhanifa's birth attest.

This shiftiness, the contingency of the ideals the stories represent, means that the same story, recounted almost identically, offers discursive space for competing forms and reconfigurations of authority and political agency. Politics, here, does not refer to electoral machinations or advocating for policy. Neither the *pir* nor Hojī Mirzo's stories engaged such concerns. Instead, their telling of stories was political because they were exercises in communal reflexivity, in which they attempted to shape the conditions of their own existence (Hirschkind 2006, 8), apart from official frameworks. The stories' specific agentive capacities come from how the narrators or editors reconfigured narrative possibilities (Barad 2007, 214). This is not agency in terms of resistance; this sort of agency not only comes from how the *pir* or Hojī Mirzo's stories implicitly or explicitly prefigure or oppose the narratives put forward by the governing elite about Abūhanifa's life (cf. Limón 1983) or even how the appropriation of state-sponsored tale collections may be indicative of folklore's use as a "weapon of the weak" (Scott 1990). Admittedly, both aspects may still be at work, but the stories' more potent agentive capacities come in the specific forms of (reconfigured) life they enable (Mahmood 2005, 24–25). This agency is not an intrinsic quality of the apple story or any other particular narrative about Abūhanifa's life or any body of hagiographic texts (Briggs 1994). Instead, it is emergent out of the stories' unique deployment within particular performance situations that they have the ability to alter qualitatively their tellers and authors understandings of the events they recount and by extension their tellers experiences of the situations in which they now live (Jackson 2013, 35).

Hannah Arendt (1958) has argued more broadly that storytelling is a strategy for transforming private into public meanings. Indeed, narratives often mediate their tellers' and hearers' relationships with worlds that extend beyond them, enabling one to negotiate a balance between the self and worlds of otherness. To an extent, that too is at work in the stories I have discussed about Abūhanifa's birth. For example, the *pir* connects the circumstances of my immediate interaction with him to larger paradigms of piety. Yet, more

20 That is not to suggest that the meanings associated with Abūhanifa are open ended. Abūhanifa's fundamental importance as someone whose example the pious should follow appears in the catechism many Central Asian learns to recite from the Chahor Kitob. See (Sattorzoda 1991, 11).

significantly the reverse move is also in play within the various versions of Abūḣanifa's life, a move from public to private. The shift embodied by a change in the ideal each story represents is akin to a move from the allegorical world of story – the public, collective notion of Abūḣanifa's importance – to the personal or local circumstances of each storytelling performance (Shuman 2005), i.e. to the worlds in which the *pir*, Mirzo, and the governing elite live, projecting its agency through the shifting spaces between the collective and individual, sameness and otherness, and allegorical and personal.

The ideal in each rendition of Abūḣanifa's birth was floating, waiting to be reconfigured, lending each teller or editor agency. Personal piety became societal perversion. Literature produced for the "Year of the Great Imom," though pure propaganda, functioned similarly. Stories about Abūḣanifa's life allowed Raḣmon and other governing elites to make a statement about what kind of society they envisioned and then legitimate it, in the same way that the *pir's* and Ḣojī Mirzo's stories did before. In extreme terms, stories about Abūḣanifa's birth simultaneously critiqued Tajik society and lauded its basis. They called attention to distinctions between the piety the stories referenced and what one can see on the streets in Dushanbe, even as they put forward a notion about patriotism and allegiance to the state. Each story held within it a space for each narrator or editor to reconfigure the ideal, allowing for pious cultivation, cultural critique, or even defense of nation. In this, stories about Abūḣanifa index some of the wider contours of contemporary public discourse on Muslim life in Tajikistan and point to the complex negotiations about and re-appropriations of the authoritative Muslim past that are inherent to the contemporary political and religious environment.

5 Abūḣanifa as Metonymy

If each performance context engendered a reconfiguration of the hagiographic ideal Abūḣanifa represents, then this chapter has also implicitly put forward its own: Abūḣanifa as metonymy. Reconfigurations of Abūḣanifa exist as microcosms of current public discourse over the meanings of Islam and what behaviors it necessarily should produce from everyday Tajik Muslims in the contemporary Tajik context. While Abūḣanifa's authority, and by extension the authority of his stories, may rest as somewhat settled, exactly how that authoritative past relates to the present remains more contentious. Significantly, discussion does not unfold over the specifics of the past, but over what it means to live in the present and the actions that one necessarily should follow because of what happened in the authoritative past. The ideals communicated by the *pir*, Ḣojī Mirzo, and the editors of Abūḣanifa's stories – personal morality, societal perversion, and the responsibilities of citizenship – all stand as discrete reflections of some of the choices pious Muslims face as they attempt to balance what they see as their duties as Muslims with the requirements of state.

For many Tajik Muslims, like the *pir*, personal piety is of foremost concern. Following the example of their pious forebears, Abūḣanifa among others, they seek to make correct ethical choices amidst a society they see as often morally fraught. For others, the relevance of Abūḣanifa's example is still broader. It does more than simply call the impious back to individual piety or work as a mirror, reflecting back the ethical imperfections of the Tajik everyday. Instead, Abūḣanifa's example suggests the moral deficiencies of Tajik society writ large. There is no Abūḣanifa today, not just because of the fraught choices of individual Tajik Muslims, but also because of the corrupt moral foundations of state. Individuals like Gulmurod Ḣalimov, the former head of a paramilitary police unit (OMON) within the Ministry of Interior and defector to ISIS, irrespective of their actual aims and motivations (Heathershaw 2015), have taken similar critiques even farther, taking Raḣmon and the secular foundations of Tajik society to task, highlighting what critics see as the perversions of Tajik Islam, and maintaining that societal perversion necessitates violent opposition. Even the portrait of Abūḣanifa as loyal citizen also embodies the tensions many pious Tajiks face regarding the possibilities for devotion within the increasing strictures put on them by the state.

The discussion in this chapter has been about the story of Abūḣanifa's birth, but it just as well could have been about any number of stories from Abūḣanifa's life or other key figures from the nearer and more distant Central Asian Muslim past and told in contemporary Tajikistan. Perhaps the localizing, contingent hagiographic ideals are distinct, but the hagiographic process operates similarly. They, too, potentially share a metonymic relationship between story particulars and ongoing negotiations in wider Tajik society. The same dialectic was at work in my friend's reference to Mavlavī at the teashop. The man emphasized the importance of a localized past, a transcendent, even global ideal made personal. Global Muslim literary tradition distilled into the local.

The localization of authority lends Tajik Muslims a multitude of political potentialities. Cultivating personal piety, offering societal critique, or enforcing the political status quo all stand as potential trajectories for action, and none need hold any purchase to transnational political ideologies. All easily derive their authority from local streams of religiosity,[21] and the roots of instability potentially come just as well come from the shiftiness of local hagiographic ideals. This instability comes not from the causes standardly proffered

21 Vera Exnerova (2017) has similarly emphasized some of the local roots of violent Islamism in the Ferghana Valley.

by scholars of politics in the region, e.g. a weak state apparatus, endemic corruption, or the absence of strong civil society institutions (Heathershaw 2014; McMann 2014). No, this instability comes from features coterminous with hagiographic authority. In the context of government-proffered hysteria, this bears repeating. The conditions for resistance, opposition, advocacy, agency, etc. are, like the apple story, ripe for reconfiguration within the contexts of local Islam, all can even derive their authority from a single text, a single story, known by most Tajik Muslims.

As Rumī sagely wrote, if one wants to know God, one need but sit with his companions. In many ways, the *pir*, Ḣojī Mirzo, and the editors of Abūḣanifa's stories suggested the same. They all told or published stories about a key intimate companion of God within the pantheon of Central Asian Islam for the consumption of pious Tajiks eager to know God better. However, as this chapter has demonstrated, what hagiographic ideal one learns from sitting, or indeed hearing or reading, about the lives of his companions is far from settled.

Acknowledgments

I want to thank Muzhdah Karimi for help with transcriptions and coding interview data. Research for this chapter was completed with the support of an IREX research grant. The Office of Student Scholarship, Creative Activities, and Research (OSCAR) at George Mason University funded Ms. Karimi's work. I am also grateful for the insightful comments I received from participants at Indiana University's Islamic Studies Program's "Authority in Islam in Muslim Eurasia" workshop.

References

Abramson, David M. 2010. "Foreign Religious Education and the Central Asian Islamic Revival: Impact and Prospects for Stability." Washington, DC: Central Asia-Caucasus Institute & Silk Road Studies Program.

Adams, Laura L. 2010. *The Spectacular State: Culture and National Identity in Uzbekistan*. Durham, North Carolina: Duke University Press.

Arendt, Hannah. 1958. *The Human Condition*. Chicago: University of Chicago Press.

Babadjanov, Bakhtiyar, and M. Kamilov. 2001. "Muhammadjan Hindustani (1892–1989) and the Beginning of the 'Great Schism' among the Muslims of Uzbekistan." In *Islam in Politics in Russia and Central Asia (Early Eighteenth to Late Twentieth Centuries)*, ed. Stephane A. Dudoignon and Hisao Komatsu, 195–219. New York: Kegan Paul.

Babadzhanov, B.M., A.K. Muminov, and A. fon Kūgel'gen, eds. 2007. *Disputy musul'manskikh religioznykh avtoritetov v T͡sentral'noĭ Azii v XX veke*. Almaty: Daĭk-Press.

Bakhtin, M.M. 1984. *Problems of Dostoevsky's poetics*. Translated by Caryl Emerson. Minneapolis: University of Minnesota Press.

Barad, Karen Michelle. 2007. *Meeting the Universe Halfway: Quantum Physics and the Entanglement of Matter and Meaning*. Durham, North Carolina: Duke University Press.

Briggs, Charles L. 1994. "The Sting of the Ray: Bodies, Agency, and Grammar in Warao Curing." *The Journal of American Folklore* 107 (423): 139–66.

DeWeese, Devin. 2009. "Authority." In *Key Themes for the Study of Islam*, ed. Jamal J. Elias, 26–52. Oxford: Oneworld Publications.

Epkenhans, Tim. 2010. "Muslims without Learning, Clergy without Faith: Institutions of Islamic Learning in Tajikistan." In *Islamic Education in the Soviet Union and Its Successor States*, ed. Michael Kemper, Raoul Motika, and Stefan Reichmuth, 313–48. New York: Routledge.

Epkenhans, Tim. 2012. "Zwischen Mythos und Minenfeld." *Osteuropa* 62 (3): 137–50.

Epkenhans, Tim. 2017. "Islam, Religious Elites, and the State in Tajikistan." In *Islam, Society, and Politics in Central Asia*, ed. Pauline Jones, 173–98. Pittsburgh, Pennsylvania: University of Pittsburgh Press.

Exnerova, Vera. 2017. "Radical Islam from Below: The Mujaddidiya and Hizb-Ut-Tahrir in the Ferghana Valley." In *Islam, Society, and Politics in Central Asia*, ed. Pauline Jones. Pittsburgh, Pennsylvania: University of Pittsburgh Press.

Gatling, Benjamin. 2013. "The Guide after Rumi: Tradition and Its Foil in Tajik Sufism." *Nova Religio* 17 (1): 1–23.

Gatling, Benjamin. 2016. "Historical Narrative, Intertextuality, and Cultural Continuity in Post-Soviet Tajikistan." *Journal of Folklore Research* 53 (1): 41–65.

Heathershaw, John. 2014. "The Global Performance State: A Reconsideration of the Central Asian 'Weak State.'" In *Ethnographies of the State in Central Asia*, ed. Madeleine Reeves, Johan Rasanayagam, and Judith Beyer, 29–54. Bloomington: Indiana University Press.

Heathershaw, John. 2015. "What Does the Halimov Defection Tell Us About Tajikistan?" *EXCAS*. http://blogs.exeter.ac.uk/excas/2015/05/31/halimov/.

Hirschkind, Charles. 2006. *The Ethical Soundscape: Cassette Sermons and Islamic Counterpublics*. New York: Columbia University Press.

Howard, Robert Glenn. 2013. "Vernacular Authority: Critically Engaging 'Tradition.'" In *Tradition in the 21st Century: Locating the Role of the Past in the Present*, ed. Robert Glenn Howard and Trevor Blank, 72–99. Logan: Utah State University Press.

Jackson, Michael. 2013. *The Politics of Storytelling: Variations on a Theme by Hannah Arendt*. Copenhagen: Museum Musculanum Press.

Khalid, Adeeb. 2007. *Islam after Communism: Religion and Politics in Central Asia*. Berkeley: University of California Press.

Limón, José E. 1983. "Western Marxism and Folklore: A Critical Introduction." *The Journal of American Folklore* 96 (379): 34–52.

Louw, Maria Elisabeth. 2007. *Everyday Islam in Post-Soviet Central Asia*. New York: Routledge.

Mahmood, Saba. 2005. *Politics of Piety: The Islamic Revival and the Feminist Subject*. Princeton, New Jersey: Princeton University Press.

Marat, Erica. 2008. "Tajik Government Regulates Wedding Splendor." *CACI Analyst* 10 (12): 14–15.

McMann, Kelly M. 2014. *Corruption as a Last Resort: Adapting to the Market in Central Asia*. Ithaca, New York: Cornell University Press.

Miles, Marintha. 2015. "Switching to Satr: An Ethnography of the Particular in Women's Choices in Head Coverings in Tajikistan." *Central Asian Affairs* 2: 367–87.

Nourzhanov, Kirill. 2015. "Nation-Building and Political Islam in Post-Soviet Tajikistan." In *Nationalism and Identity Construction in Central Asia Dimensions, Dynamics, and Directions*, ed. Mariya Y. Omelicheva, 71–90. Lanham, Maryland: Lexington Books.

Olcott, Martha Brill. 2012. *Tajikistan's Difficult Development Path*. Washington, DC: Carnegie Endowment for International Peace.

Olimova, Saodat. 2005. "The Current State of Religious Education in Tajikistan: An Overview of the Situation with Recommendations." In *From Confidence Building towards Co-Operative Co-Existence. The Tajik Experiment of Islamic-Secular Dialogue*, ed. Jean-Nicolas Bitter, 239–54. Baden Baden: Nomos.

Omelicheva, Mariya Y. 2016. "Islam and Power Legitimation: Instrumentalisation of Religion in Central Asian States." *Contemporary Politics* 22 (2): 144–63.

Paul, Jürgen. 2002. "Contemporary Uzbek Hagiography and Its Sources." *Hallesche Beiträge zur Orientwissenschaft* 32: 621–28.

Rah̊mon, Ėmomalī. 2009. *Merosi Imomi A"zam va guftugūi tamaddunh̊o*. Dushanbe: Sharqi ozod.

Rah̊monov, Ėmomalī. 2006. *Dar borai din*. Dushanbe: Sharqi ozod.

Rasanayagam, Johan. 2014. "The Politics of Culture and the Space for Islam: Soviet and Post-Soviet Imaginaries in Uzbekistan." *Central Asian Survey* 33 (1): 1–14.

Roche, Sophie. 2013. "Continuities and Disruptions in Islamic Education: Biographies of Shogirds from Tajikistan." *Anthropology of the Contemporary Middle East and Central Eurasia* 1 (1): 23–53.

Roche, Sophie. 2014. *Domesticating Youth: Youth Bulges and Their Socio-Political Implications in Tajikistan*. New York: Berghahn Books.

Ruffle, Karen G. 2011. *Gender, Sainthood, & Everyday Practice in South Asian Shi'ism*. Chapel Hill: The University of North Carolina Press.

Sattorzoda, Abdunabi, ed. 1991. *Chah̊or Kitob*. Moscow: COMIL.

Schmitt, Casey R. 2013. "Asserting Tradition." In *Tradition in the Twenty-First Century: Locating the Role of the Past in the Present*, ed. Trevor J. Blank and Robert Glenn Howard, 100–122. Logan: Utah State University Press.

Scott, James C. 1990. *Domination and the Arts of Resistance: Hidden Transcripts*. New Haven, Connecticut: Yale University Press.

Shamolov, Abdulvohid. 2009. *Ahvol, osor va afkori Imomi A"zam*. Dushanbe: Donish.

Shuman, Amy. 2005. *Other People's Stories: Entitlement Claims and the Critique of Empathy*. Urbana: University of Illinois Press.

Stewart, Susan. 1993. *On Longing: Narratives of the Miniature, the Gigantic, the Souvenir, the Collection*. Durham, North Carolina: Duke University Press.

Thibault, Hélène. 2016. "Female Virtue, Religion and State Ideology in Tajikistan." *CERIA Brief*, no. 10: 1–9.

Tucker, Noah. 2016. "Public and State Response to ISIS Messaging." *CERIA Brief*, no. 11: 1–9.

Yanagihashi, Hiroyuki. 2014. "Abū Ḥanīfa." Edited by Kate Fleet, Gudrun Krämer, Denis Matringe, John Nawas, and Everett Rowson. *Encyclopaedia of Islam, THREE*. Brill. http://referenceworks.brillonline.com/browse/encyclopaedia-of-islam-3.

Young, Katharine Galloway. 1987. *Taleworlds and Storyrealms: The Phenomenology of Narrative*. Boston: Nijhoff.

Mukhamedzhan Tazabek and Popular Islamic Authority in Kazakhstan

Wendell Schwab

Mukhamadzhan Tazabek is a star. He does everything that you expect stars to do. He appears on morning talk shows to promote his work.[1] He is popular on social media sites like Twitter and Instagram.[2] Mainstream newspapers report on scandals involving foreign funding of his media empire.[3]

Tazabek is also the most popular Islamic authority in Kazakhstan. He runs Talim TV (formerly Asyl Arna), a television network focused on conservative, family-friendly programming (Abai.kz 2020). He has a visibility and popularity that dwarf those of other Islamic figures. For example, his Instagram feed has over 1.6 million followers. To put this in context, the Kazakhstani Muftiyat's Instagram feed only has 279,000 followers; Ninety One, a popular boy band, has 564,000 followers on Instagram.[4] This chapter explores what makes Tazabek so popular and why he is an Islamic authority for many Kazakhs. I do this by examining a text excerpted from an appearance by Tazabek on "Meaningful Issues" (*Mangyzdy Masele*), an Talim TV talk show, and placing this text in the broader context of Tazabek's brand in Kazakhstani mass media.

---

1 See, for example, a July 2016 interview with Tazabek on *Sukhbat*, a program on the "Kazakhstan" national television channel (Asyl Arna TV Online 2016). Another example is Tazabek's August 2016 appearance on the women's program *Aiel Baqyty* on the same channel (Raiymbek 2016).

2 Tazabek's Twitter account can be found here: https://twitter.com/mtazabek. His Instagram account can be found here: https://www.instagram.com/mukhamedzhan_tazabek/. One measure of popularity on Twitter ranks his account as the fifth most influential account in Kazakhstan – this rating includes corporate accounts such as those of mobile phone companies – and the most influential personal account in Kazakhstan (Kaznet Magazine 2018).

3 In 2015, Zikirya Zhandarbek, an academic scholar of Islam in Central Asia, accused Talim TV of being a Wahhabi television station and receiving money from Saudi Arabia. He also argued that the Kazakhstani Muftiyat is a Wahhabi organization that harms Sufi traditions in Kazakhstan. See Zhandarbek 2015. Talim TV's response has disappeared from their website, but see the following Tweet for the original link: https://twitter.com/asylarna/status/656785366381260800. For the Mufityat's response, see Malghazhuly 2015.

4 Tazabek's Instagram page is here: https://www.instagram.com/mukhamedzhan_tazabek/. The Muftiyat's Instagram page can be found here: https://www.instagram.com/muftiyatkz/. Ninety One's Instagram page is here: https://www.instagram.com/ninetyone/.

 | DOI:10.1163/9789004527096_006

Tazabek was born in 1975 in a small village in Zhambyl Oblast in southern Kazakhstan.[5] At an early age, Tazabek started training to be an *aqyn*, a traditional bard in Kazakh culture. *Aqyns* perform in *aitys*, a competition between two *aqyns* who alternate improvising songs. *Aitys* and *aqyns* become formalized by the Soviet promotion of national cultures, and *aitys* could be seen in Houses of Culture and heard on the radio in the Soviet era, giving popular performers a mass audience. By the age of 14 Tazabek was winning regional competitions. He was discovered by Berden Baiqosharov, a regional politician and client of Dinmukhamed Qonaev, the First Secretary of Kazakhstan.[6] He subsequently learned *aitys* from several well-known *aqyns*, including Shorabek Aidarov and Serik Qaliev. In 1990, while still a teenager, he took the main prize at several competitions. Later, the Zhambyl regional television channel produced a film about his life. He was considered a prodigy and continued participating in *aitys* during the 1990s.[7] He also attended the Al-Farabi National University of Kazakhstan and graduated with a degree in Philology in 1996. He participated in the national *aitys* scene until his retirement in 2003 (Kitab.kz 2014). Since then, he has occasionally acted as a judge and organizer of *aitys* competitions (Aizhanbai n.d.).

In the late 1990s and early 2000s, Tazabek became more interested in scripturalist Islam and participated in what I have called elsewhere the "piety movement" in Kazakhstan. The piety movement is a group of Muslims preaching a vision of Islam centered on a gendered division of labor, the hijab or conservative clothing for women, the authority of the Qur'an and hadiths, and an ideology strongly hostile to saint and ancestor veneration. During this time, Tazabek also married the younger sister of Bekbolat Tileukhan, a singer, eventual Member of the Kazakhstani Mazhlis (lower house of parliament), and a prominent Islamic activist. Tileukhan and Tazabek were part of a group of *aqyns* and entertainers who began to form a network working at both the national and grassroots levels to spread their vision of Islam. At the national level, Tazabek was the deputy director of the Khalifa Altai Charitable Fund from 2001 to 2003. The Khalifa Altai Charitable Fund sponsors Islamic education and publishes books and pamphlets, often translated Arabic works from

5 I present a sketch of Tazabek's biography to provide some context for his current construction of Islamic authority. A more complete biography and analysis would tell an interesting story about the establishment of a scripturalist niche in Kazakhstan and the interaction between political patrons and scripturalist activists.

6 Tazabek was patronized by many Kazakh elites in the 1990s. See, for example, the video of Tazabek singing at Qonaev's birthday in 1992 (Qamshy 2017).

7 For examples of Tazabek's participation in aitys on national television, see Aitys TV 2016a and 2016b.

scholars in Egypt and Saudi Arabia.[8] From 2003 to 2008, Tazabek also worked as a journalist for the "Kazakhstan" radio channel and wrote and presented a program focused on Islam (Asyl Arna 2017b).

At a more grassroots level, Tazabek began to travel the country to meet with small groups of Kazakhs. I observed some of this work in the summer of 2007, when I saw Tazabek speak at a 20-person gathering in the courtyard of a wealthy businessman's house in Zhambyl Oblast; the businessman was known to give to Islamic charities and the local mosque. Tazabek spoke alongside Abdughappar Smanov, a fiery preacher who ran a medrese in southern Kazakhstan until his death in 2020.[9] Abdughappar Smanov was the brother of Abdusattar Smanov, a scholar on the Kazakhstani Muftiyat's Council of Scholars until Abdusattar's death in 2016. Tazabek worked to gather the support of these types of business and Islamic elites for his planned media projects. On this day, Tazabek drank tea and spoke for only a short time, as he was headed to a meeting for an unnamed television channel – the future Talim TV – that he was hoping to open at the time. He calmly asked those gathered to become leaders in educating Kazakhs about Islam. Tazabek said he hoped to use subjects interesting to Kazakhs, like family life, to bring Kazakhs to piety, rather than presenting theological arguments. His style contrasted with Abdughappar Smanov's style. Abdughappar was a large, overtly masculine man who drank dozens of bowls of fermented mare's milk while preaching. Abdughappar spoke for approximately three hours, quoting hadiths and the

8 Although Tazabek identifies as a member of the Hanafi school of jurisprudence, the Khalifa Altai International Charitable Fund employed several Muslims identified by the scholar Ashirbek Muminov as Salafists, including Daryn Mubarov and Didar Ospanov. Mubarov was a translator for the Khalifa Altai Charitable Fund publication *Pendege Iman Ozi Ashady Zhol* (Ibrahim et al, trans. 2006). Ospanov was an editor for the same book. I prefer grouping these men and scripturalist Hanafis, including the vast majority of imams and bureaucrats in the Kazakhstani Muftiyat, together as a single "piety movement" to show their general separation from the majority of Kazakhs, just as the term "Religious Right" denotes a particular grouping of Catholics, Protestants, and Mormons in the United States. Muminov's work is valuable in its delineation of different theological currents of scripturalist Muslims within Kazakhstan. See Muminov 2016. Since this chapter was originally written in 2017, Tazabek admitted that he associated with Salafis. In November 2020, he met with the members of the Muftiate to discuss his beliefs and the Muftiyat's new television network. Tazabek recanted any former Salafi beliefs and praised the traditional Hanafi jurisprudence of the Kazakhstani Muftiyat. See Qappas 2020. The original working agreement between the Muftiyat and Talim TV in 2007, and the appearance of imams and other Muftiyat personnel on Talim TV, show the utility of grouping all of these groups together into a single "piety movement" that works together, despite occasional theological differences.

9 For an examination of the Smanov family's role in Soviet and post-Soviet Kazakhstan, see Muminov 2014. See also Bigozhin 2019 on Abdughappar's masculine style of preaching.

Qur'an while condemning adultery, drinking, and the practice of asking ancestors for their blessings, and commending the Prophet's kindness to orphans. The Kazakhs at the gathering later commented that Tazabek presented an image more suited to a mass audience, even if they personally preferred Abdughappar's ardor and scriptural citations.

Asyl Arna was formally founded shortly after this meeting in 2007. Asyl Arna was first broadcast in Almaty, but by 2009 it was available throughout Kazakhstan (Asyl Arna 2017a). Tazabek continued promoting Asyl Arna, and his work with Islamic, business, and political elites paid off: the Kazakhstani Muftiyat and the Kazakhstani Ministry of Culture and Sport signed an official agreement to cooperate on educating Kazakhstanis on religion, promoting ethnic harmony, and combating extremism in 2015 (Muftyat.kz 2015). In addition, Asyl Arna's popularity as a television channel and a multimedia company exploded in the late 2010s. In early 2014, approximately 30,000 people followed Asyl Arna on the social networking site vKontakte (hereafter, vK). In December 2018, over 486,000 people followed Asyl Arna on vK, and by February 2021, over 550,000 followed the new brand of Talim TV. Tazabek's company continues to expand, even through scandal. In November 2020, Tazabek met with members of the Kazakhstani Muftiyat and was censured for his previous work with Salafis, and some previous Salafi-inspired beliefs (Qappas 2020). The Kazakhstani Muftiyat then announced that it would open its own television channel. However, all was quickly forgiven. The Mufti argued that Tazabek had recanted any problematic positions. Tazabek gave the Muftiyat's channel his blessings, and has changed Asyl Arna to Talim TV, which is a "conservative platform" that offers "positive role models" to its viewers (Abai.kz 2020). Talim TV continues to work with the Muftiyat; imams still appear on their programs, for example (Talim TV 2021). Tazabek directs programs and films for Talim TV, runs its business operations, and appears on its programs. Tazabek also continues to be active and popular on social media.

The text I want to analyze comes from an episode of the Talim TV television program "Meaningful Issues" (*Mangyzdy Masele*). I have chosen this text because it shows the contrast between stereotypical constructions of authority in scripturalist movements and the ways that Tazabek constructs his authority. In this episode, Tazabek sits down with Ardaq Baighabul, the host of the program, and Anuar Izimbai, the head imam of the Arafat mosque in Almaty. There is a clear coffee table with white legs in front of the guests, who sit in white chairs. Baighabul sits on a white loveseat. Tea cups on saucers rest in front of the guests. Behind the guests, there is an angled wall in front of a large television screen which displays graphics throughout the episode. Tazabek wears a suit and tie, while Baighabul has on a sports jacket and dress pants. Izimbai, in contrast, has on the official imam's turban of the Kazakhstani Muftiyat and the accompanying official white robe. The excerpt below is from the opening statements of Izimbai and Tazabek.

> Ardaq Baighabul: Generally, we have not looked at [men's duties] because we discuss women's duties more often. We have not said what men's duties are in detail. Today we will start discussing these things, live, on air. Generally, marrying a woman, starting a family, loving children, and giving them a religious upbringing and education are some of the things that men do that are most pleasing to God. For example, the Prophet (p.b.u.h.) says: if you raise three girls and give them a proper upbringing, you will go to Heaven. We could go on with similar things [said by the Prophet]. Let's start by saying some general words about what a man's duties are in a family. What kind of duties are there?
>
> Anuar Izimbai: [Arabic benediction] Respected Ardaq, the topic raised today is, of course, a fundamental issue. Truthfully, in the Sacred Qur'an, [it is said that] God the Most Exalted created men and women, made them into a pair, and welcomed them. In the Sacred Qur'an, [it is said that] God named the particular qualities of both men and women. But God the Most Exalted gave men elevated status compared to women in one regard. In the Sacred Qur'an, in the Nisa surah, God the Most Exalted says [Arabic quotation], or "men are the rulers of women." Truthfully, the idea of this [decree] is that, in whatever society you are in, there must be a responsible figure in the family. God the Most Exalted has placed this responsibility on men's shoulders. Therefore, it is considered the duty of men, given by the Creator, to feed, clothe, and shelter their families.
>
> Ardaq Baighabul: Understandable. May God be pleased [with your answer]. Older brother Mukhamedzhan, related to this topic, you are yourself a father, a husband, you found a wife, you made a family. But we say "it is easy to marry, but hard to make a home." And connected to that, we know about the duties of a father, but not as much about the duties of a husband. We make mistakes because we think about [these duties] too late. So, as a husband yourself, what can you say about a husband's duties to his wife?
>
> Tazabek: Thank you, brother Ardaq. Our brother the imam spoke well because, on this topic, no one can speak better than the Lord of the Worlds, Allah, and no one can be a better example than our Prophet (p.b.u.h.). Therefore, our Kazakh traditional [child-rearing] skills and family customs start from these two bases. In our history, we, the Kazakh

> people, have never been in a place to be ashamed of our model of a family. But, unfortunately, recently we have been limping away from these things. Why? In the past, starting from when they came into the world, men were raised to say that tomorrow I will be responsible, I will raise a family. When they were circumcised, boys were made to ride a horse. This has great meaning because, grabbing the horse's mane, seeing those ordinary [people on the ground] from up high, these things were done in the hope of turning the child into someone who thinks about what is far off. So, from when they were young, boys were given the chance to govern with their own hands when they grabbed a horse's mane. But, we don't mean just directing the government or the nation by "governing," but to govern and raise a family. [A man] governs his family. Governing is not just demanding; it means to work, to be kind, to provide everything for one's family to achieve good outcomes. Therefore, we, as fathers, understand the example that has come down to us from our ancestors, and it is very important to define a man's duties. If every man hugged his wife and children, loved them, provided for them at the necessary material level, even [national] governmental problems would be solved. We have taken our [national] independence in many ways, but many of our problems that have taken a long time to solve can be attributed to men's weakness in their families. Because, every man must raise his children [well], he must give them an education so that they are not unnecessary lumps but essential to the homeland. And if he [teaches his children], then whether that a child goes to university, or another institution of higher education, or even simply goes to work, he will be turned into a person who does not abuse trust, who raises everyone's level, and who is welcome in the people's hearts. Therefore, what our imam said is not that men arbitrarily govern their wives, but that being a governing man means taking responsibility, managing [the household], and thinking about his wife.

I approach the ways that Tazabek's authority is constructed by using the theoretical framework proposed by Devin DeWeese, who argues that "establishing authority is essentially a process of reference; it is the set of footnotes, in effect, to religious life ..." (DeWeese 2010, 33–34). These footnotes are rarely explicit in everyday speech, but help to tell broader stories about people, places, and things. Think about the types of authority constructed by an ex-football player during a football broadcast. He might reference his playing career to establish his authority as a football expert. He is different than the implied audience because he ran faster, threw better, and hit harder. He knows more about what high-level football feels like. He is, in effect, implying a larger story about himself while telling the more immediate story of live football game. A Viagra commercial during the same broadcast featuring the same ex-football player might show him performing household tasks, adding to the previously referenced playing career by constructing the visual argument that he now lives just like the intended consumer. He might have run faster in the past, but he now has the same difficulties as other middle-aged men, and is an authority on everyday struggles.

So what kind of stories does Tazabek tell about himself? The first story that Tazabek tells about himself is that he is an interpreter of expert opinion. On "Meaningful Issues," Tazabek begins rhetorically nodding towards Izimbai's discussion of Qur'an and the example of the Prophet. However, Tazabek does not cite the Qur'an like Izimbai does. On this program, Izimbai plays the role of expert on scripture. Izimbai shows his mastery of Arabic by starting with an Arabic benediction, implying that an Islamic authority should know Arabic, which itself implies that a Muslim should engage with the Qur'an in the original language. Next, Izimbai paraphrases the Qur'an twice, and then quotes the Qur'an in Arabic and provides a translation. What makes Izimbai authoritative is his ability to reference the Word of God. What makes Tazabek authoritative is his ability to make the knowledge of the imam understandable to Kazakhs. He does not interpret the Qur'an. Rather, he cites and interprets an imam's words. He is close to an expert, both literally and metaphorically. Tazabek sits near the imam. He references the imam's textual knowledge and the imam's interpretation of the Qur'an. But he then goes on to interpret the imam's interpretation.

Similarly, on his Instagram feed, Tazabek presents images of hadiths and Qur'anic verses, but does not comment on them. An August 16, 2016 post shows a Kazakh translation of Baqarah 216 (Tazabek 2016a). (See Figure 1.) An October 11, 2016 shows text on the same background as the August 16, 2016 post and juxtaposes the difference between the everyday thoughts of a Muslim – "don't

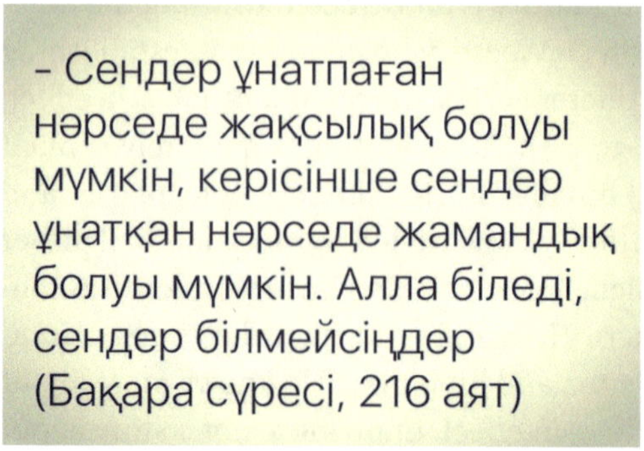
- Сендер ұнатпаған
нәрседе жақсылық болуы
мүмкін, керісінше сендер
ұнатқан нәрседе жамандық
болуы мүмкін. Алла біледі,
сендер білмейсіңдер
(Бақара сүресі, 216 аят)

FIGURE 1
A verse from the Qur'an on Tazabek's Instagram feed

forget me" – and the answers of God found in the Qur'an – "remember me and I will remember you" (2:152) (Tazabek 2016b). He also reposts fatwas from the Kazakhstani Muftiyat, such as a 2020 fatwa on transgender identity (Tazabek 2020a). Scripture stands near Tazabek on his social media feeds, but he does not interpret it. That is a job for the imams and other experts.

The second story that Tazabek tells is that he is a man of the people. Even before he speaks on "Meaningful Issues," Tazabek is positioned as an authority because of his similarities to the program's imagined audience. While Izimbai is distinguished by his turban and robe, Tazabek dresses as a stereotypical middle-class Kazakh. Baighabul introduces Izimbai and Tazabek in ways that reinforce their roles of textual expert and man of the people. Tazabek is an authority because, as Baighabul says, "you are yourself a father, a husband, you found a wife, you made a family." Baighabul repeats this idea when he poses his question to Tazabek, "So, as a husband yourself, what can you say about a husband's duties to his wife?" Compare this to how Baighabul prompts Izimbai to speak about the Prophet and the Qur'an, saying "For example, the Prophet (p.b.u.h.) says: if you raise three girls and give them a proper upbringing, you will go to Heaven. We could go on with similar things [said by the Prophet]." The presenter pushes Izimbai to reference the Qur'an and the Prophet, not his own experience. Izimbai might be a father and a husband, but that is not why we listen to him. We listen to him for Qur'anic quotations. If we want to know about the experience of someone like us, we should turn to Tazabek.

Tazabek does not show his mastery of Arabic by beginning with an Arabic benediction. The national frame that Tazabek places on his answer is Kazakh. After nodding to the importance of the Qur'an and sunnah, Tazabek focuses on historical Kazakh practices like the tradition of placing a boy on a horse on the day of his circumcision. Part of this explanation's power comes from its reference of a bygone golden era. The other part stems from the Kazakhness of the reference. The Qur'an has good ideas, even divine templates for living, but the Kazakh audience does not need to know these. They need to know how Kazakhs have lived in accordance with the Qur'an without all the scriptural bells and whistles the imam uses. Tazabek establishes his authority for Kazakh Muslims by substituting lessons on Kazakh history for scriptural references. The audience should listen to him not because he knows Islamic scripture, but because he is Kazakh like them.

Tazabek's former life as an *aqyn* also establishes him as a man of hte people. Early in the program, Baighabul introduces Tazabek as "an *aqyn* and an Honored Worker of Kazakhstan." On his Instagram account, Tazabek provides a similar introduction: "Director of the Asyl Arna Teleradio Company, Honored

Worker of Kazakhstan. Psychology Sciences Ph.D. *Aitys aqyn*." *Aqyns* think of themselves as speakers for the people in Kazakhstan. Dubuisson, after three years of research with *aqyns* in Almaty, writes that "All the poets with whom I spoke believe it is their duty and obligation to speak *khalyqtyng shyndyghy* (the people's truth)" (Dubuisson 2010, 107). By referencing Tazabek's past as an *aqyn*, Baighabul and Tazabek brings Tazabek into a larger story of *aqyns* speaking for the people. In an article on the role of *aqyns* in Islam, Tazabek cites another writer's argument that one reason Kazakhs are Muslims is because *aqyns* played a special role in making Islam intelligible to the people (Tazabek n.d.a.). Tazabek is a father, a husband, a man like those in his audience, but he also has a special bond with his audience as an *aqyn*. He is someone who understands them and can make things clear to them.

An October 1, 2016 post illustrates how Tazabek combines images with short, poetic, *aqyn*-like statements to create an everyman persona. (See Figure 2.) In the photo posted, he stands near a rough hay barn next to homemade ladders. The image evokes a nostalgic sense of returning to the land. Tazabek's accompanying post reads, "The village, where one's fate is determined by labor, is my homeland!" (*Engbekpen tapkan nesibin, auylym - altyn besigim!*) (Tazabek 2016c) This short couplet, with a near rhyme, accomplishes several things. It references "labor," calling to mind Soviet refrains on the importance of the people and their labor. It asserts that Tazabek does his own labor, and combines with the image in the post to show that Tazabek is like rural Kazakhs. And it repeats the well-known phrase "*auylym - altyn besigim*," literally "my village is my golden cradle," thus showing Tazabek's mastery of Kazakh language and idiom. In short, the couplet exemplifies an *aqyn*'s art. It shows knowledge of Kazakh culture and pithily states a message in a way memorable and understandable to the people.[10]

Tazabek's authority as a man of the people works in parallel with his role as interpreter of expert Islamic opinion. On "Meaningful Issues," Tazabek speaks as the everyman in contrast to the the imam Izimbai on "Meaningful Issues" and, through this juxtaposition, identifies himself as someone who acts out the scriptural injunctions of imams in his everyday life. On his Instagram feed, Tazabek visually shows his common touch in juxtaposition to an iconography of scripturalist Islam. He posts quotes from the Qur'an and hadiths next to pictures of himself relaxing in nature near his hometown (Tazabek 2016d), watching the 2016 Olympics (Figure 3) (Tazabek 2016e), and drinking tea at restaurants (Figure 4) (Tazabek 2016f). He posts mundane videos

10 See Dubuisson 2010 for a longer description of the art of aqyns. Tazabek's words also play a large role in Talim TV's social media. For material on how Talim TV presents Tazabek in comparison to the Head Mufti of Kazakhstan, see Schwab 2016.

FIGURE 2 A man of the people: Tazabek in the village

FIGURE 3 Just like you: Tazabek watching boxing

of "the first snow [of the season] in Shymkent" (Tazabek 2016g) and of shoveling show in Zhangaqorghan (Tazabek 2021a). His Instagram followers identify with Tazabek in these images, writing comments discussing their own television viewing habits such as "the real spectacle will be the Paralympics" in response to the picture of Tazabek watching the 2016 Olympics, and more

FIGURE 4 Tazabek drinking tea at a restaurant

direct identifications with Tazabek like "I live in your hometown … A warm hello from home" in response to the photo of Tazabek drinking tea. The first commenter engages in a conversation about TV with Tazabek, while the second identifies as his compatriot. They don't praise his scriptural knowledge or liken him to a Sufi saint. They treat Tazabek like someone they met on the train from Almaty to Shymkent. By bringing together images of the Qur'an as an object or the Qur'an as text with images of his own everyman lifestyle, Tazabek makes the visual argument to Kazakhs that he is just like them, only closer to scriptural Islam. Like you, but a bit better.

Relatable Muslim intermediaries are attractive to many Kazakhs because Kazakhs lack self-confidence in their own Islamic knowledge and practice. This lack of self-confidence is furthered by discussions of Kazakh history in the media.[11] Tazabek does not think many Kazakhs are ready for the scriptural citations of imams and scholars. Kazakhs might misinterpret scripture. Tazabek speaks of the need to correct Kazakhs who have studied Islam abroad and believe Kazakh traditions are un-Islamic (Tazabek 2015). He also speaks of the need to teach scripture to Kazakhs who have been influenced by 70 years of Soviet atheism. For Tazabek, Kazakhstan may have made great strides in technological progress during the Soviet era, but "from the standpoint of ordinary morality, we are going backwards" (Tazabek n.d.b.). The result is that "the Kazakh nation had great qualities, but these are now asleep" (Bitore 2014).

11 I have discussed Kazakhs' lack of self-confidence in their Islamic practice and belief at length in the past. See Schwab 2011, 2012, 2015. See also Privratsky 2001.

70 years of Soviet atheism made it so that people could not "separate religion from tradition." He argues that "People will smear soot on a child's face to ward off the evil eye and wear a wolf's tooth around their neck to be brave. These have no place in the school of the Great Imam [Abu Hanifa]" (Aizhanbai n.d.). In addition to the damage caused by the Soviet era and foreign Islamic ideas, contemporary entertainment on TV and the radio lure young people into sexual immorality (Tazabek n.d.b.). This potent combination of immoral, foreign, and atheist influences means that, even if Tazabek wants to "wake the noble qualities" of Kazakhs, he cannot, "in a single day, to turn everyone into a person who preaches well, wears a headscarf, prays five times a day, and gives charity" (Bitore 2014). Kazakhs simply cannot make such a transition. They need an everyman to show them how Islam can fit into their lives. Tazabek is not some highfalutin imam, but someone who has found his own wife and had his own struggles.

The third story that Tazabek tells about himself is that he is an upper-class knowledge worker. He is an authority on how to be economically successful in contemporary Kazakhstan. On "Meaningful Issues," after establishing himself as a man of the people, Tazabek elaborates what he means by "governing:" working hard, being kind, and providing for one's family. However, the justification for these actions is made not by referencing their innate worth or Qur'anic verse, but by referencing their end result. Children with such fathers would not be corrupt. They would be useful to the homeland. Policy problems could be solved because children would contribute to society after graduating from universities and moving into professional or managerial work, or "even" if they just went to work after secondary school. In short, they would be respectable citizens contributing the economy. Tazabek is not a man of the people as they are, but as they want to be. He is an Ordinary Joe who has done well.

Tazabek's popular Instagram account references his own upper-class work and lifestyle. For example, on July 12, 2016, Tazabek posted a picture "from a meeting on Asyl Arna's new projects" (Figure 5) (Tazabek 2016h). In this photo, Tazabek sits on a leather couch in front of a wooden table. He wears casual clothes: a short-sleeved dress shirt, a black watch, and khaki pants. Four male Talim TV employees sit around him. One shares the couch with Tazabek, while three others are in leather chairs. The wooden table has gaps in the stain, giving it a vintage look popular with middle- and upper-class urbanites. Floor to ceiling glass windows and a chandelier appear behind the men. If these men were in the United States, they would be busy gentrifying Brooklyn.

Other images depict Tazabek in similar ways. In an October 3, 2016 post, Tazabek sits in the lobby of the Almaty Towers, an expensive new shopping and residential complex (Tazabek 2016i). In a May 16, 2016 post, Tazabek strolls through the streets of Frankfurt (Figure 6) (Tazabek 2016j). A November 15, 2016 post shows Tazabek, and a friend just returned from studying in the USA, eating at a trendy coffee shop in Almaty that goes by the name "Breakfast at Tiffany's" (Tazabek 2016k). A January 31, 2021 post shows him sitting in a fancy lobby in Almaty, accompanied by text quoting the Caliph Ali (Tazabek 2021b). A February 2, 2017 post shows him drinking coffee, a drink notable for its cosmopolitan and non-traditional image in Kazakhstan, at the Astana Airport (Tazabek 2017a). The combined effect of these images is of a man who works at cafes planning media campaigns, wears casual but stylish clothes, uses an iPad, goes out to eat, and vacations abroad. His lifestyle is the endpoint of what Osmonova describes as the "dream" of many migrants to Astana: getting a loan, buying an apartment, shopping in malls, and socializing in bars and cafes.[12] These migrants go to great lengths to realize this dream: they live in non-registered apartments with three to four people in a room and struggle to find stable middle-class jobs. In contast, Tazabek does not show himself pouring concrete or living with ten other labor migrants in a small apartment. Instead, he offers a model of what happens when you live an Islamic lifestyle: you have leisure time and consumer goods, go out to eat in fashionable restaurants in Almaty, and drink coffee before jet-setting around the world.

A key feature of this knowledge work and an upper-class lifestyle is its association with and promotion of "development." Learning technical skills from developed nations will enrich individual Muslims as well as Muslim nations. In January 2017, Tazabek promoted the work of the Talim TV screenwriter and journalist Murat Eszhan, who writes about his travels to the USA. Tazabek argues that it is not enough see films about the USA, but that Kazakhs must go there and see the good and bad, and determine what can be emulated and what must be shunned (Tazabek 2017b). In December 2016, Tazabek traveled to London to participate in a BBC media development workshop. He described his meeting with and learning from "global experts" (Tazabek 2016l). Learning from global experts will "raise Asyl Arna to a new level" (Tazabek 2016m). This cultural complex combining development and Islam is a continuation of the program of the Jadids in the late 19th century and early 20th century in Central Asia. Jadids were enamoured with progress, civilization, and Islam (Khalid 1998, 2015). These three concepts were tied together in a virtuous bundle. The key to a better Islam was scientific progress and abandoning superstition in favor of textual knowledge. The key to scientific progress was learning from

12 Osmonova 2016. See also the analysis of gender and consumption among young Kazakhstanis in Aktobe in Jager 2016.

FIGURE 5
White-collar work: Tazabek managing a meeting of his workers

FIGURE 6
The perks of success: Tazabek strolling through Frankfurt

more developed civilizations, such as those in Europe. The key to improving on European morals was Islam. Tazabek and Talim TV similarly argue that the key to a better Islamic life is to learn secular skills from developed nations, become richer as individuals and as a society, and focus on scripturalist Islamic knowledge.

The idea that Islamic piety is a path to economic wealth is often explicitly stated by Tazabek. He reposts Talim TV content on hard work, such as the content posted on Talim TV's social media during a week devoted to the topic "if you want to be rich" (See Figure 7).[13] For example, Tazabek reposted an image showing a man lifting an impossibly heavy stone while wearing a tie and suit

13 "If you want to be rich" was the theme for the week between October 9th and 15th, 2016. See Asyl Arna Teleradiokompaniyasy 2016b.

АПТАЛЫҚ ТАҚЫРЫП:
БАЙ
БОЛҒЫҢЫЗ КЕЛСЕ...
АСЫЛ АРНА

FIGURE 7 "If you want to be rich ..."

pants. (Figure 8) (Asyl Arna Teleradiokompaniyasy 2016c). The caption reads, "A pot never boils without sweat on a forehead." In other words, you have to work hard to get ahead. However, the image is not of a mason installing a brick wall or sanitation worker or shepherd in the field. The image depicts a man with a tie. Tazabek's company, Talim TV, includes tips on how to organize your time to be productive, such as making three categories of activity: very important, somewhat important, and less important. Start with the very important things, and once you finish them, and only if you finish them, move on to the somewhat important things (Asyl Arna Teleradiokompaniyasy 2016a).[14] Good

14 For a different example of Talim TV's promotion of business self-help tips, see their summary of of the 19th and 20th century Canadian journalist Herbert Casson's thoughts on

FIGURE 8 The path to success: work hard and listen to Tazabek

Muslims know how to prioritize their time and be productive. Even a Kazakh with one arm and no legs can achieve his economic dreams, if he works hard and plans (Tazabek 2020b). This is part of a wider change in Kazakhstani culture which focuses on self-management and self-governing in a market-oriented economy (Adams and Rustemova 2009). Tazabek's presentation of an upper-class lifestyle and his promotion of the skills necessary to achieve a middle or upper-class life appeal to Kazakhstanis whether or not they are seeking to learn more about Islam. How do you achieve your middle-class dream? Tazabek will tell you: work hard and prioritize.

The particular genius of Tazabek is to then answer the implied question: What helps you to work hard and prioritize? The answer is Islamic scripture and Islamic ethics. And, as we know from above, Tazabek is just the man to distill Islam into a modern lifestyle for his audience. The model for achieving this lifestyle includes the type of self-discipline described above, but also includes following the tenets of scripturalist Islam. The Talim TV post on organizing

business: "Seven Rules of Getting Rich" (Asyl Arna 2017c), promoted on social media here: https://vk.com/asyl_arna?z=photo-51948252_440328178%2Falbum-51948252_00%2Frev.

time includes non-religious examples such as "getting up to exercise in the morning," and religious examples like "going to the mosque for noon prayers" (Asyl Arna Teleradiokompaniyasy 2016a). Scripturalist activists like Tazabek sacralize middle- and upper-class behaviors. A wife at home and the importance of educational achievement are both encouraged by Islam, in Tazabek's view. If we follow the entirety of the discussion between Tazabek and Izimbai excerpted above, we can see that running a middle-class family in accordance with scripturalist dictates on gender roles will probably help you get your child into a university. On his Instagram feed, Tazabek brings together images of Qur'anic injunctions – "remember me and I will remember you" – with images of his lifestyle and makes the visual argument that the Qur'an is both part of and a guide to an economic success. One of his Instagram posts asks, "[Do you] need advice? The answers to difficulties are in the Qur'an" (Tazabek 2017c). It is not just difficulties that the Qur'an has answers to. The answers to the questions implied by the topic "If you want to be rich …" are also found in the Islamic textual tradition.

The fourth story that Tazabek tells about himself is that he is close to the government of Kazakhstan. On "Meaningful Issues," Tazabek references his connection to the government in his discussion of governing a family. He makes the connection between governing a family and governing the nation. If fathers governed their families as good Muslims, the government's problems would be solved. Good Muslim fathers and husbands will prevent corruption, increase social cohesion, and increase economic output by raising children who follow Islamic morals, respect others, and excel in school. Hugs will make Kazakhstan a better place: "If every man hugged his wife and children, loved them, provided for them at the necessary material level, even [national-level] governmental problems would be solved."

Tazabek's reference to solving governmental problems is part of a strategy to connect Tazabek to the government of Kazakhstan. Tazabek was the driving force behind an Talim TV online video praising Nursultan Nazarbaev, the former President of Kazakhstan (Asyl Arna TV Online 2014). This video was a viral hit on the Kazakh-language internet. The poem recited in the video asks why people expect Nazarbaev to be perfect, and then goes on to argue that, whatever else, Nazarbaev is a Kazakh patriot who has helped Kazakhstan achieve independence. The video shows Nazarbaev singing with the people, walking in fields of grain, and visiting factories. In an interview about the clip, Tazabek stresses that this project is not an attempt to flatter the president. Rather, he hoped to bring common Kazakhs and "the authorities" into dialogue (Bitore 2014). If common Kazakhs follow political elites, and political elites hear the moral concerns of common Kazakhs, economic and Islamic development will result.

Tazabek's story of working with the government is popular with Kazakhs who worry about how the government will react to their practice of Islam, as well as to Kazakhs who worry about terrorism. In response to acts of violence, the government of Kazakhstan has increased its control over Islamic practice. On May 18, 2011, as a response to a May 17, 2011 attack in Aqtobe, the Kazakhstani government created the Agency for Religious Affairs (Aubakirov and Sarybai 2013). This agency was tasked with enforcing a new law on religions passed in October 2011 (Lillis 2012). This law required all religious organizations to re-register with the Kazakhstani government. In effect, this allowed authorities to examine all religious organizations and judge if they were legal. A June 2016 attack, again in Aqtobe, and a July 2016 attack in Almaty led to the elevation of the Agency for Religious Affairs to the Ministry of Religious Affairs in September 2016. The new Ministry for Religious Affairs was led by a former secretary of the National Security Committee (Lillis 2016).

Many Kazakhs worry that the practice of Islam will exceed the bounds of what the government considers acceptable. The question is, as one journalist put it, how to "be a normal Muslim" (Aidabosyn 2016). After the passage of the October 2011 law, I had email conversations with Kazakh men who worried that the government might ban beards. The government did not ban beards, but these men's fears show the extent to which some Kazakhs worry about deviating from official dictates on religion. I have had conversations with Kazakh women who wondered if they would lose their jobs if they continued wearing their headscarves.

Even more concerning to the majority of Kazakhs is the possibility of terrorism. In 2013, one young woman related that she had "heard rumors that if someone on the bus had 'short pants' [considered a sartorial sign of Salafism], it means they were carrying something explosive, and were dangerous." Maria Louw relates similar attitudes in Kyrgyzstan. One Kyrgyz woman spoke of a friend's son who started going to the mosque and saying the daily prayers. He was well-behaved – he did not drink, for example – and everyone was pleased. But then he grew out his beard and made more stringent arguments against things like television. In the end, she thought this young man "looked like a Taliban warrior." She pitied him and his parents because, in her judgment, he had thrown away a life with good prospects for a life excessively devoted to religion (Louw 2013).

Tazabek's references on "Meaningful Issues" to solving governmental problems, and his references to the achievements of the government and Nazarbaev, show that he is an authority on what kind of Islamic belief and practice are acceptable to authorities in Kazakhstan. After the June 2016 shootings in Aktobe, Tazabek gave an interview in which he addresses accusations that he and Talim TV are spreading Salafist ideology (Kunanbaiuly 2016). He interprets and elaborates on a speech of President Nazarbaev on terrorism and Salafis. He stresses that the most dangerous part of Salafist ideology is the tendency to criticize the government and national traditions. He goes on to state that Talim TV has been audited by the government since 2007. He highlights the relationship between Talim TV, the Kazakh Muftiyat, and Ministry of Culture and Sport. (The Ministry of Culture and Sport was home of the Agency for Religious Affairs until September 2016). Tazabek implies that if you listen to him or watch his television channel, you will not get in trouble with the government. Even after admitting, in November 2020, to Salafi influences in his past, Tazabek is still portrayed as an unthreatening man. Qairat Zholdybaiuly, the head imam of one of the largest mosques in Astana, said Tazabek can be a model for learning from his mistakes, and that Tazabek's eloquence will help win over similarly mistaken Kazakhs (Qappas 2020). In the end, if your son watches Talim TV or follows Tazabek on Instagram, he will not become a terrorist or Salafi. Tazabek is a safe authority.

There are several effects of the widespread acceptance of Tazabek's authority. One effect is the expansion of Islamic and traditionalist discourses in Kazakhstani media. Another effect is a backlash against Tazabek and his allies. (See Schwab 2019 for an article-length discussion of this type of backlash.) A third effect is the production of cultural content for those pious Muslims who cannot reach the middle class. Kazakhs in this position may deny the connection between economic success in the 21st century and Islam. The feelings of scripturalist Muslims who do not meet expectations of entering the middle class and fulfilling gender expectations are similar to lower to middle-class Republicans in the United States. Arlie Hochschild uses an extended metaphor to summarize these Republicans' "deep story." They are waiting in line on a hill. The hill is the American Dream of a middle or upper-class lifestyle: a house, kids, cars, vacations. The line is not moving forward very quickly. It may even be moving backwards. They, and their parents, and their parents' parents, have been in the line for generations. But other people are skipping forward in the line due to governmental practices. Members of minority, immigrant, and LGBTQ communities are cutting ahead. All of this breeds resentment (Hochschild 2016). Scripturalist Muslims in Kazakhstan have a similar story. They are obeying God's dictates after a long period of enforced atheism. They are moral in an immoral society. They listen to successful Muslim leaders whose piety God has rewarded with a nice house, meaningful work, and vacations abroad. So why are their own efforts not being rewarded by God?

Here I want to make a diversion to the videos and social media posts of Namys TV, a social media brand in Kazakhstan with pages on vKontakte, Instagram, and YouTube. Namys TV could be called an Islamic conspiracy theory site and be dismissed by scholars. I assume that most readers of this chapter do not think that the Illuminati are, in fact, part of Satan's army (Namys TV 2017c). But this would deny the seriousness of Namys TV's arguments, and its connections to broader Kazakh and global culture. Mosques from Oral and Astana in the north to Saryaghash in the south link to Namys TV's posts (Musylmane G. Ural'sk 2017; Bozaryq Nasriddin Baba Meshiti 2017; Saqy Ata Meshit 2017). More than 102,000 people follow Namys TV on vK.

Namys TV provides an answer to the question, "why are pious Muslims' efforts not being rewarded by God?" The answer is that there are sinister forces out there conspiring to break up middle-class families with gendered divisions of labor. Immoral atheists, Jews, Russians, Westerners, and homosexuals are taking jobs and resources. Satanic conspiracies deny Muslims the possibility for a happy life by turning men into homosexuals and women into prostitutes. The break up of families makes middle-class lifestyles impossible for Muslims. This type of conspiracy theory is made clear in "The Politics of Depopulation: Chapter 4 – Feminism," a Namys TV video that translates global conspiracy videos on feminism into Kazakh. This video presents the argument that feminism and gender politics are the result of wealthy elites' worries about Malthusian disaster and their plans to dominate the world economy. To give an example of this type of discourse, here is an excerpt from the video:

> One of the clearest manifestations of [these policies] is feminism, or gender politics. Throughout the world, various feminist groups have emerged and the trend is for women holding a feminist worldview to strive for authority and political power. They are prevailing in every area of society. Feminism's general ideology is, "women are independent from men, and do not have to raise children and sit in the kitchen." Or, they should work together with men, they should move out from the confines of family life and into other places. There are even radical feminist groups completely opposed to childbirth. They implement their hatred and fear of family life through film.
>
> It is increasingly apparent that the development of feminism and women's striving for power and professional careers have affected birth rate indicators. A clear example of this is the aging continent of Europe. Feminist politics are funded by the Rockefeller family and the Rockefeller Foundation. And the Rockefeller family is among the most influential people behind the idea of population reduction.
>
> NAMYS TV 2017b

The article goes on to translate part of an interview with Aaron Russo, an American conspiracy theorist advertised as a "producer, director, and political activist." Russo argues that the Rockefeller family decided to promote feminism, particularly women working in paying jobs, in order to increase tax revenue and promote early childhood education to indoctrinate children. Women's liberation was intended to break up families and cause children to look to the government as responsible for their welfare. Namys TV concludes:

> This is how the global system prepares women for careers and employment. And now television and the internet are responsible for raising children. Or, [put otherwise,] this is the most important factor in the degradation of society and the collapse of people's religiosity. Which, in its own way, is another method to control the population!

The exact connection between taxing women and indoctrinating children with depopulation, spiritual degradation, and the collapse of religion is unclear. What is clear, however, is that someone – the Rockefellers most specifically, but by extension, the Zionist-Satanic conspiracy – is trying to break up your family and take economic advantage of you, your wife, and your children.

Namys TV asserts that this conspiracy has made it into Kazakhstani mass media as well. The boy band Ninety One is part of a global Satanic ideology which seeks to trample on Kazakh manhood (Namys TV 2016). The popular internet portal, Nur.kz, disparages traditional, moral, Islamic gender relations (Namys TV 2017a). A Namys TV video asserts that Nur.kz publishes or links to articles which denigrate women who wear headscarves, and never mentions the "positive effects of the headscarves on society and the people's spirituality, and its anti-adultery influences." It never discusses the "victims of feminism" whose lives have been ruined by adultery or prostitution. Namys TV connects this "anti-Islamic" viewpoint with foreign influences. Other articles on anti-headscarf policies or media also argue that Russia has colonized the minds of Kazakh elites (Namys TV 2017d). These foreign influences want to increase immorality in Kazakhstan. Why else would Nur.kz have a section on dating and sex? Talking about sex and dating only serves to lead Muslims to adultery and prostitution. Adultery and prostitution lead to the the breakdown of society. And the breakdown of society leads to the impoverishment of Muslims. If you can't find a good job or you don't like your daughter's clothes, it is not your fault. Satan and the Illuminati are oppressing you.

Just as Namys TV translates and localizes global conspiracy theory culture, Tazabek has analogues elsewhere in the Islamic world. Television personalities such as Amr Khaled and Moez Masoud in Egypt (Moll 2010) and Muslim business gurus such as Ary Ginanjar in Indonesia promote a similar link between piety and economic success. Capitalism and Christianity have similarly been linked throughout the world (Connolly 2008). What makes Tazabek unique is his use of Kazakh cultural forms. He uses his cultural position of an *aqyn* as well as his mastery of Kazakh proverbs and styles of speech to address unique challenges of post-Soviet Kazakhstan, including cultural anxieties about the effect of the Soviet era on religion and governmental insecurities about Islam. To sum up: the particular appeal of Tazabek is that he combines four authoritative characteristics in a single package. Tazabek is the model of a man who follows scripture, is a Kazakh like you, has found economic success, and will stave off terrorism and political pressure on Islam. These characteristics speak to the anxieties of Kazakhs and provide a sacralized model for living a middle-class life in a politically stable country. Kazakhs may recognize the authority of imams such as Izimbai, but imams are not models of or for modern life. Imams think about Islam all day and work at a mosque. Tazabek works an office job and is someone who you can talk about television with. He is someone from your hometown. And he can show you how to make money.

Bibliography

Abai.kz, 2020. "'Asyl Arna' Zhabyldy, 'Khalyq Arnagha' Aq Zhol!" Abai.kz/post/123509, accessed 2/16/2021.

Adams, Laura L., and Assel Rustemova. 2009. "Mass spectacle and styles of governmentality in Kazakhstan and Uzbekistan." *Europe-Asia Studies* 61(7): 1249–1276.

Aidabosyn, Esbolat. 2016. "Salafit, Sopy, Gulenshi … Zhai Ghana Musylman Bolugha Bolmai Ma?" 365info.kz, July 27. https://kaz.365info.kz/s-l-fit-sopy-g-lenshi-zhaj-ana-m-sylman-bolu-a-bola-ma-217068, accessed August 4, 2017.

Aitys TV. 2016a. Mukhamedzhan Tazabek pen Quanysh Maqsutov. YouTube video, 21:09, January 5, 2016. http://www.youtube.com/watch?v=uKciAQhvW8k, accessed August 4, 2017.

AITYS TV. 2016b. Mukhamedzhan Tazabek pen Serik Qaliev. YouTube video, 20:13, January 5, 2016. http://www.youtube.com/watch?v=uKciAQhvW8k, accessed August 4, 2017.

Aizhanbai, Gulbarshyn. N.d. "Mukhamedzhan Tazabekov: Buryn Aitys Aqyny Atansam, Qazir Aitys Menedzheri Bolyp Zhurmin." Aiqyn. http://www.elarna.com/koru_kk.php?tur=20&id=151086, accessed August 4, 2017.

Asyl Arna. 2017a. "Biz Turaly." http://asylarna.kz/about, accessed August 4, 2017.

Asyl Arna. 2017b. "Mukhamedzhan Orazbaiuly Tazabek." http://asylarna.kz/ujym/Asylarnaujymy/1, accessed August 4, 2017.

Asyl Arna, trans. 2017c. "Bai Bolydyng Zheti Qaghidasy." http://www.asylarna.kz/maqala/maqalainfo/286, accessed August 4, 2017.

Asyl Arna Teleradiokompaniyasy. 2016a. "Isim Retin Tapsyn Desengiz." vK post, July 11, 2016. https://vk.com/asyl_arna?w=wall-51948252_101335, accessed August 4, 2017.

Asyl Arna Teleradiokompaniyasy. 2016b. "Aptalyq Taqyryp: Bai Bolghynyz Kelse." vK post, October 10, 2016. http://vk.com/asyl_arna?z=photo-51948252_439380526%2Falbum-51948252_00, accessed August 4, 2017.

Asyl Arna Teleradiokompaniyasy. 2016c. "Mangdaiy Terlemegenning Qazany Qainamaidy." vK post, October 13, 2016. https://vk.com/asyl_arna?z=photo-51948252_439829667%2Falbum-51948252_00, accessed December 11, 2018.

Asyl Arna TV Online. 2014. "Kit Aitypty Minsiz Dep Nuraghamyz?" YouTube Video, 4:57, November 14, 2017. https://www.youtube.com/watch?v=FjsD2TRxyRY, accessed August 4, 2017.

Asyl Arna TV Online. 2016. "'Arnaiy Sukhbat' Mukhamedzhan Tazabekov." YouTube Video, 37:37, July 30, 2016. https://www.youtube.com/watch?v=oCOh1ofF4So, accessed September 14, 2021.

Aubakirov, Arnur and Yelden Sarybai. 2013. "Religious Affairs Agency Works to Protect Freedoms, Stop Extremist Ideologies." Astana Times, July 10. http://astanatimes.com/2013/07/religious-affairs-agency-works-to-protect-freedoms-stop-extremist-ideologies/, accessed August 4, 2017.

Bigozhin, Ulan. 2019 "'Where is Our Honor?' Sports, Masculinity, and Authority in Kazakhstani Islamic Media." *Central Asian Affairs* 6 (2–3): 189–205.

Bitore, Ali. 2014. "Mukhammedzhan Tazabek: Qazir – Alasapyran Uaqyt. Erkim Zhasyna Zharaspaityn Zhuk Koterip Zhur." *Zhaqsy*, June 6. https://web.archive.org/web/20160324172644/http://www.jaqsy.kz/article/view?id=383, accessed August 4, 2017.

Bozaryq Nasriddin Baba Meshiti, "Qalauym," vK post, September 23, 2017. https://vk.com/wall-111576025_1974, accessed October November 2017.

Connolly, William E. 2008. *Capitalism and Christianity, American Style*. Durham, North Carolina: Duke University Press.

DeWeese, Devin. 2010. "Authority," in *Key Terms for the Study of Islam*, 26–52, edited by Jamal J. Elias. Oxford: Oneworld.

Dubuisson, Eva-Marie. 2010. "Confrontation in and through the Nation in Kazakh Aitys Poetry." *Journal of Linguistic Anthropology* 20 (1): 101–115.

Hochschild, Arlie Russell. 2016. *Strangers in their Own Land: Anger and Mourning on the American Right*. New York: The New Press.

Jäger, Philipp Frank. 2016. "Where the Whole City Meets: Youth, Gender and Consumerism in the Social Space of the MEGA Shopping Mall in Aktobe, Western Kazakhstan." *Central Asian Survey* 35 (2): 178–194.

Kaznet Magazine. 2018. “Reiting Klout.” http://kaznet.me/rating/, accessed December 10, 2018.

Khalid, Adeeb. 1999. *The politics of Muslim cultural reform: Jadidism in Central Asia*. Berkely: University of California Press.

Khalid, Adeeb. 2015. *Making Uzbekistan: Nation, Empire, and Revolution in the Early USSR*. Ithaca: Cornell University Press.

Kitab.kz. 2014. “Mukhamedzhan Tazabek: Biz Turaly Oraghandar, Tumaghandar, Fariza Apalarymyz Zhazatyn …” Kitab.kz, April 11, 2014. http://kitap.kz/suqbat/entry/2014-04-11-10-24-32, accessed August 4, 2017.

Kunanbaiuly, Asylbek. 2016. “Bizdi Salaf Dep Aiytaugha Quzyrly Mekemening Ghana Quqyghy Bar.” Baq.kz, June 27. https://baq.kz/kk/news/ruhaniyat/muhamedzhan_tazabek_bizdi_salaf_deitinder__otpen_oinap_zhur, accessed August 4, 2017.

Lillis, Joanna. 2012. “Kazakhstan: Places of Worship Closed Under New Religion Law.” Eurasianet.org. http://www.eurasianet.org/node/66289, accessed August 4, 2017.

Lillis, Joanna. 2016. “Kazakhstan: Rearranging Chairs on the Ship Astana.” Eurasianet.org. http://www.eurasianet.org/node/80531, accessed August 4, 2017.

Louw, Maria. 2013. “Even honey may become bitter when there is too much of it: Islam and the struggle for a balanced existence in post-Soviet Kyrgyzstan.” *Central Asian Survey* 32 (4): 514–526.

Malghazhuly, Erzhan qazhy. 2015. “‘Asyl Arna’ Hem Sayat Ybyrai Zhyry’ Zhauaby.” Abai.kz, October 16, 2015. http://abai.kz/post/41806, accessed August 4, 2017.

Moll, Yasmin. 2010. “Islamic Televangelism: Religion, Media and Visuality in Contemporary Egypt.” *Arab Media & Society* 10: 1–27.

Muftyat.kz. 2015. “QMDB: Ush Zhaqty Keleisimge Qol Qoiyldy.” Muftyat.kz, July 5, 2015. https://www.muftyat.kz/kk/news/qmdb/2015-07-05/4784-kmdb-ush-zhakty-kelisimge-kol-koiyldy-foto/, accessed September 14, 2021.

Muminov, Ashirbek. 2014. “From Revived Tradition to Innovation: Kolkhoz Islam in the Southern Kazakhstan Region and Religious Leadership (through the Cases of Zharti-Tobe and Oranghay since the 1950s).” In *Allah's Kolkhozes: Migration, De-Stalinisation, Privatisation, and the New Muslim Congregations in the Soviet Realm (1950s–2000s)*, ed. Stephane A. Dudoignon, and C.U. Noack: 307–366. Berlin: Klaus Schwarz.

Muminov, Ashirbek. 2016. “Foreign Influence and the Development of Islamic Education in Kazakhstan: Causes, Success, and Consequences of Foreign Education Institutions.” YouTube video, 23:53, March 28, 2016. http://www.youtube.com/watch?v=S-fjB8dpUQU, accessed August 4, 2017.

Namys TV. “Ninety One Toby Nemese Antiqazaqtyq Sayasat,” vK post, December 27, 2016. https://vk.com/namystvpro?w=wall-74436962_1616, accessed December 13, 2017.

Namys TV. 2017a. “Nur.kz Aqparattyq Portalyna Zhuieli Kozqaras” vK video, January 1, 2017. https://vk.com/namystvpro?w=wall-74436962_1618, accessed November 27, 2017.

Namys TV. 2017b. "Qalyq Sanyn Qysqarty Sayasaty: 4-Bolim – Feminizm." vK video, May 25, 2017. https://vk.com/namystvpro?w=wall-74436962_1683, accessed November 16, 2017.

Namys TV. 2017c. "Shaitannyng Armiyasy: Lyutsiferler, Masondar, Illyuminattar," vK post, September 23, 2017. https://vk.com/namystvpro?w=wall-74436962_1776, accessed December 13, 2017.

Namys TV. 2017d. "Qudaidan Qoryqpaghan Oramaldy Syilaidy Ma?" vK video, November 22, 2017. https://vk.com/namystvpro?w=wall-74436962_1830, accessed November 27, 2017.

Osmanova, Kishimjan. 2016. "Experiencing Liminality: Housing, Renting and Informal tenants in Astana." *Central Asian Survey* 35 (2): 237–256.

Privratsky, Bruce. 2001. *Muslim Turkistan: Kazak Religion and Collective Memory*. London: Routledge Curzon.

Qamshy. 2017. "Mukhamedzhan Tazabek 25 Zhul Buryn Qonaevtyng Tughan Kuninde Tusirilgen Ekcluyuzivti Videony Zhariyalady." http://www.qamshy.kz/article/muxamedzhan-25-zhil-burin-qonaevtinh-twghan-kuninde-tusirilgen-eksklywzyvti-vydeoni-zharyyaladi, accessed August 4, 2017.

Qappas, Quanysh. 2020. "Tazabekov: Salafilerden Mendei Zardap Korgen Adam Zhoq." www.abai.kz/post/123580, accessed 2/16/2021.

Raimbekov, Zhanadil. 2016. "Mukhamedzhan Tazabek/Axhyrasudyng Qalai Aldyn Alamyz?/Aiel Baqyty?" YouTube Video, 4:44, August 17, 2016. https://www.youtube.com/watch?v=kDp-_qu33Ok, accessed September 14, 2021.

Saqy Ata Meshit, "Ulttyq Ideologiyagha Ainaluy Tiis Uran," vK post, March 12, 2017. https://vk.com/wall-139431451_25, accessed December 13, 2017.

Schwab, Wendell. 2011. "Establishing an Islamic Niche in Kazakhstan: Musylman Publishing House and Its Publications." *Central Asian Survey* 30 (2): 227–242.

Schwab, Wendell. 2012. "Traditions and Texts: How Two Young Women Learned to Interpret the Qur'an and Hadiths in Kazakhstan." *Contemporary Islam* 6 (2): 173–197.

Schwab, Wendell. 2015. "Islam, Fun, and Social Capital in Kazakhstan." *Central Asian Affairs* 2 (1): 51–70.

Schwab, Wendell. 2016. "Visual Culture and Islam in Kazakhstan: The Case of Asyl Arna's Social Media." *Central Asian Affairs* 3 (4): 301–329.

Schwab, Wendell. 2019. "The Rhetoric of Islamic Debate in Kazakhstani Media." *Central Asian Affairs* (2–3): 166–188.

Talim TV. 2021. "Imam Bolmasang Da, Imandy Bol!" YouTube Video, 1:06:05, September 1, 2021, https://www.youtube.com/watch?v=uJoyXmdOnO8, accessed September 14, 2021.

Tazabek, Mukhamedzhan. N.d.a. "Aqyndyqtyng Islamdaghy Orny." Asyl Arna. http://www.asylarna.kz/maqala/maqalainfo/23, accessed August 4, 2017.

Tazabek, Mukhamedzhan. N.d.b. "Ult Bolyp Qalamyz Ba?' Degen Suraq Manyzdy." Asyl Arna. http://www.asylarna.kz/maqala/maqalainfo/42, accessed August 4, 2017.

Tazabek, Mukhamedzhan. 2015. "Bizding Kushimiz – Kelesim men Turaqtylyq." Egemen Qazaqstan, September 5. Originally at http://egemen.kz/2015/09/05/75154. Also found at http://www.elarna.com/koru_kk.php?id=494229&qolfon=jok, accessed August 4, 2017.

Tazabek, Mukhamedzhan. 2016a. Instagram post. August 16, 2016. http://www.instagram.com/p/BJL1SBNBns1/, accessed August 4, 2017.

Tazabek, Mukhamedzhan. 2016b. Instagram post, October 11, 2016. http://www.instagram.com/p/BLawGrEBS9V/, accessed August 4, 2017.

Tazabek, Mukhamedzhan. 2016c. vK post, October 1, 2016. http://vk.com/wall235948813_24065?reply=24090 accessed December 11, 2018.

Tazabek, Mukhamedzhan. 2016d. Instagram post, June 17, 2016. https://www.instagram.com/p/BGweUIoHpHv/, accessed August 4, 2017.

Tazabek, Mukhamedzhan. 2016e. Instagram post, August 17, 2016. https://www.instagram.com/p/BJORYMuhBfC/, accessed August 4, 2017.

Tazabek, Mukhamedzhan. 2016f. Instagram post, July 27, 2016. https://www.instagram.com/p/BIXfxEnh54v/, accessed August 4, 2017.

Tazabek, Mukhamedzhan. 2016g. Instagram post, October 13, 2016. https://www.instagram.com/p/BLgS_SiByvZ/, accessed August 4, 2017.

Tazabek, Mukhamedzhan. 2016h. Instagram post, July 12, 2016. https://www.instagram.com/p/BHxLkGMBb6A/, accessed August 4, 2017.

Tazabek, Mukhamedzhan. 2016i. Instagram post, October 3, 2016. https://www.instagram.com/p/BLFmFaKh_3t/, accessed August 4, 2017.

Tazabek, Mukhamedzhan. 2016j. Instagram post, May 16, 2016. https://www.instagram.com/p/BFems-6HpIX/, accessed August 4, 2017.

Tazabek, Mukhamedzhan. 2016k. Instagram post, November 15, 2016. https://www.instagram.com/p/BM18QAthWnR/, accessed August 4, 2017.

Tazabek, Mukhamedzhan. 2016l. Instagram post, December 8, 2016. https://www.instagram.com/p/BNwfVSkBRab/, accessed August 4, 2017.

Tazabek, Mukhamedzhan. 2016m. Instagram post, December 6, 2016. https://www.instagram.com/p/BNq3XF4BzbL/, accessed August 4, 2017.

Tazabek, Mukhamedzhan. 2017a. Instagram post, February 1, 2017. https://www.instagram.com/p/BP99hHWhKc-/, accessed August 4, 2017.

Tazabek, Mukhamedzhan. 2017b. Instagram post, January 3, 2017. https://www.instagram.com/p/BOyoOTNB1Mc/, accessed August 4, 2017.

Tazabek, Mukhamedzhan. 2017c. Instagram post, January 23, 2017. https://www.instagram.com/p/BPm_QZ_hYcB/, accessed August 4, 2017.

Tazabek, Mukhamedzhan. 2020a. Instagram post, December 6, 2020. https://www.instagram.com/p/CId_VNZlFQf/, accessed February 18, 2021.

Tazabek, Mukhamedzhan. 2020b. Instagram post, December 15, 2020. https://www.instagram.com/p/CIoFGb-nupc/, accessed February 18, 2021.

Tazabek, Mukhamedzhan. 2021a. Instagram post, January 30, 2021. https://www.instagram.com/p/CKqzjz2F2g4/, accessed February 18, 2021.

Tazabek, Mukhamedzhan. 2021b. Instagram post, January 31, 2021. https://www.instagram.com/p/CKtnJf4lSoM/, accessed February 18, 2021.

Ural'sk, Musylmane G. "Hidzhab Allanyng Buiryghy nemese Turkan Khanymnyng Zhazasy," vK post, October 15, 2017. https://vk.com/wall-59846424_2791, accessed December 13, 2017.

Zhanderbek, Zikiriya. 2015. "'Asyl Arna' Hem Sayat Ybyrai Zhyry." Abai.kz, October 15, 2015. http://abai.kz/post/41806, accessed August 4, 2017.

PART 3

Authority Embodied: Lives and Histories of Holy Persons and Lineages

ʿAbd al-Raḥmān Khalīfa and the Contest for Merv

A Sufi Shaykh's Authority among the Sarïq Turkmens in the 19th Century

William A. Wood

In the late summer of 1827, the Khivan ruler Allāh Qulī Khan received the disturbing news that the governor of his distant outpost in the Merv oasis had been murdered by rebellious Turkmens from the Sarïq tribe. As the Khivan khan's advisors deliberated how best to respond to this development, there appeared before them a delegation from Merv, led by a local religious notable whom Āgahī, the official court historian of the Qongrat rulers of Khiva, calls "Khalīfa ʿAbd al-Raḥmān Īshān."[1] This is the first mention in the historical record of this individual, a man who would play a significant political role among the Sarïq Turkmens of Merv for at least a quarter century, and whose sons continued to demonstrate some authority into the 1880s.

While occasional references have been made in the literature to the role of holy men among the Turkmen tribes, generally this has been either Tsarist imperialists seeing them as a threat,[2] or 20th century Soviet atheist propaganda viewing them as bastions of conservatism and backward thinking.[3] In this chapter I will examine one specific example of a Turkmen Sufi saint and his descendants from the 19th century in order to better understand the role

1 Āgahī, *Riyāż al-dawla*, f. 98b; cf. *Materialy po istorii turkmen i Turkmenii*, vol. II, *XVI–XIX vv. Iranskie, bukharskie i khivinskie istochniki*, edited by V.V. Struve, A.K. Borovkov, A.A. Romaskevich and P.P. Ivanov (Moscow-Leningrad: AN SSSR, 1938) [hereafter, *MITT*], p. 441.

2 See for example: F.A. Mikhailov, "Religioznye vozzreniia turkmen Zakaspiiskoi oblasti," in *Sbornik materialov po musul'manstvu*, vol. 2 (Tashkent, 1900), pp. 87–103.

3 See especially the publications of S.M. Demidov: *Turkmenskie ovliady* (Ashkhabad: Ylym, 1976); *Sufizm v Turkmenii (Evoliutsiia i perezhitki)* (Ashkhabad: Ylym, 1978); and *Legendy i pravda o "sviatykh" mestakh* (Ashkhabad: Ylym, 1988). In addition, see: [Sev], "Zametki o turkmenskom dukhovenstve," *Turkmenovedenie*, 1928 (no. 3–4), pp. 5–20; A.A. Rosliakov, "K voprosu o miuridizme u turkmen," *Izvestiia AN Turkmenskoi SSR*, 1952 (no. 5), pp. 21–25; V.N. Basilov, "Honour Groups in Traditional Turkmenian Society," in *Islam in Tribal Societies: From the Atlas to the Indus*, ed. Akbar S. Ahmed and David M. Hart (London: Routledge and Kegan Paul, 1984), pp. 220–243; M.B. Durdyev, "Dukhovenstvo v sisteme obshchestvennykh institutov turkmen kontsa XIX–nachala XX v.," *Vestnik Moskovskogo Universiteta: Istoriia*, 1970 (no. 4), pp. 27–42.

 | DOI:10.1163/9789004527096_007

these individuals played as the bearers of religious authority within their local society.[4]

1 ʿAbd al-Raḥmān Khalīfa

All that Āgahī tells us initially is that ʿAbd al-Raḥmān is "the deputy (*naib*) and successor (*khalīfa*) of the martyred Shaykh al-Islām," and that he is a recluse and man of prayer (*khalvat guzin va sajjada nishin bolub*) occupied with instructing students (*taliblar*) in the Merv region.[5] Concerning ʿAbd al-Raḥmān's spiritual lineage, the "martyred Shaykh al-Islām" is certainly a reference to the Naqshbandī *pīr* Ṣūfī Islām, who was also known as Islām Shaykh, a somewhat controversial and enigmatic figure who was active in Bukhara and Herat in the latter part of the 18th century, before dying in battle against the Shi'a Qajars.[6] Indeed, an Afghan envoy on his way to the court of Persia in 1837 refers to ʿAbd al-Raḥmān simply as Khalīfa Ṣūfī Islām.[7]

This connection of ʿAbd al-Raḥmān with Ṣūfī Islām is confirmed by the British officers James Abbott and Arthur Conolly, who passed through Merv on

4 I first discussed the role of ʿAbd al-Raḥmān (down to 1854) in the context of my larger work: cf. William A. Wood, "The Sariq Turkmens of Merv and the Khanate of Khiva in the Early Nineteenth Century" (PhD diss., Indiana University, 1998). There I extensively deal with the prominent place of religious notables, especially Sufis, in rural and nomadic societies (see esp. pp. 12–33). For further observations on Sufis as distinct examples of religious authority within Islam see: Gudrun Krämer and Sabine Schmidtke, "Introduction: Religious Authority and Religious Authorities in Muslim Societies. A Critical Overview," in *Speaking for Islam: Religious Authorities in Muslim Societies*, ed. Gudrun Krämer and Sabine Schmidtke (Leiden: Brill, 2006), pp. 9–10; Devin DeWeese, "Authority," in *Key Terms for the Study of Islam*, ed. Jamal J. Elias (Oxford: Oneworld, 2010), pp. 47–50; Orkhan Mir-Kasimov, "Introduction: Conflicting Synergy of Patterns of Religious Authority in Islam," in *Unity in Diversity: Mysticism, Messianism and the Construction of Religious Authority in Islam*, ed. Orkhan Mir-Kasimov (Leiden: Brill, 2014), pp. 6–7.

5 Āgahī, *Riyāż al-dawla*, f. 98b; cf. *MITT*, pp. 441–442. Note, however, that the translators badly garble this passage. They imply that ʿAbd al-Raḥmān is connected to the Shaykh al-Islām of Khiva, leaving out the critical information that he is the *khalifa* of the "martyred" (*shahid*) Shaykh al-Islām. Also, the *MITT* translators insert the word "murid," which nowhere appears in the text.

6 His shrine is located at Kurukh, near Herat. I dealt with Ṣūfī Islām in more detail in Wood, pp. 101–105. However, much more thorough information is now to be found in Christine Noelle-Karimi, *The Pearl in its Midst: Herat and the Mapping of Khurasan (15th–19th Centuries)* (Vienna: OAW, 2014), pp. 155–159.

7 Mahomed Hoosain Kashee, "Account of an Embassy to the King of Persia from the Ameer of Ka'bul in 1837–38," in George W. Forrest, ed., *Selections from the Travels and Journals Preserved in the Bombay Secretariat* (Bombay, 1906), p. 56.

separate occasions on their way from Herat to Khiva in 1840. Abbott, who dined with ʿAbd al-Raḥmān in January, 1840, notes that the other guests included the son of Islām Ṣūfī ("Sufi al-Islam"), who at that time had received refuge in Merv after fleeing from Khushk to escape the persecution of Muhammad Zeman Khan, the Jamshedi chief of that area. Abbott learned that Islām Ṣūfī, "a man of very extensive power in the spiritual world," had given the title of Khalīfa to ʿAbd al-Raḥmān's father, who had in turn passed it on to his son.[8] In November, 1840, Conolly also met with ʿAbd al-Raḥmān Khalīfa, whom he describes as "a very influential vicar of Soofee Islam's sect settled at Merv."[9]

A recently discovered hagiography of Ṣūfī Islām also makes brief mention of ʿAbd al-Raḥmān Khalīfa, called here "Marwazi." This is the *Vāqiʿāt-i Islāmī*, written by one of Ṣūfī Islām's sons named Mirza Junayd Allāh. This source states that "the noble Ḥażrat-i Khalīfa ʿAbd al-Raḥmān Marwazī was very generous (*karīm*) and forbearing (*ḥalīm*); he possessed [spiritual] states (*aḥwāl*)."[10]

Finally, a later Teke Turkmen poem, recorded by the Russian orientalist A.N. Samoilovich in 1906, also alludes to ʿAbd al-Raḥmān's ties to Ṣūfī Islām.[11] This poem, which describes the "evils" of the Sarïqs from a Teke perspective, includes a line calling upon the son of the "ishan" (i.e. ʿAbd al-Raḥmān) to leave Merv and, "drink your water from Karrukh." Samoilovich in his note to

8 James Abbott, *Narrative of a Journey from Heraut to Khiva, Moscow, and St. Petersburgh, During the Late Russian Invasion of Khiva; with some Account of the Court of Khiva and the Kingdom of Khaurism*, vol. 1 (London: W.H. Allen and Co., 1843), pp. 47–48. Note that according to one Persian source Ṣūfī Islām had 1,001 *khalīfas* (see Noelle-Karimi, *The Pearl in its Midst*, p. 155, note 97).

9 Arthur Conolly, "Part II: Extract from a letter from Captain A. Conolly, on a mission to Khiva, to the address of the Envoy and Minister, dated 26th December 1840," in *India Office Library* (hereafter *IOL*), V/27/69/3 [censored report], p. 1. Conolly's meeting with ʿAbd al-Raḥmān was motivated by a desire to obtain information about the fate of Colonel Stoddart in Bukhara. Conolly here states that the Khalīfa maintained valuable contacts with Bukhara, in particular with a son of Ṣūfī Islām named "Meerza Shibhee" (Mirza Shiblee?), who is said to have been much in favor with the Bukharan Amir. It is not clear whether this is the same individual who Abbott met, or another son.

10 A copy of this manuscript is now in the possession of Alan Godlas, who kindly provided me with this reference. The mention of ʿAbd al-Raḥmān is found on f. 21b. While the author of this hagiography was executed by Amir Naṣrallāh in 1259/1843–44, he does not appear to be the same individual mentioned by Conolly. See Noelle-Karimi, *The Pearl in its Midst*, p. 158, for information on two other sons of Ṣūfī Islām.

11 Samoilovich transcribed this and other Turkmen poems while in Yolotan in 1906. His manuscript of this text is preserved St. Petersburg, No. 13, ff. 27–28. The text, with a Russian translation, appears in: Abdu-s-Sattar kazy [ʿAbd al-Sattar Qazi], *Kniga rasskazov o bitvakh tekintsev: Turkmenskaia istoricheskaia poema XIX veka*, edited and translated by A.N. Samoilovich (St. Petersburg, 1914), pp. 105–108.

the published version of this text adds that, according to oral sources, the "Pir of Khalifa-ishan" had lived in this village near Herat.[12]

Several sources point to the influence of Ṣūfī Islām among the Turkmens and surrounding Sunni Muslims. For example, according to Hamid Algar, Ṣūfī Islām founded a distinctive branch of the Naqshbandī *ṭarīqat* based at Kurukh, which "extended a powerful influence across the border among the Hanafis of Khurasan."[13]

ʿAbd al-Raḥmān Khalīfa of Merv would appear to be an example of this influence. Unfortunately, our sources provide very little information concerning ʿAbd al-Raḥmān's teachings, his disciples (besides his sons – see below), or the extent of his following. Nor have I found additional references to any other individual Turkmen shaykhs who can be tied directly to Ṣūfī Islām. Lacking such evidence, we must for the time being postpone any firm conclusions regarding large-scale activity by the disciples of Ṣūfī Islām among the Turkmens. Instead, we will turn to other sources which describe some of the activities and personal characteristics of ʿAbd al-Raḥmān Khalīfa.

The Khivan historian Āgahī (mentioned above) is very sparing in his description of ʿAbd al-Raḥmān. This is not unusual for the type of court chronicle which Āgahī was composing, where one rarely encounters more than the most basic of biographical details concerning individuals outside the royal family. Fortunately for us, ʿAbd al-Raḥmān is virtually unique among inhabitants of the area at this time in that on several occasions he met with European travelers, who subsequently left written accounts describing the Khalīfa of Merv. These include, besides the above-mentioned James Abbott and Arthur Conolly, the missionary Joseph Wolff, the British officer Richmond Shakespear, the British diplomat W. Taylour Thomson, and others.

---

12 Abdu-s-Sattar kazy, p. 106 (note 1).

13 See Hamid Algar, "Religious Forces in Eighteenth- and Nineteenth-Century Iran," in *The Cambridge History of Iran*, vol. 7: *From Nadir Shah to the Islamic Republic*, ed. Peter Avery, Gavin Hambly and Charles Melville (Cambridge: Cambridge University Press, 1991), p. 730. Algar claims elsewhere that this "branch" is still active, with its main centers now at Kurukh, Badghis and Mazar-i Sharif (see his "Silent and Vocal *dhikr* in the Naqshbandī Order," in *Akten des VII. Kongresses für Arabistik und Islamwissenschaft*, ed. Albert Dietrich [Göttingen: Vandenhoeck & Ruprecht, 1976], p. 45). See also Hasan K. Kakar, *Government and Society in Afghanistan: The Reign of Amir ʿAbd al-Rahman Khan* (Austin: University of Texas Press, 1979), p. 152; and Asta Olesen, *Islam and Politics in Afghanistan* (Richmond, Surrey: Curzon Press, 1995), p. 48. The latter states that the followers of Ṣūfī Islām were, and still are, to be found among the Jamshidi, Taimuri, Firozkohi, Uzbeks, and Turkmens, as well as other Sunnis of Central Asia.

The first European reference to ʿAbd al-Raḥmān Khalīfa is from a most unusual and problematic source, the travel accounts of Joseph Wolff.[14] Wolff passed through Merv on two occasions, in 1832 and again in 1844, during his travels in Central Asia and on both trips he enjoyed the hospitality of the Khalīfa. In his memoirs, written after his return to England, he gives a good deal of descriptive information concerning his host. To be frank, the difficulty in using Wolff's accounts arises from his tendency to assume that he had the ability to describe in detail an individual's personality and character traits after only the briefest of visits. Despite this caveat, however, we must acknowledge that Wolff gives us a unique insight into the Khalīfa which is not found in the rather dry historical chronicles of Khiva and thus should not be overlooked as a source.

Wolff first arrived in Merv on February 16, 1832, while on a missionary journey to the Jews of Bukhara. While at Merv he met a certain Jewish mystic who lived there, named Joseph (Yusuf) of "Talkhtoon" (Talkhatan – see below). Wolff notes that this Jewish mystic was originally from Mashhad, but had withdrawn from the world and now "lives in a house with a Turkomaun Priest, (who has the title of Khaleefa of Talkhtoon) where he spends his time in reading the Bible in the Hebrew tongue, and in meditating on the works of God, and in prayer … in unison with the Mussulman Khaleefa, for higher light from above,"[15] as well as discussing the meaning of an un-named Persian manuscript on "Divine Love."[16] Wolff claims at this time that the Khalīfa preached against the system of plundering caravans and refused to accept the usual vow promised after a successful raid (but see below).[17] According to Wolff, the Khalīfa

---

14 For more on Wolff see Wood, pp. 36–37 (and references).

15 Joseph Wolff, *Researches and Missionary Labours Among the Jews, Mohammedans, and Other Sects, during his travels between the years 1831 and 1834*, First American Edition (Philadelphia: Orrin Rogers, 1837), p. 113; and Joseph Wolff, *Travels and Adventures of the Rev. Joseph Wolff*, 2 vols. (London: Saunders, Otley, and Co., 1860–61), vol. 1, p. 528. Wolff is here reporting information which he received while at Sarakhs, but he later confirms this for himself in person at Merv. Elsewhere Wolff comments that the Jews at Merv, who are from Herat or Mashhad, "are great favourites with the Khaleefa." See Joseph Wolff, *Narrative of a Mission to Bokhara in the years 1843–1845, to ascertain the fate of Colonel Stoddart and Captain Conolly*, 2 vols. (London: J.W. Parker, 1845), vol. 1, p. 274; and p. 281, where Wolff states that Jews who had been forced to become Muslims elsewhere are allowed to return to their former practices at Merv. For more on the Jewish community at Merv see Wolff, *Researches*, p. 124–126; *Narrative*, vol. 2, p. 154; and *Travels*, vol. 1, pp. 519–520; Albert Kaganovich, *The Mashhadi Jews (Djedids) in Central Asia* (Halle: ANOR 14, 2007) *passim*.

16 Wolff, *Researches…*, p. 123.

17 Ibid., p. 114. I assume by "vow" that Wolff means tribute offerings.

accompanied him as far as the Bukharan frontier town of Charjuy to insure his safe travel.[18]

We see several activities here which connect ʿAbd al-Raḥmān Khalīfa with some of the common roles of Muslim saints in tribal societies. Wolff points out his obvious literacy, including a knowledge of Persian, as well as alluding to what must have been an uncommon intellectual breadth for his time and place due to his interactions with the Jewish mystic. Further, we see the role of ʿAbd al-Raḥmān's *baraka* in ensuring safe passage for Wolff, as well as other caravan travel in the region, though his role in the common Turkmen practice of raiding caravans is somewhat unclear at this point. Perhaps most interesting is Wolff's reference to ʿAbd al-Raḥmān as the Khalīfa of Talkhatan, the only place in any source that I have found which connects ʿAbd al-Raḥmān with a specific locality in Merv, and which happens to be a well-known shrine.

The shrine of Talkhatan-baba, also known apparently as Taliqan-baba, dates from the eleventh or twelfth centuries.[19] It is located approximately 40 kilometers south of the modern city of Mary and 13 kilometers northwest of Yolotan, near the main road connecting the two cities.[20] While it is tempting to speculate that ʿAbd al-Raḥmān Khalīfa was in some way connected to this shrine, perhaps even as the shrine's keeper, at this point we lack the hard evidence to prove this. It would certainly, however, be in keeping with his role as a religious notable in a tribal area for him to draw part of his influence from administering an established shrine, and would also help explain some enigmatic references in other sources to his offering sanctuary in his "house" to political refugees. That Talkhatan-baba was particularly important to the Sarïqs is shown by

18 See Wolff, *Travels…*, vol. 1, p. 532. Note that Wolff does not mention this fact in his earlier work (see his *Researches*, p. 126, where he lists those who accompanied him from Merv to Charjuy; no mention is made here of ʿAbd al-Raḥmān).

19 While consistently referred to as Talkhatan-baba by Russian and later Turkmen sources, this shrine is almost certainly the same which Āgahī calls the "*mazār* of Shaykh Aḥmad Ṭāliqānī" (see *Riyāż al-dawla*, f. 212b), or, elsewhere, "Ṭāliqān-bābā" (see *Zubdat al-tavārīkh*, f. 398b). For the location of Ṭāliqān in northern Afghanistan, see W. Barthold, *An Historical Geography of Iran*, translated by Svat Soucek (Princeton: Princeton University Press, 1984), p. 24 (but also pp. 35 and 37, "Talaqan," along the Murghab but apparently another location). For the shrine itself, see V.A. Zhukovskii, *Drevnosti Zakaspiiskogo kraia: Razvaliny starogo Merva* (St. Petersburg, 1894), p. 190; A.M. Pribytkova, "Mavzolei Talkhatan-baba," *Soobshcheniia instituta istorii i teorii arkhitektury*, 8(1947), pp. 25–34; as well as the same author's *Pamiatniki arkhitektury XI veka v Turkmenii* (Moscow: Gos. izdat. literatury po stroitel'stvu i arkhitekture, 1955), pp. 77–110; G.A. Pugachenkova, *Puti razvitiia arkhitektury iuzhnogo Turkmenistana pory rabovladeniia i feodalizma* (Moscow: AN SSSR, 1958), pp. 248–256.

20 I visited this shrine in 1994 while traveling north from Yolotan and found the site well marked and in good repair at the time.

Alikhanov's reference to the site as late as the 1880's as "a sacred place of the Sarïqs – the tomb of Talkhatan-baba."[21]

The complex at Talkhatan-baba included not only a shrine, but also a mosque and a madrassa. This is interesting in light of the fact that a Persian engineer, who passed through the Merv oasis sometime before 1850, mentioned both a "palace" and a "mosque of the Khalīfa ʿAbd al-Raḥmān," not far from the Khivan fortress at Merv.[22] No other sources mention any such buildings with ʿAbd al-Raḥmān's name attached to them, and indeed, it would be unusual for a Turkmen to construct such edifices. However, it may be that at the time of the Persian engineer's visit, the Khalīfa's name had come to be associated with older structures in the oasis, perhaps even those at Talkhatan-baba.[23] Again, we must acknowledge that this is only speculation at this point, but it is certainly quite possible that ʿAbd al-Raḥmān had come to be associated with this shrine.

Wolff elsewhere makes mention of the Khalīfa's sons maintaining a school at Merv in which they instruct the children in Arabic and Persian languages.[24] The Turkmens are said to claim that a school has been kept at Merv since the time of Niẓām al-Mulk (i.e., the eleventh century). Since Wolff is unclear as to the location or the exact ages of the students involved in this school, it is impossible to say for certain if he is referring to a madrassa or a maktab (primary school). Still, the role of ʿAbd al-Raḥmān Khalīfa in providing education

---

21 [M.] Alikhanov, *Mervskii oazis i dorogi, vedushchie k nemu* (St. Petersburg, 1883), p. 95.

22 See [L.] Sédillot, "Notice sur une carte routière de Meschhed à Bokhara et de Bokhara à Balkh, suivie d'un plan de Bokhara et de ses environs, par un ingénieur persan, d'après la traduction de M. Garcin de Tasssy," *Bulletin de la société de géographie*, 4(1854), p. 225. See also Zhukovskii's comments on this publication (pp. 98–99), where he mentions that the original map was now lost. Zhukovskii was also at a loss to identify the locations of ʿAbd al-Raḥmān's palace and mosque.

23 In fact, Talkhatan-baba is a relatively short distance to the west of the fort which the Persian engineer describes, that of Niyāz Muḥammad Bāy, first begun in 1832. The Persian engineer, as cited in the article by Sédillot, calls this fort "the new Merv of Muhammad Hurkandji" (i.e. Muḥammad Urgenchī). While this name is not found in other sources, it is almost certainly a reference to Niyāz Muḥammad's fort.

24 Wolff, *Narrative...*, vol. 1, p. 280. ʿAbd al-Raḥmān Khalīfa had at least two sons, one named Raḥmān Berdī and a second named Jumʿa Īshān. Both will be discussed later in this article, but note that while the former appears in numerous sources, especially Āgahī, I have only found the latter's name in British sources from the 1880s (see below). Abbott would report dining with two of the Khalīfa's sons, stating that the eldest was about 22-years-old at that time (1840), but provides no names. [At one point Wolff (*Narrative...*, vol. 1, p. 271) refers to the Khalīfa's eldest son as "Kereem Werde," but this appears to be an error on his part. Cf. the appendix to the same volume, written by Wolff's companion Abdul Wahab Mirza, where it states that ʿAbd al-Raḥmān's eldest son was named Raḥmān Berdī (see vol. 2, p. 305; and Wolff's own statement in vol. 2, p. 156).]

for the local population is clearly seen, which is in keeping with his saintly duties. Whether this schooling is connected with Talkhatan-baba is, however, impossible to say at this point.[25]

Wolff provides considerably more information on ʿAbd al-Raḥmān Khalīfa after his second visit in 1844.[26] At that time Wolff was traveling en route to Bukhara to ascertain the fate of two British officers who had been interned there by the Bukharan amir, Captain Arthur Conolly and Colonel Charles Stoddart.[27] In offering himself for this mission, Wolff had publicly expressed confidence in his ability to successfully carry out such a venture with the help of his "Turcoman friends in the desert of Khiva, and one of the Dervishes," no doubt a reference to ʿAbd al-Raḥmān.[28] He found Merv in a state of turmoil following the recent murder of the Khivan governor by the Sarïqs, an act for which the locals fully expected Khivan revenge at any moment. Concerning his arrival at Merv Wolff writes that the Khalīfa came from his tent with bread and sherbet and asked for a blessing from Wolff. He then hosted Wolff in his tent until another could be prepared for him.[29]

Wolff describes the influence of ʿAbd al-Raḥmān Khalīfa in lavish terms. He states that this

> … friend in the desert of Merw, in the kingdom of Khiva, whose autograph Wolff considers an ornament to his Bible, whose name is Abd-Arrahman, which means, slave of the merciful God, because his mother said, on the day of his birth, 'Thou shalt be a slave of the most merciful God all the days of thy life,' has also a royal title. He is called Shahe-Addaalat, 'King of Righteousness'.… And when he makes peace between kings, he bears the title Shahe-Soolkh, i.e. 'King of Peace.'[30]

25 See Pugachenkova, *Puti*, p. 474, for a late 19th century madrassa belonging to the Sarïqs at Talkhatan-baba.

26 Including a drawing of ʿAbd al-Raḥmān, which is found in Wolff, *Narrative*…, vol. I, facing p. 270.

27 The fate of Conolly and Stoddart has been the subject of much scholarly interest. See, for example, M.E. Yapp, *Strategies of British India: Britain, Iran and Afghanistan, 1798–1850* (Oxford: Oxford University Press, 1980), pp. 401–413.

28 This comment was made by Wolff in a letter published in a newspaper in July, 1841, under the title, "Proposal for the Liberation of Colonel Stoddart and Captain Conolly." For the complete contents of this letter see, Captain [John] Grover, *The Bokhara Victims*, Second edition (London: Chapman and Hall, 1845), pp. 66–67.

29 Wolff, *Travels*, vol. II, p. 377; and Wolff, *Narrative*, vol. I, p. 268.

30 Wolff, *Travels*…, vol. I, p. 484–485.

Elsewhere, Wolff claims that the Turkmens are so unruly, no caravan would dare cross the deserts near Merv

> … if there was not one man in that desert who knew how to restrain the Turkomauns. This man is the great derveesh, who has the title of Khaleefa, or successor of the Prophet, and is addressed by the royal epithet of Hasrat, i.e. Majesty, and to whom are paid all the honours due to royalty by the Turkomauns. His blessing they invoke previous to their going on any expedition, and to him they give the tenth of all their spoil. He receives all the caravans under his protection, and shows hospitality to all the wanderers. His blessing is the most ardent desire of the Turkomauns, and his curse their deepest dread. He inculcates among them the rites of hospitality.… Even the Kings of Bokhara, Khiva, Khotan, and Khokand, and even the Governor of Yarkand in Chinese Tartary, send him presents, and give him the title of King.… This is the man sent by Providence to keep the Turkomauns in order to a certain degree.[31]

In a letter sent from Merv to Captain Grover, Wolff described ʿAbd al-Raḥmān as the spiritual guide of all the Turkmens, and even of the above mentioned rulers, adding those of Tashkent and Shahrisabz as well for good measure.[32]

Wolff is no less complimentary in his estimation of ʿAbd al-Raḥmān's personal qualities. He describes him as a "venerable old Turkmen, worthy of his office; a man without many words, without covetousness, given to prayer, and a friend of hospitality."[33] Wolff does concede, with some regret, that ʿAbd al-Raḥmān does nothing to prevent the Turkmens' slave-raiding in Iran (though note his statements to the contrary cited above). In fact, the Khalīfa himself, according to Wolff, "encourages them to fight and spoil the Sheea, which he tells them is more acceptable to God than the performance of pilgrimages to Mecca or to Masaur, near Balkh, where ʿAli's camel ascended to heaven."[34] Still, the missionary has ʿAbd al-Raḥmān repent somewhat, quoting him as saying:

---

31 Wolff, *Narrative…*, vol. 1, pp. 270–271.

32 Ibid., p. 277.

33 Ibid., p. 268.

34 Wolff, *Narrative*, vol. 1, p. 271. "Masaur" (or "Mazaur," as Wolff sometimes writes) is a reference to Mazar-i-Sharif and the ʿAlid shrine there. Wolff himself visited this shrine in 1832, when traveling from Bukhara to Afghanistan. See his description in his *Researches*, pp. 149–150, which includes his version of the camel miracle. See R.D. McChesney, *Waqf in Central Asia: Four Hundred Years in the History of a Muslim Shrine, 1480–1889* (Princeton: Princeton University Press, 1991), especially pp. 33–34, for some insightful comments on the persistent veneration of ʿAli (along with the rest of Muhammad's family) among the Sunni population of Central Asia.

"God rewards integrity. The English are a people of integrity, and therefore God rewards their integrity. We Turkomauns are thieves, and therefore God is displeased with us."[35]

Thus, to summarize Wolff's description of ʿAbd al-Raḥmān Khalīfa, we see the Turkmen holy man functioning as a key figure in the conduct of trade through the region, offering protection to caravans which seek his aide and, at least by implication, threatening dire consequences to those which ignore his good offices. The Khalīfa would certainly have been paid for this service in the form of donations from the travelers. In addition, we see examples of ʿAbd al-Raḥmān's *baraka* being expended in the form of blessings to those Turkmens setting out on raids, for which he was perhaps paid in advance but certainly at the conclusion of successful forays. Finally, Wolff again emphasizes the Khalīfa's ties with neighboring sedentary powers and his ability to exert influence across a broad spectrum of Central Asian society, not just within the Merv oasis. Wolff's description of the Khalīfa's personality as rather reserved is also in keeping with a standard view of those religious notables who preferred quiet contemplation over political involvement, but who found themselves drawn into the profane world by their responsibilities to their communities. Indeed, even allowing for some exaggeration on the part of this European missionary, ʿAbd al-Raḥmān appears to be a classic example of a rural religious notable possessing the *baraka* which allowed, or perhaps even compelled, him to mediate between his community and outsiders, as well as between his followers and God.

Between Wolff's first visit to Merv in 1832 and his second in 1844, several other Europeans had occasion to deal with ʿAbd al-Raḥmān and they all appeared to regard him in a similar, positive, light. As noted above, Abbott was his guest in January of 1840, and engaged the Khalīfa in conversation concerning the political situation in Central Asia at that time from the British perspective. During his visit, Abbott presented to the Khalīfa, whom he calls "a priest of great reputation," a Book of Prayers in Arabic from the British envoy at Herat, Major Todd, with whom ʿAbd al-Raḥmān had enjoyed some friendly contact.[36] On another occasion Sir John Login, the surgeon to the British Mission, gave a New Testament in Turki to the Khalīfa, whom he describes as "a man of considerable sanctity among the Turcomans," when the latter

35 Wolff, *Narrative*, vol. II, p. 151.

36 Abbott, p. 42. Wolff reports that one of ʿAbd al-Raḥmān's sons knew Major Todd well. See his, *Narrative*..., vol. I, p. 268. [This is apparently Raḥmān Berdī – see below.]

visited Herat.[37] In these contacts we see both the Khalīfa's role as a collector and disseminator of information from the outside world, including in this case Europe, as well as perhaps further evidence of his intellectual breadth via his interest in and interactions with Christian sacred texts.[38]

Yet another Englishmen, Lieutenant (later Sir) Richmond Shakespear, when passing through Merv en route to Khiva in May 1840, called on the Khalīfa, whom he describes as:

> another greybeard, but a very different character [from the Khivan governor]; he received me like a patriarch. This old gentlemen has very great influence with all Turcomans, by whom he is much respected and trusted; he is considered almost a saint; and the Turcomans are only too glad to make him the distributor of their charitable donations. I believe he is well worthy of the trust, though they say that some of his *attaches* eat an unconscionable share of the poor-rates. The Khuleefa is a very small man, of very quiet and retiring manners – a *rara avis* – a bashful Turcoman. His face is pleasing, notwithstanding the loss of the bridge of his nose, which was caused by frost.[39]

Much of Shakepsear's opinion was echoed by Arthur Conolly, who, as mentioned previously, also had occasion to meet with ʿAbd al-Raḥmān during his travels through Merv in November, 1840. Conolly, who refers to the Khalīfa as "apparently our friend," states that he sent ʿAbd al-Raḥmān 20 ducats in exchange for his assistance in obtaining information from Bukhara, asking only that the Khalīfa distribute these funds as charity. Conolly continues by stating that:

---

37 See the footnote by Sir John Login, in J.P. Ferrier, *Caravan Journeys and Wanderings in Persia, Afghanistan, Turkistan, and Beloochistan; with Historical Notices of the Countries Lying Between Russian and India*, trans. by William Jesse (London: J. Murray, 1857), p. 185; Wolff mentions that on one occasion, ʿAbd al-Raḥmān threatened to leave Merv and settle at Herat if some recalcitrant Turkmens did not obey his wishes. See Wolff, *Narrative…*, vol. II, p. 148. These references to Herat may be connected with ʿAbd al-Raḥmān's ties to the *khānaqāh* of Ṣūfī Islām at Kurukh.

38 Granted, we cannot know if ʿAbd al-Raḥmān actually read any of the Christian materials given to him, but considering his interactions with the Jewish mystic mentioned by Wolff, it seems likely that he was indeed genuinely interested in the spiritual experiences of other religious traditions.

39 Sir Richmond Shakespear, "A Personal Narrative of a Journey from Heraut to Ourenbourg, on the Caspian, in 1840," *Blackwood's Edinburgh Magazine*, 51(1842), p. 697.

> Afterwards, calling upon this person, I took an opportunity of carefully explaining to him our policy towards the Persians, Afghans, and Usbegs, and requested that, when he next wrote to Meerza Shibhee, he would mention his having seen the English envoy going to Khiva, and ascertained from him that the views of the British Government were only preservative and friendly, with any other remark that he thought might induce the Ameer to repent of his unwise conduct. The Khalifah promised that he would do so.[40]

Again, we see ʿAbd al-Raḥmān's role in the political realm emphasized, as well as Shakespear's description of him, in keeping with Wolff, as a model of the retiring saint. But we also in these accounts see his activity as the supporter of the poor. Shakespear and Conolly, who by this time had gained considerable experience in the Muslim world, clearly understood the Khalīfa's traditional role as a religious notable in the redistribution of wealth among the less fortunate members of his community, and therefore Conolly's stipulation that his donation be used to help the poor. This responsibility as distributor of charity within his community both gave the Khalīfa control over considerable wealth, as well as additional influence stemming from the fact that a portion of his community was beholden to him for their well-being.

As a final European observer, we have the account of William Taylour Thomson, secretary to the British Legation in Persia, which supports the descriptions left by earlier English travelers. In 1842, Thomson traveled from Persia to Khiva in the company of a Persian envoy to the Khivan khan, and a Khivan ambassador who was returning home.[41] En route they passed through Merv, where Thomson met ʿAbd al-Raḥmān and about whom he gives the following description:

> Among so barbarous a race it is gratifying to find that there is one individual in whom interest can be felt – this is a Toorkoman Moola, who is known by the title of the Caliph. He is a man of mild disposition,

40 Conolly, *IOL*, pt. II, p. 1. Wolff, *Narrative…*, vol. 1, p. 268, mentions that Conolly had visited ʿAbd al-Raḥmān, apparently obtaining the information from the Khalīfa himself. The published extracts of Conolly's manuscript notes do not mention ʿAbd al-Raḥmān. See "The Country between Bamian and Khiva," *Calcutta Review*, 15 (1851), pp. 1–35.

41 The Qajar envoy has left an account as well; see Muḥammad ʿAlī Khān Ghafūr, *Rūznāma-yi safar-i Khwārazm* (Tehran: Vizārat-i Umūr-i Khārija, 1373/1994). See also Christine Noelle-Karimi, "On the Edge: Eastern Khurasan in the Perception of Qajar Officials," *Eurasian Studies* 14 (2016): 135–177, and Jeff Eden, *Slavery and Empire in Central Asia* (Cambridge: Cambridge University Press, 2018), pp. 40–47.

> respected by the chiefs of the neighbouring principalities; and although active in repressing to the best of his ability the system of kidnapping and traffic in slaves, practised by the people of his tribe, has maintained a degree of influence over them amounting to veneration. On paying him a visit I was much pleased with the gentleness and courtesy of his manners ...[42]

Yet another traveler's example of ʿAbd al-Raḥmān Khalīfa's influence is provided by the Afghan envoy mentioned previously.[43] This individual came to Merv in the company of a Bukharan ambassador in the fall of 1836. Upon arriving at the oasis, the Khivan governor Niyāz Muḥammad Bāy refused to allow the Bukharan envoy to proceed until he received instructions from Allāh Qulī Khan in Khiva. When the Bukharan learned of this decision, he went immediately to ʿAbd al-Rahman to sue for his good offices. The Khalīfa in turn went to Niyāz Muḥammad and, pointing out the recent good relations between Bukhara and Khiva, asked that the governor allow the ambassador to continue on his way to Persia. Niyāz Muḥammad reportedly replied, "who will be answerable to Allāh [Qulī] Khan when he asks me?" ʿAbd al-Raḥmān said that he would be responsible to the khan, and with this assurance, the Khivan governor gave the envoy his permission to proceed. We see in this event both the influence of ʿAbd al-Raḥmān with the Khivan governor and with the Khivan khan himself, as well as the awareness by outsiders such as the Bukharan envoy that the Turkmen Khalīfa wielded considerable authority at Merv.

What are we to make of these traveler's descriptions of ʿAbd al-Raḥmān? First, we must acknowledge that none of the sources of these accounts spent more than a few days at Merv. Their descriptions, therefore, of ʿAbd al-Raḥmān, are often very impressionistic. Secondly, while our European travelers appear to be of like mind in their positive estimation of the Khalīfa, note that they are viewing him as bearing the qualities of a holy man *as they understand them*. In other words, something about ʿAbd al-Raḥmān's personality "fit" with what these Europeans thought a spiritual leader should be like. However, this does not tell us if the Turkmen Khalīfa's Muslim peers saw him in the same manner.[44]

---

42 [W.T. Thomson] in Lady Sheil, *Glimpses of Life and Manners in Persia* (London: John Murray, 1856), Note (F.), "Khiva," p. 361.

43 The following event is described in Mahomed Hoosain Kashee, p. 56.

44 See Ernest Gellner, *Muslim Society* (Cambridge: Cambridge University Press, 1981), pp. 40–41, for insightful comments on the differences between Christian and Muslim notions of sanctity.

These reservations being duly noted, however, it is still evident from both these and indigenous sources that ʿAbd al-Raḥmān was a man of considerable distinction among the Merv Turkmens, a position which he derived primarily from his recognized spiritual authority. This places the Khalīfa in the traditional role of a religious notable in rural society and also contrasts him with the other common route to leadership among the Turkmens, namely success in leading raiding parties. While the latter type of leader would certainly continue to play a key role at Merv, ʿAbd al-Raḥmān Khalīfa serves as an example of the Muslim saint who skillfully employs his possession of *baraka* to guide his own community, as well as to influence the politics of the world in which he lives. Thus, recalling the events of 1827 and the initial Sarïq uprising at Merv, we can see just how significant the appearance of ʿAbd al-Raḥmān at the Khivan court was for the Khivan khan, and how important it would become for the Khivan authorities to cultivate and maintain a close relationship with ʿAbd al-Raḥmān, making him their key ally among the Sarïqs for the next twenty years.

That ʿAbd al-Raḥmān demonstrated a close relationship with the Khivan authorities from 1827 until the mid-1840's is seen in my earlier work, though as noted there it comes as no surprise that the Khivan sources often downplay or overlook his role.[45] His importance received broader notice during Persia's attack on Herat in 1837–1838 due to the assistance given to Kāmrān Shah of Herat by the Turkmens and the Khivan ruler Allāh Qulī Khan. The Afghan and Qajar sources repeatedly point to the central role of ʿAbd al-Raḥmān as the leader of the Turkmens who came to Herat's aid early on in this crisis.[46] One source observes that his success in raising troops to aid Herat was because "he was considered so holy that the dust from his feet was believed to heal all ailments."[47] While Āgahī notes the presence of ʿAbd al-Raḥmān in the Khivan army later dispatched to assist Herat, he is mentioned only in passing, along with several other leading people of Merv.[48] Again it is important to note that, in the view of outsiders, in this case Afghans, ʿAbd al-Raḥmān Khalīfa was

---

45 Wood, pp. 119–124 and 156 (note 66).

46 See Wood, pp. 158–160; Noelle-Karimi, *The Pearl in its Midst*, pp. 159–161; Faiz Muhammad Katib, *Siraj al-Tawarikh*, vol. 1, (Kabul, 1913), pp. 132–134 (see McChesney/Khorrami, vol. 1 [2013], pp. 221–222); and Jonathan E. Lee, *The 'Ancient Supremacy': Bukhara, Afghanistan and the Battle for Balkh, 1731–1901*, (Leiden: Brill, 1996), pp. 149–154. Āgahī makes no mention of this initial support for Herat from the Merv Turkmens in the fall of 1837, i.e. before the arrival of forces from Khiva in 1838.

47 Lisān al-Mulk, as cited in Noelle-Karimi, *The Pearl in its Midst*, p. 160. This is the only reference I have found to the miraculous healing power of ʿAbd al-Raḥmān, a common quality of religious notables in the Islamic world.

48 Āgahī, *Riyāż al-dawla*, f. 212a. See Wood, pp. 161–163.

the most influential Turkmen at Merv, despite Āgahī's tendency to downplay his role.

While serving as a key supporter of Khivan rule in Merv, ʿAbd al-Raḥmān was significantly unable to prevent the murder of the Khivan governor Niyāz Muḥammad Bāy in 1843 by Sarïq Turkmens seeking to assert their independence from Khivan authority.[49] A most interesting version of these events, one which highlights the role of ʿAbd al-Raḥmān Khalīfa, was recorded by Joseph Wolff during his travels through Merv in April, 1844, less than a year after the Sarïq uprising.[50] Wolff states that the Turkmens had conspired against Niyāz Muḥammad Bāy and killed him, along with several hundred other Khivans. However, about 300 Khivan troops escaped and took refuge "in the house" of ʿAbd al-Raḥmān Khalīfa.[51] When the Turkmens rushed to this location and demanded that the Khalīfa hand over the Khivans, ʿAbd al-Raḥmān boldly confronted them and said, "First you must put to death your [Khalīfa], and then those unfortunate men who took refuge under my roof." Furious, the Turkmens withdrew, and during the night ʿAbd al-Raḥmān escorted the remaining Khivans away from the oasis of Merv until they were safe from being pursued by the Turkmens.

Wolff's version of events would appear to support the image of ʿAbd al-Raḥmān Khalīfa as generally favoring good relations with Khiva at this time. We have already noted ʿAbd al-Raḥmān's pro-Khiva stance as exhibited in 1827, as well as the good relations that he seems to have enjoyed with the Khivan governor Niyāz Muḥammad Bāy throughout the 1830's. It should not surprise us, therefore, that he tried to intervene on the behalf of the Khivan garrison in 1843. The Khalīfa had determined for some time that a friendly relationship with the Khivan Khanate offered greater benefits than drawbacks for the Sarïqs, and thus was a strong advocate of maintaining these cordial ties. In addition, as was common with Sufi elites and other religious notables elsewhere, it is likely that ʿAbd al-Raḥmān preferred social order over disorder (as

49 I deal with this extensively in my dissertation; cf. Wood, pp. 184–193. I note there that Khivan sources highlight the role of Bukhara in instigating this rebellion. For Qajar views, see Noelle-Karimi, *The Pearl in its Midst*, pp. 273–274.

50 See Wolff, *Narrative*, vol. 1, p. 272. Wolff would be the last European to visit Merv until Edmund O'Donovan, almost forty years later. Thus his importance as a source, though, as noted previously, his narrative can be somewhat problematic.

51 It is not clear what "in the house" here refers to: perhaps to the shrine at Talkhatan-baba (?). Compare the role of religious edifices such as shrines and Sufi *zāwīyas* as *ḥaram* (sacred) space, and thus politically neutral zones where sanctuary could be sought, in North Africa. See Julia Clancy-Smith, *Rebel and Saint: Muslim Notables, Populist Protest, Colonial Encounters (Algeria and Tunisia, 1800–1904)* (Berkeley: University of California Press, 1994), pp. 137 and 142–145.

long as the shari'a was upheld). In general, the ideal of saintliness included the avoidance of violent confrontations, and this may in part explain 'Abd al-Raḥmān's opposition to the events in Merv in 1843.

However, 'Abd al-Raḥmān's inability to prevent the Turkmen uprising against Khivan rule also demonstrates the limitations which religious notables contend with within their own communities. While very influential, they are generally speaking unable to reverse a course of action, especially rebellion, once the vast majority of the population has determined that such action is desirable. Indeed, as Clancy-Smith has argued, since one of the "social indicators of sainthood" was collective recognition of piety expressed in the form of popular followings, saintly leaders such as 'Abd al-Raḥmān Khalīfa had to be responsive to the demands and needs of their clienteles.[52] In the case of 'Abd al-Raḥmān, once the bulk of his Turkmen followers had determined that Khivan rule was too oppressive to be further tolerated, he was under tremendous pressure, even obligation, to join them in rebellion, or else risk losing his position of authority and influence at Merv. Thus, as we shall see from Āgahī's later accounts, 'Abd al-Raḥmān would indeed assume a position of leadership among the rebel Sarïqs, despite his initial reticence and even direct opposition to the overthrow of the Khivan governor.

For several years, from 1843–1849, the Khalīfa tried to balance Khivan and Bukharan interests in Merv, while avoiding conflict with both, all the while maintaining a level of autonomy for the Sarïqs of Merv.[53] According to Wolff, during this time 'Abd al-Raḥmān's protection was essential for all caravans traveling through the region, thus pointing out the commercial role of this Turkmen saint.[54] Wolff also indicates that the Khalīfa, as with rural religious notables elsewhere, maintained a network of contacts with outsiders, particularly within nearby urban centers.[55] The Khalīfa's ability to assist Wolff in his stated goal of reaching Bukhara was made possible by his established contacts in this city.[56] 'Abd al-Raḥmān also took advantage of Merv's location on a major trade route to maintain contacts with areas further afield. An example,

52 Clancy-Smith, pp. 3 and 109.

53 See Wood, pp. 193–219 for more details. Bukhara had exercised authority in Merv from 1785 to 1822, and thus remained an alternative source of support for Turkmens there.

54 See Wolff, *Narrative*, vol. I, pp. 270–271. See also Wood, pp. 200–202 for 'Abd al-Raḥmān's role in protecting a caravan, including Qajar and Bukharan envoys, that Wolff joined on his return journey through Merv.

55 Especially Herat; see Wolff, *Narrative*, vol. I, p. 268. Later we will see 'Abd al-Raḥmān's ties to Mashhad.

56 Ibid., vol. I, pp. 268, 271, 274, 277; and vol. II, p. 35, where Wolff claims that the Khalīfa is the only one in the region able to safely forward letters to Bukhara.

which Wolff witnessed during his brief sojourn, was the visit of a group of Sufis from Yarkand at the Khalīfa's residence.[57] Visitors such as these allowed the Khalīfa to obtain information from, and interact with, the much larger Islamic world.

After several years of experiencing annual campaigns against them from Khiva, often led by the new Khivan ruler Muḥammad Amīn Khan (r. 1846–1855), in 1848 the rebel Sarïqs finally indicated a willingness to negotiate, sending none other than the son of ʿAbd al-Raḥmān Khalīfa to the Khivan camp to request the return of prisoners.[58] According to Āgahī, the Khivan khan received this offspring of the famous Sarïq holy man with honor, granting him and his companions gold daggers and robes, and releasing some Sarïq prisoners to his care. Muḥammad Amīn Khan then designated Ata Naẓar, one of the *mutawallīs* of the tomb of Pahlavān Maḥmud, as his representative and sent him along with the Sarïq envoys to the rebel fort.[59] However, according to Āgahī, not only was the khan's request for submission refused; the *mutawallī* was detained for 24 hours and treated very roughly by the inhabitants of the fort, before being sent back to the Khivan camp.

It is not inconceivable, based on Āgahī's account, that ʿAbd al-Raḥmān Khalīfa was acting on his own, or at least a minority's, initiative in sending his son to the Khivan camp, to judge from the response which the majority of the Sarïqs in the fort gave to the Khivan demands.[60] It would, of course,

57 Ibid., vol. I, p. 272. Wolff states that this group of "dancing dervishes" stripped themselves and danced about until they sank to the ground. One of the Khalīfa's sons also stripped and danced with them. Another example of these types of contacts is reported by Wolff on his return journey through Merv, when he states that the Khalīfa recommended to his care a pilgrim from Qoqand bound for Mecca (see ibid., vol. II, p. 152).

58 Āgahī, *Jāmiʿ al-vāqiʿāt-i sulṭānī*, f. 476b. This is the first mention of ʿAbd al-Raḥmān Khalīfa in Āgahī's accounts since well before the death of Niyāz Muḥammad Bāy. It is unclear what the Khalīfa's role had been to this point but, despite the fact that Āgahī refers to him here as a rebel leader, it is quite likely that he had up to this time been reluctant to identify himself with those Sarïqs opposed to Khivan rule. Āgahī does not mention which of ʿAbd al-Raḥmān's sons is referred to here, but it is most likely his eldest, Raḥmān Berdī.

59 This was the principal shrine of Khiva, the tomb of the "patron saint" of the city. It is surely significant that this individual, the keeper of the most sacred shrine in the city of Khiva, was chosen by the khan to negotiate with the Sarïqs and their own holy-man, ʿAbd al-Raḥmān. On the veneration of this saint in Khorezm see G.P. Snesarev, *Khorezmskie legendy kak istochnik po istorii religioznykh kul'tov Srednei Azii* (Moscow: Nauka, 1983), pp. 169–185. On the shrine itself see Ia.G. Guliamov, *Pamiatniki goroda Khivy* (Tashkent: Fan, 1941), pp. 24–29; and L. Man'kovskaia and V.A. Bulatova, *Pamiatniki zodchestva Khorezma* (Tashkent: Izd. literatury i iskusstva, 1978), pp. 169–175.

60 At the same time, it is also possible that ʿAbd al-Raḥmān and the Sarïqs never had any intention of coming to terms with the Khivan ruler at this time, but simply were using the offer of negotiations as a delaying tactic while they considered other options.

be appropriate for a religious notable in ʿAbd al-Raḥmān's position to attempt to mediate an end to hostilities and thus shield his community from further harm, but it appears that the bulk of the Sarïqs were not yet willing to concede defeat and accept Khivan rule. However, this situation soon changed for in May 1849 the Merv Sarïqs once again indicated their willingness to accept Khivan rule.[61]

Taking advantage of the renewed submission of Merv, in the fall of 1849 Muḥammad Amīn Khan marched to Tezhen, where he gathered supplies and reinforcements from the Teke of Tezhen and Sarakhs, in preparation for a planned campaign in the mountains of Khurasan.[62] While camped along the Tezhen, a detachment of Sarïqs arrived from Merv, led by Raḥmān Berdī, the son of ʿAbd al-Raḥmān Khalīfa, and presented themselves to the Khivan khan. However, this force also included a bedraggled Muḥammad Amīn Bek, the newly appointed Khivan governor over the Salor Turkmens of Yolotan, south of Merv. According to Āgahī, when Muḥammad Amīn Bek reached the fort of Yolotan after being sent there by Muḥammad Amīn Khan, some of the Salor clans sought to kill him, while others rallied to his side.[63] In the end, after hiding for several days among some friendly Salors, the Khivan officer managed to flee by night to Merv, where he received the protection of ʿAbd al-Raḥmān Khalīfa. The Khalīfa in turn put him with the detachment under his son and sent him on to Muḥammad Amīn Khan at Tezhen, where Muḥammad Amīn Bek reported all that had taken place.[64]

Soon after, Muḥammad Amīn Khan broke camp and set out with his army toward Persian territory. The khan's officers, however, took him aside and dissuaded him from undertaking a winter campaign in Khurasan when the Salors where in rebellion and, according to these officers, the Sarïqs and Tekes were only pretending to be loyal.[65] Instead, the Khivan officials argued for a surprise strike in the direction of "Pend" (Penjdeh) and Maruchaq, with the goal of plundering the herds sent there by the Turkmens to hide them from the Khivan army, and thus delivering a deadly blow to the rebellious Turkmen tribes. This plan appealed to Muḥammad Amīn Khan who, after giving gifts

61 Though significantly, without the restoration of a Khivan governor or garrison at Merv: Wood, pp. 218–219.

62 Āgahī, *Jāmiʿ al-vāqiʿāt-i sulṭānī*, f. 482a.

63 While Āgahī does not tell us, it seems likely that these hostile Salors still remembered an earlier tenure of Muḥammad Amīn Bek as governor with some bitterness. See Wood, pp. 185–187 and 219–220.

64 See Āgahī, *Jāmiʿ al-vāqiʿāt-i sulṭānī*, f. 482a.

65 Ibid. No indication is given here of any specific reason for these officers doubting the Sarïq's and Teke's loyalty.

to the Tezhen, Akhal and Sarakhs Teke and thanking them for their service, dismissed them to their homes, while the rest of the Khivan army turned in the direction of Penjdeh.

After traveling one day's march, the Khivan khan suddenly ordered his troops to surround the Sarïq detachment led by Raḥmān Berdī Makhdūm, take all their horses and weapons, and make them prisoners.[66] The Khivan force was then divided into three parts, and each detachment sent in a different direction in search of plunder, with the goal of meeting up near the confluence of the "Mor" (Kushk) and Murghab Rivers.[67] According to Āgahī, these forces gathered tremendous amounts of loot, although one, due to their own carelessness, was ambushed by Salor, Sarïq and Sarakhs Teke horsemen and suffered heavy casualties.[68] All three forces met up again with Muḥammad Amīn Khan on December 20, 1849, at a spot above the bridge across the Kushk River.[69]

We can understand the Sarïqs' anger when, in response to their willing cooperation, Muḥammad Amīn Khan turned on their detachment, accused

66 Ibid., f. 483a. We can assume that prisoners traveling on foot with the Khivan army were treated very poorly.

67 The "Mor" river mentioned here by Āgahī is the Kushk River, which flows into the Murghab at Aq-tepe, just north of Penjdeh. See Wood, p. 222 [note 105].

68 See Āgahī, *Jāmiʿ al-vāqiʿāt-i sulṭānī*, f. 483a–b for the account of these plundering expeditions. The ambushed party was the first to arrive at the rendezvous point, where they reportedly became preoccupied with their loot and thus were caught unawares by the Turkmens. They were forced to flee to a second detachment led by Muḥammad Amīn Khan himself, but not before losing 200 killed. The rebel Turkmens then reportedly fled out of fear of the Khivan khan.

69 In February, 1885, the English officer Maitland visited a spot about 40 miles west of Aq-tepe (which is near Penjdeh), in the direction of Sarakhs, called "Tatung Ori," or "Or Muhammad Amin." He was told that this means the "entrenchment of the Tatar," or the "entrenchment of Muhammad Amin," and dates from the Khivan khan's campaign in this area. One of Maitland's guides claimed to have served in the Khivan army, which he states consisted of 10,000 horsemen, plus 10,000 others (camel-drivers, etc.). The description which Maitland records generally fits Āgahī's, with the exception that he states that the flocks of the Sarakhs Teke, rather than those of the Sarïqs, were the object of the Khivan campaign. He further claims that the Merv Sarïqs were then nominally subjects of Khiva, and that about 100 served with the expedition (no doubt having in mind Raḥmān Berdī's force), which was primarily composed of Khivan Turkmens, along with a large number of Jamshidi. See "Captain Maitland to Lieutenant-General Sir P. Lumsden, March 5, 1885," in *Central Asia: Further Correspondence respecting Central Asia*, no. 4 (London, 1885), p. 8. (Unfortunately, this "Tatung Ori" is not marked on the accompanying map). However, the same info from Maitland is published in Peter Lumsden, "Countries and Tribes bordering on the Koh-i-Baba Range," *Proceedings of the Royal Geographical Society* 7, no. 9 (Sept., 1885): 561–583, pp. 571–572. This article's map does show Tatung Ori.

them of harboring secret hostilities, made them his prisoners, and then set out to plunder their herds. Indeed, in Āgahī's account it appears as if the Khivan officers were looking for any excuse to avoid a relatively dangerous campaign in Persian Khurasan and instead raid the unsuspecting Turkmens. That the Sarïqs thus humiliated were led by Raḥmān Berdī, the son of a religious personage with the status of ʿAbd al-Raḥmān Khalīfa among the Sarïqs, only exacerbated the situation. While this is partly speculation, it is very likely that the resolute hostility and uncompromising attitude which ʿAbd al-Raḥmān Khalīfa would demonstrate from this time forward toward the Khivan Khanate, stems in large part from his feeling personally betrayed by Muḥammad Amīn Khan. In any case, following the imprisonment of his son and continuing until his death, ʿAbd al-Raḥmān Khalīfa would disavow his former role of holy man mediating between the urban state and the rural tribe, and instead, take up the mantle of the "warrior-saint," resolutely opposed to the Khivan Khanate's efforts to extend its control to the Merv Sarïqs.

From 1849 to 1854 the Khivans again engaged in annual plundering expeditions to Merv.[70] By 1853 the situation for the Merv Sarïqs was without doubt serious and, therefore, in an effort to hold off the Khivan onslaught, ʿAbd al-Raḥmān Khalīfa decided at this time to appeal to Iran for help. He sent his son, Raḥmān Berdī, with fifty of the leading Sarïqs of Merv to Mashhad to offer their submission to the Qajars if the latter would protect them from the Khivan khan.[71] The irony of the "man-stealing" Merv Sarïqs turning to their usual victims, the Persians of Khurasan, for aid, is only matched by the willingness of the Qajars to come to the Sarïqs assistance. Naturally, the Qajars were primarily interested in undercutting the growing power of Muḥammad Amīn Khan in the region, who they saw as a much greater threat than the Sarïqs, and thus their willing acceptance of ʿAbd al-Raḥmān's offer. According to the Qajar sources, the governor of Mashhad, Sulṭān Murād Mirza, sent this request on

70 Wood, pp. 219–245.

71 See *MITT*, pp. 249–250; and Noelle-Karimi, *The Pearl in its Midst*, p. 274. Raḥmān Berdī is said to have asserted that Merv lay within the domains of the Qajar shah, and thus requested the latter to send a governor to rescue the population of the oasis. Another source names a second individual, named Yazbeg Garyn, who accompanied Raḥmān Berdī (called here "ishan") to Mashhad and who then went on to deliver the Sarïqs' request to the Qajar Shah personally. This person reportedly stayed in Iran for six years as the representative of the Sarïqs and even married there. See Umur Esen, "Meshkhur 'Maru-shakhu-jahan' barasynda," in *Merv v drevnei i srednevekovoi istorii vostoka V: "Merv drevnii--Mary sovremennyi": Tezisy dokladov nauchnoi konferentsii,* (Mary: Izd. Tipografiia Maryiskogo veliata, 1994), pp. 107–108.

to the shah in Teheran, who then dispatched ʿAbbās Qulī Khan Deregezi with 150 horsemen to govern Merv.[72]

2 The Death of ʿAbd al-Raḥmān and the Conquest of Merv by Khiva

The precise date of ʿAbd al-Raḥmān Khalīfa's death is uncertain, though all indicators point to death by natural causes. Āgahī makes no mention of this key event, but Bayānī records that, shortly before the fall of Merv to the Khivan forces, ʿAbd al-Raḥmān Khalīfa died, leaving the Merv Sarïqs without a leader (*bī-bash*).[73] The anonymous "History of the Sarïqs," which also records the Khalīfa's death as just before the fall of Merv, further mentions an unspecified epidemic which broke out at Merv at that time, perhaps claiming the Khalīfa as one of its victims.[74] Samoilovich's informants simply state that the Khalīfa died one and a half years before Muḥammad Amīn Khan.[75]

The extent of ʿAbd al-Raḥmān Khalīfa's influence among the Merv Sarïqs is indicated by the speed with which the opposition to Khivan rule collapsed among the Sarïqs after the Khalīfa's death. By the time of ʿAbd al-Raḥmān's passing in 1854, the Sarïqs' confrontation with Khiva over control of the Merv oasis had grown extremely costly. While they had managed to hold off the Khivan army more or less continuously for 12 years, this had not come without a high price. Especially in the years after 1849, the annual Khivan campaigns against the Merv oasis became increasingly destructive, while the will of the Sarïqs to oppose Khivan rule grew increasingly weaker, as evidenced by the defections of various Sarïq groups to the Khivan side. Only the respect and veneration which the majority of Sarïqs held for ʿAbd al-Raḥmān Khalīfa ensured their continuous opposition to Khiva despite the heavy costs.

At the same time, however, it must be pointed out that the benefits of independence for the Sarïqs, while diminished, continued as well, and this certainly played a role in the ongoing support for ʿAbd al-Raḥmān's position. Throughout these years of struggle with Khiva, the Sarïqs paid no taxes or duties to any state, while exacting their own payments from the merchants and caravans which continued to ply the trade route between Mashhad and Bukhara. Indeed, never in the period that we have been investigating does it

72 Noelle-Karimi, *The Pearl in its Midst*, p. 274.

73 Bayānī, *Shajara-i Khwārazmshāhī*, f. 346a.

74 *Sarïq khalqïnïng tarikhi*, p. 17.

75 A.N. Samoilovich, "Iz Turkmenskoi stariny. II. Mervskiia vospominaniia," *Zhivaia starina*, 18 (1909), p. 83. This would indicate that he died in late 1853, since the khan died in March, 1855.

appear that the caravan trade stopped completely, despite the risks. While we lack hard data, we can assume that, at least to some extent, this commercial activity lessened the impact of the Khivan depredations on the Merv oasis. Combined with the revenues from raiding and the slave trade, the profits of which went directly to the Turkmens after the overthrow of the Khivan garrison, these various sources of income certainly contributed to the force of ʿAbd al-Raḥmān's arguments for resisting Khivan rule.

Whether or not ʿAbd al-Raḥmān utilized religious grounds for opposing Khivan rule is unknown due to the lack of sources. To my knowledge there exists no extant text purporting to express the Khalīfa's religious views. On the one hand, it is unlikely that religious justifications would have carried great weight with the Sarïqs, who, despite their opposition to Khivan (and Bukharan) rule, nevertheless acknowledged both as centers of true Islamic faith and learning. This is not to say, on the other hand, that the Khalīfa could not draw on the perception that the Khivan rulers were oppressive, and thus unjust (from an Islamic perspective), in their exactions. At this point, the distinction between economic and religious motivations becomes difficult to determine and, lacking the sources, we can only suggest that both may have played a role in the Sarïqs following ʿAbd al-Raḥmān Khalīfa.

Of course, any religious argument which ʿAbd al-Raḥmān Khalīfa may have advanced would have been undercut by his turning to Shiʾite Iran for aid against the Sunni Khivan Khanate. While this may have been understandable, and even justifiable, given the desperate situation which Merv faced in the early 1850's, orthodox Sunnis such as the historian Āgahī were quick to point out the error of turning to the "evil Qizilbash."[76] The regular Turkmen assertion that enslaving Persians was acceptable because the latter were not true Muslims only adds to the irony. Yet, it must be mentioned, none of our sources indicate that the appeal to Iran induced any of ʿAbd al-Raḥmān's Sarïq followers to abandon him before his death, and thus we should probably not make too much of these events.

The real basis for ʿAbd al-Raḥmān Khalīfa's influence among the Sarïqs is probably best seen not in economic terms or even in religious motivations, if by the latter we mean only appeals to Islamic conceptions of orthodoxy and justice. Rather, the Khalīfa's position was based on his community's belief that he, in a powerful sense, possessed that *baraka* which gives one special access to the spiritual world and to Allah himself. Thus, even when the Sarïqs were faced with overwhelming hardship due to the Khivan army's depredations, to the point that some were unwilling to resist any longer, the majority of the

76 See Āgahī, *Jāmiʿ al-vāqiʿāt-i sulṭānī*, f. 498b.

Sarïqs remained loyal to ʿAbd al-Raḥmān Khalīfa and his determined opposition to Khiva, seeing in the Khalīfa the most powerful, tangible, representation of Allah's will that they knew of. When ʿAbd al-Raḥmān died, however, no one with his spiritual authority was able to replace him and lead the resistance to Khivan rule, and thus Merv quickly fell again under complete Khivan control in the summer of 1854.[77]

Khivan success was short-lived as in the following year the Teke defeated a Khivan force near the Tezhen River, killed Muḥammad Amīn Khan, and set in motion a series of events that forced the Khivans to abandon Merv and plunged the khanate into a decade long crisis.[78] The Sarïqs fared little better, as they also soon faced pressure from the Tekes, who began migrating into the Merv region. While a peaceful coexistence was at first attempted, the Sarïqs soon found themselves at odds with the numerically superior Tekes and, after several conflicts, fled the oasis in the direction of Yolotan.[79] The Sarïqs in turn drove the Salors from Yolotan, as well as from higher up the Murghab at Penjdeh, and occupied these regions. These areas remained the tribal lands of the Sarïqs into the twentieth century.

3 ʿAbd al-Raḥmān's Sons

In the conclusion of my dissertation I stated that the Khalīfa's sons did not appear to retain his influence among the Sarïqs.[80] Instead, I argued that the final subjugation of the Sarïqs by Khiva in 1854, followed by their later expulsion from the Merv oasis after 1857 due to Teke pressure, likely left the Sarïqs in such a state of defeat and disarray that the traditional relationship between the saintly family and the Sarïqs was disrupted, along with the entire economic and social order of this community. While some wealth was portable, any agricultural resources which the Khalīfa's family might have controlled would have been lost. In addition, defeat at the hands of Khiva may have dealt a blow to the Khalīfa's prestige, who after all had been the primary proponent of opposition to Khiva in his later years. As a result, some of the suffering which resulted from this failed policy may have been blamed on the Khalīfa and his family by the surviving members of the community, thus diminishing their influence.

---

77 Wood, pp. 249–252.

78 Wood, pp. 253–255.

79 Wood, pp. 255–256.

80 I also noted that this may have been in keeping with Wolff's negative assessment of them (Wolff, *Narrative*, vol. II, p. 148): "his sons, however, imitate ill their noble father."

At the time of my dissertation research, I knew of only two references to his sons after the Khalīfa's death: a brief notice of one of the Khalīfa's sons mentioned in an oral tradition as one of a group of Sarïqs at Porsu-qala who sought the aid of Persia at the time of the Teke invasion of Merv in 1857;[81] and, as noted earlier, a reference to a son of the Khalīfa in a Teke poem from the 1860s describing the evils of the Sarïqs.[82] Otherwise, I found no mention of a role for the offspring of ʿAbd al-Raḥmān Khalīfa among the Sarïqs after their father's death. However, since that time I have discovered more information which has caused me to rethink their role.

One example comes from the Afghan historian Riyāżī, who states that when ʿAbd al-Raḥmān died, "[t]he clans of the Salvar [Salor] and Saruq [Sarïq] selected his son instead of the Caliph as their leader, and fought with the Khan of Khwarazm, forcing him back. He could not raid the areas around Marv."[83] While I believe that the chronology is wrong (Riyāżī has ʿAbd al-Raḥmān dying in 1851), this does indicate the immediate leadership role of one (un-named) son of ʿAbd al-Raḥmān after the latter's death, something neither Āgahī nor any other source mentions.

The son in question is no doubt Raḥmān Berdī who, along with a brother named "Juma Ishan," appears in the accounts of several British officers involved with the Afghan Boundary Commission surveys and, in particular, in the clash which occurred with Russian forces at Penjdeh in March 1885, i.e. 30 years after ʿAbd al-Raḥmān's death and 25 years after the Sarïqs had been driven from Merv by the Teke.[84] For example, General Peter Lumsden reports meeting Raḥmān Berdī (who he calls Rahman Mahdi),[85] "a son of the late Khalifah of Merv, and himself the Khalifah of Penjdeh," who showed him testimonials from Dr. J.S. Login of the Herat Mission dated 1840, and from Joseph

81 Samoilovich, "Iz turkmenskoi stariny," p. 84.

82 See Abdu-s-Sattar, p. 0106. The son is not named in the poem, though Samoilovich suggests that it was Raḥmān-berdī Īshān (see p. 0105).

83 Michael O'Rourke Patterson, *A Partial Translation of* ʿAyn al-Vaqayiʿ (*Wellspring of Events*)*: The Third of Twelve Works in* Bahr al-Fava'id: Kuliyat-i Riyazi (*Unlimited Benefits: The Complete Works of Riyazi*) *of Muhammad Yusuf*, Master's Thesis, New York University, 1988 (p. 177; MS p. 115) [refers to events of 1268/1851].

84 On the Penjdeh Incident, see Lee, pp. 459–473; and Robert A. Johnson, "The Penjdeh Incident 1885," *Archives* 24, no. 100 (1999): 28–48. The Afghan Boundary Commission findings were compiled in five volumes between 1888 and 1891, and extant copies are very rare (cf. Lee, p. 446). I consulted a set in the British Library which has physical copies of 3 volumes (numbers 2, 4 and 5: see MSS EUR F112/388/1–5) and microfilm copies of the remaining volumes (1 and 3: see OMF/IOR Neg 9037 and 9038).

85 British sources variously refer to Raḥmān Berdī as Mahdi, Wardi or Verdi.

Wolff dated April 14, 1844.[86] Elsewhere it is stated that Raḥmān Berdī's "father and grandfather were Khalifas of the tribe before him," and that when he was "quite young he accompanied Dr. Wolff to Bokhara, and thence to Mashad; and Abbott lived in his house."[87] While British sources describe him in 1885 as "Khalifa, or spiritual guide, to the whole tribe, and as such possessed with much influence," they also note that he was growing senile at the time and that as a result his influence was waning.[88] Indeed, these sources assumed that his brother Juma Ishan likely replaced him as Khalīfa shortly after the British visit.

In 1885 the British describe Juma Ishan as the most influential man in the Sokhti sub-division of the Sarïqs.[89] This connection of the family of Abd al-Raḥmān with the Sokhti is perhaps significant since elsewhere this clan is described as both the wealthiest of the Sarïqs and, as a result, the first to flee from Merv upon the arrival of the Teke, in order, it is implied, to protect their considerable assets.[90] Charles E. Yate in his *Northern Afghanistan* affirms the oft-repeated statement that "the Sariks have no hereditary chiefs or rulers." Yet he also states, in describing the Sarïq settlement at Penjdeh, that "[t]he only building of any sort in use that I know of is a small, low, flat-roofed *musjid*, built of mud, at the northern end of the valley in the Sokti settlements, the peculiar property of Juma Eshan, the head priest of the Sariks, one of the men who behaved so staunchly to the British officers, and who stuck by them so faithfully when matters looked so threatening after the Russian attack."[91] We should note in passing that the mention of this mosque structure reminds us of the Khalīfa's connection to the shrine of Talkhatan-baba in Merv. Since we can assume that buildings were a rarity among the Sarïqs, it is noteworthy that the Khalīfa's family continued to be connected with such physical representations of Islamic authority as this mosque.

---

86 Lumsden, "Countries and Tribes bordering on the Koh-i-Baba Range," p. 576; and "Diary of Major Maitland" in *Records of Intelligence Party, Afghan Boundary Commission*, vol. I (Simla, 1888), pp. 209 and 221. In his published article Lumsden states that the meeting took place in December 1884 but Maitland places it on 9–10 January 1885.

87 "Report on the Tribes" in *Records of Intelligence Party, Afghan Boundary Commission*, vol. IV (Simla, 1891), p. 30.

88 *Records of Intelligence Party*, vol. IV, p. 30; and vol. I, pp. 209 and 221.

89 *Records of Intelligence Party*, vol. IV, p. 30.

90 *Records of Intelligence Party*, vol. IV, p. 23.

91 C.E. Yate, *Northern Afghanistan, or Letters from the Afghan Boundary Commission* (London: Cambridge Scholars Press, 2003 [original 1888]), p. 138.

In recounting the clash with Russian forces at Penjdeh, Lieutenant Arthur C. Yate, after again asserting that the Sarïqs recognize certain religious leaders' authority, "known as Ishan and Khalifa,"[92] states that Captain [= Charles E.] Yate rode down from Penjdeh to Ak-tapa on the evening of March 25, 1885, and visited Afghan positions. A.C. Yate continues: "In the evening, on his return from Ak-tapa, he visited Juma Ishan, the chief Mulla, and his brother the Khalifa, the most influential men in Panjdeh, and sons of the former Khalifa of Merv. They promised to persuade the Saruks to remain quiet and interfere neither with the Russians nor Afghans."[93] Elsewhere, in describing this same visit, Yate calls Juma Ishan "the spiritual head of the Saruks."[94] When matters became heated the next day with the Sarïqs anxious to attack the Russians, Yate states that the Afghan commander (Naib Salar) sent "for Juma Ishan and his Kuran to pacify them."[95] Later, the Sarïq "headmen, including Juma Ishan, Khalifa Rahman Verdi …" and others "of the most influential men, arrived" at the British camp, following a clash with the Russians.[96] In the end, Juma Ishan (along with another chief named Aqa Muhammad) escorted the remaining Afghan forces away from the Russia positions to safety.[97] This is the final mention of the Khalīfa's heirs that I have found in the historical record.

While there is no reason to assume that the sons of ʿAbd al-Raḥmān Khalīfa exercised anything approaching their father's authority after 1854, nonetheless their activity thirty years later in the 1880's would indicate that they continued to have some influence among the Sarïqs in both spiritual and political realms. This in spite of all of the upheavals that the Sarïqs had experienced due to their defeat by Khiva and subsequent expulsion from Merv up the Murgab River to Penjdeh by the Teke.[98]

92 A.C. Yate, *England and Russia Face to face in Asia: Travels with the Afghan Boundary Commission* (Edinburgh: W. Blackwood, 1887), p. 234.

93 Ibid., p. 324.

94 Ibid., p. 347.

95 Ibid., p. 348. Cf. DeWeese, "Authority," p. 35 for the Qur'an as talisman, "charged with sacrality in its physical presence …"

96 A.C. Yate, p. 353.

97 Ibid., p. 357.

98 Granted, since our only sources for the activity of the sons are British, it is possible that the Sarïq community put forward the sons in this instance due to their perceived influence with foreigners, rather than actual ongoing authority among the Sarïqs. But this is equally speculative.

4 Conclusion

While this is clearly just one example and perhaps an isolated case, the role of ʿAbd al-Raḥmān Khalīfa and his sons does raise some interesting possibilities. For a period from the 1820's to the mid-1880's (i.e. at least 60 years) they exercised some measure of influence if not necessarily (in the case of the sons) actual authority among the Sarïq Turkmens. As has been shown, the family drew its religious authority from a number of sources, including: ties to Ṣūfī Islām of Kurukh and the Naqshbandī tradition; their personal piety and charisma; prestige and resources from the (probable) control of a local shrine at Talkhatan; gifts and 'tithes' from Turkmen raiding parties and passing caravans; diplomatic roles vis-à-vis both surrounding states and other Turkmen groups; expertise regarding the external world; and finally, their literacy and knowledge of sacred texts.

As Waleed Ziad has recently stated, both the newly formed states of post-Nadir Shah Central Asia and their subject populations looked to Naqshbandī Sufis and their institutions to provide a range of religious services. Indeed, "both states and their subject populations were in need of political and commercial mediation," which as Ziad notes was "best provided by an outside party with significant transregional, historically grounded symbolic capital across rural, tribal, and urban environments."[99] Though not definitively tied to the Naqshbandī-Mujaddidī networks described by Ziad, it is quite likely that ʿAbd al-Raḥmān Khalīfa and his sons are an example of this type of religious authority.

While the nature of our sources allows us to explicate this family's use of their religious authority in the political and, to some extent, economic life of the Sarïqs, these same sources do not provide insight into the family's religious authority in other realms such as the personal, social, or theological views and customs prevalent among the nineteenth century Sarïq Turkmens. However, perhaps it is time to reconsider the oft repeated maxim that the Turkmen resisted hereditary rule from either noble or religious lineages and consider again the sources we have available to us reflecting the authority of Sufis and other religious notables over multiple generations.

99 Waleed Ziad, "Transporting Knowledge in the Durrani Empire: Two Manuals of Naqshbandi-Mujaddidi Sufi Practice," in *Afghanistan's Islam: From Conversion to the Taliban*, ed. Nile Green (Oakland: University of California Press, 2017), pp. 105–126 (quotes from p. 112). Unfortunately, I have found no examples of texts tied to ʿAbd al-Raḥmān Khalīfa similar to the "manual genre" described by Ziad for other Naqshbandī groups in the region.

Bibliography

Manuscripts

Āgahī, Muḥammad Riżā Mīrāb. *Jāmiʿ al-vāqiʿāt-i sulṭānī*. MS Institute of Oriental Studies, St. Petersburg E 6/VI, ff. 441b–523a.

Āgahī, Muḥammad Riżā Mīrāb. *Riyāż al-dawla*. MS Institute of Oriental Studies, St Petersburg D 123.

Āgahī, Muḥammad Riżā Mīrāb. *Zubdat al-tavārīkh*. MS Institute of Oriental Studies, St. Petersburg E 6/VI, ff. 387b–439b.

Bayānī, Muḥammad Yūsuf. *Shajara-i Khwārazmshāhī*. MS Tashkent, IVANRUz, inv. no. 9596.

Sarïq khalqïnïng tarikhi. MS Institute of Oriental Studies, St. Petersburg B 725/I.

Published Works

Abbott, James. *Narrative of a Journey from Heraut to Khiva, Moscow, and St. Petersburgh, During the Late Russian Invasion of Khiva; with some Account of the Court of Khiva and the Kingdom of Khaurism*, vol. I. London: W.H. Allen and Co., 1843.

Abdu-s-Sattar kazy [ʿAbd al-Sattar Qazi], *Kniga rasskazov o bitvakh tekintsev: Turkmenskaia istoricheskaia poema XIX veka*. Edited and translated by A.N. Samoilovich. St. Petersburg, 1914.

Algar, Hamid. "Religious Forces in Eighteenth- and Nineteenth-Century Iran." In *The Cambridge History of Iran*, vol. 7: *From Nadir Shah to the Islamic Republic*, edited by Peter Avery, Gavin Hambly and Charles Melville. Cambridge: Cambridge University Press, 1991, pp. 705–731.

Algar, Hamid. "Silent and Vocal dhikr in the Naqshbandī Order." In *Akten des VII. Kongresses für Arabistik und Islamwissenschaft*, edited by Albert Dietrich. Göttingen: Vandenhoeck & Ruprecht, 1976, pp. 39–46.

Alikhanov, [M.] *Mervskii oazis i dorogi, vedushchie k nemu*. St Petersburg, 1883.

Barthold, W. *An Historical Geography of Iran*. Translated by Svat Soucek. Princeton: Princeton University Press, 1984.

Basilov, V.N. "Honour Groups in Traditional Turkmenian Society." In *Islam in Tribal Societies: From the Atlas to the Indus*, edited by Akbar S. Ahmed and David M. Hart. London: Routledge and Kegan Paul, 1984, pp. 220–243.

Central Asia: Further Correspondence respecting Central Asia. Nos. 1–4. London, 1885.

Clancy-Smith, Julia. *Rebel and Saint: Muslim Notables, Populist Protest, Colonial Encounters (Algeria and Tunisia, 1800–1904)*. Berkeley: University of California Press, 1994.

Conolly, Arthur. "Part II: Extract from a letter from Captain A. Conolly, on a mission to Khiva, to the address of the Envoy and Minister, dated 26th December 1840." In *India Office Library*, V/27/69/3 [censored report].

"The Country between Bamian and Khiva." *Calcutta Review* 15(1851): 1–35.

Demidov, S.M. *Turkmenskie ovliady*. Ashkhabad: Ylym, 1976.

Demidov, S.M. *Sufizm v Turkmenii (Evoliutsiia i perezhitki)*. Ashkhabad: Ylym, 1978.

Demidov, S.M. *Legendy i pravda o "sviatykh" mestakh*. Ashkhabad: Ylym, 1988.

DeWeese, Devin. "Authority." In *Key Terms for the Study of Islam*, edited by Jamal J. Elias. Oxford: Oneworld, 2010, pp. 26–52.

Durdyev, M.B. "Dukhovenstvo v sisteme obshchestvennykh institutov turkmen kontsa XIX-nachala XX v." *Vestnik Moskovskogo Universiteta: Istoriia*, 1970 (no. 4), pp. 27–42.

Eden, Jeff. *Slavery and Empire in Central Asia*. Cambridge: Cambridge University Press, 2018.

Esen, Umur. "Meshkhur 'Maru-shakhu-jahan' barasynda." In *Merv v drevnei i srednevekovoi istorii vostoka V: "Merv drevnii – Mary sovremennyi": Tezisy dokladov nauchnoi konferentsii*. Mary: Izd. Tipografiia Maryiskogo veliata, 1994, pp. 105–108.

Ferrier, J.P. *Caravan Journeys and Wanderings in Persia, Afghanistan, Turkistan, and Beloochistan; with Historical Notices of the Countries Lying Between Russian and India*. Translated by William Jesse. London: J. Murray, 1857.

Gellner, Ernest. *Muslim Society*. Cambridge: Cambridge University Press, 1981.

Ghafūr, Muḥammad ʿAlī Khān. *Rūznāma-yi safar-i Khwārazm*. Tehran: Vizārat-i Umūr-i Khārija, 1373/1994.

Grover, Captain [John]. *The Bokhara Victims*. Second edition. London: Chapman and Hall, 1845.

Guliamov, Ia.G. *Pamiatniki goroda Khivy*. Tashkent: Fan, 1941.

Johnson, Robert A. "The Penjdeh Incident 1885." *Archives* 24, no. 100 (1999): 28–48.

Kaganovich, Albert. *The Mashhadi Jews (Djedids) in Central Asia*. Halle: ANOR 14, 2007.

Kakar, Hasan K. *Government and Society in Afghanistan: The Reign of Amir ʿAbd al-Rahman Khan*. Austin: University of Texas Press, 1979.

Katib, Faiz Muhammad, *Siraj al-Tawarikh*. 3 vols. Kabul, 1913–1915.

Katib, Fayz Muhammad. *The History of Afghanistan: Fayż Muḥammad Kātib Hazārah's* Sirāj al-tawārīkh. *Volume 1, The Sadūzāʾī Era 1747–1843*. Translation and notes by R.D. McChesney and M.M. Khorrami. Leiden: Brill, 2013.

Krämer, Gudrun, and Sabine Schmidtke. "Introduction: Religious Authority and Religious Authorities in Muslim Societies. A Critical Overview." In *Speaking for Islam: Religious Authorities in Muslim Societies*, edited by Gudrun Krämer and Sabine Schmidtke. Leiden: Brill, 2006, pp. 1–14.

Lee, Jonathan E. *The 'Ancient Supremacy': Bukhara, Afghanistan and the Battle for Balkh, 1731–1901*. Leiden: Brill, 1996.

Lumsden, Peter. "Countries and Tribes bordering on the Koh-i-Baba Range." *Proceedings of the Royal Geographical Society* 7, no. 9 (Sept., 1885): 561–583.

Mahomed Hoosain Kashee, "Account of an Embassy to the King of Persia from the Ameer of Ka'bul in 1837–38, Part I." In *Selections from the Travels and Journals*

Preserved in the Bombay Secretariat, edited by George W. Forrest. Bombay, 1906, pp. 53–59.

Man'kovskaia, L. and V.A. Bulatova, *Pamiatniki zodchestva Khorezma*. Tashkent: Izd. literatury i iskusstva, 1978.

Materialy po istorii turkmen i Turkmenii, vol. II, *XVI–XIX vv. Iranskie, bukharskie i khivinskie istochniki*, edited by V.V. Struve, A.K. Borovkov, A.A. Romaskevich and P.P. Ivanov. Moscow-Leningrad: AN SSSR, 1938.

McChesney, R.D. *Waqf in Central Asia: Four Hundred Years in the History of a Muslim Shrine, 1480–1889*. Princeton: Princeton University Press, 1991.

Mikhailov, F.A. "Religioznye vozzreniia turkmen Zakaspiiskoi oblasti." In *Sbornik materialov po musul'manstvu*, vol. 2. Tashkent, 1900, pp. 87–103.

Mir-Kasimov, Orkhan. "Introduction: Conflicting Synergy of Patterns of Religious Authority in Islam." In *Unity in Diversity: Mysticism, Messianism and the Construction of Religious Authority in Islam*, edited by Orkhan Mir-Kasimov. Leiden: Brill, 2014, pp. 1–20.

Noelle-Karimi, Christine. "On the Edge: Eastern Khurasan in the Perception of Qajar Officials." *Eurasian Studies* 14 (2016): 135–177.

Noelle-Karimi, Christine. *The Pearl in its Midst: Herat and the Mapping of Khurasan (15th–19th Centuries)*. Vienna: OAW, 2014.

Olesen, Asta. *Islam and Politics in Afghanistan*. Richmond, Surrey: Curzon Press, 1995.

Patterson, Michael O'Rourke. *A Partial Translation of* ʿAyn al-Vaqayiʿ (*Wellspring of Events*)*: The Third of Twelve Works in* Bahr al-Fava'id: Kuliyat-i Riyazi (*Unlimited Benefits: The Complete Works of Riyazi*) *of Muhammad Yusuf*. Master's Thesis, New York University, 1988.

Pribytkova, A.M. "Mavzolei Talkhatan-baba." *Soobshcheniia instituta istorii i teorii arkhitektury* 8 (1947): 25–34.

Pribytkova, A.M. *Pamiatniki arkhitektury XI veka v Turkmenii*. Moscow: Gos. izdat. literatury po stroitel'stvu i arkhitekture, 1955.

Pugachenkova, G.A. *Puti razvitiia arkhitektury iuzhnogo Turkmenistana pory rabovladeniia i feodalizma*. Moscow: AN SSSR, 1958.

Records of Intelligence Party, Afghan Boundary Commission. 5 vols. Simla, 1888–1891.

Rosliakov, A.A. "K voprosu o miuridizme u Turkmen." *Izvestiia AN Turkmenskoi SSR*, 1952 (no. 5), pp. 21–25.

Samoilovich, A.N. "Iz Turkmenskoi stariny. II. Mervskiia vospominaniia." *Zhivaia starina* 18 (1909): 78–85.

Sédillot, [L.] "Notice sur une carte routière de Meschhed à Bokhara et de Bokhara à Balkh, suivie d'un plan de Bokhara et de ses environs, par un ingénieur persan, d'après la traduction de M. Garcin de Tasssy." *Bulletin de la société de géographie*, 4(1854): 221–235.

[Sev], "Zametki o turkmenskom dukhovenstve." *Turkmenovedenie*, 1928 (no. 3–4), pp. 5–20.

Shakespear, Sir Richmond. "A Personal Narrative of a Journey from Heraut to Ourenbourg, on the Caspian, in 1840." *Blackwood's Edinburgh Magazine* 51(1842): 691–720.

Snesarev, G.P. *Khorezmskie legendy kak istochnik po istorii religioznykh kul'tov Srednei Azii*. Moscow: Nauka, 1983.

[Thomson, William Taylour]. In Lady Sheil, *Glimpses of Life and Manners in Persia*. London: John Murray, 1856, Note (F.), "Khiva," pp. 358–370.

Wolff, Joseph. *Researches and Missionary Labours Among the Jews, Mohammedans, and Other Sects, during his travels between the years 1831 and 1834*. First American Edition. Philadelphia: Orrin Rogers, 1837.

Wolff, Joseph. *Travels and Adventures of the Rev. Joseph Wolff.* 2 vols. London: Saunders, Otley, and Co., 1860–61.

Wolff, Joseph. *Narrative of a Mission to Bokhara in the years 1843–1845, to ascertain the fate of Colonel Stoddart and Captain Conolly*. 2 vols. London: J.W. Parker, 1845.

Wood, William A. "The Sariq Turkmens of Merv and the Khanate of Khiva in the Early Nineteenth Century." PhD diss., Indiana University, 1998.

Yapp, M.E. *Strategies of British India: Britain, Iran and Afghanistan, 1798–1850*. Oxford: Oxford University Press, 1980.

Yate, A.C. *England and Russia Face to face in Asia: Travels with the Afghan Boundary Commission*. Edinburgh: W. Blackwood, 1887.

Yate, C.E. *Northern Afghanistan, or Letters from the Afghan Boundary Commission*. London: Cambridge Scholars Press, 2003 [original 1888].

Zhukovskii, V.A. *Drevnosti Zakaspiiskogo kraia: Razvaliny starogo Merva*. St. Petersburg, 1894.

Ziad, Waleed. "Transporting Knowledge in the Durrani Empire: Two Manuals of Naqshbandi-Mujaddidi Sufi Practice." In *Afghanistan's Islam: From Conversion to the Taliban*, edited by Nile Green. Oakland: University of California Press, 2017, pp. 105–126.

Advice from a Holy Man

Īshāns *in Nineteenth-Century Khwārazm*

Ulfat Abdurasulov

1 Introduction[1]

This chapter opens with an anecdote from the *Gulshan-i saʿādat*, a chronicle compiled by Ḥasan-Murad Laffasī, a Khivan author of the early 20th century. The events in question took place in the Khanate of Khiva, a Muslim principality in the lower delta of the Amu Darya, on the territory of historical Khwārazm. The khanate was ruled by members of the Qonghrat dynasty from the late eighteenth century through 1920, when it was eventually liquidated in a pro-Bolshevik *coup d'état*. The events described in the episode recounted below unfolded in January 1916, and reflect a much larger confrontation between the ruling dynasty and its Turkmen subjects. This conflict marked one of the most severe political crises in the history of Qonghrat rule in Khwārazm. The culmination of the siege of Urgench – the largest city and economic hub of the khanate – by rebel groups, mostly Turkmen clans, under the leadership of a certain Muḥammad Qurbān Sardār, better known as Junayd Khān (1857–1938),[2] is described thus:

> Then Muḥammad Ṣāliḥ Īshān went to Junayd Khān and Khān Īshān, asking them to forgive the trespasses of the dwellers of Urgench. Yet Khān Īshān, who was a mischief-maker and a despotic *īshān*, refused to accept [this request]. Thereupon, [the whole community] of *īshān*s of Urgench, having gathered together, declared that if they [= Junayd Khān and Khān Īshān] intended to destroy Urgench, they would have first to eliminate the whole community of the *īshān*s. Ultimately, [it was only thanks to this declaration as well as the payment of a ransom of] 60,000 *tilla* to

1 The current chapter originates from the paper read at the international workshop "Authority in Islam in Muslim Eurasia," Indiana University, March 24–25, 2017. I would like to thank Devin DeWeese, James Pickett, Paolo Sartori, Nuryoghdi Toshov, and Thomas Welsford for their thoughtful comments on the earlier drafts of the text. All errors contained herein are mine and mine alone.

2 On Junayd Khān and on the events described here, see further Ulfat Abdurasulov, "Konflikt kak resurs: anatomiia turkmenskikh besporiadkov v Khorezme, 1914–1916 gg.," *Ab Imperio*, 2018, No. 3: 141–86.

 DOI:10.1163/9789004527096_008

> them [= J.Kh. and Kh.I.] that those *īshāns* managed to keep the town of Urgench intact.[3]

What is remarkable about this description is the power the author attributes to the *īshāns*. The account makes it eminently clear that it was only due to the *īshāns*' involvement that the Turkmen leaders agreed to lift the siege of Urgench. As a consolation prize, the Turkmens confined themselves to collecting monetary contributions from the city's inhabitants, and refrained from plundering the city.

The episode also highlights the participation of a further *īshān*, albeit on the opposite side of the conflict. This was the figure referred to in the text as Khān Īshān, whom we encounter in numerous records of the Russian colonial administration in the region, where he is singled out for his "religious authority" among various Turkmen groups, especially the Yomut tribe. Some scholars suggest in fact that Khān Īshān's "religious authority" was instrumental in the rapid political ascendance of the Turkmen leader Junayd Khān in Khwārazm during the turbulent 1910s and early 1920s.[4] Continuing the story given by Laffasī, it is worth mentioning here that a few days later the same Junayd Khān and his detachment approached the capital of the khanate – the city of Khiva – where he besieged the very palace of the Khivan ruler Isfandiyār Khān (r. 1910–8). As one of the eyewitnesses – this time a Russian colonel – put it, after a short skirmish between the defenders of the palace and the attackers, a great calm fell over the participants as a "long string of *īshāns*" came forth from the inner court of the Khivan dynast, where they apparently had been holding negotiations. After some time, the officer continued, Isfandiyār Khān was brought out into the yard and "kissed Junayd's hand," whereupon the latter generously agreed to save the ruler's life. As in the previous instance, an *īshān* ensured that the marauders limited themselves to financial extraction, and refrained from spilling blood. "The Turkmens believe that the Khan's life was spared at the insistence of the influential Uzbek ishan Jalāl" (*nastoianiiami vliiatel'nogo uzbekskogo ishana*), concluded our author.[5]

---

3 Ḥasan-Murād Laffasī, *Gulshan-i sa'ādat*, MS Tashkent, Institute of Oriental Studies, inv. no. 7797, f. 45a.

4 G.I. Karpov and D.M. Batser, *Khivinskie turkmeny i konets Kungradskoi dinastii* (*Materialy po istorii turkmen*) (Ashkhabad: Turkmenskoe Gosudarstvennoe Izdatel'stvo, 1930), pp. 91–92, 108.

5 Geitsig, *Raport*, cited from Karpov and Batser, *Khivinskie turkmeny i konets Kungradskoi dinastii*, pp. 114–5. See also [Fedor Martson] *Voennomu ministru. 04.07.1916.*, TsGARUz, f. I-1, op. 31, d. 1104, l. 109.

Accounts such as this one are far from unique over the course of the history of Qonghrat-ruled Khwārazm. Various sources – from court chronicles to documents from the Khivan royal chancellery to colonial officers' notes – describe other conflicts between political and social groups, more often than not with specific emphasis on the participation of *īshān*s. In some instances, the *īshān*'s role is implicit or behind the scenes, as in the abovementioned episode, where their presence was noticed only by virtue of the Russian colonial officer's vigilance. In other cases, such as in Laffasī's aforementioned account, their presence is depicted more explicitly. In such testimonies the *īshān*s appear as principal intermediaries in conflicts between central authorities in Khiva and various population groups, whether within the Khwārazmian oasis or far beyond it (such as in Sarakhs or in the Qazaq steppe). What all these accounts have in common is the suggestion that the *īshān*s were able to transform their religious authority into an ability to motivate and persuade conflicting parties to come together to negotiate.

The *īshān*s of Central Asia are broadly recognized as spiritual leaders with Sufi communal affiliation. Their participation in conflicts and ability to attract parties to peace is often taken for granted, understood as deriving from their moral capital, the prestige which they attained by dint of their piety, as well as the role that "holy men" play in Muslim societies. Often their influence is portrayed as transcendental, somehow beyond the political processes and concrete power relations of the day. In the meanwhile, as Peter Brown puts it, such understandings "illustrate the prestige the holy man had already gained, they do not explain it."[6] Indeed, such descriptions of authority and power attributed to the holy men cannot alone explain their agency to mediate in conflicts between different Khwārazmian populations during periods of conflict. How might we better understand the nature of this political-religious authority?

Newer historiographical approaches, many of which have emerged from South Asian studies, might be utilized by scholars of Central Asian history to expand an analytical framework and broaden insights on technologies of government and on processes of power relations in the Central Asian khanates. Sanjay Subrahmanyam, for instance, argues in favor of shifting our analytical focus from "structures" and "forms" to "processes."[7] Farhat Hasan similarly broadens the scope of the *processual* approach by taking into consideration

6 Peter Brown, "The Rise and Function of the Holy Man in Late Antiquity," *The Journal of Roman Studies* 61 (1971), p. 81.

7 Sanjay Subrahmanyam, "The Mughal State – Structure or process? Reflections on Recent Western Historiography," *The Indian Economic and Social History Review* 29:3 (1992), pp. 291–321.

"the local experience of imperial sovereignty" through intricate levels of "interconnectedness between the imperial sovereignty and local power relations."[8] He also suggests that instead of searching for sources of saintly authority, we should rather focus on the process through which religious groups participated in the local networks of control and dominion.[9]

My own research builds on these historiographical trends to reconsider the role of *īshāns* as religious leaders *vis-à-vis* the broader power relations in which they were enmeshed. That is to say, I attempt to situate *īshāns*' religious authority through the lens of the processual character of the political field. In so doing, I shall focus on the intermediary activities of *īshāns*, and shall argue that their agency to act as mediators was facilitated not so much by their religious authority, as some autonomous force, as by a broader range of cultural conventions and pre-assigned political behaviors. The *īshāns* and the military elite alike were playing from a shared script, one that was shaped by the local exigencies of the day, and in which everyone had a role. Religious authority in this sense emerged from participation in a dynamic and volatile processes, and from the *īshāns*' individual ability to invoke the script at the proper moment.

2 Who Were the *Īshāns*?

As the authors of the article 'Īshān' in the *Encyclopaedia of Islam* put it, the term was widely in use in Central Asia and "always had honorific significance" in the sense of a *shaykh* or *murshid* who "lived with his followers in … [a] *khānqāh*, and sometimes at the tomb of a saint."[10] Sergey Abashin, drawing upon extensive ethnographical research, also suggests that the very utilization of the term "*īshān*" (lit. "they") was associated with the belief – prevalent in Central Asia – that uttering the personal names of "the spiritual leaders" was considered taboo, and that taking such names in vain could bring about "all sorts of misfortunes" for lay people.[11]

---

8 Farhat Hasan, *State and Locality in Mughal India. Power Relations in Western India, c. 1572–1730* (Cambridge: Cambridge University Press, 2006), pp. 1–8.

9 Ibid., p. 91.

10 W. Barthold, and [G.E. Wheeler], "Is̱hān," in *The Encyclopaedia of Islam. New Edition*, vol. IV (Leiden: Brill, 1997), p. 113.

11 See Sergey Abashin, "Ishan," in *Islam na territorii byvshei Rossiiskoi imperii. Èntsiklopedicheskii slovar'*, vol. 2, ed. S.M. Prozorov (Moscow: Vostochnaia literatura, 1999), pp. 40–1.

Īshāns are depicted in a similar manner in the rare Sufi works of the nineteenth century which have come down to us from Khwārazm.[12] They appear as recognized masters of the mystical path – *shaykhs* or *pīrs* (terms that were often used interchangeably with *Īshān*), who led the Sufi lodges (*khānaqāh-nishīn*) with a number followers (*ṣūfī; khalīfa*) and disciples (*murīd*). *Īshāns* often appear as the founders of madrasahs, where they would train students (*mullā-lār; ṭalaba-i ʿulūm*) and 'teach the Sufi path to the seekers' (*ṭalaba-lärgha taʿlīm-i ṭarīqat qïlïb*).[13]

Without going into details of the doctrine, or detailing the practices and organizational structure of Central Asian Sufi groups in the eighteenth and nineteenth centuries,[14] it is nevertheless worth noting that by the period under

12 Bakhtiyar Babajanov, editor and translator of the *Risāla-yi khalvat-i ṣūfīhā*, had earlier noted that by the 19th century in the region of Khwārazm, the tradition of compiling Sufi hagiographical works "gradually began to fade;" see Baxtiyar M. Babadžanov, "Xalwat-i ṣūfīhā (The Religious Landscape of Khorezm at the Turn of the 19th Century)," in *Muslim Culture in Russia and Central Asia*, vol. 3: *Arabic, Persian and Turkic Manuscripts (15th–19th Centuries)*, ed. Anke von Kügelgen *et al.* (Berlin: Klaus Schwarz Verlag, 2000), p. 119. Today, however, along with the *Risāla-yi khalvat-i ṣūfīhā*, we know about other hagiographical texts from nineteenth-century Khwārazm. One is the *Khwārazm taʿrīfi* ("Description of Khwārazm"), an anonymous text in Chaghatay verse on the Sufi landscape in Khwārazm, an analysis of which has recently been published by Devin DeWeese; see his "Encountering Saints in the Hallowed Ground of a Regional Landscape: The 'Description of Khwārazm' and the Experience of Pilgrimage in 19th-Century Central Asia," in *Saintly Spheres and Islamic Landscapes*, ed. Daphna Ephrat *et al.* (Leiden: Brill, 2021), pp. 183–218. Another is the *Riyāż al-dhākirīn* ("The Garden of the *Dhikr*-Performers"), an extensive hagiographical work on the Sufis of Khwārazm, authored by Dāmullā Allāh-yār Makhdūm Khudāy-berdi-oghlï. The single known manuscript of the work is currently in private hands in the province of Khorezm in Uzbekistan; see also Alfrid K. Bustanov, "The Bulghar Region as a 'Land of Ignorance:' Anti-Colonial Discourse in Khwarazmian Connectivity," *Journal of Persianate Studies* 9 (2016), p. 189, and Devin DeWeese, "Mapping Khwārazmian Connections in the History of Sufi Traditions. Local Embeddedness, Regional Networks, and Global Ties of the Sufi Communities of Khwārazm," *Eurasian Studies* 14 (2016), p. 88, n. 77. To the best of my knowledge, Alfrid Bustanov and Paolo Sartori are currently working on publishing an edition of the manuscript's text.

13 See, for instance, Dāmullā Allāh-yār Makhdūm Khudāy-berdi-oghlï, *Riyāż al-dhākirīn*, MS Urgench, Private Collection of Ahmadjon Rahmatullaev, ff. 123a, 144a–144b.

14 These topics are well covered in the historiography: see Bakhtiar Babadzhanov, "On the History of Naqshbandiya Mujaddidiya in Central Mawara'nnahr in the Late 18th and Early 19th Centuries," in *Muslim Culture in Russia and Central Asia from the 18th to the Early 19th Centuries*, ed. Anke von Kügelgen *et al.* (Berlin: Klaus Schwarz, Verlag, 1996), pp. 385–413; Devin DeWeese, "Organizational Patterns and Developments within Sufi Communities," in *The Wiley Blackwell History of Islam*, ed. Armando Salvatore *et al.* (Hoboken, New Jersey: John Wiley & Sons, 2018), pp. 329–50; idem, "Re-Envisioning the History of Sufi Communities in Central Asia: Continuity and Adaptation in Sources and Social Frameworks, 16th–20th Centuries," in *Sufism in Central Asia: New Perspectives on*

study the previous form of Sufi communal affiliations known in the forms of brotherhoods (*ṭarīqa*) – e.g. Yasavī, Kubravī, Qādirī – had ceased to exist as discrete entities.[15] Nevertheless, those designations "persisted in the popular imagination as ideals and inclusive lineages."[16] Furthermore, by the nineteenth century, the categories of "Sufis" and "Ulama" had all but collapsed into one another, as nearly all ulama were also Sufis in one sense or another.[17] For the purposes of the present article, the important point emerging from this larger body of research is that *īshān*s were not sectarian leaders of narrowly defined Sufi orders, but rather wielded numerous kinds of authority within a current of piety that enjoyed broad popular support.

Thus in the Khivan Khanate, Sufis were employed far beyond the walls of the *khānaqāh*, appearing first and foremost in the office of "official" legists, i.e. *qāżī/ra'īs/muftī*s.[18] Moreover, apparently in contrast with other regions of Central Asia, in Khwārazm the term "*Īshān*" was often explicitly appended to the formal legal positions buttressing the khanate. For instance, top jurists at the court of the Qonghrat khans bore titles such as *qāżī kalān-īshān*,[19] *qāżī-'askar- īshān*,[20] *qāżī al-khāṣṣ-īshān*.[21] Lest these titles be understood as the honorifics carried exclusively by the super elite, it is important to note that even humbler figures in remote provincial settlements, such as Ambar-Manaq,[22] or Shahabad,[23] boasted similar titles.

Sufi Tradition, 15th–21st Centuries, ed. Devin DeWeese and Jo-Ann Gross (Leiden: Brill, 2018), pp. 21–74. For the long-durée historical perspective on Sufi traditions in Khwārazm, see also DeWeese, "Mapping Khwārazmian Connections," pp. 37–97.

15 Moreover, Sufi adepts often "obtained initiation from several different masters" at the same time; Devin DeWeese, "Dis-Ordering' Sufism in Early Modern Central Asia: Suggestions for Rethinking the Sources and Social Structures of Sufi History in the 18th and 19th Centuries," in *History and Culture of Central Asia*, ed. Bakhtiyar Babadjanov and Kawahara Yayoi (Tokyo: The University of Tokyo, 2012), pp. 268–9; idem, "Mapping Khwārazmian Connections," p. 86.

16 James Pickett, *The Persianate Sphere during the Age of Empires: Islamic Scholars and Networks of Exchange in Central Asia 1747–1917* (Ph.D. dissertation, Princeton University, 2015), p. 185.

17 James Pickett, "Enemies beyond the Red Sands: The Bukhara-Khiva Dynamic as Mediated by Textual Genre," *Journal of Persianate Studies*, 9 (2016): 161. For a critique of the conceptual binary of Sufi and ulama see also his *Polymaths of Islam: Power and Networks of Knowledge in Central Asia* (Ithaca and London: Cornell University Press, 2020), pp. 130–41.

18 See Paolo Sartori, "On Madrasas, Legitimation, and Islamic Revival in 19th-Century Khorezm: Some Preliminary Observations," *Eurasian Studies* 14 (2016), pp. 108–9.

19 TsGARUz, I-125, op. 2, d. 633, l. 114.

20 TsGARUz, I-125, op. 2, d. 633, l. 24–24 ob.; l. 190–190ob.

21 Laffasī, *Gulshan-i sa'ādat*, f. 6a.

22 TsGARUz, f. I-125, op. 1, d. 498, l. 44.

23 TsGARUz, f. I-125, op. 1, d. 498, l. 86; Laffasī, *Gulshan-i sa'ādat*, ff. 6a, 32a.

A certain Dāmullā Allāh-yār Makhdūm Khudāy-berdi-oghli̊ authored an important work called *Riyāż al-dhākirīn* ("The Garden of the *Dhikr*-Performers"), one of the few works of the genre of hagiography known from the region of Khwārazm during the nineteenth century. While narrating the biographical accounts of various Sufi leaders who dwelled with their followers in the different places of the oasis, the author often reports about the madrasahs led by those *īshāns*.[24] This information is also confirmed by documents of the Khivan royal chancellery, which demonstrate that the foundations of such madrasahs were often in the name of famous *īshāns*, often also under the sponsorship of the Qonghrat dynasts.[25] One may safely conclude then that graduates of those madrasahs that were led by individual *īshāns*, who had a "Sufi background," were subsequently widely employed in various fields of activity, as official legists, scribes, clerks, and suchlike.

Īshāns and Sufi groups were thus integrated into the administrative and bureaucratic environment of the khanate, and were able to establish themselves and attract adherents from scholarly and literary circles, as well as representatives of the ruling house. For instance, Bābā Jān Thanāʾī, a Khivan writer of the second half of the nineteenth century, noted that Muḥammad Raḥīm Khān I (r. 1806–24), one of the most prominent representatives of the Qonghrat dynasty, was married to the daughter of Ādīna Īshān, an influential Sufi shaykh of the time.[26] According to Sayyid Ḥāmid Tūra Kāmyāb, yet another Khivan author and a Qonghrat prince, his father, the ruler Sayyid Muḥammad Raḥim Khān (r. 1856–64), maintained close relations with "the venerable *īshāns* of the time," and even was on "father-son terms" with some of them.[27] The prince, by his own admission, had been cultivating a relationship with influential Sufi leaders since his earliest days, and overtly emphasized their transformative impact on his education and worldview. Describing the years during which he administered the madrasah and mosque which he had

---

24 Dāmullā Allāh-yār Makhdūm, *Riyāż al-dhākirīn*, ff. 122b–123a.

25 See for instance: TsGARUz, f. I-125, op. 2, d. 3, l. 1. A recent study by Paolo Sartori eloquently demonstrates how the Qonghrats pursued a large-scale project of establishing madrasahs in order to train a corps of qualified officials for the maintenance of the new bureaucratic apparatus: Sartori, "On Madrasas," 98–134.

26 Bābā Jān Thanāʾī, *Tawārīkh-i Khwārazmshāhīya*, MS Berlin, Staatsbibliothek, inv. no. Or. quart. 1605, f. 141.

27 Sayyid Ḥāmid Tūra Kāmyāb, *Tawārīkh al-khawānīn*, MS Tashkent, Institute of Oriental Studies, inv. no. 7717, f. 197b–198a. The work is also available in a Cyrillic-script edition; see Sayid Homid Tura Komyob, *Taworikh ul-Khavonin*, ed. N. Norqulov *et al.* (Tashkent: Akademiya, 2002). On similar evidence of Qonghrat rulers' engagement in "the Sufi path," see for instance Devin DeWeese, "Encountering Saints in the Hallowed Ground," pp. 188–9.

founded, Kāmyāb recalls that he often "invited *īshāns* and *murshids*," "deriving great spiritual pleasure from verbal communication (*ṣuḥbat*) with them as well as [from the rituals of] vocal recitations (*jahr*) [performed] in the mosque."[28]

The *īshāns* were also deeply integrated into local power structures, and their influence was especially palpable among the various Turkmen and Qaraqalpaq tribal groups that lived in the Khwārazm region.[29] Russian authors also emphasized the influence of sacred lineages, particularly that of the *īshāns*, among Turkmen clans.[30] Khivan court chronicles also provide information regarding particular *īshāns* living among the Turkmens, making special note of the considerable influence they wielded among them. As an especially vivid example, we might consider the famed Khwāja Aḥmad Īshān, whom the nineteenth-century Khivan chronicler Āgahī described as "a defender, spiritual mentor, and guide of all the Turkmens, notably those of the Yomuts and Chowdurs."[31] It was due primarily to Khwāja Aḥmad Īshān's mediation, says Āgahī, that a negotiation process between Khivan authorities and rebel Turkmen groups emerged during the height of the political crisis in the mid-1850s, as discussed below.

No less important was the case of a certain Qutluq Khwāja Īshān (d. 1878), as depicted in the *Riyāż al-dhākirīn*. After the death of his spiritual mentor, the prominent Muḥammad Sharīf Īshān (a.k.a. Nāghāy Īshān, d. 1841),[32] Qutluq Khwāja dwelled in a small village next to Qonghrat – the northernmost province of Khwārazm, where he led a Sufi lodge and "instructed adepts in

28 Kāmyāb, *Tawārīkh al-khawānīn*, f. 197b.

29 On the "deep embeddedness" of Khwārazmian Sufi communities in local social topography, as well as their engagement in wider trans-regional networks, see DeWeese, "Mapping Khwārazmian Connections," pp. 37–97.

30 Sergei M. Demidov, *Turkmenskie owliady* (Ashkhabad: Ylym, 1976), pp. 20, 24. A mid-19th-century Russian author notes that a certain Nūr Muḥammad Īshān, "also known as Sary-ishan," son of Biktirlī Īshān, had been acting in the capacity of *qāżī* among Turkmen Chowdur groups of Manghïshlaq: see M.N. Galkin, *Ėtnograficheskie i istoricheskie materialy po Srednei Azii i Orenburgskomu kraiu* (St. Petersburg: Izdanie Ia.A. Isakova, 1868), pp. 34–5. Another Russian author describes the same *Īshān* as "the main spiritual person among the Manghïshlaq Turkmens," who often acted as a "reconciler in the quarrels between the Kirghiz (= Qazaqs) and the Turkmens," and whom "both [Turkmens and Qazaqs] equally respected;" see "Raport komendanta Novo-Petrovskogo ukrepleniia maiora I.A. Uskova. 09.02.1856," in *O slukhakh i sobytiyakh v Srednei Azii. Sbornik dokumentov*, vol. 1, ed. B.T. Zhanaev (Karaganda: TOO Kazakhskoe obshchestvo slepykh, 2016), p. 192 (doc. no. 84).

31 Muḥammad Rižā Mīrāb Agahī, "*Jāmiʿ al-Vāqiʿāt-i Sulṭānī*," ed. Nouryaghdi Tashev (Samarkand/Tashkent, 2012), 229.

32 On Muḥammad Sharīf Īshān see Bustanov, "The Bulghar Region as a 'Land of Ignorance,'" pp. 189–92.

the Sufi path."[33] In the meantime, the Qaraqalpaq clans in the vicinity invited the holy man to settle among them. The author describes the many "disputes and conflicts" among the Qaraqalpaq elders that had erupted immediately preceding Qutluq Khwāja Īshān's arrival, as each of them sought to entice the holy man to settle on the territory of his own clan. Upon his arrival, however, the Īshān decided to dwell in a relatively neutral territory next to the locality of Qarāqūm:

> [His Holiness said:] "We [the "royal 'we,'" referring to himself] have deigned to stay in this particular abode, but we will offer prayers for the sake of *all* your people (*jamāʿa*).... If your decision is to follow our faith from now on, then erect a mosque and a madrasah in this place." Most of the [Qaraqalpaqs] found this proposal worthy of approval, as [the place] was equally accessible for all [clans]. Therefore, they erected a worthy madrasah and mosque and ... lived for many years under the shadow of the blessing of His Holiness, cultivating those lands and giving their tithing (*dahyak*) in his favor.[34]

Judging from the further narration of the author, one may also conclude that, upon the aforementioned insurrection of a number of Qaraqalpaq clans against the Khivan central authorities in 1855–1856, Qutluq Khwāja Īshān would provide his support and, apparently, intercession in support of Ér Nażar Bīy, one of the leaders of the rebel Qaraqalpaq insurrection.[35]

This case may serve as an illustration of the dynamics underlying cooperation between the holy men and local groups in nineteenth-century Khwārazm. The *īshān*'s presence among the Qaraqalpaq clans enabled them to have not only a spiritual guide, but also a political intermediary – an intercessor and patron who could provide protection from the central authorities. The holy man, in turn, acquired social support and material resources, which allowed

33 Dāmullā Allāh-yār Makhdūm, *Riyāż al-dhakirīn*, f. 143b.

34 Dāmullā Allāh-yār Makhdūm, *Riyāż al-dhākirīn*, ff. 144a–144b. The existence of Qūtlūq Khwāja Īshān's mosque in the locality of Qarāqūm is also supported by ethnographic data; see Makset Karlybaev, "L'instruction musulmane et les îshân chez les Karakalpaks du XIXe siècle," in *Karakalpaks et autres gens de l'Aral: Entre rivages et déserts* (Tashkent/Aix-en-Provence: Édisud, 2002; *Cahiers de l'Asie centrale*, 10), p. 183.

35 Dāmullā Allāh-yār Makhdūm, *Riyāż al-dhākirīn*, ff. 145a; for a detailed description of those events, see Muḥammad Riżā Mīrāb Āgahī, *Gulshan-i dawlat*, MS Tashkent, Institute of Oriental Studies, inv. no. 7572, ff. 40b–65a.

him to expand the number of his followers, and consequently to accumulate further influence and authority.[36]

It is worth noting here that the local sources often distinguish various *īshān*s and *īshān*-groups not only according to their Sufi affiliation or the type of recitation (*dhikr*) – whether vocal or silent – they exercised, but also according to their political orientation or the social groups they represented. More specifically, they refer to those who lived, for instance, among Turkmens as "the Turkmen *īshān*s" (*turkmān īshānlari*)[37] or "the Yomut *īshān*s" (*yamūt īshānlari*),[38] thus differentiating at the sub-tribal level. Meanwhile, references to "the Khivan *īshān*s" (*Khīvaq īshānlari*)[39] hints at the latter group's political inclination towards Khiva, and their access to the authority of the khan.

3 "And the *Īshān*'s Consciousness Flew away from His Head:" On Mediation

In the following part I focus on the intermediary activities of *īshān*s in conflicts between various population groups in the Khanate of Khiva. As noted previously, more often than not the descriptions of conflict between various groups in Khwārazm mention the participation of *īshān*s as mediators, envoys (*élchī*) or intercessors (*shafīʿ*). Instances of such activity can be seen both inside the "core" oasis of Khwārazm and far beyond its borders.

One illustrative example involves the return of the remains of the body of the Khivan ruler Muḥammad Amīn Khān. During an ill-fated military campaign to Sarakhs in March 1855, Muḥammad Amīn Khān was killed by a group of Teke Turkmens, who then took possession of his corpse.[40] But then, thanks to the intervention of "a certain *īshān* from among the Sarïq [Turkmens]," the Khivan ruler's corpse was returned to Khiva, together with prisoners taken from his entourage, for the sake of a decent burial.[41]

The involvement of *īshān*s in the resolution of conflicts among ruling groups has appeared to be pivotal. In his monumental *Firdaws al-iqbāl*, the

---

36 On the roles of *īshān*s in the Qaraqalpaq environment in the 19th-century, see further Karlybaev, "L'instruction musulmane et les îshân chez les Karakalpaks du XIXe siècle," pp. 177–91.

37 Muḥammad Yūsuf Bayānī, *Shajara-yi Khwārazmshāhī*, MS Tashkent, Institute of Oriental Studies, inv. no. 9596, f. 369b.

38 Laffasī, *Gulshan-i saʿādat*, ff. 44a, 45b.

39 Bayānī, *Shajara-yi Khwārazmshāhī*, f. 369b.

40 Bayānī, *Shajara-yi Khwārazmshāhī*, ff. 347a–352a.

41 Bayānī, *Shajara-yi Khwārazmshāhī*, f. 353b.

local court chronicler Shīr Muḥammad Mūnis narrates the story of Niyāz Bék, a political opponent of the ruler Muḥammad Raḥīm Khān I, who in 1811 escaped from the latter's clutches and sought asylum with an influential *shaykh* from Khwāja-Éli – Sayyid Tursūn Khwāja Īshān. The Īshān not only provided shelter for the fugitive, but also interceded for him before the Qonghrat dynast, securing forgiveness both for Niyāz Bék himself and for his other family members.[42] Thanks to Sayyid Tursūn Khwāja Īshān's intercession (*shafāʿat*), Muḥammad Raḥīm Khān I additionally "absolved the sins" of a further political opponent of the time, a certain Mullā Dawlat Naẓar.[43]

Yet the most frequent accounts of holy men's intercession and mediation involve various Turkmen groups, whether between one another or between the Turkmens and the Khivan authorities. There was ample opportunity: insurrection by Turkmen groups was a constant political reality in the Khivan Khanate, throughout the entire period of Qonghrat rule. These uprisings could be quite large in scale. This happened, for example, during the Turkmen insurrection in 1915–6, a few episodes of which were considered in the opening part of this essay. An even larger-scale Turkmen uprising occurred a half-century earlier, in the second half of the 1850s, constituting one of the most severe political crises in the history of the khanate. Over the course of twelve months in 1855, the Qonghrat dynasty lost two of its leaders in battle with various Turkmen groups. At the same time, the Qaraqalpaq chieftains of the Aral Sea littoral proclaimed as khan a certain Zarlïq Töre, a Chinggisid prince, and repudiated their former submission to Khivan authority. The leaders of various Jamshidi groups, who had in recent years provided a bulwark of military support to Khiva, also repudiated their submission and plundered a number of fortresses in the central part of the khanate. Of all these opposition groups, however, it was the Turkmen clans of the Yomuts, Chowdurs, and Yemrelis that displayed the strongest resistance.[44]

In December 1855, after several months of turbulence, the newly enthroned Khivan ruler Qutluq Murād Khān (r. 1855–6) sought to initiate a negotiation process with rebellious Turkmen chieftains. The most influential *īshān*s from both the Khivan and the Turkmen sides were involved. To illustrate these events, let us turn to two descriptions left by the Khivan authors Muḥammad Riżā Āgahī (1809–74) and Muḥammad Yusūf Bayānī (1858–1923), which provide

42 Shir Muhammad Mirab Munis, and Muhammad Riza Mirab Agahi, *Firdaws al-iqbāl: History of Khorezm*, tr. Yuri Bregel (Leiden and Boston: Brill, 1999), p. 382.

43 Mūnis and Āgahī, *Firdaws al-iqbāl*, tr. Bregel, 382.

44 See Iu.È. Bregel', *Khorezmskie turkmeny v XIX veke* (Moscow: Izdatel'stvo vostochnoi literatury, 1961), pp. 197–225.

us with two distinct perspectives on the *īshāns*' participation in the negotiation process.

It is noteworthy that Āgahī attributes the very initiation of these negotiations to the merits of Khwāja Aḥmad Īshān, whom, as noted above, he calls "a defender, spiritual mentor, and guide of all the Turkmens, notably those of the Yomuts and Chowdurs."[45] This influential *īshān* threatened the rebellious Turkmens with heavenly punishment for their mutiny, and refused to participate in their funeral ceremonies (*janāza*), and furthermore "forbade other [*īshāns*] from participating" as well.[46] Such arguments proved expedient and, according to the chronicler, prompted the Turkmen elders to beg Khwāja Aḥmad Īshān to be their intermediary (*shafīʿ*), and to go to Khiva and ask the ruler Qutluq Murād Khān to forgive their misdeeds. Qutluq Murād Khān acceded to the requests of the holy man and, in response, provided this intermediary with a supplementary group of *īshāns* who would accompany Khwāja Aḥmad Īshān. The whole group of holy men was then dispatched to the various Turkmen localities, where they succeeded in persuading the elders of the "mutinous" Yomuts and Chowdurs to appear before the khan in order to "repent of their crimes and beg [a royal] pardon."[47] Judging from this account it appeared that the *īshāns*' intervention into the conflict was instrumental in bringing the parties to the negotiating table. Yet, Āgahī's rather rosy account of events does not match with descriptions of the conflict in other sources.

The account of the same story by Muḥammad Yūsuf Bayānī, another Khivan author, is of considerable interest, since Bayānī provides us with specific details of the episode and negotiation process undertaken by this group of *īshāns* with the various Turkmen elders. Bayānī based his depiction on evidence provided by a certain Jumʿa Niyāz Dīwān, a Khivan court official, who took part in that mission alongside the holy men. According to the chronicler, it was Qutluq Murād Khān rather than the *īshāns* who initiated the negotiations. Qutluq Murād Khān instructed his officials "to gather there all the Turkmen and Khivan *īshāns*," who then should be sent to the Turkmens as envoys (*élchī*).[48] Meanwhile, a large group of Khivan troops approached the Turkmen settlements next to the fortress of Hilali. Only *after* the display of military force was a group of envoys numbering 25 persons, consisting of "*īshāns* and Ṣūfīs" as well as several Khivan officials, including the aforementioned Jumʿa Niyāz Dīwān, dispatched toward the Turkmens. Bayānī does not say anything about

45 Āgahī, *Jāmiʿ al-Vāqiʿāt-i Sulṭānī*, 229.
46 Ibid.
47 Ibid.
48 Bayānī, *Shajara-yi Khwārazmshāhī*, f. 369b.

the personality of the "Turkmen *īshāns*" who participated in the mission, but he does list those whom he distinguishes as "Khivan *īshāns*" – ʿAbdullāh Īshān, ʿUmar Īshān, Muḥammad Karīm Īshān from Özbék-Yaf, another Muḥammad Karīm Īshān from Vazir, and Jumʿa Niyāz Īshān from Yumru.[49] As soon as the group left the Khivan camp and approached the fortress (*qalʿa*) of the Turkmens of Yemreli, they were immediately surrounded by 500 armed, aggressive horsemen from that clan. Bayānī's informant reports that the riders turned their blades towards the envoys, and that it was thanks only to the *īshāns*' statement that "we are envoys and envoys should not be murdered" (*bular élchidur élchighä ölüm yoqdur*) that they escaped with their lives. As the author puts it, the *īshāns* were so frightened that "their hearts had leapt into their mouths" or, in the literal Turkī, their "consciousness flew away from their heads" (*īshānlarnïng hūshï bashlarïdïn uchtï*).[50] It seems that the presence of the *īshāns* was *necessary*, but perhaps not by itself *sufficient*.

The whole group of envoys then proceeded to the Yemreli fortress, where they conveyed to the leader of the clan, ʿAważ Muḥammad Wakīl, the Khivan ruler's offer "to relinquish past grievances" and to assist the envoys in persuading the other Turkmen clans to obey the khan. The answer from the Yemreli was that the Turkmens were ready to consider the proposals of the Khivan ruler – but only on one condition. They suggested that until the negotiations were resolved, the Khivan authorities should provide the Yemreli clan with food and money for their equipment as a gesture of good will.[51] Only after the requested tribute and payments were delivered would the Yemreli chieftain ʿAważ Muḥammad Wakīl agree to accompany the *īshān* group to the other Turkmen clans in order to fulfil their mission.

Next the envoys proceeded to the settlement (*oba*) of the Yomut clan of Orus Qoshchi, the leader of which, Khwāja Niyāz Wakīl, met with the *īshāns* and even declared his readiness to go to Khiva and express his obedience to the khan. However, negotiations with other Yomut clans proved to be by far less successful. Suffice it to say, the elders of the majority of the Yomut groups not only rejected any suggestions of reconciliation with the Khivan authorities, but they even refused to meet with those *īshān* envoys (*bizlär yarashmaymïz wa barïb īshānlarnï ham körmäsmiz*). Even the sons of the same Khwāja Niyāz Wakīl expressed utter reluctance to reconcile themselves with Khiva, stating

49 Āgahī's list of *īshāns* slightly differs from Bayānī's – ʿUmar Īshān, ʿAbdullāh Īshān, Sāʿat Īshān, Muḥammad Karīm Īshān; see Āgahī, *Jāmi al-Vāqiʿāt-i Sulṭānī*, 229.

50 Bayānī, *Shajara-yi Khwārazmshāhī*, f.369b–370a.

51 Ibid., f. 370a–b.

that "if our father intends to make peace [with the khan], then let him [alone] go to Khiva."[52]

The embassy had been among the Yomuts for 12 full days attempting to exhort them, but the latter flatly refused to accept any terms of truce. Having failed to achieve positive results among the Yomuts, the *īshān* envoys continued further to the locality of Chash-Tepa, the main area of residence of the Chowdur Turkmens. The elders of the Chowdurs also rejected the envoys' suggestions to reconcile with Khiva, thereby expressing their solidarity with the Yomut leaders on this matter (*yāmūt né ṭarīqada bolsa bīzlār āndāqmïz*). However, this was not the end of the *īshāns*' adventures. As soon as the envoys rode away from the Chowdurs' encampments, they were attacked by people of one of the Chowdur clans. The robbery of the *īshān*s was prevented due to the intervention of a Chowdur chieftain, who, according to Bayānī's informant, "managed to calm down those [Chowdurs] with great difficulty."[53] If we take the results of this mission at face value, it becomes evident that only a few groups of Turkmens agreed to go to Khiva, whereas the majority of Yomuts and Chowdurs expressed their reluctance to negotiate and disregarded the *īshāns*' attempts at mediation. Even ʿAważ Muḥammad Wakīl, the aforementioned leader of Yemreli, who previously had received gifts and payments from the khan, also refused to accept a truce with the Khivan authorities.

Thus, Bayānī's description of negotiations with the Turkmen clans as facilitated by the *īshān*s differs substantially from that offered by his predecessor Āgahī. Not only did the *īshān*s' mission fail to achieve complete success, but the very lives of the holy men had been repeatedly under the threat of physical violence. The behavior and actions of the Turkmens leaves no doubt that they regarded the *īshān*s neither as neutral parties, nor as untouchable holy men. On the contrary, it turned out that in this specific context, Turkmen leaders considered the *īshān*s as partisan political agents representing Khiva's interests. This less than auspicious version of the story is corroborated by a handful of similar accounts in the Khivan chronicles, where the *īshān*s' attempts to intercede in the conflict between Turkmens and Khiva ended in vain, resulting only in humiliation and insults at the hands of the Turkmens.[54]

This case illustrates the highly instrumental character of the *īshān*s' involvement in the mediation and negotiation process. Numerous rescripts and reports among the documents of the Khivan chancellery paint a similar picture, showing that the success or failure of dialogues and agreements between

52 Bayānī, *Shajara-yi Khwārazmshāhī*, f. 370b.
53 *ba-zūr ularghä taskīn bérdi*, Bayānī, *Shajara-yi Khwārazmshāhī*, f. 371a.
54 See Āgahī, *Gulshan-i dawlat*, f. 52a.

conflicting groups was often determined by the real-world political circumstances of the day. For instance, documents provide evidence of discussions over numbers of Turkmen hostages – *āq-oylī* – to be handed over to Khiva, or the sum of compensation which rebel groups of Turkmen were demanded to pay to the communities whom they plundered, or on reciprocal obligations of Khivan agencies toward the Turkmens. It is clear that the negotiation process involved various actors from both the Khivan and Turkmen sides, and not just the *īshān*s alone. But by remaining quietly "visible," the *īshān*s frequently enabled negotiations that might otherwise have been impossible.

4 The Power of Convention: The Case of the Qazaq Sulṭān Élikay

The *īshān*s, it seems quite clear, functioned as an effective instrument for initiating the negotiation process. The spiritual profile of the *īshān*s, derived from a piety manifest in their spiritual activities, furnished their ability to precipitate and maintain communication between the conflicting parties. The *īshān*s' participation was of particular importance in circumstances where conflicting parties were *already* favorably inclined toward the idea of negotiation for separate reasons. In such cases, mediation by holy men offered an opportunity to begin negotiations. In a state of conflict, establishing direct dialogue between warring parties would have been extremely difficult, since any such move by either party might be perceived as a manifestation of weakness, to the detriment of their standing. The status of *īshān*s as spiritual figureheads allowed the parties to obey the *īshān*s' "admonitions" and "exhortations," and thereby "save face" while entering into negotiations or compromise. Hence, it was more about the authority of the *īshān*s, conditioned by certain cultural conventions and accepted, adopted, and implemented within this political culture.

An episode involving the Qazaq chieftain Ér Muḥammad Qāsim-oghlï, otherwise known as Sulṭān Élikay, provides an illustration of how this often worked in practice. Ér Muḥammad was a Chinggisid Sulṭān, one of the leaders of the Qazaq groups of the lower reaches of the Syr Darya.[55] This region was of strategic importance for the Qonghrat rulers of Khiva, who, since the establishment of their power over Khwārazm in the early nineteenth century,

---

55 For further details of Sulṭān Ér Muḥammad's biography, see Irina V. Erofeeva, "Kazakhskie khany i khanskie dinastii v XVIII–seredine XIX vv.," in *Kul'tura i istoriia Tsentral'noi Azii i Kazakhstana: Problemy i perspektivy issledovaniia* (Almaty: Fond Sorosa-Kazakhstan, 1997), pp. 140–1.

persistently sought to maintain their influence there.[56] In their policy in the lower Syr Darya, the Khivan authorities exploited local leaders as intermediaries, regularly switching their support from one such individual to another. Thus it was that Sulṭān Élikay, with Khivan backing, was able to expand his power and maintain control over the area in the mid-1840s.[57] In 1849, however, on the pretext of receiving an audience with the Khivan ruler Muḥammad Amīn Khān, Élikay was summoned to Khiva, and thereupon was taken into custody. After a few years of 'honorable' captivity in Khiva, in early 1852, he managed to flee to the lower Syr Darya and was subsequently able to re-establish his influence in the area.[58]

After his escape from Khivan imprisonment in 1852, Élikay undertook various initiatives to rescue his family members who were still imprisoned. According to various sources, his mother, three of his wives, and two children, as well as a group of looser dependents, were still kept by the Khivan authorities.[59] The return of family members, apparently, was a matter of prestige for Sulṭān Élikay. In seeking his dependents' release, he tried to involve in negotiations the Russian administration in Orenburg headed by General Vasilii Perovskii (second term in office: 1851–7). Consequently, a group of Qazaq notables was dispatched to Khiva on behalf of both the Orenburg administration and Sulṭān Élikay to negotiate with the Khivan authorities about this matter. The Orenburg administration suggested that the Khivan administration pay a sum of money (200 *chervonets*) as a ransom for Élikay's family members.[60]

Upon the Qazaq envoys' arrival, the Khivan officials were clearly confronted with a dilemma. To return Élikay's family upon the first request of the Russian administration (even though it was dressed in the form of redemption) was

56 On Khivan policy in the lower Syr-Darya basin, see A.I. Dobromyslov, "Turgaiskaia oblast:' Istoricheskii ocherk," in *Izvestiia Orenburgskogo otdela IRGO* 17 (Tver': Tipo-litografiia N.Rodionova, 1902), pp. 258–471.

57 In 1846 Sulṭān Ér Muḥammad was entrusted by the Khivan ruler Muḥammad Amīn Khān with a warrant that recognized him as khan of some of the Qazaq clans in the lower Syr Darya. In 1847, the sultan was appointed head of the Khwāja Niyāz Qalʿa fortress – the principal Khivan outpost in the lower Syr Darya; see Erofeeva, "Kazakhskie khany i khanskie dinastii," p. 95.

58 L. Meier, *Kirgizskaia step' Orenburgskogo vedomstva* (St. Petersburg: Tipografiia E. Veimara i F. Perona, 1865), p. 73; Iskander Batyrshin, "Zapiska mladshego perevodchika Orenburgskoi pogranichnoi komissii Iskandera Batyrshina o Khivinskom khanstve i khane prisyrdar'inskikh kazakhov Ermukhamede (Ilikee) Kasymove," in *Istoriia Kazakhstana v russkikh istochnikakh XVI–XIX vv.*, ed. I.V. Erofeeva and T.B. Zhanaev (Almaty: Daik-Press, 2007), pp. 304–5.

59 *O slukhakh i sobytiyakh v Srednei Azii*, pp. 648–9.

60 "[Osmalovski I.Ya.] Raport Orenburgskomu i Samarskomu General-Gubernatoru V.A. Perovskomu, 30.04.1853," in *O slukhakh i sobytiyakh v Srednei Azii*, pp. 19–20.

obviously unacceptable in terms of maintaining their prestige and authority, particularly among Qazaq groups. Furthermore, the initiation of direct negotiations with Élikay was also hardly inappropriate for the Khivans, as it could be perceived as a sign of weakness. On the other hand, it was also a vital issue for Khivan policy, especially in the face of growing Russian expansion, to restore relations with Sultan Élikay in order to drive him back into his formerly subjugated state and to utilize his potential for maintaining Khiva's influence in the lower reaches of the Syr Darya. It took Khivan officials forty-five days from the time of the Qazaq envoys' arrival in Khiva to come up with their decision. Ultimately, the Qazaq envoys were informed that Sulṭān Élikay's family was being held in captivity "for the sake of maintaining the stability of state affairs and governance,"[61] and that they could not be released upon the demand of Russian administration.[62] However, the envoys were also informed that if Sulṭān Élikay really wished to restore good and peaceful relations with Khiva, he should communicate via someone called ʿAzīz Khwāja Chaghatāy-oghlï.

> The Sulṭān [Élikay] should contact a certain ʿAzīz Khwāja, the son of Chaghatāy, to seek his advice, and then let us know about his intention to be in peace with us and not in enmity. Furthermore, he [Élikay] should provide [us] with a letter on his behalf [with appropriate content] stamped by his seal; then perhaps we shall return his mother and children …[63]

One may wonder who exactly this ʿAzīz Khwāja was. Among the materials of the Khivan royal chancellery we managed to find a handful of references to this individual, where he is designated as an *īshān*, and is accorded the epithets "the sign of faith" and "the imprint of the Sharīʿa."[64] According to information from the Orenburg administration, ʿAzīz Khwāja had been a "religious

61 *mamlakat niżāmï wa padishāhlïgh mahāmï intiżāmï üchün*, see *Ūrūnbūrgh maḥkamasīnīnk jān ārālīgha*, Institute of Oriental Manuscripts, St. Petersburg, *Arkhiv Vostokovedov*, f. 61, op. 1, d. 13, l. 48.

62 "*oruṣ sözi bilän sulṭānnïng ana jamāʿatlarin bérmäymïz*," see *Buyūk afżalatlūk Ginirāl Gūbirnāṭur ʿażīm ḥażratlārigha* Institute of Oriental Manuscripts, St. Petersburg, *Arkhiv Vostokovedov*, f. 61, op. 1, d. 13, ll. 50–51.

63 *Buyūk afżalatlūk Ginirāl Gūbirnāṭur ʿażīm ḥażratlārigha* Institute of Oriental Manuscripts, St. Petersburg, *Arkhiv Vostokovedov*, f. 61, op. 1, d. 13, l. 50–51.

64 *Sharīʿat shiʿār, diyānat āthār ʿAzīz Khwāja īshānimīz*, TsGA RUz, f. 1-125, op. 2, d. 213, ll. 1.

figure" "respected by Khivans," and lived among the Qaraqalpaq and Qazaq groups in the lower Syr Darya. The Russians' informants also reported that this individual was "nothing else but a Khivan scout."[65] Therefore, one may safely suppose that ʿAzīz Khwāja was someone who maintained close ties with Khivan officials without being designated by any administrative (official) titulature. I suggest, then, that the involvement of such a figure as ʿAzīz Khwāja Īshān enabled the parties to open space for negotiation. It is likely that the religious status of such figures was instrumental for the parties in conflict in finding a better pretext to start negotiation in an indirect way. This enabled them to avoid possible moral debasement – in this case by appearing to be at the beck and call of Russia – in a situation where direct talks would hardly be possible.

That is certainly how this message by Khivan authorities was understood by Sulṭān Élikay, who within a short time initiated communication with ʿAzīz Khwāja Īshān. In his letter, ʿAzīz Khwāja reports that the Élikay's envoys reached his locality and conveyed the Sulṭān's readiness to enter into discussions with the *īshān* regarding the return of his family members. Azīz Khwāja also informs Élikay that he would visit him at his convenience to discuss multiple issues in person, as such matters "cannot be put down in writing."[66] We know little regarding the outcome of the negotiations between Qazaq Sulṭān and the Khivan authorities brokered by the holy man. Yet one may easily judge from further developments that with the passage of time, Sulṭān [Élikay]'s formal excuses would have been delivered to the Khivan palace by ʿAzīz Khwāja.[67] Consequently, his family members would have been released,[68] while the Khivan authorities again would find in Ér Muḥammad Sulṭān a relatively loyal, but still instrumental ally in pursuing their policy among the Qazaqs of the lower Syr Darya.[69] Thus, the authority of the holy man proved consequential for exactly the same reasons as illustrated in previous examples.

---

65 "[Osmalovski I.Ya.] *Raport*, 30.04.1853," in *O slukhakh i sobytiyakh v Srednei Azii*, pp. 19–20.

66 *Sulṭān Ér Muḥammad janāb-i ʿālīlārī-gha*, Institute of Oriental Manuscripts, St. Petersburg, *Arkhiv Vostokovedov*, f. 61, op. 1, d. 13, l. 51.

67 See L.A. Abdurasilova *et al.*, ed., *Istoriia Kazakhstana v dokumentakh i materialakh: Al'manakh. Vyp. 3* (Karaganda: PK Ekozhan, 2013), pp. 72–3 (doc. no. 54).

68 Meier, *Kirgizskaia step' Orenburgskogo vedomstva*, pp. 73–4.

69 See for instance Abdurasilova *et al.*, ed., *Istoriia Kazakhstana v dokumentakh*, pp. 81–2 (doc. no. 58).

5 "We Do Not Need Gold:" Between Spiritual Service and Material Patronage

If we turn now to the *Khalwat-i ṣūfīhā*, we find a telling illustration of how Qonghrat ruling dynasts relied on various Sufi groups to consolidate their power.[70] This symbiotic relationship between the ruler and Sufi authorities has been well illustrated in numerous contexts and time periods. As Bakhtiyar Babajanov, the editor of the *Khalwat-i ṣūfīhā*, puts it, the dynasty sought to keep Sufi groups under control, and one of the ways to do so was by allocating endowments (*awqāf*) in favor of certain groups and families, and thus stimulating competition among the leaders of rival Sufi groups.[71]

In order to give a sense of power relations between the Qonghrat dynasty and Sufi leaders, an account by the Khivan historian Thanāʾī may serve as an illustrative example. Muḥammad Raḥīm Khān I, one of the most prominent members of the dynasty, had been faced by challenges early in his reign both from fellow Qonghrat dynasts and from rival tribal groupings. The most severe resistance was from a certain Töre Murād Ṣūfī, a leader in the northernmost province of Khwārazm – also known as the province of Aral (*Ārāl diyārī*).[72] In 1811, in the midst of this confrontation, before launching yet another campaign against the fortress of Qonghrat, the main stronghold of the Aral province, Muḥammad Raḥīm Khān took a curious step. He dispatched one Ṭāhīr Khwāja Īshān with a purse filled with gold to deliver to *pīr* Ṭayyib Īshān, an influential Sufi leader (*pīr wa murshid-i arshadī*)[73] from Khāwja-Éli, asking the *īshān* to deploy his miraculous power (*karāmatlārīdīn madad wa istiʿānat ṭalab qīlib*) against Muḥammad Raḥīm I's political opponent. Ṭāhīr Khwāja Īshān, who conveyed the Khivan ruler's alms (*nadhr wa niyāz*) and request to Ṭayyib Īshān, received the following answer:

---

70 *Xalwat-i ṣūfīhā*, 113–217.

71 Babadžanov, Introduction, *Xalwat-i ṣūfīhā*, p. 123.

72 Ulfatbek Abdurasulov, "The Aral Region and Geopolitical Agenda of the early Qongrats," *Eurasian Studies* 14 (2016), pp. 3–36.

73 According to Thanāʾī, this Ṭayyib Ishān was a direct descendant of the eighteenth-century Naqshbandi shaykh Muḥammad Ṭāhīr Īshān (or Ṭāhīr Īshān), who was also prominent due to his authorship of a number of Sufi works; including a large hagiographical compendium, the *Tadhkira-yi Ṭāhīr Īshān*; see on his writings B. Babadzhanov et al., ed., *Katalog sufiiskikh proizvedenii XVIII–XX vv. iz sobraniia Instituta vostokovedeniia im. Abu Raikhana al-Biruni Akademii nauk Respubliki Uzbekistan, VOHD 37* (Stuttgart, 2002), pp. 163–166 (nos. 76, 77, 78, 79), see also DeWeese, "Encountering Saints in the Hallowed Ground," p. 193.

> "We do not need gold: it is [an expression of] faith (*iʿtiqād*) that is [really] needed. But a condition for [such] faith is the following: we will present (*pīshkash*) the head of Töre Ṣūfī, but [in exchange] a *tarkhān yarlïq* should be granted to our Sufis (*allāhgūy ṣūfīlär*)." Having said that, he did not even touch the gold with his hands, [but] ordered that [Ṭāhīr Khwāja Īshān] should take this gold [back] and restore a mausoleum and a well at [the tomb of] Shaykh ʿAbdullāh Nārinjānī.

Muḥammad Raḥīm Khān I, encouraged by Ṭayyib Īshān's response, ordered the construction of a mausoleum at the grave of Shaykh ʿAbdullāh Nārinjānī,[74] and promised that a warrant with a conferral of *tarkhān* status would be given to Ṭayyib Īshān's followers and dependents. Only thereafter did the Khivan ruler move to besiege his opponent in the fortress of Qonghrat. With the passage of a few days, "Töre Ṣūfī's men cut off his head and presented it to the [Muḥammad Raḥīm] Khān … and thus the miracle performed by Ṭayyib Īshān became clear." The khan then granted Ṭayyib Īshān, "together with all his descendants and dependents," the royal warrant (*yarlïq*) that would confer upon them *tarkhān* status.[75] "That was the first such warrant granted by the [Muḥammad Raḥīm] khan," concludes the author.[76]

Thanāʾī's anecdote is important in that it demonstrates a clear connection between spiritual services and material patronage. The *tarkhān yārlīq*s mentioned by Thanāʾī granted a tax exemption privilege to Ṭayyib Īshān's Sufi community, following a practice that had been broadly utilized by the Qonghrat dynasts while supporting various other descent groups, including those of *īshān*s. The conferral of such royal warrants seems to have endowed the recipient with the right to enjoy fiscal privileges in any kind of activity, ranging from agriculture to handicrafts to trade.[77] A cadastral survey compiled by the Khivan chancellery in 1907 noted 68 descent groups across

74 The tomb of ʿAbdullāh Nārinjānī (Nārinjān Bābā) is about 22 km north of Turtkul; *Firdaws al-iqbal*, p. 657, note 1141.

75 A *tarkhān* grant was a conferral of fiscal priviledges. The procedure usually involved descent groups such as *sayyid*s, *khwāja*s and *shaykh*s; cf. William Wood, "A Collection of Tarkhan Yarliqs from the Khānate of Khiva," *Papers on Inner Asia*, 38 (Bloomington, 2005), p. 30.

76 Thanāʾī, *Tawārīkh-i Khwārazmshāhīya*, ff. 144a–145a. An account of this anecdote is given by Yuri Bregel; see *Firdaws al-iqbāl*, p. 636, note 849.

77 William Wood suggests that *tarkhān* grant holders were also freed from obligation to military service and received a sort of immunity with regard to a number of infractions; see Wood, "A Collection of Tarkhan Yarliqs," p. 29. Though many royal warrants for the conferral of *tarkhān* status have been published, little is known of the way in which these grant-holders exploited their fiscal privileges and how they made use of them.

Khwārazm – identified variously as *īshān*s, *sayyid*s, *khwāja*s and *shaykh*s – whose members were identified as *yarlïqdär*s, that is to say, as *tarkhān* grantees.[78] The register relates to the land properties of those individuals. From the lists of landholders who belonged to the community of each particular holy man listed in the register, it becomes apparent that *tarkhān* privileges extend not only to a holy man's descendants and followers, but also to his servants (*khidhmatkär*), tenants (*käranda*) and sharecroppers (*waqfkär*). So the conferral of *tarkhān* status provided the recipient with ample opportunities for generating income and economic resources. This simple fact explains the abundance of formal appeals for *tarkhān* status among the documents of the Khivan chancellery by representatives of sacred families and Sufi groups leaders. Moreover, in Khivan political tradition *tarkhān* status was not given once and for all, but rather required periodic re-confirmation by each newly enthroned ruler.[79] This had the added benefit of serving as a powerful tool to create sympathizers and loyal constituencies among descent groups and *īshān*s *inter alia*.

An account in Dāmullā Allāh-yār Makhdūm's *Riyāż al-dhākirīn* about the activities of Shaykh Khalīfa Walidān Ishān is equally illustrative of the intersection between material compensation and the power of piety. After the death of his spiritual mentor Muḥammad Sharīf Īshān, we read, Khalīfa Walidān erected a madrasah and mosque at his mentor's grave. There he oversaw a Sufi lodge, "taught in the madrasah," and "every Friday morning he would address [the needs of] the Sufis" (*ṣūfīlärghä har jumʿa ṣabāḥi tawajjuh bérib tururlar*). Things changed, however, when Muḥammad Sharīf Īshān's son Muḥammad Bāqī Makhdūm, who by that time had completed his education in Bukhara, decided to head back to Khwārazm. Before his return, he sent Khalīfa Walidān a missive, asking him to leave his late father's mosque and madrasah. Khalīfa Walidān found he had no choice but to accept Makhdūm's will. He moved then to his small estate, consisting just of "three or four *ṭanāb*s of land," whereupon he dwelled there together with his family and followers. When the Khivan ruler Muḥammad Amīn Khān (r. 1845–55) learned about Khalīfa Walidān's troubles, he granted to the *īshān* three hundred *ṭanāb*s of land on the bank of the Yarmïsh channel and a similar amount of land on the bank of the Bazsu channel. By the Bazsu channel the *īshān* built a new mosque and madrasah, and here he settled together with his people. As the author

---

78 *1325 tāzadīn yārlīqdārlārnīng awlādī kurulub wa yārlīq yir bīlib tanga ālinghān daftarī*, TsGARUz, f. I-125, op. 2, d. 491.

79 Ulfatbek Abdurasulov, "Atā'ī-Mulk and Yārlīqlī-Mulk: Features of Land Tenure in Khiva," *Der Islam* 88:2 (2012), p. 320.

put it, soon the number of mullahs teaching at his madrasa (*dars uqītūrghān mullālārī*) reached 120, whereas "the number of his Sufis was so great that it was known only to God."[80] This case provides us certain insights into possible ways of competition among holy men for the right to administer properties and associated Sufi communities. It also illustrates how instrumental the support of a holy man could be for obtaining rights from a khan, as a means of obtaining physical resources and increasing the number of followers and, hence, in enforcing his influence and the authority.

The following events, which unfolded in Khwārazm in the mid-nineteenth century in the midst of the wide-scale Turkmen upraising, demonstrate a similar dynamic. According to the chroniclers Āgahī and Bayānī, on February 11, 1856, the Khivan ruler Qutluq Murād Khān came up with an initiative aimed at pacifying his subjects who were in revolt. In response to the Khivan authorities' decision to bestow a reward (*qonuq wa in'ām wa sarpāy*) upon every Turkmen warrior who came before the court and expressed his loyalty to the khan, numerous Turkmens "crowded the streets of the city of Khiva."[81] Among those who came was a certain Muḥammad Niyāz Bīy, one of Qutluq Murād Khān's close relatives. Muḥammad Niyāz Bīy had previously been held in captivity by the Salakh clan of Yomut Turkmens, and now came to Khiva with a group of forty Turkmen warriors of that clan, apparently to convey their willingness to submit to the khan's authority. During his audience with Qutluq Murād Khān, however, Muḥammad Niyāz Bīy assassinated him, and then proclaimed himself as the new ruler of Khiva.[82] Meanwhile, a group of Khivan officials managed to block Muḥammad Niyāz Bīy's rebellious party in the audience hall of the palace (*körünüsh-khāna*), and in the nearby palace courtyard they instead elected Sayyid Muḥammad Töre, yet another member of the dynasty, as the new khan.[83] In order for Sayyid Muḥammad Töre to be successfully enthroned, however, it was crucial to eliminate the rebels in the audience hall. But numerous attempts to seize them brought little success. It was decided then to initiate negotiations with the involvement of a certain Muḥammad Karīm Īshān from the locality of Özbék-Yaf. Both Āgahī and Bayānī repeatedly identify Muḥammad Karīm Īshān as one of the key mediators in conflicts between the Khivan authorities and various Turkmen groups living in the oasis. Something similar happened on this occasion; the *īshān* got involved in negotiations (*aragha tushub*) and, on the basis of guarantees that he had

80 Allāhyār Makhdūm, *Riyāż al-dhakirīn*, f. 123a.

81 Āgahī, *Jāmi'*, 239–240; Bayānī, *Shajara-yi Khwārazmshāhī*, 372a.

82 Āgahī, *Jāmi'*, 240–241; Bayānī, *Shajara-yi Khwārazmshāhī*, 374a–b.

83 Āgahī, *Gulshan-i dawlat*, f. 12a–13a; Bayānī, *Shajara-yi Khwārazmshāhī*, 376b–377a.

given, Muḥammad Niyāz Bīy and his Turkmen supporters agreed to leave their refuge in the palace. As soon as the rebels came out, however, they were immediately executed by the order of the newly elected Sayyid Muḥammad Khān.[84]

Particularly striking in this description by the Khivan chroniclers is the character of Muḥammad Karīm Īshān's involvement. It is evident that the *īshān*'s guarantees to the rebel group of Muḥammad Niyāz Bīy were easily disregarded by the Khivan authorities. One can only imagine how much this eroded his political capital in future negotiations, his guarantees having been so thoroughly debunked. Nevertheless, the very same *īshān* would be repeatedly employed by the Khivan authorities over the further negotiation process with the rebellious Turkmen clans almost throughout the entire reign of Sayyid Muḥammad Khān (r. 1856–64).

In order to provide context for the actions and motives of Muḥammad Karīm Īshān, it might be worthwhile to turn to the background of the Sufi community to which he belonged. Muḥammad Karīm was the son of one Qurbān Naẓar Īshān (d. 1848), a founder of a Sufi community in the locality of Özbék-Yaf near Ghaziabad in Khwārazm. Writing in *Riyāż al-dhākirīn*, Dāmullā Allāh-yār Makhdūm recounts that Qurbān Naẓar Īshān's disciples (*khalīfa*) went to all different parts of Khwārazm, and far beyond it, conducting Sufi activities. Among Qurbān Naẓar Īshān's disciples Dāmullā Allāh-yār Makhdūm notes such shaykhs as ʿAṭā-Allāh Īshān, who was prominent among the inhabitants of the Aral Sea littoral, or ʿAbd al-ʿAẓīm Īshān, who was active among Turkmens, or Adḥam Īshān, active among the Göklen Turkmens in the Qara-Qalʿa region.[85] It was perhaps this broad network established by Qurbān Naẓar Īshān's disciples that allowed his son Muḥammad Karīm Īshān to intercede in various conflicts between the Khwārazmian central authorities and various local population groups.

No less illustrative for our purposes here are the materials of a private collection compiled by the Sufi community in Özbék-Yaf that was founded by Qurbān Naẓar Īshān and continued after his death in 1848 by his son Muḥammad Karīm Īshān. This rather unique collection consists of 88 documents,[86] including notarial deeds, royal warrants conferring fiscal privileges, land grants, and *waqfīya*s, together clearly illustrating how the members of an individual Sufi community were able to concentrate and broaden their ownership and control

84 Āgahī, *Gulshan-i dawlat*, 15a; Bayānī, *Shajara-yi Khwārazmshāhī*, 377a–377b.

85 Dāmullā Allāh-yār Makhdūm, *Riyāż al-dhakirīn*, f. 123a.

86 The collection was previously kept by descent groups in the locality of Özbék-Yaf. Since 2013 the whole collection has been held at the Ichan-Qalʿa State Museum in Khiva (Ichan-Qalʿa Museum, Khiva, MS inv. nos. KP 2661/1–2661/88).

of material resources over the course of the nineteenth century. It becomes evident that since the time of Allāh Qulī Khān's reign (r. 1825–42)[87] through the early twentieth century, Qonghrat dynasts systematically conferred and re-confirmed *tarkhān* status upon members of Qurbān Naẓar Īshān's Sufi community. One may also note that these fiscal privileges extended to not only the immediate descendants and Sufis, but also to a broader community, obviously including dependents and servants (*aqrabā wa khudamā*).[88] The collection also includes royal warrants regarding the conferral of land upon various members of the community, as well as notarial deeds of pious donation (*waqf*) by numerous individuals in the favor of Qurbān Naẓar Īshān's mosque and madrasah. Judging from the documents of this collection, it becomes evident that there was a marked increase in the number of such investitures in favor of the community during the reign of Sayyid Muḥammad Khān (r. 1856–64), whom Muḥammad Karīm Īshān had done so much to assist in the above-described negotiations with Muḥammad Niyāz Bīy's rebels.

Muḥammad Karīm Īshān, following the death of his father Qurbān Naẓar Īshān in 1848, not only succeeded in preserving and expanding the property and economic interests of his father's community in Özbék-Yāf, but also managed to establish his own community, as well as to obtain authorization for the erection of a madrasah and a mosque in his own name. This is evidenced by the *waqfīya* stamped by Sayyid Muḥammad Khān in November 1864. It certifies the donation by Sayyid Muḥammad Khān of two plots of land, comprising respectively 600 and 400 *ṭanāb*s (more than 300 hectares in total), in favor of Muḥammad Karīm Īshān's madrasah and mosque. Both the donated lands as well as the newly erected madrasah and mosque were located on the right bank of the Amu Darya River in the locality of Bālpāqchik. Judging from the further contents of the *waqfiya*, the mosque and madrasa were formally sanctioned in the name of Muḥammad Karīm Īshān. It was Muḥammad Karīm who, according to the will of the donor, i.e. Sayyid Muḥammad Khān, was appointed to the position of *imām* and *mudarris* of the madrasah. Muḥammad Karīm was also granted lifelong and hereditary authority as trustee (*mutawallī*), which enabled him to exercise control over all the donated property.[89] It is not

87 See *Tarkhān yārlīq* of 1825 r., Ichan-Qalʿa Museum, Khiva, MS inv. no. 2661/87.

88 See, *Tarkhān yārlīq* of 1866, Ichan-Qalʿa Museum, Khiva, MS inv. no KP 2661/86.

89 According to the stipulations of the *waqfīya*, Muḥammad Karīm was entitled, after receiving from sharecroppers (*kāranda*) the proportion of the harvest that was due to the *waqf* (*ḥiṣṣat al-waqf*), to withdraw that share which was due to him as trustee (*tawliya ḥaqqi*). He was additionally entitled to withdraw in his favor as much as half of the remaining harvest as payment for fulfilling the duties as *imām* at the mosque and professor at the madrasah (*imāmat wa mudarris haqqi*). It was only from what money that remained that

difficult to discern that the conditions of the *waqf* document are stipulated in such a way that the main beneficiary of all donations was Muḥammad Karīm Īshān, who was enabled to actually dispose a significant part of the revenues from these lands as well as to lead the mosque and madrasah. Furthermore, the same privilege was afforded to his descendants.[90] As we can learn from the above-cited land register compiled in 1907, the immediate descendants of Muḥammad Karīm Īshān, notably his son Dāmullā Artūq Īshān, were able to secure the interests of both communities well into the beginning of the twentieth century.[91] Obviously, such a close interaction with the dynasty enabled the Sufi community in Özbék-Yaf to retain its status as one of the most influential and most far-reaching Sufi groups in nineteenth century Khwārazm.

Bibliography

Archival Fonds

Central State Archive of the Republic of Uzbekistan (TsGARUz = Tsentral'nyi Gosudarstvennyi Arkhiv Respubliki Uzbekistan):

Fond I-1 *Opis'* 31 – "The Chancellery of the Turkestan Governor-General."

Fond I-125; *Opis'* 1 – "Archive of the Khans of Khiva"; Opis' 2 – "The Chancellery of the Khan of Khiva."

Institute of Oriental Manuscripts, Russian Academy of Sciences, St. Petersburg, *Arkhiv Vostokovedov*:

Fond 61 – "Grigor'ev Vasili Vasilievich," *Opis'* 1 and 2.

Ichan-Qal'a State Museum, Khiva, Uzbekistan, MS inv. nos KP 2661/1–2661/88.

Unpublished Sources

Āgahī, Muḥammad Riżā Mīrāb, *Gulshan-i dawlat*, MS Tashkent, Institute of Oriental Studies, the Uzbek Academy of Sciences, inv. no. 7572.

Bayānī, Muḥammad Yūsuf, *Shajara-i Khwārazmshāhī*, MS Tashkent, Institute of Oriental Studies, the Uzbek Academy of Sciences, inv. no. 9596.

Kāmyāb, Sayyid Ḥamid Tura, *Tawārīkh ul-khawānīn*. MS Tashkent, Institute of Oriental Studies, the Uzbek Academy of Sciences, inv. no. 7717.

---

he was required then to issue payments for service staff as well as for the students at the madrasah (*ṭalaba-i ʿulūm*).

90 TsGARUz, f. I-125, op. 2, d. 3, l. 1.

91 *1325 tāzadīn yārlīqdārlārnīng awlādī kurulub wa yārlīq yir bīlib tanga ālinghān daftarī*, TsGARUz, f. I-125, op. 2, d. 491, l. 70 ob. – 71.

Laffasī, Ḥasan-Murād, *Gulshan-i sa'ādat*, MS Tashkent, Institute of Oriental Studies, the Uzbek Academy of Sciences, inv. no. 7797.

Makhdūm, Dāmullā Allāh-yār Makhdūm Khudāy Berdi Oghlī, *Riyāż al-dhakirīn*. MS Urgench, Private Collection of Ahmadjon Rahmatullaev.

Thanā'ī, Bābā Jān, *Tawārīkh-i Khwārazmshāhīya*. MS Berlin, Staatsbibliothek, inv. no. Or. quart. 1605.

Published Sources and Catalogues

Abdurasilova, L.A., *et al.*, eds. *Istoriia Kazakhstana v dokumentakh i materialakh: Al'manakh. Vyp. 3* (Karaganda: PK Ekozhan, 2013).

Āgahī, Muḥammad Rižā Mīrāb. *Jāmi' al-Vāqi'āt-i Sulṭānī*, ed. Nouryaghdi Tashev. Samarkand/Tashkent: IICAS, 2012.

Babadžanov, Baxtiyar M., ed. and tr. "Xalwat-i ṣūfīhā (The Religious Landscape of Khorezm at the Turn of the 19th Century)." In *Muslim Culture in Russia and Central Asia*, vol. 3: *Arabic, Persian and Turkic Manuscripts (15th–19th Centuries)*, ed. Anke von Kügelgen, Aširbek Muminov, and Michael Kemper (Berlin: Klaus Schwarz Verlag, 2000), pp. 113–217.

Babadzhanov, B., *et al.*, eds. *Katalog sufischer Handschriften aus der Bibliothek des Instituts für Orientalistik der Akademie der Wissenschaften, Republik Usbekistan*. Stuttgart: Franz Steiner Verlag, 2002; Verzeichnis der orientalischen Handschriften in Deutschland, Supplementband 37.

Batyrshin, Iskander. "Zapiska mladshego perevodchika Orenburgskoi pogranichnoi komissii Iskandera Batyrshina o Khivinskom khanstve i khane prisyrdar'inskikh kazakhov Ermukhamede (Ilikee) Kasymove." In *Istoriia Kazakhstana v russkikh istochnikakh XVI–XIX vv.*, t. VI, ed. I.V. Erofeeva and B.T. Zhanaev (Almaty: Daik-Press, 2007), pp. 300–319.

Komyob, Sayid Homid Tura. *Taworikh ul-Khavonin*, ed. N. Norqulov, *et al.* Tashkent: Akademiya, 2002.

Munis, Shir Muhammad Mirab, and Muhammad Riza Mirab Agahi. *Firdaws al-iqbāl: History of Khorezm*, tr. Yuri Bregel (Leiden and Boston: Brill, 1999).

O slukhakh i sobytiyakh v Srednei Azii. Sbornik dokumentov, t. 1, ed. B.T. Zhanaev. Karaganda: TOO Kazakhskoe obshchestvo slepykh, 2016.

Urunbaev, A., *et al.*, ed. *Katalog sredneaziatskikh zhalovannykh gramot iz fonda Instituta Vostokovedeniia im. Aby Raikhana Beruni Akademii nauk Respubliki Uzbekistan*. Halle: Orientwissenschaftliche Hefte, 2007.

Secondary Literature

Abashin, Sergey. "Ishan." In *Islam na territorii byvshei Rossiiskoi imperii. Entsiklopedicheskii slovar'*, ed. S.M. Prozorov, t. 2 (Moscow: Vostochnaia Literatura, 1999), pp. 40–41.

Abdurasulov, Ulfatbek. "The Aral Region and Geopolitical Agenda of the early Qongrats." *Eurasian Studies* 14 (2016): 3–36.

Abdurasulov, Ulfatbek. "Atā'ī-Mulk and Yārlīqlī-Mulk: Features of Land Tenure in Khiva." *Der Islam* 88:2 (2012): 308–323.

Abdurasulov, Ulfat. "Konflikt kak resurs: anatomiia turkmenskikh besporiadkov v Khorezme, 1914–1916 gg." *Ab Imperio*, 2018, No. 3: 141–86.

Babadzhanov, Bakhtiar. "On the History of the Naqšbandīya Muǧaddidīya in Central Māwarā'nnahr in the Late 18th and Early 19th Centuries." In *Muslim Culture in Russia and Central Asia from the 18th to the Early 19th Centuries*, ed. Michael Kemper, Anke von Kügelgen, and Dmitriy Yermakov (Berlin: Klaus Schwarz Verlag, 1996), pp. 385–413.

Barthold, W., and [G.E. Wheeler]. "Is̲h̲ān." *The Encyclopaedia of Islam, New Edition*, vol. IV, Leiden: Brill, 1997, p. 113.

Bregel', Iu. È. *Khorezmskie turkmeny v XIX veke.* Moscow: Izdatel'stvo Vostochnoi Literatury, 1961.

Brown, Peter. "The Rise and Function of the Holy Man in Late Antiquity." *The Journal of Roman Studies*, 61 (1971): 80–101.

Bustanov, Alfrid K. "The Bulghar Region as a 'Land of Ignorance:' Anti-Colonial Discourse in Khwarazmian Connectivity." *Journal of Persianate Studies* 9 (2016): 183–204.

Demidov, Sergei M., *Turkmenskie owliady*. Ashkhabad: Ylym, 1976.

DeWeese, Devin. "'Dis-Ordering' Sufism in Early Modern Central Asia: Suggestions for Rethinking the Sources and Social Structures of Sufi History in the 18th and 19th Centuries." In *History and Culture of Central Asia*, ed. Bakhtiyar Babadjanov and Kawahara Yayoi (Tokyo: The University of Tokyo, 2012), pp. 259–79.

DeWeese, Devin. "Encountering Saints in the Hallowed Ground of a Regional Landscape: The 'Description of Khwārazm' and the Experience of Pilgrimage in 19th-Century Central Asia." In *Saintly Spheres and Islamic Landscapes*, ed. Daphna Ephrat, Ethel Sara Wolper, and Paulo G. Pinto (Leiden: Brill, 2021), pp. 183–218.

DeWeese, Devin. "Mapping Khwārazmian Connections in the History of Sufi Traditions: Local Embeddedness, Regional Networks, and Global Ties of the Sufi Communities of Khwārazm." *Eurasian Studies* 14 (2016): 37–97.

DeWeese, Devin. "Organizational Patterns and Developments within Sufi Communities." In *The Wiley-Blackwell History of Islam*, ed. Armando Salvatore *et al.* (Hoboken, New Jersey: John Wiley & Sons, 2018), pp. 329–350.

DeWeese, Devin. "Re-Envisioning the History of Sufi Communities in Central Asia: Continuity and Adaptation in Sources and Social Frameworks, 16th–20th Centuries." In *Sufism in Central Asia: New Perspectives on Sufi Tradition, 15th–21st Centuries*, ed. Devin DeWeese and Jo-Ann Gross (Leiden: Brill, 2018), pp. 21–74.

Dobromyslov, A.I. "Turgaiskaia oblast'. Istoricheskii ocherk." In *Izvestiia Orenburgskogo otdela Imperatorskogo Russkogo Geograficheskogo Obshchestva* 17 (Tver': Tipolitografiia N.Rodionova, 1902), pp. 257–524.

Erofeeva, Irina V. "Kazakhskie khany i khanskie dinastii v XVIII–seredine XIX vv." In *Kul'tura i istoriia Tsentral'noi Azii i Kazakhstana: Problemy i perspektivy issledovaniia* (Almaty: Fond Sorosa-Kazakhstan, 1997), pp. 46–144.

Galkin, M.N. *Ètnograficheskie i istoricheskie materialy po Srednei Azii i Orenburgskomu kraiu*. St. Petersburg: Izdanie Ia.A. Isakova, 1868.

Hasan, Farhat. *State and Locality in Mughal India. Power Relations in Western India, c. 1572–1730*. Cambridge: Cambridge University Press, 2006.

Karlybaev, Makset. "L'instruction musulmane et les îshân chez les Karakalpaks du XIXe siècle." In *Karakalpaks et autres gens de l'Aral: Entre rivages et deserts* (Tashkent/Aix-en-Provence: Édisud, 2002; *Cahiers de l'Asie centrale*, 10), pp. 177–191.

Karpov, Georgii I., and Dmitrii M. Batser. *Khivinskie turkmeny i konets Kungradskoi dinastii* (*Materialy po istorii turkmen*). Ashkhabad: Turkmenskoe Gosudarstvennoe Izdatel'stvo, 1930.

Meier, L. *Kirgizskaia step' Orenburgskogo vedomstva*. St. Petersburg: Tipografiia E. Veimara i F. Perona, 1865.

Pickett, James. "Enemies beyond the Red Sands: The Bukhara-Khiva Dynamic as Mediated by Textual Genre." *Journal of Persianate Studies* 9 (2016): 158–82.

Pickett, James. "The Persianate Sphere during the Age of Empires: Islamic Scholars and Networks of Exchange in Central Asia 1747–1917." Ph.D. dissertation, Princeton University, 2015.

Pickett, James. *Polymaths of Islam. Power and Networks of Knowledge in Central Asia*. Ithaca, New York, and London: Cornell University Press, 2020.

Sartori, Paolo. "On Madrasas, Legitimation, and Islamic Revival in 19th-Century Khorezm: Some Preliminary Observations." *Eurasian Studies*, 14 (2016): 98–134.

Subrahmanyam, Sanjay. "The Mughal State – Structure or process? Reflections on Recent Western Historiography." *The Indian Economic and Social History Review* 29:3 (1992): 291–321.

Wood, William. "A Collection of Tarkhan Yarliqs from the Khānate of Khiva." *Papers on Inner Asia*, No. 38 (Bloomington, Indiana: Research Institute for Inner Asian Studies, 2005).

Shāh-i Aḥmad al-Ṣabāwī and His Descendants

A Tatar Khoja *Dynasty in Southern Kazakhstan*

Allen J. Frank

1 Introduction

The explosion of publishing in Kazakhstan since its independence in 1991, and especially since 2000, has resulted in the emergence of an impressive number of memoirs, genealogical treatises, and biographical dictionaries. These are almost exclusively written in Kazakh and cover religious, and geographic communities located throughout Kazakhstan. They provide a wealth of information about Kazakh social history, illuminating aspects of Kazakh life that particularly during the Soviet era were suppressed and little-known outside of the communities the works derive from. These sources are for the most part based on manuscripts derived from Kazakh oral tradition, which while lauded during Soviet period for its "democratic character," was for the most part highly controlled in terms of what it transmitted. Much Kazakh oral tradition is still preserved in privately-owned manuscripts, which in Kazakhstan is only beginning to receive sustained attention as an aspect of Islamic culture.[1] The emergence of memoirs, genealogical treatises, and biographical dictionaries has provided us with an entirely new body of sources to examine the religious history of the Kazakh Steppe, both to extract biographical information on the Kazakh *ʿulamāʾ*, and to understand the social history of Muslim communities before Russian rule, as well as under Russian and Soviet rule.[2] Among the most

1 Publications of manuscript sources from Kazakhstan include the following works: *Islamizatsiia i sakral'nye rodoslovnye v Tsentral'noi Azii*, vol. I, ed. Devin DeWeese, Ashirbek Muminov et al. (Almaty: Daik-Press, 2013); vol. II, ed. Ashirbek Muminov, Anke von Kügelgen, Devin DeWeese, and Michael Kemper (Almaty: Daik-Press, 2008); Ashirbek K. Muminov, *Rodoslovnoe drevo Mukhtara Auezova*, (Almaty: Zhĭbek zholĭ, 2011); Saduaqas Ghĭlmani, *Zamanĭmĭzda bolghan ghŭlamalardĭng ömĭr tarikhtarĭ/Biographies of the Islamic Scholars of Our Times*, ed. Ashirbek Muminov, Allen J. Frank, and Aitzhan Nurmatova (Istanbul: Research Centre for Islamic History, Art and Culture [IRCICA], 2018); Qurbān-ʿAlī Khālidī, *An Islamic Biographical Dictionary of the Eastern Kazakh Steppe, 1770–1912*, Allen J. Frank and M.A. Usmanov, eds., (Leiden: E.J. Brill, 2005).

2 Recent *khoja* genealogical treatises include: S. Qŭrbanqozhaŭlĭ *et al.*, eds., *Ŭlĭ payghambar zhäne ŭrpaqtarĭ* (Astana: Foliant, 2014); Ä. Äbdimomĭnov, *Qarakhan äuletĭ* (Taraz: n.p., 2012); Tŭrsĭnbek Basbayŭlĭ, *Äbu Bäkĭr as-Sĭddĭq ŭrpaghĭ Hisamĭddĭnnĭng (Sŭnaq-Ata) tolĭqtĭrĭlghan*

 | DOI:10.1163/9789004527096_009

promising sources are genealogical treatises, containing elaborate compilations of personal recollections and narratives, devoted to holy lineages referred to as "*ishans*." The *ishans* are generally, but not necessarily from *khoja* lineages, and are commonly, but by no means exclusively, concentrated in southern Kazakhstan. These sources are particularly important because as essentially internal documents, they offer us a chance to obtain a deeper understanding of religious communities in Kazakhstan outside of the limiting lens of state archives.[3]

This chapter will examine one such *khoja* lineage based in the town of Sozaq, located in the Qaratau region north of the city of Türkistan. Although centered in Sozaq, members of this lineage trace their origins as *pīrs* to Kazakh communities to the town of Ayagöz, in modern day East Kazakhstan *oblast*, as well as to Taraz *oblast*, and elsewhere in Kazakhstan. Our knowledge of this lineage derives almost entirely from a genealogical treatise published in 2000, whose title can be translated as "The Saintly Lineage: The Holy Shāh-i Aḥmad and his Younger Brother Fātiḥ Imām and the Genealogy of their Descendants."[4] It offers insights into the social history of Muslims communities in Kazakhstan, including *khojas*, Kazakhs, Tatars, and Bashkirs in the 19th and 20th centuries. The source provides extensive information on the question of religious authority on the Kazakh steppe, illuminating social relations

---

shezhĭresĭ (Almaty: n.p. 2010); by comparison, the genealogies devoted to Kazakh tribes and clans are beyond enumeration. Important genealogical treatises include: Zharïlqap Beysenbayŭlï, *Qazaq shezhĭresĭ* (Almaty: Atamŭra-Qazaqstan, 1994); Khamit Madanov, *Kĭshĭ zhüzdïng shezhĭresĭ* (Almaty: Atamŭra-Qazaqstan, 1994); Zayïr Sädĭbekov, *Qazaq shezhĭresĭ* (Tashkent: Özbekiston, 1994); M.S. Mukanov, *Iz istoricheskogo proshlogo (rodoslovnaia plemen kerei i uak)* (Almaty: Qazaqstan, 1998); Tengĭzbay Üsenbayev, *Alshïn shezhĭresĭ* (Qïzïlorda: Tŭmar, 2003).

3 A partial list of important biographical dictionaries and biographical and hagiographical treatises include: Shaydarbek Äshĭmŭlï, *Sïr boyïndaghï äuliyeler*, (Almaty: Atamŭra, 2000); Shaydarbek Äshĭmŭlï *Sïrgha tolï Sïr boyï: tarikhi-tanïmdïq zhazbalar* (Astana: Foliant, 2009); Säden Nŭrtayŭlï, *Islam zhäne Maral Baba* (n.p., n.d.); Sotsial Zhŭmabayev, *Ŭlïlar tughan ölke* (Petropavl: n.p., 2006); Zäkĭratdin Baydosŭlï, *Qarazhĭgĭt* (Aqtöbe: A-Poligrafiya, 2008); K. Abuyev, *Nauan khazĭret* (Astana: n.p., 2001); Temĭrkhan Tebegenov, *Niyaz molda Tasbŭlatŭlï* (Almaty: Arïs, 2011).

4 Asqar Mangabay (Wäli) ŭlï, *Äziz äulet: Shakhiakhmed Khazret pen onïng ĭnĭsĭ Fatikh imamnïng häm olardïng ŭrpaqtarïnïng shezhĭresĭ* (Almaty: Öner, 2001), henceforth *Äziz äulet*. I wish to thank Ulan Bigozhin for bringing this important source to my attention and providing me access to it. For a discussion of this work in the context of Kazakh hagiography see Allen J. Frank, *Gulag Miracles: Sufis and Stalinist Repression in Kazakhstan* (Vienna: Austrian Academy of Sciences Press, 2019), 51–54 and passim.

between *khojas* and Kazakhs, especially the *pīr-murīd* relationship, which among Kazakh nomads bore particularly wide-reaching social and communal implications.[5] In the accounts preserved among Shāh-i Aḥmad's descendants the claim to religious authority is explicit. Shāh-i Aḥmad and his descendants are described repeatedly as "religious leaders" (*dĭn basshĭsĭ*) and as "functioning as religious leaders" (*dĭnĭ basshĭlĭq etu*). The source also illustrates the how *khoja* lineages were affected by and negotiated a range of Soviet policies, and sought to preserve their religious authority in the dire conditions of the Stalin era.

2 The Ancestors of Shāh-i Aḥmad al-Ṣabāwī

The central figure in this narrative, Shāh-i Aḥmad al-Ṣabāwī, came to the Kazakh steppe in the 1830s from the Volga-Ural region of Russia, and was known among Kazakhs as Noghay Ishan (the Tatar Ishan). The treatise names Shāh-i Aḥmad's birthplace as the village of Saba, a reference to the Tatar village of Ulugh Saba, at that time in Mamadysh District, Kazan Province, in the Volga Ural region. Today the village is known as Baylar Sabasï, or Bogatye Saby in Russian documents, and is in Russia's Republic of Tatarstan. Shāh-i Aḥmad's descendants reveal little information on the history of his family in the Volga-Ural region, instead simply emphasizing its Ḥusaynī *sayyid* lineage. However, from Tatar genealogical sources we know that he came from a particularly distinguished family of legal scholars in Ulugh Saba. Additionally, the Kazakh and Tatar genealogical sources for Shāh-i Aḥmad's lineage strongly broadly support each other.[6] (See Table 1)

5 In Central Asia, the melding of the *pīr-murīd* relationship with kinship relationships was not restricted to Kazakhs, or even to nomads. Yuri Bregel commented on the connection between *pīr*s and kinship groups in the Turkmen environment, as well as among Uzbek communities; see Iu. È. Bregel', *Khorezmskie turkmeny v XIX veke* (Moscow: Izdatel'stvo Vostochnoi Literatury, 1961), 171.

6 The major Tatar biographical dictionaries all contain the genealogies of Shāh-i Aḥmad's ancestors in Ulugh Saba: Shihāb al-Dīn Marjānī, *Mustafād al-akhbār fī aḥwāli Qazān wa Bulghār*, II (Kazan, 1900), 199–200, 238; Riżāʾ al-Dīn b. Fakhr al-Dīn, *Āthār*, I:2, 82; II:14, 432; Ḥusayn b. Amīrkhān, *Tawārīkh-i bulghāriya* (Kazan, 1883), 41, 44–45.

TABLE 1 Comparative genealogies of Shāḥ-i Aḥmad's ancestors from Tatar biographical dictionaries and from the *Äziz äulet*

Amīrkhān (1883)	**Marjānī (1889)**	**Fakhrutdinov (1908)**	***Äziz äulet* (2000)**
Yūllīgh Shaykh	Yūllīq Shaykh	Yūllïq Shaykh	Zhollïqozha
Khwāja Shaykh	Khwāja Shaykh	Khwāja Shaykh	Shaykhï Mŭkhammed qazhï
Yūshīh	Ayyūb Shaykh	–	Ayup
Dūlājan/Dūjān	Dūlājān	Dūlājān	Dolazhan
–	Älkāy	Īlkāy	Alkey
–	Aqmān	Aqman	Aqman
Muḥammad	Muḥammad	Mamat (Muḥammad)	Momïd
Shïghāy Ḥāfiẓ	Shïghāy	Shïghāy	Shakhï Shïghay
Dīn-Muḥammad	Dīn-Muḥammad	Dīn-Muḥammad	Dïnmŭkhammed
ʿAbd al-Ḥamīd Ḥāfiẓ	ʿAbd al-Ḥamīd	ʿAbd al-Ḥamīd	Ghabdilkhamid-ghazizi
Tāj ad-Dīn	Ḥusām ad-Dīn	Ḥusām ad-Dīn	Khisam
Shams ad-Dīn	Shams ad-Dīn	Shams ad-Dīn	Shamsi
Jamāl ad-Dīn	Jamāl ad-Dīn	Jamāl ad-Dīn	Zhamali
Muḥammad-Ḥāfiẓ	–	–	Shah-i Ahmad

The Tatar genealogies do not explicitly identify these lineage as *sayyids* but rather as simply a lineage of scholars. During the 19th and early 20th centuries *khoja* lineages, while present in the Volga-Ural region, did not play the same social role as in Kazakhstan, and claims of *khoja* origins when mentioned at all in the Tatar biographical dictionaries, at times came under criticism. In any case, Dūlājān, one of Shāh-i Aḥmad's ancestors, is said to have lived at the time of the Russian conquest of Kazan in 1552. As a result, we can place his ancestors, Yūllïq Shaykh, Khwāja Shaykh, and Ayyūb Shaykh in the Kazan Khanate before the Russian conquest. The appearance of the title "*shaykh*" in the Tatar genealogies suggests that this was in fact a *sayyid* lineage. Russian chronicles identify "*shikhs* and *shikhzadas*" as titles of the "clergy" in the 15th and 16th century Kazan Khanate, alongside *sayyids*. Here the term *shikhzada* suggests a hereditary lineage. While the specific meaning of the title *shaykh/shikh* in the Kazan Khanate remains obscure, the title in Siberia can be equated with *sayyids* with more confidence. Alfrid Bustanov has shown that Sharbatī Shaykh, an ancestor of *sayyid* families in Siberia, was a descendant of Jaʿfar as-Ṣādiq, and "a descendant of *shaykhs*" (*shaykhzada*).[7] The title of *shaykh/shikh* was also used by *sayyids* in Siberia as a surname, such as the Shikhov family of Tara. The founder of this family, Abaz-Bakchi Sheikh, had moved from Sayram, today in Kazakhstan, to Siberia in the 17th century and the family, like Shāh-i Aḥmad's family, traced their ancestry to Zayn al-ʿĀbidīn, the son of Imam Ḥusayn, and counted themselves as descended from the rulers of Sayram.[8]

The accounts from Kazakhstan do not place Zhollïqozha (Yūllïq Shaykh) in the Volga-Ural region at all, but in Central Asia at the time of the reign of Amir Timur. One of the Kazakh genealogies relates that Amir Timur expressly sought a descendant of Zayn al-ʿĀbidīn to appoint as imam in Bukhara. His descendant ʿAbd al-Ḥamīd appears in both Tatar and Kazakh sources as a historical figure active in the first half of the 18th century. In Tatar sources ʿAbd al-Ḥamīd is described as a great scholar, and as a student of the semi-legendary scholar Īsh-Muḥammad b. Ṭūq-Muḥammad al-Ādāʾī. The Kazani historian Ḥusayn b. Amīrkhān writes that ʿAbd al-Ḥamīd was skilled in logic and excelled in his mastery of the works on logic such as *Īsāghūjī* and the *Shamsīya*, and authoring a treatise on the latter work. For many years, we are told, he had been a *mudarris* among the Kazakhs [*qazāqlarda*], and eventually returned to Kazan, where he passed away.[9] He is also remembered for fathering 30 sons, many of whom became prominent scholars.

ʿAbd al-Ḥamīd's presence on the Kazakh steppe is confirmed as well in the traditions of the Sïban-Nayman Kazakhs. These accounts have been preserved in the unpublished poetry of the Nayman poet Ärip Tängïrbergenŭlï (1856–1924), who described his ancestors' relations with Shāh-i Aḥmad's family.[10] Ärip's lineage was as follows: Sïban → Zhanköbek → Narïnbay → Qŭttïbay → Bayghara-biy → Baysal → Äli → Tängirbergen → Ärip, and his accounts of ʿAbd al-Ḥamīd ʿAzīzī and Shāh-i Aḥmad narrate the relations

7 Alfrid Bustanov, "The Narrative of Ishaq Bab and the Lore of Holy Families in Western Siberia: a Preliminary Discussion," in *Islamizatsiia i sakral'nye rodoslovnye v Tsentral'noi Azii*, 1, ed. Devin DeWeese and Ashirbek Muminov (Almaty: Daik Press, 2013), 501, 506–507.

8 G.N. Potanin, "O karavannoi torgovle s dzhungarskoi Bukhariei v XVIII stoletii," *Chteniia istorii i drevnostei Rossiiskikh pri Moskovskom Universitete*, April–June 1868, Kniga 2, 71.

9 Ḥusayn b. Amīrkhān, *Tawārīkh-i bulghāriya*, 44. Strictly speaking, the text is ambiguous, and "*qazāqlarda*" could refer to a location, rather than a people. There is more than one village with the name Qazaqlar in the Middle Volga region, one of which is where the tomb of Bayrāsh b. Ībrāsh, reportedly the teacher of Īsh-Muḥammad b. Ṭūq-Muḥammad, is located. However, the reading of "*qazaqlar*" as "Kazakhs" is confirmed by Sïban-Nayman tradition.

10 Qaim Mŭkhamedkhanov, *Köp tomdïq shïgharmalar zhinaghï*, 4 (Almaty: Alash, 2005), 63.

between his direct ancestors and this *khoja* lineage. Ärip-aqïn is remembered not only as a poet, but also as a Sufi, and these accounts emphasize less the lineage's *khoja* status than its authority as a line of Sufis. In an apparently unpublished manuscript work titled *Bakharam*, Ärip-aqïn related that ʿAbd al-ʿAzīz was imam of a mosque in Türkistan around 1722, but was also the "chief of the *tariqat* path." Ärip's ancestor, Bayghara-biy (1699–1775), a prominent leader of the Sïban-Naymans, became his *murid* at the age of 16.[11] This was the time of the *Aqtaban shŭbïrïndï*, when the Kazakhs suffered from a devastating Zhunghar invasion. To protect their master, the *murids* sent ʿAbd al-Ḥamīd back to the Volga-Ural region, "which was a center of the Islamic faith and his ancestral homeland."[12] The Sïbans remember Bayghara-biy not only as a military and political leader, but also as a saint, thanks to his connection with the Naqshbandi *tariqat* through ʿAbd al-Ḥamīd. Until 1927, we are told, "the Zhanköbek people [*el*] of the Sïban-Naymans would bring their *zakāt*, recite the Qurʾan, and slaughter livestock at his [Bayghara-biy's] grave. Their war cry was 'Bayghara' if they went into battle or took part in a horse race."[13]

The Sïban account relates that ʿAbd al-Ḥamīd's great-grandson Jamāl al-Dīn (1784–1866), moved to Tashkent, and became an imam there. The reason given for his move from Russia to Tashkent was that the Russian authorities were persecuting "*shaykhs* and *khojas*," and it was no longer possible to reside in Russia. In any case, he eventually returned to the Volga-Ural region, and later instructed his son Shāh-i Aḥmad to travel to the Kazakh steppe and find a people there called Bayghara. He explained that ʿAbd al-Ḥamīd had been a *pīr* to his *murīd* Bayghara-biy, and that Shāh-i Aḥmad should rest there a while before continuing on to southern Kazakhstan, where he would find his [*khoja*] kinsmen.[14]

TABLE 2 Shaḥ-i Aḥmad's Ḥusaynī genealogy to Zhollïqozha (from the *Äziz äulet*)

Fatima → Khusayïn → Zeynelghabitdin → Mŭkhametqozha → Zhaghïparsïdïq → Smail → Älaqram → Mŭsa → Shakhïmŭkhammed → Shaykhï Ghŭla → Khasen Askeri → Mŭkhammed Mahdi → Zhollikhozha.

11 *Äziz äulet*, 52, 214.

12 In the Nayman accounts ʿAbd al-ʿAzīz and his descendants lived in "Ufa," but this usage both among the Naymans and in other Kazakh accounts, appears to signify the Volga-Ural region as a whole. The equation of the Volga-Ural region with Ufa may be because that city was the seat of the Orenburg Spiritual Assembly and the Orenburg Mufti.

13 *Äziz äulet*, 144.

14 *Äziz äulet*, 52.

3 Shāh-i Aḥmad

Äziz äulet provides no information on Shāh-i Aḥmad's life before coming to the Kazakh steppe, besides mentioning his birth in Ulugh Saba in 1812. Nor does the work mention his Sufi *silsila*. He is absent from Riżā' al-Dīn b. Fakhr ad-Dīn's biographical entry on his father or on his brother Jamāl ad-Dīn, where there is no mention is made of Jamāl al-Dīn's journey to Tashkent, for that matter. But Shāh-i Aḥmad is identified in other Tatar sources, including a compilation of *silsilas* entitled *al-Qaṭrat min biḥār al-ḥaqā'iq*, by the Orsk scholar and Sufi ʿAbdullāh al-Muʿāẕī. There he appears as Shāh-i Aḥmad b. Jamāl al-Dīn al-Ṣābawī and as a *murīd* of the Bukharan shaykh Jalāl al-Dīn Bukhārī, better known as Jalāl al-Dīn al-Khiyābānī (1785/86–1870/71). Khiyābānī was himself a Ḥusaynī, and according to one account, his Sufi lineage went back to Aḥmad Sirhindī via the Central Asian figures Mūsā Khān Dahbidī and Muḥammad-Ṣiddīq al-Samarqandī. Shāh-i Aḥmad might have traveled to Bukhara to study with Jalāl al-Dīn al-Khiyābānī, but this need not necessarily have been so, since Khiyābānī is known to have trained *murīds* in the Volga-Ural region by correspondence.[15] Al-Muʿāẕī also names a certain ʿAbd al-Majīd al-Sibirī as one of Shāh-i Aḥmad's *murīds*.[16]

In discussing Shāh-i Aḥmad's arrival to the Kazakh steppe the Sïban account relates how in his will, after ʿAbd al-ʿAzīz had departed, Bayghara-biy gave the following instructions to his descendants: "You will seek out and find the *pīr* that I had once found." To honor that request, Bayghara's youngest son, Samed, went out in search of Shāh-i Aḥmad. After he had traveled for a day Shāh-i Aḥmad appeared in Samed's dream and told him, "Don't look for me, I will come and find you." Because of that revelation [*ayan*], Samed returned to his people and instead waited in Ayagöz. In April, when the Ayagöz River was flooding, "his *pīr*" Shāh-i Aḥmad revealed to Samed in a dream that he was coming. The next day Shāh-i Aḥmad came and crossed the flooded river without incident, and arrived at the mosque of Muḥammad-Ṣādiq b. Ismāʿīl al-Ayāgūzī, the Bashkir imam in that city, who was also awaiting Shāh-i Aḥmad.[17] After his arrival, Muḥammad-Ṣādiq (Sadïq-molda in Kazakh sources) gave him his

15 On Khiyābānī, see Allen J. Frank, *Bukhara and the Muslims of Russia: Sufism, Education, and the Paradox of Islamic Prestige* (Leiden: E.J. Brill, 2012), 113–117.

16 ʿAbdullāh al-Muʿāẕī, *al-Qaṭrat min biḥār al-ḥaqā'iq fī tarjumat al-aḥwāl mashā'ikh al-ṭarā'iq* (Orenburg: Dīn wa maʿīshat maṭbaʿasī, 1907), 29.

17 On Muḥammad-Ṣādiq see Qurbān-ʿAlī Khālidī, *Tawārīkh-i khamsa-yi sharqī* (Kazan: Kazakov, 1910), 407; Qurbān-ʿAlī Khālidī, *An Islamic Biographical Dictionary of the Eastern Kazakh Steppe, 1770–1912*, ed. Allen J. Frank and M.A. Usmanov (Leiden: E.J. Brill, 2005), fol. 78ab.

daughter, Shäripzhamal. Then Samed took Shāh-i Aḥmad to the encampments of his people, who in the account are called the Zhanköbek people, after the name of Bayghara-biy's great grandfather.[18] Shāh-i Aḥmad's arrival among the Zhanköbek people, which took place in 1838, is confirmed in a Tatar source as well. Qurbān-ʿAlī Khālidī writes in his history of the town of Ayagöz that "Shāh-i Aḥmad Ishan Ṣabāwī came to the town" and the imam there, Damullā Muḥammad-Ṣādiq b. Ismāʿīl gave the *ishan* his daughter, and both the Kazakhs on the steppe and the Tatar and Bashkir townsmen became his *murīds*, and the "entire Bayqara [Bayghara] people [*el*] became his *murīds*."[19]

The Sïban account credits Shāh-i Aḥmad with several miracles during his stay among the nomads. These miracles illustrate well the collective nature of the *pīr-murīd* relationship for the "Bayghara people," since they involve Shāh-i Aḥmad's ability to confer to members of the community the ability to perform miracles themselves. For example, when Samed was accompanying Shāh-i Aḥmad from Ayagöz they stopped to eat at the home of a certain Bürbek, whose wife Zhaqay had had a spell cast on her [*zïkïr salghan*] and was in a coma. While telling amusing stories, Shāh-i Aḥmad foretold, "This Zhaqay will awaken from her sleep after three days, and she will ask for me. You'll tell her where I'm staying." Shāh-i Aḥmad rode on with Samed to the encampment of Zharqïnbay, the grandson Aqtaylaq-biy and the grandson of Bayghara-biy. Three days later, Zhaqay woke up from her coma, went to Zharqïnbay's encampment, and managed to mount a fearsome stallion named Tengbïl. She raced the stallion around the yurt where Shāh-i Aḥmad was staying, asking him to grant her husband a son (she was 50 years old at the time). Shāh-i Aḥmad gave her the blessing, and instructed her to name their son Müsapïrbek. Müsäpïrbek later became Shāh-i Aḥmad's adept (*duana*), and, we are told, when Müsäpïrbek recited the call to prayer, all the dogs nearby who heard it would look to the sky and howl.[20]

Upon arriving among the Sïbans, Shāh-i Aḥmad's status as a *pīr* to this community was cemented through marriages. While he was on the steppe, he received numerous marriage offers. In addition to marrying the daughter of the Bashkir imam in Ayagöz, Samed gave him his daughter Qïnatay. A certain Aydarkhan-molda gave him his daughter named Balzhan. Taybek-molda gave him his daughter Zhaday, who was a granddaughter of Bayghara-biy. During

18 *Äziz äulet*, 52–53; Shāh-i Aḥmad had evidently come from Russia to Sozaq first, and from Sozaq travelled to the Ayagöz region; *Äziz äulet*, 58.

19 Qurbān-ʿAlī Khālidī, *Tawārīkh-i khamsa-yi sharqī*, 409.

20 *Äziz äulet*, 53, 58.

his lifetime, he was given nine brides. He married five of them, and betrothed the remaining four to his sons.

How long he remained among the Sïbans is unclear, but the account relates that he aroused the suspicion of a local Chinggisid Sultan named Baraq-töre[21] who secretly denounced him to the Russian authorities for being a *sayyid* and a saint. As a result, the Russians exiled Shāh-i Aḥmad to Irkutsk and imprisoned him there. We are told that the Zhanköbeks gathered, and Zharqïnbay asked, "Who among the people will sacrifice his life for the sake of the unjustly punished Shāh-i Aḥmad?" A man named Kereybay volunteered to go to Irkutsk, and Zharqïnbay pledged 200 rams for the journey. Kereybay then traveled to Irkutsk, and brought Shāh-i Aḥmad back.[22]

After gaining his freedom, Shāh-i Aḥmad did not return to Ayagöz, where he had been arrested, but instead went to Sozaq. An account of one of his descendants relates that when Shāh-i Aḥmad came to Sozaq he elicited the jealousy of the local mullahs, who were unable to prevail in religious debates, so accused him of engaging in sorcery and misleading the people. One charge appears to have been that he was not performing the prayers at the correct time, and he replied that he performed them according to the time in Mecca and Medina. He argued that both the local saints buried in and around Sozaq, such as Qarabura-ata, Äzhi Ata, Zhïltïraq Ata, and Qazanshï Ata, as well as the ancestors of his critics had shared this practice. Having failed to thwart Shāh-i Aḥmad, the mullahs then brought a *qazi* from Türkistan named Qaraqazï, who tried to challenge Shāh-i Aḥmad's practice of letting his wives walk about with their faces uncovered. However, on this topic, too, Shāh-i Aḥmad prevailed over Qaraqazï in a debate.[23]

During his time in Sozaq Shāh-i Aḥmad is described as training *murīds* and performing many miracles that increase his authority and that of his descendants. However, his apparent ability to transmit to others the power to perform miracles, including to his family members and *murīds*, and even to strangers and to animals appears designed to demonstrate his authority both within his own family and within the communities that accepted him as their *pīr*. The association of miracles with authority is stated explicitly in an account told by Beyseqan Saghïndïqŭlï (1874–1973), who was from the Ayagöz region. Beyseqan had been an associate of the great Kazakh literary figure Abay Qŭnanbayŭlï, and he described a *majlis* he had attended with Abay in Semipalatinsk in 1897,

21 Evidently a reference to the Chinggisid Senior Sultan in the Ayagöz region Bārāq-tōra b. Ṣūlṭābāy-tōra; see Qurbān-ʿAli Khālidī, *Tawārīkh-i khamsa-yi sharqī*, 457.

22 *Äziz äulet*, 58.

23 *Äziz äulet*, 157–158.

in which Shāh-i Aḥmad's sanctity is affirmed in explicitly religious terms by one of the secular saints of the Soviet Kazakh pantheon. At that gathering, Abay reportedly observed:

> During my lifetime I have encountered two people who possessed the sacred quality of revealing people's internal secrets with their thoughts, and who were obviously miracle workers. What we call a miracle, typically, is making what doesn't exist exist, benefiting people who are physically deficient, in a difficult situation, or in need. Opening a beneficial path is an ability saints have. Prophets have the ability to perform prophetic miracles [*mughzhiza*] [by] revealing to people what is beyond their understanding, upholding their belief, and building an unbreakable foundation of faith and understanding. One such person was Zaynullah-hazrat [Rasulev] in Troitsk. Recently he became the imam of the Grand Mosque in Ufa,[24] and he is giving people lessons on the path of the Sufism and Islamic law. The second is the son of the three *zhüzes*, Seyd-qozha Shayakhmet Zhamali-khazïret [Shāh-i Aḥmad], who is revered by the Naymans' Sïban people. His main abode is the mosque in the city of Sozaq, and he has sons. In 1862, when I was young, my father [Qŭnanbay Öskenbayŭlï] invited him to Bayqoshqar, his summer encampment. He was my father's special guest. We greeted eather other and shook hands. He was customarily mild of speech.[25]

Even the dogs belonging to Shāh-i Aḥmad and his sons sometimes possessed miraculous, or seemingly supernatural, powers. Shāh-i Aḥmad's dog Zholqŭt cured a sick woman by opening three doors to enter an interior room and performing a *tawwaf* three times around her sickbed. This dog was said to have many holy qualities [*zhaqsï qasiyetterï köp bolghan*], such as biting the backsides of visitors to Shāh-i Aḥmad's house who were carrying snuff or tobacco. Shāh-i Aḥmad's grandson, Zeynolla owned a dog that would guard the door of the mosque on Fridays, and pull at the hems of the robes of worshipers who had bad thoughts or had not performed their ablutions.[26]

---

24 Here the narrator is confusing Zaynullāh Rasulev (1833–1917), who lived in Troitsk, with his son Gabrakhman Rasulev (1881–1950), who served as mufti in Ufa from 1943–1950.

25 *Äziz äulet*, 73.

26 *Äziz äulet*, 155,156, 205; on the phenomenon of dog saints in Central Asia, see Devin DeWeese, "Dog Saints and Dog Shrines in Kubravī Tradition: Notes on a Hagiographical Motif from Khwārazm," in, *Miracle et Karāma: Hagiographies Médiévales Comparées* 2, ed. Denise Aigle, (Turnhout: Brepols, 2000), 459–497.

Shāh-i Aḥmad remained in Sozaq with his sons, where during his lifetime they raised to money to build a large mosque. He also traveled to Tashkent frequently, where he died on in May 1878. His remains were brought back to Sozaq, and he was buried in a mausoleum in mosque, which was only completed after his death.

4 The Sons of Shāh-i Aḥmad

Shāh-i Aḥmad's authority, based among the Sïban-Naymans in eastern Kazakhstan and in Sozaq was substantially expanded by his sons and their descendants throughout southern and eastern Kazakhstan, as well as in China's Xinjiang Province. Shāh-i Aḥmad had five sons, who carried on the tradition of serving as *ishans*. These were, 1) Mukhammed Kamal-maghzŭm (1845–1905), known as Kamal, 2) Shärip; 3) Wali-maghzŭm (1855–1904), 4) Safar-maghzŭm (1861–1921), 5) Khasen-maghzŭm, 6) Shäker-maghzŭm (1855–1904), and 7) Zhollïqozha-maghzŭm (d. 1931). The first five sons were born from Shäripzhamal, the daughter of the Bashkir imam in Ayagöz, Muḥammad-Ṣādiq b. Ismāʿīl. Shäker-maghzŭm's mother was named Balzhan, the sister of Aydarkhan-molda from the Ayagöz region. Zhollïqozha's mother was Bibighaysha, the daughter of a Maralshï, also from the Ayagöz region.

Kamal-maghzŭm is remembered for being a religious leader [*dĭni basshïlïq etu*], and serving as imam of the family's mosque in Sozaq. As a young man, he travelled to Qulja, in Xinjiang, where local Kazakhs, from the Alban, Nayman, Kerey, and Qïzay people, as well as local Taranchis, became his *murīds* and devotees (*mŭqlis*). "Rain from his unstinting cloud poured onto the people after his arrival, and it was as if the land turned green." With a companion from Sozaq named Zhüdeu, he left Qulja for the Tian Shan Mountains, where they camped near the encampment of a local *törä* name Mamïrbek.[27] When Mamïrbek failed to visit Kamal's camp, Zhüdeu performed the *zikr* and rode to Mamïrbek's encampment carrying a whip. The narrator explains that at that time those approaching a *törä's* yurt would dismount, hide their whip and bow before addressing the *törä*. However, in this case, Zhüdeu came galloping right up to Mamïrbek's bed, and improvised a poem upbraiding Mamïrbek for his negligence in failing to pay respect to Kamal.

27 This is apparently a reference to Maʿmūr-tōra b. Ḥājjī Jānim-Jān-tōra, to whom the Chinese had granted the rank of *amban*. Qurbān-ʿAlī Khālidī described him as the most renowned and wealthiest of the *töräs* among the Kazakhs in Xinjiang; see Qurbān-ʿAlī Khālidī, *Tawārīkh-i khamsa-yi sharqī*, 461.

Mamïrbek became frightened and went to Kamal's camp, where he greeted Zhüdeu and found Kamal "trembling in meditation" [*murakhaba*] and he was struck by the pleasant aroma inside the tent. He promised to bring a cart the next day to bring Kamal to his encampment, where Kamal stayed for a time. At his encampment Mamïrbek and others would make offerings of livestock and receive blessings from Kamal, apparently for their children. For example, Mamïrbek gave 200 sheep and received blessings for his two sons, and another 300 sheep to obtain a blessing for himself and his wife. The Kereys were informed of his presence that day, and Kamal by the end of his stay had received 1,500 head of livestock, including 100 horses. Zhüdeu sold this livestock in Qulja and Shymkent, and contributed the proceeds toward building the family's mosque in Sozaq. Kamal then went to the Tarbaghatay region of Xinjiang, where the Bayzhïgït-Toqtanay Naymans became his *murids*.[28]

Kamal returned to Sozaq, and there became the victim of an ill-fated love-triangle involving his wife Erkezhan, who divorced him and married a Russian-appointed Senior Sultan in Auliya-Ata (today known as Taraz). The unidentified Senior Sultan, we are told, considered Kamal to be his enemy, and had him arrested and exiled to Astrakhan. During his imprisonment, Kamal is said to have performed several miracles, including saving a fishing boat and its crew from a storm on the Caspian Sea. He died in prison, and was buried in an unmarked grave.[29]

The biography of Shāh-i Aḥmad's son Safar-maghzŭm demonstrates in especially clear terms the collective aspect of the *pīr-murīd* relationship between *khojas* and Kazakh descent groups. Safar studied in Tashkent, and after completing his studies, the elders of the Nökis people in Kökbŭlaq became his *murīds*, and brought him to live amongst them as their *pīr*. "The Nökis in Kökbulaq gave him a house, built a mosque for him and gave him their daughters Äshïrkül and Shïnar as an offering for his blessings [*näzïrge batagha beredï*]." He also had *murīds* among the Sätek people, a branch of the Senior Zhüz's Ïstï tribe, who had lived near Sholaqqorghan, near Sozaq, but moved to Oyïq, in the Talas region, near Auliye-Ata. He then left his children in Kökbŭlaq, and moved to Oyïq. Although he had a particularly close relation with the Nökis and Säteks, we are told that the Oyïq, Oshaqtï, Botpay, Shïmïr, Siqïm, and Zhanïs tribes [*ru*], also held him as their *pīr*, and "gave their livestock to him, and their daughters to his sons."[30]

28 *Äziz äulet*, 73–75.
29 *Äziz äulet*, 81.
30 *Äziz äulet*, 197–199.

Shāh-i Aḥmad sent another of his sons, Khasen-maghzŭm, outside of the Sozaq region, to the Zhezqazghan area "to spread Islam," where the chiefs of the Nayman and Tama people took him in made him their *pīr*. He married there and had several children.[31] Finally, Shāh-i Aḥmad's son Shäker-maghzŭm[32] reestablished the family's bonds with the Sïbans in the Ayagöz region, and went to a place called Engrekey, where it is said he had 60 adepts (*duanas*). The youngest of his *duanas* was Arqarbay Shoqantayŭlï (1865–1948) who is remembered for owning almost no possessions and for giving away the all the offerings he was given.[33]

By the beginning of the 20th century Shāh-i Aḥmad's sons and their descendants had close kinship and religious ties to with nomadic Kazakh communities covering a vast geographic area. These included communities in the Sozaq region, along the Talas River near Awliye-Ata, in the Qulja, Tian-Shan, and Tarbaghatay regions of Xinjiang Province, in China, and among the Sïban-Naymans in the Ayagöz region. In addition, as Sufi masters the family also had connections with Tatars and Bashkirs in Ayagöz and with "Taranchis" in Qulja.

5 Shāh-i Aḥmad's Descendants in the Soviet Era

The narratives of Shāh-i Aḥmad and his sons during the pre-Soviet era present numerous examples of the difficulties they faced from Russian authorities and their Kazakh intermediaries. As we have seen, Shāh-i Aḥmad's father Jamāl al-Dīn was driven from the Volga-Ural region because the Russian authorities were persecuting the "*shaykhs* and *khojas*." Shāh-i Aḥmad himself was exiled to Irkutsk as a a result of persecution by a Senior Sultan. Kamal-maghzŭm was exiled to Astrakhan, where he died, due to the jealousy of another Senior Sultan. Shäker-maghzŭm also appears to have been briefly exiled by a tsarist general, who evidently repented, and sent him back to his people.[34]

The *Äziz Äulet* focuses attention on the travails of the Soviet era, which were borne primarily by Shāh-i Aḥmad's grandsons and great-grandsons. Like many of Kazakhstan's holy lineages and legal scholars of that time, Shāh-i Aḥmad's lineage was victimized by collectivization, famine, and mass arrests, and charged with being "mullahs" or the "descendants of mullahs." At the

31 *Äziz äulet*, 209.

32 His name appears elsewhere as Mŭkhammedshäkir and Shäkïzhan-äuliye.

33 *Äziz äulet*, 136.

34 *Äziz äulet*, 135.

same time, the wealthier members of the family, particularly in Sozaq, were stripped of their property and accused of being "*bays*," that is, members of the propertied class. Nevertheless, many of Shāh-i Aḥmad's descendants survived the 1920s and 30s, and managed to salvage, and even rebuild, their authority following the reestablishment of officially-sanctioned Islamic institutions in Kazakhstan after 1943. The family eventually reestablished its authority as *pīrs* following the Second World War.

Sozaq itself was the site of one of the largest armed uprising that protested the Soviet policies of collectivization and confiscation. The Tama people, who considered a local saint, Qarabura-äuliye, to be their *pīr*, were especially prominent among the rebellion's participants.[35] There is no evidence that Shāh-i Aḥmad's descendants were involved in the uprising, although in Sozaq the Säuirbay and Buzau branches of the Tama people had maintained kinship relations with Shāh-i Aḥmad's family, several of whom had wives and mothers from among the Tamas.[36] In 1931 the authorities accused Shāh-i Aḥmad's youngest son, Zhollïqozha of participating in the uprising. He was arrested in 1931 and subsequently taken to Shymkent, and shot. The same year Qozhakhmet, the son of Mŭkhay-maghzŭm was arrested and shot, as was Akhatay-maghzŭm. The punishment of these figures (whose wealth and status as *ishans* made them prime targets for imprisonment and confiscation) extended to their families, as well. For example, not only was all of Akhatay's livestock confiscated (876 horses, 285 camels, 217 sheep, and 87 cattle), but all of the family's household goods, including their yurts, bedding, and even kitchenware, were seized as well. This left Akhatay's family not only homeless and destitute, but also social outcasts, since the Party activists warned people not to feed these descendants of *ishans*. Akhatay's wife and 8-month old son starved to death, and his son Sŭltan was secretly taken in among the Tamas who lived to the north of Sozaq.[37] The descendants of Safar-maghzŭm were compelled to flee Sozaq and settle in Tashkent, where the children were split up and taken in by different families. The descendants of Kamal-maghzŭm and Shäker-maghzŭm were taken in by the Sïban-Naymans, and their identity as *sayyids* was concealed. Sadïq-maghzŭm was killed by Soviet troops in 1931,

35 On the Sozaq Uprising see Niccolò Pianciola, "Interpreting an Insurgency in Soviet Kazakhstan: the OGPU, Islam, and Kazakh 'Clans' in Suzak, 1930," *Islam, Society and States across the Kazakh Steppe (18th–early 20th Centuries)*, ed. Niccolò Pianciola and Paolo Sartori (Vienna: Verlag der Östereichischen Akademie der Wissenschaften, 2013), 297–340; for Kazakh traditions about the uprising, see Ötesh Qïrghïzbayev, *Sozaq köterïlïsï* (Almaty: Arqas, 2003).

36 *Äziz äulet*, 80, 159, 232–233.

37 *Äziz äulet*, 95–96, 227.

trying to flee to China with a group of 300 to 400 Kazakhs.[38] Beyond political persecution, many of Shāh-i Aḥmad's descendants were killed during Second World War. Shāh-i Aḥmad's grandson Sakhibzada Saparŭlï related that seven members of the family were reported killed during the war. A further ten were reported missing and never returned, while four came home wounded.[39]

The family's religious authority was challenged in more symbolic ways, as well. In 1936 Shāh-i Aḥmad's mosque, which was also the family mausoleum, was turned into a club. Shāh-i Aḥmad's body was ordered disinterred, and it was reburied (his remains were reportedly uncorrupted). However, the remains of his wives were left in the former mosque, and a stage was built over their graves, which resulted in the people of Sozaq warning one another not to go onto that stage.[40]

Nevertheless, even under the strictures of the Soviet system, some members of the family maintained the family's prestige simply by surviving. In 1928 Ghabdiakhmet Abuyusŭpŭlï Shakerov (b. 1914), the grandson of Shäker-maghzŭm, was declared a *bay* and his property was confiscated. In 1930 Ghabdiakhmet was arrested, and later sent to Semey, where he was put in a work brigade felling trees. In 1934, he went to Chuguchak, in Xinjiang Province, and studied in a teachers' college staffed by Tatars and Kazakhs brought from Almaty and Tashkent via the Sovetintorg trade organization. He later served as a teacher in Kazakh settlements in Xinjiang. By 1945 he had become a superintendent of schools in the Tarbaghatay region, and by 1951 he was the chairman of the association of Chinese-Soviet Citizens. However, he was made to return to Ayagöz in 1956.[41]

In Ayagöz the family was able to maintain a degree of the religious authority its members enjoyed as *sayyid*s through the establishment of official Soviet Islamic institutions during the Second World War. *Sayyid*s, in fact, maintained some of the highest positions in the Religious Administration of Central Asian Muslims (SADUM), founded in Tashkent in 1943. The most prominent of these included the Babakhan family, "Uzbek" *sayyids* from Sayram who served as muftis in Tashkent. Elsewhere in Kazakhstan one of the members of an important lineage of non-*khoja ishans* along the lower Syr Darya River was Süleyman-ishan Eseyŭlï, a descendant of Maral-ishan Qŭrmanŭlï (1783–1841); Süleyman-ishan served as imam at the mosque in Qïzïlorda from 1949 to

38 *Äziz äulet*, 83.

39 *Äziz äulet*, 136.

40 *Äziz äulet*, 136, 209.

41 *Äziz äulet*, 120–122; the Chinese communists compelled most Soviet citizens living in Xinjiang to return to the Soviet Union in the late 1950s and early 1960s; see Mirqasïym Gosmanov, *Yabïlmaghan kitap* (Kazan: Tatar kitap näshriyatï, 1996), 185–200.

1969.[42] Another figure who obtained a position as imam under SADUM was a grandson of Shāh-i Aḥmad, Mŭkhametshaykh (1891–1977), known as Shaykhan Qari-Ata, who was the sixth son of Kamal-maghzŭm; he studied in Tashkent, and later in "the mosque of the Holy Zaynullah in Ufa," (evidently a reference to a Rasuliya Madrasa in Troitsk). After the mosque was closed in Ayagöz in 1936, he "organized the community" and in the absence of a formal mosque, held religious services in his home. The story goes that in 1943 his daughter-in-law translated an appeal he had written "in Arabic," and sent it to Voroshilov and Stalin, and in 1945 they authorized opening a mosque in the town. Shaykhan served as imam of that mosque for 32 years, until 1977.

While an important aspect of Shaykhan's religious authority resided in his connections to the official Soviet establishment, and the personal recognition of his authority by Stalin and Voroshilov, he continued to retain the older authority of an *ishan*, *sayyid*, and Sufi through the continuance of the *pīr* relationship with the local community, and through his status as a Muslim saint. The *Äziz äulet* records several of his miracles, including performing *zikr* over a bowl of milk that cured a patient after he drank it. Another miracle occurred in 1953, when he cured a woman afflicted rather dramatically with mental illness. He was remembered as "our *ishan-pĭr*," and the people of Ayagöz "offered him their hands," and thus became his *murīds*. He also had Sufi adepts (*pĭrädarlar*). Shaykhan also associated with saints. One of his friends, Senbay-sopï, is remembered for his own miracles. Senbay reportedly was witnessed walking over juniper coals barefoot in the family's cemetery in Qoytas and not suffering from any burns. He could also heal patients by spraying water on them after licking a piece of red-hot iron.[43]

6 Conclusions

The *Äziz äulet* is one of several hagiographical treatises produced in independent Kazakhstan providing multi-generational accounts of holy lineages which providing information on the enduring social and religious roles of

42 Nŭrtayŭlï, *Islam zhäne Maral Baba*, 69; Maral Baba and his descendants were neither *sayyids* nor *qozhas*, but Kereys. Nevertheless, they functioned as *ishans* while competing with local *sayyids* and *khojas* for authority and income. This dynasty was particularly influential in Qïzïlorda and Qostanay *oblasts*.

43 *Äziz äulet*, 89–91; such dramatic displays of religious power would in much Soviet and post-Soviet ethnography be classified as a manifestation of "Kazakh shamanism" (*baqsïlïq*). However nowhere in their accounts do these *sayyids* identify themselves *baqsïs*.

these lineages in Kazakh society, from before the Russian conquest down to the present era. Focusing on a lineage with longstanding ties to both the Volga-Ural region and to sedentary and nomadic communities in various portions of the Kazakh steppe and Eastern Turkestan, the story of Shāh-i Aḥmad's lineage demonstrates the long-standing religious ties – in this case involving *khojas* – that connected the Volga-Ural region with Central Asia. The case of this lineage is compelling because it offers an alternative to the prevailing view that examines Islamic religious bonds between Volga-Ural Muslims and Central Asians almost exclusively as features of Russian imperialism, or more simplistically, as vectors of "modernity" for Central Asians (in contrast to the Volga-Ural region, the religious bonds between Siberia and Central Asia have been ably discussed by Alfrid Bustanov). In the case of the *Äziz äulet*, the relationship between these *khojas* and the Russian (or Soviet) state is consistently problematic for these khojas, if not dangerous, and it was punitive state policies that repeatedly determined the migrations and fates of the members of this dynasty. More broadly, however, the *Äziz äulet* should encourage us to appreciate the depth of religious connections between the Volga-Ural region and Central Asia (including the little-remarked presence of Syr Darya *khojas* in the Volga-Ural region), and should make us question the utility of segregating the Islamic history of the Volga-Ural region from that of Central Asia.

More broadly, the hagiography addresses issues relating to the question of religious authority in Central Asia. Thanks to works like the *Äziz äulet*, we can see precisely how the collective relationship between holy lineages and Kazakh descent groups functioned as manifestations of the *pīr-murīd* relationship, including as kinship relations, and as arrangements of collective mutual obligation. At the same time, we have also seen the role of the state, whether Imperial Russian or Soviet, in disrupting these bonds. The *Äziz äulet* provides a timely corrective to an unqualified view of the Imperial Russian state as a champion of "Tatar" Muslim religious authority among the Kazakhs. Clearly, the Russian state (and the Tatar bourgeoisie) privileged some types of religious authority over other types. We can also see among Shāh-i Aḥmad's descendants the importance of maintaining their authority and bonds as *pīrs* with Kazakh communities through the Soviet era and into the 21st century. Clearly, the authority of these sorts of descent groups remains relevant.

Finally, the *Äziz äulet* speaks to some broader issues touching on the history of Sufism in Russia and Central Asia in the 18th, 19th, and 20th centuries. First, it raises the issue of how we can more clearly the collective *pīr-murīd* relationship between lineages. To what degree did such relationships reflect engagement in the Sufis discipline, and to what degree did were they more metaphoric? Did these relationships change over time? The decline and blurring of exclusive *silsila* affiliations appear to have been resisted in the Volga-Ural region, where Sufis like Aḥmad al-Barangawī and ʿAbdullāh al-Muʿāẕī in the 20th century were especially meticulous in tracing *silsila* affiliations. At the same time, the Kazakh sources across the board (which are admittedly later sources) downplay or even ignore *silsila* affiliations.

Bibliography

Äbdimomïnov, Ä. *Qarakhan äuletĭ*. Taraz: n.p., 2012.

ʿAbdullāh al-Muʿāẕī. *al-Qaṭrat min biḥār al-ḥaqāʾiq fī tarjumat al-aḥwāl mashāʾikh al-ṭarāʾīq*. Orenburg: Dīn wa maʿīshat maṭbaʿasī, 1907.

Abuyev, K. *Nauan khazĭret*. Astana: n.p., 2001.

Äshĭmŭlï, Shaydarbek. *Sïr boyïndaghï äuliyeler*. Almaty: Atamŭra, 2000.

Äshĭmŭlï, Shaydarbek. *Sïrgha tolï Sïr boyï: tarikhi-tanïmdïq zhazbalar*. Astana: Foliant, 2009.

Basbayŭlï, Tŭrsïnbek. *Äbu Bäkĭr as-Sïddïq ŭrpaghï Hisamĭddĭnnĭng (Sŭnaq-Ata) tolïqtïrïlghan shezhĭresĭ*. Almaty: n.p. 2010.

Baydosŭlï Zäkĭratdin. *Qarazhĭgĭt*. Aqtöbe: A-Poligrafiya, 2008.

Beysenbayŭlï, Zharïlqap. *Qazaq shezhĭresĭ*. Almaty: Atamŭra-Qazaqstan, 1994.

Bregel', Iu. È. *Khorezmskie turkmeny v XIX veke*. Moscow: Izdatel'stvo Vostochnoi literatury, 1961.

Bustanov, Alfrid. "The Narrative of Ishaq Bab and the Lore of Holy Families in Western Siberia: a Preliminary Discussion." In *Islamizatsiia i sakral'nye rodoslovnye v Tsentral'noi Azii*, 1, ed. Devin DeWeese and Ashirbek Muminov (Almaty: Daik Press, 2013), 496–533.

DeWeese, Devin. "Dog Saints and Dog Shrines in Kubravī Tradition: Notes on a Hagiographical Motif from Khwārazm." In *Miracle et Karāma: Hagiographies Médiévales Comparées* 2, ed. Denise Aigle (Turnhout: Brepols, 2000), 459–497.

Frank, Allen J. *Bukhara and the Muslims of Russia: Sufism, Education, and the Paradox of Islamic Prestige*. Leiden: E.J. Brill, 2012.

Frank, Allen J. *Gulag Miracles: Sufis and Stalinist Repression in Kazakhstan*. Vienna: Austrian Academy of Sciences Press, 2019.

Ghïlmani, Saduaqas. *Zamanïmïzda bolghan ghŭlamalardïng ömĭr tarikhtarï/ Biographies of the Islamic Scholars of Our Times*, ed. Ashirbek Muminov, Allen J. Frank, and Aitzhan Nurmatova. Istanbul: Research Centre for Islamic History, Art and Culture (IRCICA), 2018.

Gosmanov, Mirqasïym. *Yabïlmaghan kitap*. Kazan: Tatar Kitap Näshriyatï, 1996.

Ḥusayn b. Amīrkhān. *Tawārīkh-i bulghāriya*. Kazan, 1883.

Islamizatsiia i sakral'nye rodoslovnye v Tsentral'noi Azii: vol. I, ed. Devin DeWeese, Ashirbek Muminov et al. (Almaty: Daik-Press, 2013); vol. II, ed. Ashirbek Muminov, Anke von Kügelgen, Devin DeWeese, and Michael Kemper (Almaty: Daik-Press, 2008).

Madanov, Khamit. *Kĭshĭ zhüzdĭng shezhĭresĭ*. Almaty: Atamŭra-Qazaqstan, 1994.

Mangabay (Wäli) ŭlï, Asqar. *Äziz äulet: Shakhiakhmed Khazret pen onïng ĭnĭsĭ Fatikh imamnïng häm olardïng ŭrpaqtarïnïng shezhĭresĭ*. Almaty: Öner, 2001.

Marjānī, Shihāb al-Dīn. *Mustafād al-akhbār fī aḥwāl Qazān wa Bulghār*, II. Kazan, 1900.

Mukanov, M.S. *Iz istoricheskogo proshlogo (rodoslovnaia plemen kerei i uak)*. Almaty: Qazaqstan, 1998.

Mŭkhamedkhanov, Qaim. *Köp tomdïq shïgharmalar zhinaghï*, 4. Almaty: Alash, 2005.

Muminov, Ashirbek K. *Rodoslovnoe drevo Mukhtara Auezova*. Almaty: Zhĭbek zholï, 2011.

Nŭrtayŭlï, Säden. *Islam zhäne Maral Baba*. N.p., n.d.

Pianciola, Niccolò. "Interpreting an Insurgency in Soviet Kazakhstan: the OGPU, Islam, and Kazakh 'Clans' in Suzak, 1930." In *Islam, Society and States across the Kazakh Steppe (18th–early 20th Centuries)*, ed. Niccolò Pianciola and Paolo Sartori (Vienna: Verlag der Östereichischen Akademie der Wissenschaften, 2013), 297–340.

Potanin, G.N. "O karavannoi torgovle s dzhungarskoi Bukhariei v XVIII stoletii." *Chteniia istorii i drevnostei Rossiiskikh pri Moskovskom Universitete*, April–June 1868, Kniga 2, 21–113.

Qïrghïzbayev, Ötesh. *Sozaq köterĭlĭsĭ*. Almaty: Arqas, 2003.

Qurbān-ʿAlī Khālidī. *An Islamic Biographical Dictionary of the Eastern Kazakh Steppe, 1770–1912*, ed. Allen J. Frank and M.A. Usmanov. Leiden: E.J. Brill, 2005.

Qurbān-ʿAlī Khālidī. *Tawārīkh-i khamsa-yi sharqī*. Kazan: Kazakov, 1910.

Qŭrbanqozhaŭlï, W., et al., eds. *Ŭlï payghambar zhäne ŭrpaqtarï*. Astana: Foliant, 2014.

Riżā' al-Dīn b. Fakhr al-Dīn. *Āthār*, I–II. Orenburg, 1900–1908.

Sädĭbekov, Zayïr. *Qazaq shezhĭresĭ*. Tashkent: Ozbekistan, 1994.

Tebegenov, Temĭrkhan. *Niyaz molda Tasbŭlatŭlï*. Almaty: Arïs, 2011.

Üsenbayev, Tengĭzbay. *Alshïn shezhĭresĭ*. Qïzïlorda: Tŭmar, 2003.

Zhŭmabayev, Sotsial. *Ŭlïlar tughan ölke*. Petropavl: n.p., 2006.

Shaykhs of the Sacred Mountain

A Local History of Soviet Islam

Sergey Abashin

In 2010, returning after many years to the *qishlaq* in Tajikistan where I used to conduct my anthropological studies,[1] I discovered – to my own surprise – a whole variety of new phenomena, sources, and interpretations. Private farms claimed former kolkhoz territories, most of the young men went off to work in Russia, many women changed their headscarves to more conservative hijabs, and volleyball became the main public entertainment for the locals. The social, political, and ideological discursive situation has gone through significant changes since my last visit in 1995, predetermining fundamentally different emphases – a different balance between desirable and undesirable conversation topics, different ways of self-presentation, including a different memory of the past. Some changes may be perceived as an influence of globalism, others as a reinforcement of traditionalism, and still others as new forms of dependence. These experiences were puzzling and prompted a question about whether history should be regarded as a linear progressive motion, as a set of leaps, or as periodic reversions. I could not figure out how to describe what was going on – whether I should picture it as another stage of modernization or, contrariwise, demodernization, as a post-Soviet stage, or as a reversion to Soviet practices.

One of the problems arising in this situation is analytical packaging of social and cultural phenomena. Sometimes researchers fit them in strictly delineated historical periods – pre-Soviet (and before that, pre-Russian), Soviet, and post-Soviet. The boundaries between those periods are seen as theoretical and disciplinary dividing lines that predetermine specific research questions and provide a conceptual framework for every time segment. Every period seems to start from a clean slate, follow its own logic, and create its own history. Every once in a while, however, scholars attempt to destabilize those boundaries in order to look at the social dynamics in a longer-term perspective. In some cases, these attempts are confined to the search for continuity between the late stage of one period and the early stage of the next one. In other cases, researchers build essentialist analytical models that rule out any dynamics whatsoever – or

1 Sergei Abashin, *Sovetskii kishlak: mezhdu kolonializmom i modernizatsiei* [*Soviet Qishlaq: Between Colonialism and Modernization*] (Moscow: Novoe literaturnoe obozrenie, 2015).

 | DOI:10.1163/9789004527096_010

find a unique, peculiar dynamic inherent to a single community or culture, a dynamic with its own temporal dimension.

This is especially evident in the case of Islam in pre-Soviet, Soviet, and post-Soviet Central Asia. Can we argue that Islam, in one form or another, represented the main regulatory instrument throughout the twentieth century, governing social practices and representations?[2] Or did Soviet rule, through intervention by modernization, manage to reduce Islam to insignificant, moribund practices, while the collapse of the USSR brought about artificial reconstruction of Muslim practices in the region?[3]

I chose a "will" (*vasiyatnoma*) as the starting point for my more detailed analysis. The text of the will, which I saw in 2010, was the following:

> I, Tulgon-shaykh, daughter of Erali-shaykh, have been by right of succession looking after the duties of shaykh-hood (*shaykhlik*) [for the shrine] of Abdurahman-ob, [which now] I leave to Erali-shaykh's grandson Yaqubjan and his son Sharibjan, whereof I inform in this will I make, and have passed on the status of shaykh of Abdurahman-ob, in [my] charge, as their full inheritance. In this will, as witnesses, took part and heard by their own ears, whereof they give testimony, saying that they appended their signatures and their consent. We give testimony that this will is true.
>
> Witnesses: names of 5 persons, their signatures, village council stamp, July 10, 2006

The practices described in this text were considered lost and archaic in Soviet times. It surprised me that they suddenly took the form of a legal or pseudo-legal document with reference to the state and society. What used to be presented in Soviet stories and conversations as insignificant, all of a sudden appeared as fully legitimate and vested with authority.

In view of this, I want to cover two issues in my chapter. First, I will try to look at the way the local authority of these shaykhs is created and developed within the village – a narrow community and a small group. I will examine the functions and roles attributed to this authority and the ways of legitimization

2 Sergei P. *Poliakov, Everyday Islam: Religion and Tradition in Rural Central Asia* (New York: M.E. Sharpe, 1992); Paolo Sartori, "Towards a History of the Muslims' Soviet Union: A View from Central Asia," *Die Welt des Islams* 50, no. 3/4 (2010): 315–334.

3 Gleb Snesarev, "On Some Causes of the Persistence of Religio-Customary Survivals among the Khorezm Uzbeks," in *Introduction to Soviet Ethnography*, eds. Stephen P. Dunn and Ethel Dunn (Berkeley: Highgate Road Social Science Research Station, 1974), 215–239; Adeeb Khalid, *Islam after Communism: Religion and Politics in Central Asia* (Berkeley: University of California Press, 2007).

used therewith. Second, I will try to see how this authority existed throughout Soviet times and what transformations it underwent in the years when the community found itself amid multifaceted and dramatic changes. In particular, I will show that among these changes was a transformation of gender roles, as occurred in the case of the elderly woman named Tulgon, who at first inherited the male status of caretaker of the holy place, but later returned it to her male relatives. My goal is to demonstrate the continuity of these shaykhs' authority, and the efforts to conserve it and pass it on, as well as the ruptures in the history of local shaykhs, the constant reformatting of their role and image, their new functions, and the new methods of legitimation.

1 Shaykhs

First of all, I will describe the general picture to figure out the meaning of the word "shaykh" suggested in the will.

In the Ferghana Valley, the word "shaykh" generally describes a person whose main function is to look after the *mazar*, that is, a place mentioned in legends about prominent Muslim figures and, according to locals, one with a special power (for instance, the ability to cure disease).[4] Not only do shaykhs take care of this place and keep it safe, they also welcome pilgrims, offer all necessary supplies to prepare pilgrim meals, explain what is to be done in order to show respect for the place, recite prayers as well as receive offerings for the *mazar*, and take care of them. As the practice of pilgrimage has been and continues to be very popular, service as a shaykh – especially at popular *mazar*s – takes a lot of time and can even become their main job and their primary source of income. As shaykhs communicate with many people, they are well-known persons who are familiar with social hierarchies. Consequently, they do not only have purely symbolic religious capital, but also possess social capital. Shaykhs of especially popular *mazar*s that were receiving pilgrims from the most distant places were tremendously influential people with various instruments to reinforce their legitimacy and a large network of supporters and partners. They could be big landowners or merchants, receive a good

4 Maria Elisabeth *Louw, Everyday Islam in Post-Soviet Central Asia* (London and New York: Routledge, 2007); Krisztina Kehl-Bodrogi, "'Who Owns the Shrine?' Competing Meanings and Authorities at a Pilgrimage Site in Khorezm," *Central Asian Survey* 25, no. 3 (September 2006): 235–250; Yasushi Shinmen, Minoru Sawada, and Edmund Waite, eds., *Muslim Saints and Mausoleums in Central Asia and Xinjiang* (Paris: Jean Maisonneuve Successeur, 2013); Jun Sugawara and Rahile Dawut, eds., *Mazar: Studies on Islamic Sacred Sites in Central Eurasia* (Tokyo: Tokyo University of Foreign Studies Press, 2016).

education, or be influential among politicians. Sometimes they bore titles of honor like Khoja, Sayyid, or Tura, indicating that they were members of famous Muslim dynasties, including those whose representatives were buried in the *mazar* where they served as shaykhs. They could also hold key positions in Sufi communities.[5] We can even say that such authorities combined a variety of roles and legitimacies, where being a shaykh was not necessarily key in the eyes of the society, but rather a supplement.

The case that I am describing represents a local variation, where the authority of the shaykh is narrowly specialized and is not mixed with any other roles or legitimacies. The *mazar* known as Abdurahman-ob, mentioned in the will, is located on the highest peak of the Kuramin mountain range, which separates the Ferghana Valley from the valley of the Ahangaran River.[6] The *qishlaq* in question is situated at the mountain base, along the shortest pilgrim trail leading to the top of the mountain. The pilgrim's journey up the mountain is a severe test, and not all pilgrims reach the top – many of them rest at stopover points with smaller *mazar*s. Correspondingly, every stopover point has a shaykh living next to it. There is subtle competition and a set priority of heritage distributed among the shaykhs. Tulgon-shaykh, mentioned above, took care of the highest point of this pilgrim trail situated almost at the top – whereas the top of the mountain itself is considered the Abdurahman-ob *mazar* as such, being the most famous and the most "powerful." Reaching the top is the most desired goal for pilgrims. It shows their strong motivation or faith and promises a more successful fulfillment of their aspirations. The pilgrimage usually takes place in August, when snow comes off the trail; during the rest of the year, the shaykhs of the Abdurahman-ob *mazar* go about their business.

As I said, the *mazar* has a local character; however, this is not exactly accurate. In August, pilgrims come to the *mazar* from many villages and towns across a fairly large region; in other words, the fame of the *mazar* is anything but local. Nevertheless, its symbolic attributes look very local. Few people, even among the current shaykhs themselves, can clearly explain what makes this place attractive for Muslims. The story about a certain *avliyo* named

5 Bruce G. Privratsky, "'Turkistan Belongs to the Qojas': Local Knowledge of a Muslim Tradition," in *Devout Societies vs. Impious States? Transmitting Islamic Learning in Russia, Central Asia and China through the Twentieth Century*, ed. Stéphane A. Dudoignon (Berlin: Klaus Schwarz Verlag, 2004), 161–212.

6 Sergey Abashin, "Mazars of Boboi-ob: Typical and Untypical Features of Holy Places in Central Asia," in *Muslim Saints and Mausoleums in Central Asia and Xinjiang*, ed. Yasushi Shinmen, Minoru Sawada, and Edmund Waite (Paris: Jean Maisonneuve Successeur, 2013), 91–105.

Boboi-ob/Boyob-buva or Abdurahman-ob, who climbed up the mountain and disappeared at its top, is not very unusual for Central Asia – this theme is often repeated in stories of various *mazar*s. Some of the most sophisticated adepts of the *mazar*, according to Russian researchers at the beginning of the twentieth century, mentioned a companion of the Prophet named Abdurahman-Auf, who is allegedly the same person as Abdurahman-ob.[7] However, this ended all attempts to align the legends about this *mazar* with more or less known realities of Muslim history. It is probably due to difficulty of approach that the mainstream versions of Islam found it hard to symbolically appropriate the *mazar*. As a result, we see that a rather popular *mazar* had neither any developed Muslim infrastructure nor support in books and writing, that is, it remained local.

The local character of the *mazar* is due to the fact that the authority of its shaykhs is entirely predetermined in the capacity of *mazar* keepers and pilgrim service providers, not going beyond this limited sphere. Local shaykhs are considered neither *khoja*s nor *ishan*s, nor do they fulfill the functions of mullahs or imams in mosques. They have no special knowledge of Muslim literary tradition and no personal spiritual powers. All these groups of religious authorities exist in the *qishlaq* separately from the shaykhs. However, the shaykhs also rank among religious Muslim authorities of the *qishlaq*, but only in a narrow area of social life. There are several groups of shaykhs in the *qishlaq* tied to different *mazar*s, who rank by popularity and by the significance of the places of worship under their care.

2 Shaykhs in Pre-Soviet Times

As I noted above, it is important to see how the status of *mazar* keepers has changed over time. We might be particularly interested in local *mazar* authorities, yet there are no reliable or detailed sources describing their state, for instance, a century ago. Local authorities are not always easy to identify in the historical materials available today.

There has been no detailed written evidence about the shaykhs of Abdurahman-ob, or I had no access to this evidence. In imperial times, *mazar*s and shaykhs were officially recognized through the acknowledgment of *waqf* endowments registered for the *mazar* and its keepers. However, this mechanism only involved well-known *mazar*s, while numerous local *mazar*s and their keepers were left without formal recognition. I could not find any

7 Abashin, "Mazars of Boboi-ob," 93–94.

evidence in the archives that there was a *waqf* registered for Abdurahman-ob, so this *mazar* and its shaykhs were not listed in any registers – it was a purely internal affair regulated by local rules and customs, without any intervention of imperial rule.

There are, however, several indirect sources. In 2010, Yaqubjon, to whom Tulgon-shaykh passed on the right to inherit the duties of the shaykh, showed me several documents dating back to 1910–1926 that were related to purchases and sales of land. He made these documents public, as he hoped, amid the disbandment of kolkhozes, to reclaim some irrigable, cultivated grounds that once belonged to his ancestors – through some sort of restitution. Here are two document examples:[8]

> (1) Instrument of Agreement to Sell
> The boundaries of the land located in the *qishlaq* in the Kūyūndī-būlāgh area: on the west – the Balāmālik Mountains, on the east – also the Balāmālik Mountains, on the south [extending] to the lands of ʿAlī-Muḥammad, son of Ustā-Sayyid; on the north – [extending] also to the Balāmālik Mountains. All the boundaries are clearly defined and identified by marks. The area of the land is 5 *tanāb*s [approx. one hectare]. Date of transaction – 4 Muḥarram 1329, December 23, 1910. The sellers are residents of the *qishlaq*: Mīrzā-ʿĀlim, son of the *aqsaqal* Ṭāhir-bāy, and Muḥammad-Zamān, son of Muḥammad-Kamāl. Place of transaction – Dār al-Qużāt (*qāżī* court). The land is sold with all the rights and according to Sharia law for one hundred and sixty rubles. The buyers are residents of Āshāba – Nūr-ʿAlī and Īr-ʿAlī [i.e., Erali], sons of Raḥīm-bāy shaykh. This plot of land is divided between them by the path on the land. Witnesses: Ashad-Muḥammad, son of Pīr-Muḥammad; Ghāyib-bāy, son of Ismāʿīl-bāy; ʿAshūr-Muḥammad-bāy, son of Ṣafar-mergen; Muḥammad-ʿĀlim, son of the abovementioned ʿAshūr-Muḥammad. A fixed-rate payment for the deal is noted further – 40 kopeks for the seal, the fee for *qāżī* services included, followed by document number – 88, day of week – Thursday. Qāżī seal: Mullā Ghanī Khwāja Qāżī, son of Kamāl al-Dīn Khwāja Qāżī.
>
> (There are two 5-kopek commission fee stamps glued on the right side, stating the date of document creation.)

8 Translated into Russian by Bakhtiar Babadzhanov.

(2) Instrument of Agreement to Sell
25 Jumādā al-Thānī 1342 (January 1, 1924)

The present testimony is given by us, whose names are hereunto subscribed (residents) of Namangān district, in the *volost* (*bulust*) of Bihisht in the *qishlaq* of Āshāba, that the cultivable plot of land in the settlement of Takhta-fas with boundaries as described below and a spring located on it (with the right to use) one fourth of water running out per day, is sold for the price of fifteen goats. The first one is Āy-zāda-bībī, daughter of Qalandar; the second one is ʿAsal-bībī, daughter of the aforementioned Qalandar. Both of them stated: "We, daughters of Qalandar, sold by final sale this land, the boundaries of which are noted (below), to Īr-ʿAlī shaykh [Erali], son of Raḥīm-bāy, (resident) of the abovementioned *qishlaq*, and received the named payment in full." (Boundaries.) The abovementioned land borders, on the side of *qibla* [west], with Balāmālik Mountain [which has no owner]; on the east, it borders partly with Balāmālik Mountain and partly with the abandoned land of Raḥīm-qul Ṣūfī; the north side (borders) with the abandoned land of Yūsuf-bangī; the south side (borders) with the private land of ʿAbd al-Wārith, son of Īshān Khalīfa. The second plot of land, (belonging) to us and located in the same settlement: on the side of the *qibla* it borders with (the land of) Īr-ʿAlī; on the east, with (the land of) Mullā ʿAbd al-Wārith *dāmullā*; on the north, with the highway (*katta yol*); on the south, with (the land of) the abovementioned Mullā ʿAbd al-Wārith *dāmullā*. The plots of land are sold and the goats are received in full. Calling to witness: 1. Dawlat-bāy, son of Rashīd-bāy; 2. Qarshī-bay, son of Nawās-bik; 3. ʿUmar shaykh, son of Khāl-Muḥammad-bāy. I, Chairman of the Executive Committee (*Isfalkum*) of the Jamāʿat of the township, Mīr-khāldār, son of Nūr-Muḥammad, sealed this (testimony). Signed by Mullā Maylī-bāy, son of Īsh-mīrzā-bāy.

From these documents we can learn the following details:

First, they mention Erali (Īr-ʿAlī), Tulgon-shaykh's father, referred to in her will as an important figure, the mention of which should have confirmed her own rights. Erali bore the title "shaykh" even before the Soviet regime. The duties and the corresponding title of shaykh were transferred in the family by succession. For instance, the documents also mentioned Erali's father, Raḥīm-bāy or Rahimbaba, who was also called shaykh. Somebody named ʿUmar-shaykh is also mentioned in the documents; however, we do not have any further details about him.

Second, the documents were prepared and attested by representatives of the local imperial/Soviet rule and the people's court/Sharia court, and residents of *qishlaq* signed these documents as witnesses. Thus, all of them, in fact, recognized the title of shaykh, the right to bear it, and the duties behind it as legitimate.

Finally, Erali-shaykh, the central figure in these documents, was a quite wealthy man by local standards; he had much land and bought new pieces of land, including the mentioned 5-tanab plot (almost one hectare, which is a lot for mountainous terrain). Notably, he bought land from local rich people, for example, Mīrzā-ʿĀlim, who was an *aqsaqal* in the *qishlaq* and represented one of the most influential local families. Erali-shaykh was not only a land owner but also a cattle breeder, as he paid in dozens of goats for the land that he bought up in the beginning of the 1920s.

3 Shaykhs in the Soviet Period

As we know, in Soviet times, the practice of *waqf* was abolished in the late 1920s and an anti-religious ideological and political campaign was launched.[9] *Mazar*s were publicly destroyed or, if they included any buildings, taken for public use; religious authorities were prosecuted and even repressed.[10] In the mid-1940s, religious institutes and authorities were partly reinstated, but with a limited scope of activity.[11] Some *mazar*s were declared cultural or natural monuments and thus gained conservation status, which allowed pilgrimage in the likeness of tourism and educational activities.[12] So what happened to the local *mazar* of Abdurahman-ob and its shaykhs?

I came across a "reply" from the Executive Committee of Asht Regional Council of People's Deputies dated October 20, 1977, to a request about religious life. It stated that "due to lack of mosques and 'religious places' in Asht region, we definitely have no special mullahs, so some religious ceremonies are carried out by various old people, whoever may." The "reply" states: "There are 16 unregistered mullahs living across the region, each one was given an individual talk 'On non-violation of the legislation on religions …'; we do not observe

9 Niccolò Pianciola and Paolo Sartori, "*Waqf* in Turkestan: The Colonial Legacy and the Fate of an Islamic Institution in Early Soviet Central Asia, 1917–1924," *Central Asian Survey* 26, no. 4 (December 2007): 475–498.

10 Shoshana Keller, *To Moscow, Not Mecca: The Soviet Campaign Against Islam in Central Asia, 1917–1941* (Westport, Conn.: Praeger, 2001).

11 Eren Tasar, *Soviet and Muslim: The Institutionalization of Islam in Central Asia, 1943–1991* (New York: Oxford University Press, 2017).

12 Sergei Abashin, "A Prayer for Rain: Practicing Being Soviet and Muslim," *Journal of Islamic Studies* 25, no. 2 (May 2014): 178–200.

collective '*namoz*' readings, preaching or any other religious events. Youth, students, intelligentsia, and kolkhoz members are especially indifferent toward the religious holiday. Only during the holidays, the cemetery was mostly visited by the elderly people, whose relatives died this year. Besides, we do not have so-called 'holy places.'"[13] However, the new letter from the Executive Committee two years later already contained a list of "prayer rooms and 'holy places' located on the territory of Asht region," and the Abdurahman-ob *mazar* was listed among them. I know that specialists from the Ferghana Museum of Local Lore studied the *mazar* in the 1980s and wrote about its uniqueness. This effort could have heightened interest toward the place and even turned it into a historical, cultural, and natural monument; however, this never happened.

This ambiguous reality is often documented in communications between public officials: locals undoubtedly knew about the *mazar*; but because it was local and hard to reach, there was essentially nothing to destroy there, and it was difficult to control, so it could be ignored. The practices of pilgrimage, according to memories of local residents, persisted throughout the Soviet era, although they did undergo some changes. The religious aspect of the pilgrimage was not demonstrated openly; many locals, who had received a Soviet atheist education, preferred to describe those practices as primarily recreational and social – a hiking trip to the mountains in the torrid month of August was often considered to be a pleasant and healthy vacation. At the same time, the main elements of pilgrimage persisted – the traditional route included visiting the main sacred points (trees, ponds, and stone clusters that were associated with Abdurahman's activity), touching them, preparing a special meal with wishes of health/recovery and reciting prayers. Even if some travelers did not identify their actions as religious, they still repeated the behavior models that the local community and the local Muslim authorities recognized as conventional, appropriate, and legitimate, describing them as *savob*, a charitable deed.

As all the main practices of pilgrimage persisted, the persons who were an integral part of these practices – the shaykhs – persisted, too. They located themselves in specific places along the hiking/pilgrimage route, meeting the travelers, providing them with dishes to prepare the ritual meal and with sleeping accommodation (if needed). They could also recite prayers or perform certain rituals (like cutting off children's hair – *kokil* – as a sign of commitment to the *mazar*). All the people in the *qishlaq* knew the *mazar* keepers and often

13 Khujand Regional Archive. Collection 117, Inventory 1, File 582: Letter to A. Sharipov, Commissioner of the Council for Religious Affairs under the Council of Ministers of the USSR in the Leninabad Region (Sheet 3–5).

used their services; they specifically added the title "shaykh" when discussing them among themselves, in order to emphasize who they were talking about or to show respect for them. The participation of witnesses and public officials that we see in Tulgon-shaykh's will in 2006 represented a continuation of this recognition in Soviet times.

However, oral stories that I collected in the *qishlaq* also reveal a picture of competition between shaykhs, which was apparently never manifested in the will. As I noted above, there are several stopover points along the trail toward the top of the mountain Abdurahman-ob. One of them is located on the outskirts of the *qishlaq*, next to another *mazar* – Chinar. Then, on the way to the mountain top, there is a *chaikhona*, and right next to the top there is an *oshkhona* – a small place for cooking meals and possible lodging for the night. In the end of the 1980s, Tulgon-shaykh used to live at the top waypoint in August, and Kholmat-shaykh used to live at the middle point. I saw some contradictions between their versions of how the heritage of shaykh-hood had been transferred.

According to Kholmat-shaykh – a drinker and marijuana smoker – the first shaykh of Abdurahman-ob was someone named Ashurmat-shaykh; in the twentieth century, the top waypoint was taken care of by two brothers – Ashurmat's descendants, Umar-shaykh and Qayum-shaykh. While their sons did not take up the duties of *mazar* keepers, Erali, who was the husband of Umar and Qayum's younger sister, became the shaykh. Tulgon-shaykh was Erali-shaykh's daughter, and Kholmat-shaykh himself is Umar-shaykh's matrilineal grandson. The other version proposed by Tulgon-shaykh, on the contrary, claims that Rahim and his son Erali were the original shaykhs of the mountain. In the 1930s, when Erali-shaykh was arrested and deported as a *kulak* and a religious figure, he instructed Umar-shaykh, his brother-in-law, to take care of the *mazar*. Umar began to carry out this duty together with his brother Qayum. After them, Yetmishbay (Qayum-shaykh's son) and Tulgon-kampyr (Erali-shaykh's daughter) assumed the duties of *mazar* keepers, dividing between themselves the two waypoints on the pilgrim trail. When Yetmishbay became old, he ceased going up the mountain and stayed near the mazar Chinar. Here, those pilgrims who did not reach the grave of the saint but ended their pilgrimage in the *qishlaq* sometimes asked him to recite a prayer for them. (However, Yetmishbay is not considered the chief shaykh of Chinar, as there is another, more legitimate, shaykh who takes care of this *mazar*). Then Kholmat, Umar-shaykh's matrilineal grandson, started going up the mountain instead of Yetmishbay.

This in-absentia argument reveals a conflict of genealogies going on between formerly close relatives, where each relative's lineage is presented as fundamental and most legitimate, while all the others are less legitimate and even suggest usurpatory claims. Such conflict is neither extraordinary nor unique – it is rather typical for situations related to heritage and hereditary transfer of titles, privileges, incomes, and legitimacy, that is, for anything that generally amounts to authority through kinship.[14] In this sense, such controversy demonstrates succession and recurrence, regardless of the Soviet context.

If we look for revamps or discontinuities in this line of succession, we should notice that the construction of legitimate authority of the Soviet shaykhs actively employed female lines of descent. Using matrilineage to enhance the status had always been a common practice in the past, for which many examples can be found.[15] In our case, we can note that the role of female lines is very important for all versions of genealogies; besides, for many years, the chief shaykh of the *mazar* was a woman – Tulgon, daughter of Erali-shaykh. I believe that this is largely due to the late Soviet situation, where elderly people and women found it easier to demonstrate their religiousness and perform practices that were officially considered "vestigial" and "nonexistent," being less at risk of persecution. Carrying out the duties of a shaykh – in the narrow sense, as these duties had been formed within a particular group in a particular *qishlaq* – brought but a small income and could not be regarded as part of an official social career. Being a shaykh did not give any advantages in taking certain positions or building local political networks, so this occupation lost its pragmatic attractiveness to a great extent, mostly retaining its symbolic value. Thus, the status of the shaykh was economically moved to a marginal – that is, a woman's – position in the family division of labor, which allowed for the preservation of symbolic capital without much economic and political hardship.

Tulgon-shaykh, by the way, had a younger brother named Abdumannob. He could have inherited the status of shaykh from Erali-shaykh through the male line; yet he did not do this, and never became a *mazar* keeper – apparently due to the reasons mentioned above. However, it is interesting that many *qishlaq* residents speak of Abdumannob as an extraordinary man, recounting, for instance, that he was lucky in cards and gave out his winnings to the poor. These stories are similar to hagiographies of various Sufi figures of the past, who could violate accepted behavior norms in order to pursue some unseen goals. Abdumannob even had a nickname, Avliyo, that is, "saint." It is unclear

---

14 Devin DeWeese, "The Politics of Sacred Lineages in 19th-Century Central Asia: Descent Groups Linked to Khwaja Ahmad Yasavi in Shrine Documents and Genealogical Charters," *International Journal of Middle East Studies* 31, no. 4 (November 1999): 507–530.

15 DeWeese, "The Politics of Sacred Lineages," 514, 516–517.

whether the locals in any possible way connected his originality to his belonging to the shaykh dynasty. I have never heard open assertions about this connection; however, it may be implied.

4 Shaykhs in Post-Soviet Times

I acknowledge that if Soviet rule had survived, accompanied by further intensive societal transformations, the shaykh dynasty of the Abdurahman-ob *mazar* might have discontinued and ceased its functioning as a specialized group of religious, Muslim authorities. This logic of events does not seem impossible to me, as such processes were seen in many other regions that went through more intensive Sovietization and reformation. However, the collapse of the USSR, characterized by a radical shift in political structures, ideologies, and economic strategies, set into motion an entirely new trajectory of change. Not only did Islam, or reference to Islam, become publicly acceptable, it turned into an important mechanism of building legitimacies, statuses, and careers. Of course, this has been and continues to be associated with the debate on what kind of reference to Islam is right or wrong, what is allowed and what is not, and so on. This debate is also an apparently inevitable effect of creating and re-creating religious, Muslim sociality as one of the main spheres where political, ideological, and economic interests collide and where social life takes place.

Let us return to the *qishlaq* and see what happened to the shaykhs in the post-Soviet period. The practice of pilgrimage to *mazar*s remained widespread, despite the criticism that was coming from religious Muslim authorities at that time. For this reason, some repressed rhetorical justifications for their preservation became more relevant. Pilgrims or travelers began to exclude episodes concerning miracles, allegedly performed by Abdurahman-ob, from their explanations. Instead, they started recounting the spiritual and physical efforts associated with the pilgrimage/hiking trip to show the intensity of their faith. That being said, the main actions – climbing the mountain, preparing the meal, visiting and touching the objects that symbolize the holy place, praying – all remained the same. The shaykhs' role also remained the same – they met the pilgrims and provided them with all necessary supplies, including Muslim legitimacy in its local sense.

Under these new conditions, shaykhs consciously or unconsciously chose the strategy of preserving and strengthening their specialized functions. A peculiar element of this strategy is a lack of effort on their part to expand their competence or to interpret a wider scope of questions that go beyond their narrow sphere of *mazar* service. They have not yet tried to build/invent their aristocratic heritage, to receive Islamic religious education, or to appeal to any of their special personal capacities to perform miracles. They did not even try to reconstruct any stories or legends of the Abdurahman-ob *mazar* in order to make it more acceptable from the Islamic scholastic point of view. Shaykhs were only interested in the purely utilitarian functions of the *mazar*, which was already well known far outside the *qishlaq* without any effort by the keepers. For them, it represented a source of income in the form of material offerings, a resource of social connections and arrangements, and a mechanism to support their symbolic status of local shrine keepers. Thus, they avoided direct and dangerous confrontation, staying away from the conflict that emerged among other Muslim leaders in the early 1990s and persisted – in its invisible yet no less harsh form – until 2010,[16] the year of my last visit.

However, there are other strategies demonstrated in the will of 2006, which I fully quoted in the beginning of this chapter. Having transferred the right to "the heritage of Abdurahman-ob" to the son of Abdumannob-avliyo, whom I mentioned above, and who was the patrilineal descendant of Erali-shaykh, Tulgon restored patrilineality and returned the role of the *mazar* keeper to the men. The written will, signed by witnesses and certified by the village council/ Jamaat, as well as the ritual reading of Quran organized in Yaqubjan's house on that occasion – where mullahs, elderly men, and respected figures of the qishlaq were invited – reinforced public and even official recognition of the shaykh dynasty. Of note, this new document partly copied the acts (of purchase and sale) of the 1910s and 1920s–it was also designed as a statement, confirmed with the witnesses' signatures and certified by the stamp of the local authorities – although here we see Cyrillic and not Arabic script, and the dates are indicated according to the Gregorian calendar, not the lunar Muslim calendar. These changes made a reference to the standardized, conventional norms, to the authority of the state and the community, to the customs and guidelines, and to the authority of Erali and Abdumannob that already existed in the memory of the people, thus, in turn, strengthening the legitimacy and authority of the shaykh dynasty. At the same time, Tulgon-shaykh and Yaqubjan-shaykh solved a more specific problem, weakening possible claims of another kindred line of the same dynasty, as noted above.

---

16 Bakhtiar Babadzhanov, "Islam in Uzbekistan: From the Struggle for 'Religious Purity' to Political Activism," in *Central Asia: A Gathering Storm?* ed. Boris Rumer (New York: M.E. Sharpe, 2002), 299–330.

5 Conclusion

First, I would like once more to draw attention to the fact that there are many roles and functions which can be described as "religious Muslim authorities." Some of them can be very local and narrow in their character and have limited duties that are sought after by the local community or by a certain group in everyday life. The eye of a religious studies scholar may not even recognize them as "religious figures;" experts on Islamic studies as well as some Muslim religious leaders will deny any connection between those local authorities and Islam. However, according to the local worldview, everything is imbued with references to the supernatural and evidence of the holy; so these roles and functions are perceived as necessary and vested with certain power. They may not need legitimation through the book tradition or a special theological rationale; local consensus and habits of the local residents suffice, while collective approval and inheritance by kinship can be quite an accepted way to actualize these roles and functions as Muslim.

Second, I would like to emphasize the peculiar transformation of these functions and roles in the twentieth century. They underwent significant and manifold transformations during two periods of dismantlement – the beginning of the Soviet reforms and the fall of the Soviet state. After the first period, we can see some sort of social marginalization – the status of the *mazar* keeper loses its association with social prestige in other spheres of activities; there is a change in the gender code of this status; and the rhetoric explaining the need for these actions changes – in particular, various rational arguments gain importance. After the collapse of the USSR, we see a largely opposite process, that is, a reconstruction of the previous situation: restoration of public religious motivation, defeminization and increasing significance of the status of shaykh, despite the fact that the *mazar* did not receive any official status, and remained an informal place of worship and relaxation.

Undoubtedly, we are faced with a question about how to consider what has happened. Was it an attempt to secularize the society from the outside – a superficial or failed attempt – with the result that many norms and practices, with some adjustments, were preserved and eventually restored after the inevitable collapse of the experiment? Or was secularization still a successful project that could go on – if not for the political and economic crisis, instigated by poor decisions, which entailed the restoration of previous statuses and practices as a spontaneous reaction to this crisis? I believe that both answers are working models, and the debate between them will apparently continue. In my view, it is important to consider the continuity, the time lapse of the social phenomenon related to the local ideas of Islam, along with the sequence of ruptures and various transformations of that phenomenon, as well as even the possibility of its extinction. Regarding the history of shaykhs through such a twofold lens allows one to see a wider picture of the fate of Islam in contemporary Central Asia.

Bibliography

Abashin, Sergei. *Sovetskii kishlak: mezhdu kolonializmom i modernizatsiei* [*Soviet Qishlaq: Between Colonialism and Modernization*] (Moscow: Novoe literaturnoe obozrenie, 2015).

Abashin, Sergei. "A Prayer for Rain: Practicing Being Soviet and Muslim." *Journal of Islamic Studies* 25/2 (May 2014): 178–200.

Abashin, Sergey. "Mazars of Boboi-ob: Typical and Untypical Features of Holy Places in Central Asia." In *Muslim Saints and Mausoleums in Central Asia and Xinjiang*, ed. Yasushi Shinmen, Minoru Sawada, and Edmund Waite (Paris: Jean Maisonneuve Successeur, 2013), 91–105.

Babadzhanov, Bakhtiar. "Islam in Uzbekistan: From the Struggle for 'Religious Purity' to Political Activism." In *Central Asia: A Gathering Storm?*, ed. Boris Rumer (New York: M.E. Sharpe, 2002), 299–330.

DeWeese, Devin. "The Politics of Sacred Lineages in 19th-Century Central Asia: Descent Groups Linked to Khwaja Ahmad Yasavi in Shrine Documents and Genealogical Charters." *International Journal of Middle East Studies* 31/4 (November 1999): 507–530.

Kehl-Bodrogi, Krisztina. "'Who Owns the Shrine?' Competing Meanings and Authorities at a Pilgrimage Site in Khorezm." *Central Asian Survey* 25/3 (September 2006): 235–250.

Keller, Shoshana. *To Moscow, Not Mecca: The Soviet Campaign Against Islam in Central Asia, 1917–1941*. Westport, Connecticut: Praeger, 2001.

Khalid, Adeeb. *Islam after Communism: Religion and Politics in Central Asia*. Berkeley: University of California Press, 2007.

Khujand Regional Archive. Collection 117, Inventory 1, File 582: Letter to A. Sharipov, Commissioner of the Council for Religious Affairshin under the Council of Ministers of the USSR in the Leninabad Region (Sheet 3–5).

Louw, Maria Elisabeth. *Everyday Islam in Post-Soviet Central Asia*. London and New York: Routledge, 2007.

Pianciola, Niccolò, and Paolo Sartori. "Waqf in Turkestan: The Colonial Legacy and the Fate of an Islamic Institution in Early Soviet Central Asia, 1917–1924." *Central Asian Survey* 26/4 (December 2007): 475–498.

Poliakov, Sergei P. *Everyday Islam: Religion and Tradition in Rural Central Asia,* ed. Martha Brill Olcott, tr. Anthony Olcott (Armond, New York: M.E. Sharpe, 1992).

Privratsky, Bruce G. "'Turkistan Belongs to the Qojas': Local Knowledge of a Muslim Tradition." In *Devout Societies vs. Impious States? Transmitting Islamic Learning in Russia, Central Asia and China through the Twentieth Century,* ed. Stéphane A. Dudoignon (Berlin: Klaus Schwarz Verlag, 2004), 161–212.

Sartori, Paolo. "Towards a History of the Muslims' Soviet Union: A View from Central Asia." *Die Welt des Islams* 50/3–4 (2010): 315–334.

Shinmen, Yasushi, Minoru Sawada, and Edmund Waite, eds. *Muslim Saints and Mausoleums in Central Asia and Xinjiang*. Paris: Jean Maisonneuve Successeur, 2013.

Snesarev, Gleb. "On Some Causes of the Persistence of Religio-Customary Survivals among the Khorezm Uzbeks." In *Introduction to Soviet Ethnography*, eds. Stephen P. Dunn and Ethel Dunn (Berkeley: Highgate Road Social Science Research Station, 1974), 215–239.

Sugawara, Jun, and Rahile Dawut, eds. *Mazar: Studies on Islamic Sacred Sites in Central Eurasia*. Tokyo: Tokyo University of Foreign Studies Press, 2016.

Tasar, Eren. *Soviet and Muslim: The Institutionalization of Islam in Central Asia, 1943–1991*. New York: Oxford University Press, 2017.

PART 4

Authority Mobilized: Religious Institutions and Frameworks for Contestation

The Struggle for *Sharīʿa*

The Empire, the Muftiate, and the Kazakh Steppe in the 19th and Early 20th Centuries

Pavel Shabley

1 Introduction

With the integration of the Kazakh *zhüz*es into the Russian empire in the 18th century,[1] Kazakhs' Muslimness underwent a significant and multifarious process of transformation.[2] To appreciate the significance of such a complex process, one should consider a number of factors. First, the Orenburg Mohammedan Spiritual Assembly (OMSA = the muftiate) played a major role in shaping Muslimness among the Kazakhs, for its sphere of influence included the Kazakh-populated territories.[3] Second, many emergent cities and cultural centers (Petropavlovsk,[4] Semipalatinsk,[5] Akmolinsk,[6] Kokchetav, and others[7]) expanded under the influx of Muslims from various regions of the Russian Empire and Central Asia. Third, equally important were the conditions that had developed in the Kazakh steppe before its annexation to the Russian Empire: the syncretism of legal culture (a perception of *ʿādat* and *sharīʿa* not as opposites but rather as complementary legal practices), the veneration of

1 The Junior *zhüz* and the Middle *zhüz* in the 1730s, the Senior *zhüz* in the 1820–1860s.

2 Allen J. Frank, "Islamic Transformation on the Kazakh Steppe, 1742–1917: Toward an Islamic History of Kazakhstan under Russian Rule," in *The Construction and Deconstruction of National Histories in Slavic Eurasia*, ed. Tadayuki Hayashi (Sapporo: Slavic Research Center, 2003), 261–289.

3 Danil' Azamatov, *Orenburgskoe magometanskoe dukhovnoe sobranie v kontse 18–19 vekakh* (Ufa: Gilem, 1999), 29.

4 In 1882, the Tatar population consisted of 2,389 people. Of these, 1,499 people were Kazakhs and 224 were Sarts. See *Central State Archive of the Republic of Kazakhstan* (TsGARK), F. 64, op. 1, d. 2757, ll. 23ob – 24; "Vedomost' o Naselenii Akmolinskoi Oblasti za 1882 god," in *Obzor Akmolinskoi Oblasti za 1882 god* (Omsk: Tipografiia Akmolinskogo Oblastnogo Pravleniia), 75.

5 In 1882, Muslims constituted 62.3 % of the city's population (36.6 % Kazakhs, 22.8 % Tatars, 2.9 % Sarts). See Allen J. Frank and Mirkasyim A. Usmanov, ed. and transl., *Materials for the Islamic History of Semipalatinsk: Two manuscripts by Aḥmad-Walī al-Qazānī and Qurbānʿalī Khālidī*, *ANOR*, 11 (Halle-Berlin, 2001), 5–6.

6 Zufar Makhmutov, *Istoriia Tatar Astany: pervaia polovina 19–nachalo 21 vekov* (Kazan: Tatarskoe Knizhnoe Izdatel'stvo, 2017).

7 TsGARK, F. 369, op. 1, d. 3822.

 | DOI:10.1163/9789004527096_011

ancestors (*äruaq*),[8] and the popularity of Sufi brotherhoods,[9] just to name a few. These ongoing processes heightened the diversity of Islamic religious practices and shaped the religious elite that consisted of the Kazakhs[10] (mullahs, *khojas*[11]) as well as the Tatar,[12] Bashkir, and Central Asian *ʿulamāʾ*. All these religious groups and their leaders had different levels of training in Islamic sciences and varying experiences of interacting with fellow believers within the Russian Empire and beyond. Their perception of imperial influence on Islamic communities was likewise diverse. Still, many *ʿulamāʾ* and administrative institutions (for example, OMSA) were eager both to profit from the changes that followed the Kazakh steppe's integration into the Russian Empire and to preserve conventional Muslim traditions and communications. The differential interactions among the religious elites and imperial officials ensured that authority and power relations changed more dynamically and unpredictably in the colonial context than in societies not functioning under non-Muslim rulers.[13]

Appealing to *sharīʿa* is one way to facilitate the functioning of authority and power relations in Muslim communities. In the Kazakh steppe, such appeals involved a blend of behavioral modes and strategies: contrasting *sharīʿa* and *ʿādat* as a way of fixating differences between law (i.e., written rules) and "savage

8 Kazakh ancestral spirits came to be assimilated to, and to be known by the generic designation for, the spirits (*äruaq* < Ar. *arwāḥ*) of Muslim saints and prophets; the ontological proximity of these categories manifests itself clearly in those cases where the saints, much like the ancestral spirits, appear to humans in dreams. See Bruce G. Privratsky, *Muslim Turkistan: Kazak Religion and Collective Memory* (Richmond, Surrey: Routledge, 2001), 17–18.

9 Frank, "Islamic Transformation on the Kazakh Steppe, 1742–1917"

10 Russian sources refer to Kazakhs as Kirgizes or Kirgiz-kaisaks. See Irina V. Erofeeva, "Kak Kazakhi stali Kirgizami: K istorii odnoi terminologicheskoi putanitsy," *Astana* 5 (2005): 23–27. Muslim texts (Kazakh and Tatar) preserved the designation Qazaqs. See Qurbān-ʿAlī Khālidī, *Tawārīkh-i Khamsa-yi sharqī* (Kazan: Tipografiia Kazakova, 1910), 220–267.

11 On *khojas* (in Kazakh, *qozhas*), see Privratsky, *Muslim Turkistan*, 98–102.

12 Kazakh sources referred to Tatars as Noghays. See Aqan Serï Qoramsaŭli, "Kökshetauda Nauan Molda men Khamidolla Noghay Moldasi Baqas Bolghanda, Khamidolla Aqan Serïnïň Aytqani," in *Aqan Serï Qoramsaŭli, Ükïlï Ibiray Sandibayŭli, Baluan Sholaq Baymirzaŭli. Shigharmalari* (Almaty: Nŭrli Press.kz, 2014), 97–99.

13 On attitudes of Muslims toward the Russian conquest of the Volga-Ural region and, later, of Central Asia, see the analysis of religious works and *fatwās* written in these territories by Michael Kemper, *Sufii i uchenye v Tatarstane i Bashkortostane: Islamskii diskurs pod imperskim upravleniem*, trans. Iskander Giliazov (Kazan: Rossiiskii Islamskii Universitet, 2008), 400–403, and by B.M. Babadzhanov, *Kokandskoe khanstvo: Vlast', politika, religiia* (Tashkent/Tokyo: Yangi nashr, 2010): 531–539.

custom,"[14] highlighting dissent from the established practices of a school of law (*madhhab*), and different, indeed opposite hermeneutic approaches to the scriptures when issuing legal opinions, *taqlīd*[15] and *ijtihād*.[16] The debates about *taqlīd* and *ijtihād* could grow more intense not only on purely intellectual grounds, but also when scholars and activists in general realized how these disagreements could be deployed in the public sphere.[17] The empire generally manifested pragmatism in relationships with its Muslim subjects:[18] in some instances, unsurprisingly, government officials relied upon the Jadids, and in others, upon OMSA, which endured harsh criticism from supporters of the new method.[19] It should be noted that for the empire, supporting OMSA's authority among Muslims was key to retaining control over legal and confessional diversity. This included, for example, fighting against Sufism and other religious movements whose structures and peculiarities imperial officials understood only very superficially.[20]

It becomes apparent that matters of authority among the Muslims must have required an understanding of how the relationships between the empire and its Muslim subjects were to be organized. It is important, therefore, to examine the peculiarities of these relationships. The work of Michael Kemper

14 The project of colonial officials anticipated that with the codification of *ʿādat*, *sharīʿa* was to lose its significance in Kazakh legal culture; see Paolo Sartori and Pavel Shablei, "Sud'ba imperskikh kodifikatsionnykh proektov: Adat i shariat v Kazakhskoi stepi," *Ab Imperio*, 2 (2015): 66–78.

15 The recognition of and adherence to the most authoritative legal opinion within a certain school of law.

16 Independent legal reasoning.

17 As Paolo Sartori demonstrates, Russian officials and Orientalists often embraced the Qur'ān and the Sunna, believing that "the true meaning of Islamic law was to be inferred from the Qur'ān and the Prophetic Sunna;" see Paolo Sartori, "What We Talk about When We Talk about *Taqlīd* in Russian Central Asia," in *Sharīʿa in the Russian Empire: The Reach and Limits of Islamic Law in Central Eurasia, 1550–1917*, ed. Paolo Sartori and Danielle Ross (Edinburgh: Edinburgh University Press, 2020), 315.

18 Andreas Kappeler, "Dve traditsii v otnosheniiakh Rossii k musul'manskim narodam Rossiiskoi imperii," *Otechestvennaia istoriia*, 2 (2003): 129–135.

19 Riżā al-Dīn b. Fakhr al-Dīn, *Dini vä Izhtimagiy Mäs'älälär* (Kazan: Rukhiyät, 2001), 69.

20 Marsil' Farkhshatov, ed., *"Delo" bashkirskogo sheikha Zainulli Rasuleva (1872–1917): Vlast' i sufizm v poreformennoi Bashkirii. Sbornik Dokumentov* (Ufa: Institut Istorii, Iazyka, i Literatury UNZ RAN, 2009). Here, one may agree with Robert Crews, who considers that the empire benefited from a temporary alliance with Muslim activists and OMSA that defended the "orthodox" interpretations of Islam (for example, certain opinions within the Ḥanafī *madhhab*) and thus assisted the state in reducing the sphere of Islam's social, religious, and legal diversity; see Robert Crews, *For Prophet and Tsar: Islam and Empire in Russia and Central Asia* (Cambridge: Harvard University Press, 2006), 23–24, 77–86.

plays an important role here, exploring as it does the notion of "Islamic discourse under Russian rule," which suggests that Muslims avoided participating actively in imperial life and opted to discuss their problems autonomously, that is, within the framework of Islamic forms of communication.[21] A shortcoming of Kemper's approach, however, is that it creates a series of difficulties in understanding OMSA's jurisdiction: was this institution merely an imperial invention that Muslims did not trust, or were the *fatwās* and other legal documents of the muftiate perceived through the prism of the customary Muslim significance attached to the *muftī* and *qāżī*? Another shortcoming of the Islamic discourse argument is its treatment of the *ʿādat* and *sharīʿa* opposition, which in the case of the Kazakh steppe was connected more with personal, opportunistic interests of the *ʿulamāʾ* than with the stability of the system of Islamic concepts and meanings.[22] Other attempts to develop the idea of Islamic discourse are equally problematic. One example is James Meyer's conclusion that Muslims and the empire succeeded in developing a common language for understanding one another. This was achieved by using in official paperwork such phrases as "in accordance with *sharīʿa*" and "Mohammedan law," among others.[23] However, various instances of legal practice suggest that the authors of claims, petitions, and other official documents employed these expressions without giving them any thought. As a result, concepts that had been extensively in use in administrative paperwork suddenly could become a source of conflict and friction between the empire and Muslims, the administrative entities, and OMSA.[24]

Thus, diverse approaches must be employed to examine the problem of the relationship between Muslims and the empire as well as matters of authority

21 Kemper, *Sufii i Uchenye*, 27, 43.

22 For cases in which custom (*ʿurf, ʿādat, ʿamal*) is not always contrasted with *sharīʿa*, but can be adapted to Islamic legal doctrine, see Reem A. Meshal, *Sharia and the Making of the Modern Egyptian: Islamic Law and Custom in the Courts of Ottoman Cairo* (Cairo and New York: The American University in Cairo Press, 2014), 46–55.

23 James H. Meyer, "Speaking Sharia to the State: Muslim Protesters, Tsarist Officials, and the Islamic Discourses of Late Imperial Russia," *Kritika: Explorations in Russian and Eurasian History*, 14/3 (2013), 487–493.

24 In 1864, OMSA did not support the Semipalatinsk regional government's decision to appoint Ibragim Akhmetov as the region's senior *ākhūnd*, since it believed that a more learned and educated person should take that post in accordance with Islamic principles. Russian authorities, on the contrary, approached the significance of the *ākhūnd* position within the framework of the imperial bureaucratic system, believing that the individual's efficiency and trustworthiness had to be the main factor. Even though the *ākhūnds* were incorporated in the Russian administrative apparatus in the early 18th century, the case of Ibragim Akhmetov took several years to resolve. See *Russian State Historical Archive* (RGIA), F. 821, op. 8, d. 1021, ll. 9, 12ob, 14 ob.

associated with this relationship. Legal hybridity is of key importance within this context.[25] Specifically, it illuminates a great variety of situations in which the boundaries between the use of *sharīʿa*, *ʿādat*, and Russian law were not strictly fixed. In discussing legal hybridity, I do not seek to demonstrate the signs of the collapse of the colonial government or to emphasize that pragmatism defined all aspects of Muslims' relationship with the empire and with each other. Rather, at issue is the diversity of contexts that forced the participants in local history to seek out the adaptive strategies and behavioral logic that they found most acceptable.

This chapter is divided into three sections: an introduction, the main part, a conclusion. The main part consists of three sections. The first portion of the main part examines the period (1788–1868) when the Kazakhs fell under OMSA's jurisdiction. In the Kazakh steppe, this time was marked by uneasy relationships between the appointed mullahs and local social groups (*biys*, Kazakh officials, and various marginal categories). Within this context, the opposition between *ʿādat*, and *sharīʿa* was evolving as a resource of power relations. The Tatar mullahs who accused their Kazakh rivals of following "savage customs" used *sharīʿa* as a weapon in fighting for authority in local communities. Lacking substantial bureaucratic means for controlling the situation in the Kazakh steppe, OMSA employed assorted tactics to maintain its influence: on the one hand, it promoted the image of the Russian Empire as a confessional state with laws that reflected Muslim interests, and on the other hand, it tightened procedural guidelines, thus allowing Kazakhs to use *sharīʿa* in disputes over decisions made by other judicial authorities (such as, for example, the *biys*' court).

The second section of the main part addresses the peculiarities of the legal situation in the Kazakh steppe after the administrative reforms of 1867–68. These reforms led to the exclusion of the Kazakhs from OMSA's jurisdiction. The military governor was placed in charge of appointing mullahs. An elective system was introduced into the *biys*' court, which came to be called the people's court (*narodnyi sud*). However, despite the Russian administration's efforts to limit the sphere of application of *sharīʿa* and to transform the *biys*' court into a colonial institution, local circumstances dictated otherwise: legal hybridity was preserved, and enabled both the *ʿulamāʾ* and the *biys* to appeal

25 I develop this approach based on Paolo Sartori's work; see Paolo Sartori, "Authorized Lies: Colonial Agency and Legal Hybrids in Tashkent, c. 1881–1893," *Journal of the Economic and Social History of the Orient*, 55 (2012): 688–717.

actively to *sharīʿa* as a source of their influence and authority, and in doing so, to ignore the very fact of the colonial reformations.

In the third section of the main part, I consider the situation that emerged when different approaches and principles used in the process of taking legal decisions (*taqlīd* and *ijtihād*) became parts of a complex context in which OMSA, the empire, the *ākhūnd* of the Kazakh Inner Horde, Ghŭmar Qarash, and his adversaries among the local Kazakhs, were participants. The very fact that *ijtihād*, supported by the Jadids, was closer than *taqlīd* to the officials' ideas about the colonial transformation of *sharīʿa* speaks to the ability of OMSA to act outside the framework of the colonial system of knowledge (the colonial episteme).[26] At the same time, the willingness of the local community to doubt the *fatwās* of *ākhūnd* Ghŭmar Qarash is a manifestation not only of pragmatism and subjectivity, but also of an opportunity to expand local conceptions about Islamic legal approaches – that is, to analyze personal knowledge and experience within the framework of their relevance to various legal principles and methods.

1.1 *"I Assist in Keeping Them Away from the Ancient Habit of Contracting Forced Marriages:" The Kazakhs under the Jurisdiction of the Orenburg Mohammedan Spiritual Assembly*

In 1860, OMSA held a special meeting to discuss the numerous pleas of the Siberian Kazakhs[27] that involved the customs of the levirate (*amangerlïk*).[28] Since these matters were handled by the local offices – the regional *prikazes*[29] – the muftiate wondered why "... do these complaints [to OMSA] not only not cease but, on the contrary, increase in number year by year?"[30] Wary of the local authorities, OMSA appealed to the Regional Administration of the Siberian Kirghiz (Kazakhs [P.S.]) "... to take measures that will put an end to

26 Sartori, "What We Talk about," 315.

27 Following the 1822 abolition of the khan's power in the Middle *zhüz*, the Kazakhs of the Northern, Central, and Northeastern parts of today's Kazakhstan came under the command of the West-Siberian Governorate-General, whose center was in the city of Tobol'sk, and later, after 1839, in the city of Omsk.

28 According to this *ʿādat* norm, after a husband's death, his wife was to marry one of his brothers.

29 According to the "Statute on the Siberian Kirghiz" (June 22, 1822), special district *prikazes* were formed in the Kazakh steppe of the Siberian *vedomstvo*. At the head of these *prikazes* were Kazakh senior sultans, as well as two Russian officials and two officials selected from among the local Kazakhs. See Margarita Masevich ed., *Materialy po istorii politicheskogo stroia Kazakhstana*, Tom 1 (Alma-Ata: Izdatel'stvo Akademii Nauk Kazakhskoi SSR, 1961), 93–94.

30 TsGARK, F. 345, op. 1, d. 1600, l. 1.

this evil and savage custom that is entirely against the common state laws and the Mohammedan *sharīʿa*."[31] The Spiritual Assembly also dispatched similar appeals to the *ukaz* mullahs.

The above-cited piece of bureaucratic correspondence suggests both that OMSA was part of the legal regulatory system created in the Russian Empire under Catherine II, and that departures from *sharīʿa* also meant a violation of state laws. This idea resonates with Robert Crews' model of the confessional state, which suggests that for Muslims, respect for the law constituted the foundation of "moral order."

> Petitions, denunciations, court records, police reports, and numerous Muslim sources reveal how, within the broader framework of tsarist toleration, Muslim men and women came to imagine the imperial state as a potential instrument of God's will.[32]

I believe it is an exaggeration for the relationships between Muslims and the empire to be explained solely on the basis of trust, respect for the law, or loyalty. Other particulars are at issue here. The fact that the Kazakh representatives of local administrations ignored the orders of OMSA, which in turn had to rely on local mullahs rather than on the administrative offices, reveals various interests and resources of power relations. The behavior of the empire and its officials, who in the 1850s–1860s expressed various Islamophobic views and attempted to codify Kazakh customary law by stressing its liberation from the "Islamic strata," is also essentially contradictory. Most obviously, it suggests that customary law codes formed an integral part of imperial politics, with selected *ʿādat* rules compiled and classified with discretion.[33] The pragmatic approach to relations with OMSA is therefore obvious here. By doubting the local Kazakh officials' ability to assist in eliminating *amangerlïk*, a marginal and inhuman phenomenon from the viewpoint of European laws, the empire effectively used *sharīʿa* as its temporary ally. One may assume that eventually, in the event of the codification of the norms of Kazakh customary law, the need for such an alliance would disappear.

Considering the situation with *ʿādat* and *sharīʿa* through the prism of the normative and political scenarios pursued by the imperial institutions and, to some extent, by OMSA, it is difficult to claim that the same logic characterized

31 TsGARK, F. 345, op. 1, d. 1600, l. 1.
32 Crews, *For Prophet and Tsar*, 20.
33 For further details see Sartori and Shablei, "Sud'ba imperskikh kodifikatsionnykh proektov," 90–94.

the actual people that operated within the local contexts. Examples include the Kazakhs who wrote petitions to OMSA, and the Tatar *ukaz* mullahs who could use the muftiate's guidelines to manage problems of power domination in their communities (*mahalla*). One such incident occurred in the town of Semipalatinsk. In 1861, OMSA considered a dispute between the Tatar imam of the 5th mosque of Semipalatinsk, Mukhammad Amin Mansurov (also known as Damin Ḥażrat), and Mukhammed Kulmametov, the Kazakh muezzin at the same mosque. The conflict began when a group of Kazakhs led by Kulmametov decided to overthrow their Tatar imam, and dispatched a petition about the matter to the Spiritual Assembly.[34] Trying to defend himself, Mansurov informed OMSA that the muezzin of the 5th mosque treated "adversely" the observance of "the rituals of the Mohammedan faith" and that his behavior remained unpunished because of other Kazakhs' support.[35] Presenting himself as the chief advocate of *sharīʿa* in this "uncouth" environment, the Tatar imam declared that all the complaints against him pursued a single objective: "... to defame me and to find a way of doing as they [the Kazakhs] please in the matter of reviving the ancient Kirghiz steppe rituals."[36]

Did these views evolve under OMSA's influence or were they the result of interactions with the local environment? The sources obviously support both possibilities. It is important to note, however, that the classification and generalization of these or other observations, especially during ongoing conflicts, were highly provisional. Mansurov and his adversaries did not aim to scrutinize legal culture but rather to preserve personal influence and authority. Within this context, the imam mentioned that "as instructed" by Kulmametov, some Kazakhs "contrary to Mohammedan law" lived "with women in sin as though in law."[37] Within the context of other social relations,

---

34 Since the Kazakh petition is not found among the archival files, and the description of these events is based on the report of Mukhammad Amin Mansurov, the reasons for the discontent with the imam can be discussed only provisionally. See National Archive of the Republic of Bashkortostan (NA RB), F. I-295, op. 3, d. 5111, ll. 1/ob. It is important to note that ʿAbd al-Karīm b. Abū Bakr Kūgārchīnī, the previous imam of the 5th mosque, also clashed with people of his *mahalla*, who succeeded in removing him; see Frank and Usmanov, *Materials*, 79.

35 In the 1880s, the 5th *mahalla* consisted of 800 people. Of these, 50 or 60 were from merchants' families, and the rest were Kazakhs. See Frank and Usmanov, *Materials*, 79.

36 NA RB, F. I-295, op. 3, d. 5111, l. 10b.

37 NA RB, F. I-295, op. 3, d. 5111, l. 10b. Possibly, this refers to the fact that once the *kalym* was payed, the bride's parents sometimes allowed the grooms to see their brides before marriage. However, there is no information on whether the norms of customary law permitted this practice. Therefore, the imam's indication that this lifestyle complied with *ʿādat* is an exaggeration.

however, Mansurov not only strove to adapt to Kazakh cultural tradition but also, through his personal charisma, tried to draw local society to himself and thereby to gain new resources of power influence. For instance, Mansurov was one of the wealthy and respected residents of the *mahalla* who were invited to the banquet on the day of slaughtering livestock for *soghim*.[38] Among the attendees was a feeble elderly man (*biyshara*). After talking to the man, the imam was convinced of the old man's wisdom, seated him at the place of honor, and presented him with a robe (*shapan*). This conduct was a typical manifestation of signs of respect and hospitality toward elderly and wise people.[39] Therefore, Mansurov's case exemplifies a complex situation in which a person wishing to preserve his own authority had to exhibit shifting allegiances, balancing between a conflict with and a display of loyalty to a different cultural milieu.

In the late 1840s and early 1850s, Russian authorities attempted to restrict OMSA's involvement in the resolution of Kazakh claims. In 1849, the Frontier Commission of Siberian Kazakhs barred a Petropavlosk *ākhūnd*, Sirāj al-Dīn b. Sayfullāh al-Qïzïlyārī, from investigating cases that involved the division of property and dowry (Rus. *kalym*, Kaz. *qalïng*) payments. The supporting argument stated that these "disputes and claims" were to be decided at the *biys*' court, "and not by spirituality"[40] (i.e., with the help of *sharīʿa* [P.S.]). Several years later, in 1852, V. Perovskii, the governor-general of Orenburg and Samara, advised OMSA "not to intervene in Kirghiz conjugal matters."[41] By supporting projects for the codification of Kazakh customary law, involving the necessity of separating the norms of *ʿādat* from *sharīʿa*, the official at the same time cast himself in the role of the defender of the interests of the local inhabitants, who were themselves unable to fight against the external influence of Islam. In particular, he wrote that "… every tribe and every people, not excluding the pagans, are permitted to contract matrimony according to the rules of their law …"[42]

If imperial officials erected insuperable barriers between *ʿādat* and *sharīʿa*, OMSA provided more diversified approaches to local legal culture. Eager to treat the levirate as a ritual and prejudice rather than a legal norm, the empire refrained from challenging OMSA's involvement in the *amangerlïk* cases;

38 Meat preserved for the winter.

39 Qurbān-ʿAlī Khālidī, *An Islamic Biographical Dictionary of the Eastern Kazakh Steppe (1770–1912)*, ed. and transl. Allen J. Frank and Mirkasyim A. Usmanov (Leiden/Boston: Brill, 2005), 29, 72, 115.

40 State Archive of Orenburg Region (GAOO), F. 6, op. 6, d. 12681, l. 3.

41 RGIA, F. 832, op. 8, d. 602, l. 6 ob.

42 RGIA, F. 832, op. 8, d. 602, l. 6 ob.

however, cases involving *qalïng* payments, marriage contracts (*ʿaqd*), property division, and so on, became a "stumbling block" in the muftiate's attempt to preserve its influence over the Kazakh steppe. Muslim spiritual leaders, for example, were authorized to use the concepts of "*qalïng*" and "*mahr*" as identical.[43] Equating *qalïng* and *mahr* was not a matter of principle for OMSA and the *ukaz* mullahs. Aware of the fact that *qalïng* was an important part of social and familial relations, OMSA tried neither to exclude this concept from legal practice nor to oppose it to *mahr*, which more than *qalïng* was associated with a woman's ability to separate from her husband's family for any reason. Here, I share S.N. Abashin's opinion that for the Central Asian *ʿulamāʾ*, the distinction between *qalïng* and *mahr* was provisional because these practices represented not a legal norm but a fiction, a ritualistic formula. The very essence of ritual determines the distinction – for example, the need to highlight the Muslim character of a wedding or, conversely, to reference an ancestral custom.[44] OMSA likewise did not seriously differentiate between *qalïng* and *mahr* in those cases when *qalïng* was not only part of a verbal agreement between Kazakhs, but also a stipulation written by a mullah into a marital contract. If such a contract was not processed as a legal document, then any claims about violating marriage conditions could be invalidated or interpreted based on their compatibility with existing circumstances.

The 1855 case "about the unlawful actions of the Kirghiz Murzaliev" illustrates this.[45] Chorman Murzaliev, a resident of Kushmurun district in the region of Siberian Kirghiz (Oblast' Sibirskikh kirgizov), entered in a marital agreement (a spoken one) with a Kazakh woman named Chalsa Sargina. According to this agreement, the *qalïng* (to the amount of 700 rubles and 47 horses) was

43 Azamatov, *Orenburgskoe magometanskoe dukhovnoe sobranie*, 126. H.G.Ishankulov and N.A. Kisliakov fundamentally differentiated between *kalym* and *makhr* (Ar. *mahr*), considering them as representing different stages of social development; see Nikolai Kisliakov, *Ocherki po istorii sem'i i braka u narodov Srednei Azii i Kazakhstana* (Leningrad: Nauka, 1969), 70–77, and Khadzhikurban Ishankulov, *Brak i svad'ba u naseleniia Khodzhenta v Novoe Vremia* (Dushanbe: Donish', 1972), 97. Adhering to this point of view, N.P. Lobacheva denies the existence of *makhr* among the nomadic Kazakhs, arguing that this norm of *sharīʿa* was characteristic only for sedentary societies; see Nadezhda Lobacheva, "*Makhr*," in *Islam na territorii byvshei rossiiskoi imperii*, ed. Stanislav Prozorov, Tom 1 (Moscow: Vostochnaia Literatura, 2006), 265–266.

44 Sergei Abashin, "Kalym i makhr v Srednei Azii: Pravo ili ritual?" *Otechestvennye zapiski*, 5 (2003): 34–48. https://strana-oz.ru/2003/5/kalym-i-mazr-v-sredney-azii-pravo-ili-ritual (accessed February 15, 2021).

45 NA RB, F. I-295, op. 4, d. 2978, l.1.

paid and Sargina's daughter Amancha was to marry Murzaliev upon achieving legal age. However, when the time came to contract the marriage twelve years later, Murzaliev changed his mind. In his defense, he stated that he had "heard of the evil actions of this daughter [Amancha] of hers, and because of this separated her from himself."[46] In view of these circumstances, Murzaliev attempted to recover the *qalïng* property. OMSA in principle did not object to the return of the *qalïng*. After studying all the details of the case, however, the muftiate decided that the marital agreement made by the Kazakhs did not have legal value, and therefore all the resulting circumstances, including the demand to return the *qalïng*, were voided.

> ... the said agreement, effected by the aforementioned Kirghiz, Chorman Murzaliev, to receive in marriage the maiden Amancha, is to be considered unlawful, being not a marital provision but merely a private deal. Even though Chalsa Sargina and Chorman Murzaliev acknowledge that an agreement was made for contracting marriage when she [the daughter] was underage, such deal of theirs, according to Mohammedan law, does not mean the marriage contract [*ʿaqd*] or the act of marriage, and if, in fact, an underage female and a male contract matrimony, by the force of Russian law this contract is dissolved.[47]

Could the analysis of this case take into an account that such a definition of marriageable age made OMSA part of the imperial system for regulating Islam? I believe so. However, there is also no doubt that OMSA's position regarding marriageable age could be completely different. In other words, in some instances, the muftiate toughened the legal requirements for contracting marriage according to *sharīʿa* (especially in the Kazakh steppe, where the preference was given to the oral rather than the written agreement). On other occasions, when the violation of a marriage contract's stipulations was not so obvious to each of the parties and represented a debatable situation, decisions did not rely upon the simplified formulas adapted to the colonial context, but rather were based on a detailed analysis of the opinions of Muslim scholars of the Ḥanafī *madhhab*. As D.D. Azamatov's study demonstrates, the imperial law regulating the legal capacity to marry (eighteen years of age for men and

46 NA RB, F. I-295, op. 4, d. 2978, l.1.
47 NA RB, F. I-295, op. 4, d. 2978, l. 5.

fifteen for women[48]) could not always be observed. Most frequently, OMSA cited fifteen years as the legal age for both men and women.[49]

Appealing to imperial administrative and legal resources became especially urgent in areas in which OMSA's control was not very effective, allowing the local courts (the *biys*' court, for example) and administrative offices to gain substantial advantage where influence over the Kazakhs was concerned. Therefore, by stiffening the requirements for observing *sharīʿa*, the Spiritual Assembly pretended to act as a court of appeals, presuming that Kazakhs unhappy with the decisions of the *biys*' court could submit their claims to OMSA. For the Kazakhs themselves, these practices did not always translate into the prospect of finding a more authoritative and competent jurisdiction. This was often determined by circumstances. Thus, in 1853, Tokash Dianasybekov, a citizen of the Kokchetav *okrug* of West Siberian General-Governorate, did not risk having his case reviewed at the *biys*' court, but submitted a claim to OMSA. This choice was justified by the fact that the *biy* Temirlan Muinakov, accused by Dianasybekov of violating a marriage agreement, was a very influential man and enjoyed the support of the *volost'* ruler Chukei Dishigarin.[50]

An analysis of several cases in which OMSA exercised influence on the Kazakh steppe reveals a complex scenario of interactions among various actors whose understanding of the legal norms was not always the source of an objective evaluation of the situation. On the one hand, forum shopping allowed one to choose the rules of the game. As a result, clashes between the Tatar and Kazakh *ʿulamāʾ* could turn the differences between *ʿādat* and *sharīʿa* into fiction, a convenient mechanism for eliminating one's adversaries during the struggle for authority. If such a strategy was indisputable for the imperial establishments, the legal manipulation became, for the mullahs, an enforced necessity rather than a genuine behavioral norm. The Tatar *ʿulamāʾ*'s attitude towards Kazakh rituals was subject to revisions depending upon the benefits they gained from each specific situation. On the other hand, pressured by administrative offices and local courts, OMSA was obliged to strengthen the requirements to observe *sharīʿa*, providing at the same time approaches to transforming customary law that were more flexible than those of colonial institutions.

---

48 *Svod zakonov Rossiiskoi imperii. Grazhdanskii polozheniia.* Tom 10. Chast' 1. Stat'ia 63 (Sankt-Petersburg, 1887), 7.

49 Azamatov, *Orenburgskoe*, 127. For other cases in which the colonial context of Khodzhent *uezd* of the Syrdarya region influenced interpretations of the *sharīʿa* definitions of the age of majority, see Sartori, "What We Talk about," 317–319.

50 TsGARK F. 345, op. 1, d. 337, ll. 17–18.

1.2 *"The People's Court Judges Now Have Turned to* sharīʿa*:" The Legal Environment after 1868*

On February 26, 1901, Husain Tastanov of Kokchetav *uezd* of Mizgil *volost'* submitted a complaint addressed to the *uezd* chief, A.I. Troitskii.[51] This document stated that Tastanov's wife, whom he inherited from a brother [or an uncle], left him for another Kazakh, Abai Khudaibergenov. The *uezd* chief forwarded the claim to Mizgil *volost'* ruler Dzhanaly Murzalin, instructing him to have the matter heard at the people's court.[52] The court reached the following decision: if the woman did not wish to live with Tastanov, she could choose another husband for herself, upon returning the *qalïng* property. The court decision was confirmed by a corresponding order of the *uezd* chief. Husain Tastanov obviously was not satisfied and reached out to other influential Kazakhs for advice. One of them was the *volost'* chief's brother, Baial Murzalin, who sent the plaintiff to mullah Talasov.[53] The mullah's ruling, formulated in accordance with *sharīʿa*,[54] differed from the *uezd* chief's order. As a result, Husain Tastanov faced a dilemma: to whom should he listen – the *uezd* chief or the mullah?[55]

51 A.L. Troitskii occupied various posts within the administrative system for governing the Kazakh steppe for over 30 years; he was Akmolinsk *uezd* governor (ca. 1894–1901), and Kokchetav *uezd* governor (1901–1903). Troitskii presented various radical proposals for fighting against Islam, and enjoyed a scandalous reputation as a result of disagreements with other officials of the colonial administration; he stood out for his diligence and excessive zeal in fulfilling imperial directives, for example, in matters of fighting against so-called Pan-Islamism. On him see TsGARK, F. 369, op. 1, d. 3728, ll. 10b-2; d. 780, ll. 19–27ob.

52 This institution was created following the adoption of the 1868 Temporary Provision. Jurors of the people's court – *biys* – were elected in the same way as *volost'* leaders. Cases had to be resolved on the basis of customary law. See Margarita Masevich ed., *Materialy*, 332–333.

53 Nauryzbai Talasov (1843–1916), or Nawan Ḥażrat in Muslim sources, studied in one of the *madrasas* of Petropavlovsk, and later studied in Bukhara and Baghdad. In 1886, following the new administrative rules, he was confirmed as imam of the cathedral mosque of Kokchetav by the Akmolinsk district government. He had wide influence among the Kazakhs. In 1902, the Kazakhs of Kokchetav *uezd* submitted a petition requesting that all *volost'* mullahs be placed under Nawan Ḥażrat and that his status be similar to that of a metropolitan in the Russian orthodox church. The image of Nawan Ḥażrat as a defender of *sharīʿa* and Islam is widely reflected in Kazakh poetry. In particular, Aqan Serï Qoramsaŭli, a famous poet (*aqïn*) and dombra player (*küyshi*), who was the relative of a Kokchetav imam, dedicated many works to him. For further details, see Saduaqas Ghïlmani, *Zamanamïzda bolghan ghŭlamalarding tarikhtarï*, Tom 1, trans. and ed. Ashirbek Muminov and Allen Frank (Almaty: Daik-Press, 2013), 61–71; Qadirjan Äbuev, *Nauan Khazïret. Kökshe Aristari* (Astana, 2001), 24–39; TsGARK, F. 369, op. 1, d. 3822, l. 16ob.; Aqan Serï Qoramsaŭli, "Kökshetauda Nauan Molda," 97–99.

54 So in original. See TsGARK F. 369, op. 1, d. 3822, l. 38ob.

55 TsGARK, F. 369, op. 1, d. 3822, l. 38ob.

Naturally, after the 1868 reform and the judicial restrictions on Islamic influence,[56] such a situation provoked outrage among some officials. Troitskii, however, refused to hold mullah Talasov responsible on the grounds of article 289 ("Code of penalties"[57]), arguing that his own administrative opinion might differ from that of a professional judge. In addition, the *uezd* chief was wary of putting himself in an ambiguous situation, in case the mullah should cite the practice of resolving family- and marriage-related cases among the Kazakhs in various offices (people's court, *qāżī*) that existed, regardless of the imperial reforms, under the previous *uezd* administration.[58] Therefore, Troitskii acknowledged that Talasov's reference to the experience of interacting with the colonial administration, which authorized the mullah to hear Kazakhs' claims, could be serious grounds for doubting the hegemony of the colonial judiciary.

The case I have just outlined demonstrates that for Troitskii, the people's court was part of the colonial system. In the Russian official's understanding, therefore, this institution had to act in accordance with *ʿādat* norms. However, while acknowledging the power of the *uezd* chief, Husain Tastanov did not oppose *ʿādat* to *sharīʿa*, and in some way the Kazakh may have perceived appealing to a mullah as a "de facto" practice accepted by the imperial officials themselves. Nauryzbai Talasov, in turn, using his knowledge of both the local reality[59] and Russian laws, was able to exert significant pressure upon local officials and to defend the views of *sharīʿa*.[60]

56 The 1868 Temporary Provision excluded Kazakhs from OMSA's jurisdiction, and mullahs were to be appointed by the military governor, figuring one mullah for one *volost'*; see Masevich, *Materialy*, 339–340.

57 Section 289 states that any individual who assumes judicial or government functions is subject to a punishment of four to eight months of imprisonment. See Nikolai Tagantzev, ed., *Ulozheniia o nakazaniiakh ugolovnykh i ispravitel'nykh* (St. Petersburg, 1898), 342.

58 State Councillor F.F. Konovalov. It was not possible to unearth any information about his attitude towards Islam. TsGARK, F. 369, op. 1, d. 3822, l. 390b.

59 It is known that Nawan Ḥażrat knew Russian well; yet he avoided direct contacts with the Russian administration and acted through his confidants. See TsGARK, F. 369, op. 1, d. 3822, l. 19.

60 In the beginning of 20th century, Muslims organized a series of petitionary campaigns. This was facilitated by the approval of both the December 12, 1904 decree "On Precepts for Improving Government Order" and the April 17, 1905 decree "On Strengthening the Foundations of Religious Tolerance." In October of 1905, Shaimardan Koshchegulov, the representative of the Kazakhs of Kokchetav *uezd* and Nawan Ḥażrat's assistant (in his madrasa), presented a memorandum addressed to A.P. Ignat'ev, the chairman of the commission on religious affairs. This paper stated that the Kazakhs wished to have a *muftī* resident in Kokchetav, and that it was necessary to change the people's court and decide cases according to *sharīʿa*, etc. See *RGIA*, F. 832, op. 10, d. 29, ll. 286b–287a. For more details

What does this example add to our understanding of the transformation of legal life in the Kazakh steppe after the 1868 and 1891 reforms? First, we must consider the people's court within its operating context. According to Zhanar Dzhampeisova, the people's court, a brainchild of the Russian reforms, both formed part of the colonial system and embodied its many shortcomings. The low efficiency of the people's court contributed to its unpopularity among the residents and signaled its inevitable demise.[61] In drawing these conclusions, however, Dzhampeisova does not consider the fact that the *biy*s may have represented an expert community that was an alternative to imperial influence,[62] and used more diversified legal experience than Russian law allotted them. A different view, developed by Virginia Martin, rests on the assumption that the 1868 and 1891 reforms enabled the Kazakhs to employ diverse legal alternatives. For example, when doubting a *biy*'s legal expertise (in *ʿādat* and *sharīʿa*), the Kazakhs appealed to the Russian administration, the Russian court, or a mullah.[63] For Martin, the significance of law as procedural norm determined the Kazakhs' choice of one legal system over another. Thus, familiarity with imperial law explains the preference for the Russian court, and the loss of a *biy*'s prestige as an expert in *ʿādat* and *sharīʿa* accounts for the dismissal of the people's court.[64]

I adhere to a different viewpoint. The situation that existed in the Kazakh steppe in the second half of the nineteenth and early twentieth centuries speaks more for the legal hybridity and unpredictable consequences of the Russian reforms than for the recognition of the superiority of law as a form of searching for one's identity within the empire, which in turn determined the choice of legal alternatives. In other words, I believe that following the 1868 and 1891 reforms, the legal situation in the Kazakh steppe included many exceptions and contradictions. Regardless of their conceptions about the transformation of local society and the rigorous demands of the law, the

---

about the petitionary campaigns see Paul Werth, *The Tsar's Foreign Faiths. Toleration and the Fate of Religious Freedom in Imperial Russia* (Oxford: Oxford University Press, 2014), 216–224.

61 Zhanar Dzhampeisova, *Kazakhskoe obschestvo i pravo v poreformennoi stepi* (Astana: ENU imeni L.N. Gumileva, 2006), 208–209.

62 S. Ghïlmani wrote on how *biy*s were guided by *sharīʿa* not only in hearing lawsuits but also in shaping public opinion. For example, during the 1916 revolt, the *biy*s spent all night discussing the relationship between this event and *sharīʿa*. See Ghïlmani, *Zamanamïzda*, 392.

63 Virginia Martin, *Law and Custom in the Steppe. The Kazakhs of the Middle Horde and Russian Colonialism in the Nineteenth Century* (London and New York: Routledge, 2001), 104–106.

64 Martin, *Law and Custom*, 105–106.

Russian authorities were obliged to recognize the existence of legal diversity and even to employ practices based on *ʿādat* and *sharīʿa* in civil law courts.[65] My work interprets the dilemma between acknowledging legal diversity and abiding by the policy of Russification as an opposition between different levels of administrative power and personal ambitions, rather than as imperial policies being turned into a principle. Another point is that when the Kazakhs appealed to Russian courts, people's courts, or a *qāżī*, they were not necessarily searching for a more competent court. Rather, they used diverse legal traditions and practices for achieving personal gain, and a familiarity with Russian law offered a convenient means of dialoguing with imperial officials with an intent to preserve their local interests and statuses.

Considering the people's court from the standpoint of its legal hybridity allows an evaluation of its role more broadly than merely as part of a colonial system or as an unconvincing legal alternative. Let us again consider the situation in Kokchetav *uezd*. In June of 1901, Troitskii organized a convention of people's judges in Kokchetav. The purpose of this gathering was to explain to the *biy*s the 1891 Steppe Statute. In Troitskii's opinion, the activity of the people's judges revealed their "complete ignorance" of the Steppe Statute, and instead of *ʿādat* they employed *sharīʿa*. The indignant official supposed that such a practice was unacceptable for the *biy*s,[66] whose court was to become the transitional stage toward introducing all-Russian civil courts.[67] The *uezd* chief blamed everything upon the actions of mullah Talasov, who with the compliance of the previous *uezd* administration, had interfered in the affairs of the people's court, and handled most claims himself.[68] Believing that administrative methods could restrict the influence of *sharīʿa*, Troitskii proposed to abolish the procedure of taking an oath in the presence of a mullah, and replace it with a "customary Kirghiz oath."[69]

Troitskii's position evoked indignation on the part of the *biy*s. In their appeal to Steppe Governor-General N.I. Sukhotin, the *biy*s reported that the oath-taking practice agreed with Russian laws and was "age-old and

65 Thus, D.V. Kudrevetskii, magistrate of the first district of Kokchetav *uezd*, sent witnesses to mullah N. Talasov for administration of the oath; see TsGARK, F. 369, op. 1, d. 3822, l. 19ob.

66 TsGARK, F. 369, op. 1, d. 3822, l. 35ob.

67 For further details about these views see Ivan Kraft, *Sudebnaia chast' v Turkestanskom krae i stepnykh oblastiakh* (Orenburg: Tipo-Litografiia P.N. Zharinova, 1898), 91.

68 TsGARK, F. 369, op. 1, d. 3822, ll. 37ob-38.

69 It is hard to tell what the official meant. I.Ia. Osmolovkii's record of customary law states that in the middle of the 19th century references to swearing an oath at a sacred place (a grave, a kurgan) and to kissing the sharp edge of a sword or the muzzle of a rifle survived only as legends. See *RGIA*, F. 853, op. 2, d. 65, ll. 51 ob., 83.

long-standing, but not based on some ancient immutable customs."[70] The reason for Troitskii's view of the people's court was not his professional diligence and desire to demonstrate his knowledge of laws,[71] but his personal animosity towards mullah Talasov, who was "a well-educated and honorable man, respected by all the Kirghiz."[72] In conclusion, the *biys* asked for the countermanding of those orders by the *uezd* chief that "violated their rights as *biys* and practicing Muslims."[73] After considering the situation of Islam in Kokchetav *uezd*, Steppe Governor-General Sukhotin remained unsupportive of several of Troitskii's initiatives. He specifically opposed the closing of the mosque in Kokchetav, observing that "this was an extreme measure" that "would not be in accordance with the highly humanistic views of his Most Gracious Majesty the Emperor."[74] This not only attests to the ambivalence of Russian policy, but also demonstrates the possibility for Muslims to have significant influence upon colonial officials and thereby to secure the functioning of Islam and of its institutions within the context of various legislative restrictions.

Thus, after the adoption of the 1868 and 1891 Steppe Statutes, the situation with the restriction of *sharīʿa* was not following the scenario intended by the empire. Not only did the people's court, portrayed by the authorities as an appendage of the colonial system, actively use *sharīʿa*, but the *qāżī* court also continued to function. This hybridity, which some officials presented as a paradoxical situation, was made possible by the following circumstances: first, the

70 Although V. Martin believes that an oath on the Qur'ān was a novelty, no precise data exists on the forms of oath that the *biys*' courts employed during the period prior to the annexation of the Kazakh Steppe to the Russian Empire. It is known that the form of the oath among the Kazakhs was legalized by the empire during the first third of 19th century; see Virginia Martin, "Kazakh Oath-Taking in Colonial Courtrooms: Legal Culture and Russian Empire-Building," in *Orientalism and Empire in Russia*, ed. Michael David-Fox, Peter Holquist, and Alexander Martin (Bloomington: Indiana University Press, 2006; *Kritika* Historical Studies, 3), 341, 344. In this context, the *biys*' position represents a notion of pragmatic flexibility and an ability to manipulate Russian law rather than a realistic analysis of legal history.

71 The *biys* thought that with his actions, the *uezd* leader violated sections 239, 248, and 249 of the "Turkestan Statute of Governance" (1886). The Statute sections that concerned the activity of the people's court also applied to the Steppe Governorate-General. See TsGARK, F. 369, op. 1, d. 3822, l. 44 ob.; "Polozhenie ob upravlenii Turkestanskogo kraia," In *Svod zakonov Rossiiskoi Imperii*, Tom 2 (St. Petersburg, 1912), 427–446.

72 TsGARK, F. 369, op. 1, d. 3822, l. 44 ob.

73 First of all, they demanded the release from custody of Nawan Ḥażrat, who was accused of anti-government activity and arrested in June of 1903, as well as the removal of the ban that closed mosques and madrasas. In addition, the *biys* requested that the *uezd* chief be prohibited from appointing on his own authority the chairmen of the emergency convention. See Äbuev, *Nauan*, 36–37; TsGARK, F. 369, op. 1, d. 3822, l. 44 ob.

74 TsGARK, F. 369, op. 1, d. 3696, l. 82 ob.

support of some representatives of the Russian administration, who avoided open confrontation with Islam and agreed to certain concessions; and second, the dynamic activity of Muslims who, having mastered the system of colonial knowledge, not only understood the imperial laws but also could contextualize them depending upon personal advantage. A third reason could be the fact that the local Kazakh officials (*volost'* chiefs, *aul* elders) actively supported the interests of legal experts from amidst their own kin or from subordinate territories; at the same time, they were able to adapt the language of bureaucratic documents so as to be acceptable for the Russian chanceries.

1.3 *Incident in the Inner Horde: Ākhūnd Ghŭmar Qarash and His Opponents*

On February 19, 1914, the first- and second-most senior Kazakhs[75] from the Talovka district (first and second *starshinstva*) of the Inner Horde[76] petitioned OMSA for a *fatwā* that clarified whether the actions of the *ākhūnd* of first *starshinstva*, Ghŭmar Qarash (1875–1921), were in accordance with *sharīʿa*. It turned out that this man was issuing his own *fatwās*, the contents of which elicited conflicting reactions among the Kazakhs. The petitioners drew OMSA's attention to five *fatwās*. In the first, Qarash spoke against Muslim participation in *badal ḥajj* ("pilgrimage by proxy").[77] The second *fatwā* suggested that boys were not to undergo circumcision (*khiṭān*). The third addressed the need to abolish payments for the sins of a deceased person (*fidya*). In the fourth, the *ākhūnd* insisted on ending the rite of sacrifice (*Qurban ayt*) and distributing the cost of the offering among the poor (*kedeyler*). In the fifth *fatwā*,

---

75 Sadrilislam Valeev, Dzhumagalii Araslanov, Gainei Pirgaliev, Mukai Zhalmurzin, and mullah Muhammadsharif Gumarov.

76 The Inner Horde was formed in 1801 in the lower interfluvial region of the Ural and the Volga. Following the death of Jahāngīr Khan in 1845, the administration of the horde was handed over to a Temporary Council chaired by a Russian official. In the 1860s, OMSA's power spread to the territory of the Inner Horde. See *Istoriia Bukeevskogo Khanstva. 1801–1852*, ed. Bolat Zhanaev, Viacheslav Inochkin, and Saniia Sagnaeva (Almaty: Daik-Press, 2002); Allen J. Frank, *Muslim Religious Institutions in Imperial Russia: The Islamic World of Novouzensk District and the Kazakh Inner Horde, 1780–1910* (Leiden-Boston-Köln: Brill, 2001).

77 "Pilgrimage by proxy" refers to cases in which a special person was hired to perform the *ḥajj* for a Muslim, who for some reason was unable to perform it himself. As a proof of pilgrimage, the hired individual brought back the evidence of the *ḥajj* (*ḥajjnama*). See Kasim Bikkulov, *Bädälche* (Kazan, 1909); I am grateful to Norihiro Naganawa for an opportunity to work with this book.

Qarash advised the donation of zakat (*zakāt*) to the poor, the mosque, and the madrasa.[78]

Before examining OMSA's reaction to this petition, I shall focus in more detail on Ghŭmar Qarash's personality; this will allow a better understanding of the context in which the *ākhūnd*'s *fatwā*s may have been read. After graduating from Ghabdullah Ghalikeev's *madrasa*,[79] Qarash spent several years teaching the new method in his own *aul* (Talovka). In 1909, he graduated from the Kazan Teachers' Seminary. He learned Russian.[80] In addition to teaching, Qarash was actively engaged in popular publishing; a few of his articles appeared in *Shura* and *Qazaq*, the reform periodicals published in Orenburg.[81] He also published works on *sharīʿa* and *kalām*, as well as poetry collections, in Kazan, Ufa, and Orenburg.[82] If in this context it would go too far to speak of Ghŭmar Qarash as a partisan of the ideas of progress and the fight against backwardness, he nevertheless was fully in accord with Jadid discourse[83] with his criticism of the traditional system of education, of the position of women, of "bad" Sufism,[84] and of ignorant mullahs.[85] Occasionally, he spoke out more radically, claiming that some books on Islam contained inaccurate explanations, and that only works of Muḥammad ʿAbduh (1849–1905) and Jamāl al-Dīn Afghānī (1839–1897) were correct.[86] Thus, the connection between Jadidism and fundamentalism based on the ideas of Muslim reformers meant not only criticism of the contemporary moral state of Islamic society through an appeal

---

78 NA RB, F. I-295, op. 6, d.3248, ll. 2–3.

79 Serïk Mäshïmbaev, *Qos özen aralighindaghi Kaztalov audanining tarikhi* (Almati: Nurpress, 2016), 66.

80 Mäshïmbaev, *Qos*, 67.

81 Ākhūnd Ghŭmar Qarash, "Zan mäselesï (Sharighi mäsele)," *Qazaq*, 50 (1914): 2–3.

82 Ghŭmar Qarash, *Bädel-Khaji.* (Kazan: Elektro-Tipografiia "Umid," 1913); idem, *Örnek* (Upï, 1911); idem, *Oygha kelgen pïkïrlerïm* (Orinbor, 1910); idem, *Bala Tŭlpar: Öleng Zhinaghi* (Upï, 1911); for a modern Cyrillic edition see idem, *Zamana* (Almaty: Ghïlïm, 2000).

83 On attempts to portray Qarash as a Kazakh variant of Jadidism, see Baqtili Boranbaeva, *Ghŭmar Qarashting ömïrï men qoghamdiq-sayasi qizmetï (1875–1921)*. Tarikh Ghilimi Kandidatï Aftoreferatï (Oral: Batis Qazaqstan Memlekettï Universitettï, 2009); Maqsat Täj-Mŭrat, *Ghŭmar Qarash: Ömïrï men Shigharmashilighi* (Aktöbe: Poligrafiia, 2004).

84 Qarash criticized certain Sufis, rather than Sufism as such. In his opinion, although the number of Sufis and *murīd*s keeps increasing, this does not benefit the public. Many of them are ignorant, steal, and spread evil. Only true Sufi preaching benefits the people. See Qarash, *Zamana*, 174–175. Compare these views with the Jadidist criticism of Sufism in Allen Frank's book: Allen J. Frank, *Bukhara and the Muslims of Russia: Sufism, Education, and Paradox of Islamic Prestige* (Leiden & Boston: Brill, 2012), 161.

85 Seemingly, these ideas can be easily correlated with the direction in historiography that regards Jadidism as a national treasure and the activity of Muslim intellectuals as a "heroic narrative" that traces efforts to resist traditionalism and backwardness.

86 See Qarash, *Zamana*, 176, 167–168, 172.

to early Islamic tradition, but also a renovation of the legal and theological principles of Islam.[87] At the same time, sharing the views of Muslim reformers, Qarash also called for adapting to the imperial situation, particularly with the help of the Russian language.[88]

Why did the local Kazakhs question the legality of Qarash's *fatwās*? One obvious explanation is that Russian cultural influence posed a threat far more serious than the debate between Jadids and Qadimists unfolding on the pages of newspapers. Qarash's foes – such influential people as his uncle mullah Ghumarov,[89] Ishan Sadïr *khal'fa*, and Baiet Zhumaliev – may have used both the *ākhūnd*'s connection with the Russians and his ideas about the significance of the Russian language to question the sincerity of his feelings about Islam.[90] Taking advantage of their authority, they spread rumors against Qarash; for example, "Having been baptized, this Russian mullah has hung Russian pictures in the madrasa at his house. During *khutba* at the mosque, he spreads propaganda among Kazakhs."[91]

One can also speculate that financial pragmatism was another issue raised by the debate between Qarash and influential local Kazakhs. The *ākhūnd* of Talovka was indignant that other *ukaz* mullahs and Kazakh *bays* (wealthy people) pressed the local population to contribute to *badal ḥajj*, which cost between 500 and 1000 rubles.[92] Convinced that more important problems

87 Devin DeWeese lays out a connection between Salafism and Jadidism. In particular, he arrives at this conclusion while analyzing the views of Muḥammad 'Abduh, who advocated the restoration of *ijtihād* and the emergence of a new *ijmā'* (the consensus of opinion or decision among authoritative *'ulamā'* on an issue under discussion), based on the Qur'ān and the "true Sunna;" See Devin DeWeese, "It was a Dark and Stagnant Night ('til the Jadids Brought the Light): Cliches, Biases, and False Dichotomies in the Intellectual History of Central Asia," *Journal of the Economic and Social History of the Orient* 59 (2016): 75.

88 Qarash wrote that a minimum of 10 years of study in a Russian school is necessary. This would allow one to adjust to life and open one's eyes to what was happening. However, this did not prevent him from expressing other views of his, as when he wrote that man cannot live without religion and must entrust himself to God's will. See Qarash, *Zamana*, 174–175, 178.

89 This likely refers to mullah Mukhammadsharif Ghumarov, i.e., one of the authors of the complaint against Qarash submitted to OMSA. It cannot be ruled out that this could be a reference to Ghabdullah Ghumarov, the *ākhūnd* of second *starshinstva* in Talovskii district.

90 The threat of Russian cultural influence was an integral part of the local Muslim narrative of the Russian Empire. See, for example, Frank and Usmanov, ed., *Materials*, 35; Khālidī, *An Islamic Biographical Dictionary*, trans. Frank and Usmanov, 59, 91.

91 "*Bül oristi quattap shoqinghan molda, uyïne medresege oristarding suretïn ïlïptï, meshïtte khutba ornina qazaqsha ugït aytadi.*" Quoted after Atash and Ölzhan, *Ghŭmar Qarash*, 192.

92 There is no evidence that OMSA controlled the process of raising funds for *badal ḥajj*.

than "pilgrimage by proxy" required attention, Qarash proposed to redistribute these contributions to the poor and to children in need.[93]

The language that the defendant used also deserves attention. When he explained his *fatwās* to OMSA, the *ākhūnd* adopted a dual stance. On the one hand, he tried to argue that his goal had been to clarify to the Kazakhs provisions of *sharīʿa* that had been distorted by local mullahs.[94] This argument was supposed to help Qarash persuade the muftiate that he followed the main provisions of *ahl al-Sunna*.[95] On the other hand, pointing to the ignorance and lack of schooling of his opponents (other *ukaz* mullahs of OMSA) reflected the local social context. While in one part of his explanation, he could write that he had said nothing about the ritual of circumcision, and that this accusation was merely a tactical maneuver by the *ākhūnd*'s enemies – in other words, slander[96] – in another part he argued more forcefully, accusing his adversaries of ignorance of the dogmas of Islam and criticizing the ritual of making payment for the sins of the dead (*fidya*) among the Kazakhs. On this point, Qarash wrote:

> I never said that "*ṣadaqa fidya*" for the deceased was a harmful innovation (*bidʿa*) or that there should be no *fidya* donations for the deceased. Every charitable act, especially "*nāfila ṣadaqa*,"[97] given wherever, whenever, and to whomever, is a God-pleasing deed. [However,] I definitely consider the rite of giving *fidya* among our people, and its elevation, together with its [related] rituals, to the status of a dogma of Islam, to be *bidʿa*.[98]

Positioning himself here as a critic of "bad customs" that became Islamic for some reason, Qarash probably intended to effortlessly win over his enemies, as he was also aware of the vulnerability of OMSA's own position on this question.

93 Qarash, *Bädel-Khazhi*, 13–14.

94 NA RB, F. I-295, op. 6, d. 3248, ll. 7–8ob.

95 Used here in the meaning of following the Sunna of the Prophet Muḥammad and his followers.

96 NA RB, F. I-295, op. 6, d. 3248, l. 7ob. It is possible that such an explanation was connected not only with the desire to enhance an understanding of the personal motives behind legal disagreements, but also with the possible need to withdraw one's words and thereby to alleviate the scenario of interactions with OMSA.

97 *Nāfila* is a notion with both legal and theological meanings; it is used in various senses in the Qurʾān and in hadiths. For example, it can refer to a supplementary ritual of worshipping God, and it can also be used in reference to the month Ramadān. See Arent Jan Wensinck, "*Nāfila*," in *The Encyclopaedia of Islam. New Edition*, ed. C.E. Bosworth, E. van Donzel, W.P. Heinrichs and Ch. Pellat, vol. 7 (Leiden-New York: Brill, 1993): 878–879.

98 NA RB, F. I-295, op. 6, d. 3248, ll. 7ob-8.

Thus, on another occasion, in responding to a question from imam Maḥmūd Jalīl al-Dīn Oghlï, from the village of Kumbash, about whether, after a person's death, money should be payed as an "expiatory charity" (*fidya*), the Spiritual Assembly was obliged to acknowledge that according to *sharīʿa* such an obligation did not exist. Noting that some Muslim scholars (not naming anyone in particular [P.S.]) recommended setting aside a certain amount only in the case of receiving an inheritance, OMSA nonetheless did not require this rule to be observed.[99] In fact, such an ambivalent response by OMSA opened the doors to *ijtihād* on the part of the local *ʿulamāʾ*.

In another fatwā – on the Festival of Sacrifice (*Qurban ayt*) – Qarash implied that the disagreement between him and other Kazakh *ʿulamāʾ* was a matter not so much of ignorance or of lack of schooling, but rather of reaching the most expedient conclusions in the process of interpreting Muslim legal sources. Switching in this case to a rationalist stance, he declared that since livestock meat could not be stored in the summer heat under nomadic conditions, the sacrifice should be replaced by paying the equivalent of its value to the poor (*kedeyler*). A reference to the Qur'ān (*ayat* 38, *sūrat al-Ḥajj*) substantiated the legal authority of this fatwā.[100]

In examining the conflict between Ghŭmar Qarash and members of the local Kazakh community, I must note that the participants in the discussions on *sharīʿa* were able to manage the resolution of their questions without the influence of OMSA. It was not only the *ākhūnd* who could, if necessary, use his connections to Muslim intellectuals in Orenburg, Ufa, and Kazan; other residents of Talovka as well were not unwavering conservatives who sought to avoid some sort of broad social attention to their problems and tried thereby to isolate themselves from change. Thus, in 1910, the editors of the Orenburg journal *Dīn va maʿīshat*[101] received a letter from Talovka.[102] This letter contained a request to clarify certain provisions of *sharīʿa* that had elicited controversy among residents of Talovka. One of the most critical questions addressed to the journal was the problem of the permissibility of eating the meat of animals butchered by Orthodox Russians.[103]

99 "Fidya dur khakinda," *Mäg'lümat*, 17 (1908), 372–373. I am grateful to Diliara Brileva for copying this material for me.

100 NA RB, F. I-295, op. 6, d. 3248, l. 8. Actually, the passage cited is 22.36 (*sūrat al-Ḥajj*, *ayat* 36); see Magomet Osmanov, trans, *Koran* (Sankt-Petersburg: Dilia, 2009), 303.

101 The journal *Dīn va maʿīshat* was published between 1906 and 1918.

102 The journal did not give the senders' names.

103 The magazine staff reported that *sharīʿa* does not allow the consumption of the meat of animals that were slaughtered by Russians. See "Mäs'älä," *Dīn va maʿīshat* 13 (1910): 194–195. Shihāb al-Dīn Marjānī issued the same *fatwā*; see G. Giliazov and G. Akhmet'ianova,

Let us now revisit the situation of Ghŭmar Qarash and see how this incident ended. As a reminder, OMSA had to decide whether the *fatwā*s of the *ākhūnd* of Talovka were in accordance with *sharīʿa*. From the five *fatwā*s presented to the Spiritual Assembly, only one entailed an official investigation.[104] It was the *fatwā* dealing with *badal ḥajj*. As is known, Qarash considered this practice a *bidʿa*, arguing that there was no direct and undisputed indication for *badal hajj* in the *sharīʿa*.[105] In a special book he wrote on the subject,[106] the following could be found:

> If (*badal ḥajj* [P.S.]) is an obligation or an indisputable obligation, then it must be mentioned in at least one of the *ayat*s of the Qurʾān. Not a single word about it has been sent down in the Qurʾān. Consulting the hadith (about Hāshima[107] [P.S.]), there is no other (authentic) hadith among the *riwayat*s about that Arab woman. This hadith is weak because it contradicts an *ayat* of the Qurʾān. It contradicts an *ayat* from the *sūrat* of al-ʿImrān. Therefore, this hadith is not correct.[108]

Thus, according to Qarash, one was to search the Qurʾān and the hadiths for answers before consulting the books containing the *riwayat*s on Muslim law. Could it be said that this approach ignored the Ḥanafī tradition? Clearly, this is not the case. Even if only formally, Qarash tried to emphasize that Ḥanafism was important for the people of the Kazakh steppe. Qarash opens his *Badal Ḥajj* book with an analysis of authoritative Ḥanafī texts, such as *Fatḥ al-qadīr*[109]

---

trans, *Sbornik statei, posviaschennykh stoletiyu Shikhab ad-Din Mardzhani, izdannyi v Kazani v 1915 godu* (Kazan': Tatarskoe Knizhnoe Izdatel'stvo, 2015), 237–238. This speaks to the need to seek other perspectives for the analysis of *fatwās*, beyond one that views Marjānī's language through the prism of modernist style and the reply of *Dīn va maʿīshat* only within the fundemantalist context.

104 No references to how OMSA reacted to Qarash's other *fatwā*s are found among the archival files.

105 Critiques of *badal ḥajj* appear also in other works, the authors of which are in one way or another portrayed as Jadids. See Bikkulov, *Bädälche*.

106 The book *Bädel-Khazhi* was published in Kazan in 1913.

107 I was unable to identify this hadith.

108 "*Eger pariz yäki uäzhïp bolsa, ol uaqitta älbette Qüran kärimde burin khaqinda bïr ayät kärime aytkan bolar edï. Qüran kärimde büniň khaqinda söz zhoq ekenï zhogharida aytiladi. Khadiske kelsek, älgï arab äyelïnïň riwayatinan basqa khadis taghi zhoq. Bü khadistïň özï sendï jikhatindan dagufadaghi ustende, maghina zhaghimen qaraghanda ayät kärimge mukhallif bolghan qayshi khadis. Bül äl ghimran suresïndegï ayätina khalif. Bü sebeptï bü khadis düris bolmaydi.*" Quoted after Qarash, *Bädel-Khazhi*, 9.

109 This refers to the commentary on Marghīnānī's *al-Hidāya* by Ibn al-Humām (d. 1457), a prominent Ḥanafī jurist regarded as a *mujtahid*.

and *al-Hidāya*,[110] among others. While he recognized the authority of these sources, the *ākhūnd* was nevertheless opposed to *taqlīd*,[111] believing that contradictions in books of fiqh (if it is difficult to choose a clear answer from among the decisions of the *mujtahids*) would open the way to *ijtihād*.[112] One can be sure that such an approach weakened OMSA's influence in the Inner Horde, and contributed to heightened tensions in relations between Qarash and the local *ʿulamāʾ* who advocated other principles and methods in taking decisions regarding *sharīʿa*. To better represent this context, I shall share another story. In 1911, the journal *Shura* published Qarash's article on a specific problem of *sharīʿa*.[113] The author pondered the question: could a woman contract a new marriage two months after[114] her husband went missing or disappeared without word? Noting that "our imams (i.e., Kazakhs [P.S.]) did not give any clear *fatwā*" regarding this issue, Ghŭmar Qarash called on OMSA to involve itself in this matter. However, the Muslims' appeal to the Ufa *muftiate* was fruitless. OMSA did not produce a single *fatwā* on the issue. Upon the request of one of his friends, Qarash took the matter in his own hands and published a separate book, entitled *Majalla ḥukkām sharīʿa* ("Compilation of provisions of Islamic law").[115] In this work, he made recourse to *ijtihād* by saying that a woman's demand to contract a new marriage upon the disappearance of her husband did not conflict with the Qurʾān, since the foundation of the family included both spiritual and material sides.[116]

Was Qarash again able to gain victory over OMSA and his Kazakh adversaries? Qarash's case was entrusted to the OMSA *qāżī* Ghinayatullah Qapkaev.[117] He was charged with verifying the expertise of the *ākhūnd*'s book on *badal ḥajj*. Qapkaev enjoyed great authority with OMSA.[118] Besides Qarash's case, this *qāżī*

110 This was the key work of Burhān al-Dīn al-Marghīnānī (d. 1196).

111 OMSA followed *taqlīd* in composing its *fatwās*; see "Bāb al-Fatāwī," *Mäg'lümat*, 52 (1910), 1352–1353.

112 Qarash, *Bädel-Khazhi*, 9.

113 In 1911–1913, Qarash was not yet an *ākhūnd*. He contributed to publishing of the newspaper *Qazaqstan*. About this, see Atash and Ölzhan, *Ghŭmar Qarash*, 71.

114 Normally, the period – i.e., *ʿidda*, the period of time after a divorce or her husband's death during which a woman cannot contract a new marriage – was three months. However, this term rarely applied to cases of a husband's disappearance. Since Muslim scholars' opinions on this subject differed substantially, OMSA hesitated in regulating such divorces. See *NA RB*, F. I-295, op. 8, d. 748, ll. 46ob-49; op. 3, d. 6023.

115 Apparently, this was a manuscript book. I was unable to locate it.

116 Gh. Qarash, "Mäzlumälär khakinda," *Shura*, 9 (1911), 260–261.

117 This interesting character deserves separate research.

118 Interestingly, Fakhr al-Dīn did not define Gh. Qapkaev as a Qadimist (as is done in contemporary studies); see Rižā al-Dīn b. Fakhr al-Dīn, *Asar. 3–4 Tomnar* (Kazan: Rukhiyät, 2010), 383–387.

handled other claims of Kazakhs of the Inner Horde.[119] He was a very educated man, and was the author of several works on problems of *sharīʿa*, as well as on history and regulation of the spiritual administration of the Muslims of the Russian Empire and the Soviet Union.[120]

Having familiarized himself with Qarash's book, Qapkaev submitted resolution in the name of OMSA. Acknowledging that certain *riwayat*s, though produced on the basis of the *ahl al-Sunna*,[121] in the end conflicted with the doctrinal principle of the Ḥanafī *madhhab*, the *qāżī* spoke against the Kazakh *ākhūnd*'s *fatwā*. According to Qapkaev, the positions of Qarash's work were analogous to the views of the Muʿtazilites, and therefore did not correspond to the understanding of the Sunna accepted by Muslims in the Russian Empire.[122] Considering the fact that the Muʿtazilites were concerned more with *kalām* than with legal problems associated with the notion of *badal ḥajj*, a question arises: which arguments did the *qāżī* use to cast doubt on the work of Qarash? According to Qapkaev's view, "in Sunni interpretation, a good deed by one person for another is not forbidden in *sharīʿa*, and only the Muʿtazilites, who separated from the Sunnīs, contradict this."[123]

Most probably, deep theological disagreements were not of essential importance in this argument. Rather, other conclusions can be suggested. One of them is that there must have been a certain bias. This line of thought becomes relevant when viewing the relationships between OMSA and the empire as a sort of alliance intended for the defense of "traditional Islam," i.e., the struggle against ideas and currents that contradicted the doctrinal principles of the Ḥanafī *madhhab*. However, to adopt this point of view without any sort of specificity would imply that the Muslims who appealed to OMSA also believed

---

119 NA RB, F. I-295, op. 5, d.1628, ll. 11–12ob.

120 Ghinayätullah Qapkaev, "Mäkhkämäi Shärgiyädän," *Mäg'lümat*, 15 (1908), 314; idem, "Röeyäte Hilyäle Khosusinda," *Mäg'lümat*, 6 (1916), 10; idem, "Vakiflardan Khisabnamäkär," *Mäg'lümat*, 55 (1910), 1452; idem, "Täwarikh vä Anlarning Mälbäeläre Khakinda Täkhkiykat'," *Mäg'lümat*, 23 (1909), 521; idem, "Bägze söällärgä Jävab Urinında," *Dianat*, 1 (1926), 8; idem, "Ghibadät vä Mönajat," *Dianat*, 3 (1926), 48–49.

121 So in original.

122 NA RB, F. I-295, op. 6, d. 3248, ll. 20–22. In other words, Gh. Qapkaev's position essentially came down to acknowledging the divergence between the Māturīdī symbol of faith and the Muʿtazilites. One of the chief disagreements between them is that for the Māturīdīs, reason is an instrument that may help us understand decisions regarding *sharīʿa*, while for the Muʿtazilites, reason itself produces decisions. Therefore, in the historical context, this debate generated contradictions between representatives of different ideological and religious currents. In our history, I begin from a different perspective, in which theological foundations have only an indirect significance. I am grateful to A.D. Knysh for his clarification; Alexander Knysh, e-mail message to author, October 29, 2016.

123 NA RB, F. I-295, op. 6, d. 3248, l. 20.

in the reality of this alliance.[124] I would proceed in a different direction. As already argued here, relations between OMSA and the imperial authorities often bore an instrumental character, based among other factors on mutual pragmatic benefits. Muslims could resolve various matters of *sharīʿa* without the Spiritual Assembly, especially given the low administrative effectiveness of this institution and the lack of clear legal guidelines. The local *ʿulamāʾ* used this situation to their advantage, resorting to rhetoric about the ignorance and lack of education of their competitors – other *ukaz* mullahs – to increase their own authority. In these instances, *ijtihād* became a weapon for this kind of dominance. In a few cases, realizing that *taqlīd* could not always withstand reformers such as Qarash, OMSA was obliged to take repressive measures.[125] For reasons that need not concern us here, in 1915 the *muftiate* removed Qarash from his post.[126] Almost concurrently with these events, from 1914 to 1915, the influence of Qarash's adversary – *ākhūnd* Ghabdullah Ghumarov – grew. In the OMSA journal I discovered this fact: in 1915, Abdullah Gumarov was the Spiritual Assembly's chief trusted consultant for organizing charitable contributions among the Muslims of the Inner Horde.[127] Apparently, the responses of local Muslims to OMSA's attempt to control such payments were not without problems. This is confirmed by Qarash's *fatwā*[128] about maintaining control over the distribution of charitable proceeds (*zakāt* and *ʿushr*) within the Muslim community itself.[129]

---

124 Crews, *For Prophet and Tsar*, 20.

125 Accusations of Muʿtazilism could often be explained by personal animosity. One example is the case of Shihāb al-Dīn Marjānī, whose student, Ḥāfiẓ al-Dīn b. Naṣr al-Dīn al-Barangavī, wrote a letter to OMSA accusing Marjānī of "belonging to the sect of the Muʿtazilites" after Marjānī made an unfavorable comment about his (Ḥāfiẓ al-Dīn's) grandfather; see Rižā al-Dīn b. Fakhr al-Dīn, *Asar*, 614. On the exaggeration, in reformist literature, of the significance of the Muʿtazilites' views in the context of the ideological struggle among Muslims of the Russian empire, see Frank, *Bukhara*, 19.

126 M. Täzh-Mŭrat believes that disagreements between Qarash and local religious leaders who continued writing denunciations about him to OMSA played the decisive role. However, the researcher does not cite any documentary confirmation for this point of view; see Täzh-Mŭrat, Tŭrlausiz, 171.

127 *Mäg'lümat*, 7–8 (1916), 33–34.

128 NA RB, F. I-295, op. 6, d. 3248, l. 80b.

129 On the increased tendency among Muslims of the Russian empire, after 1905, to avoid OMSA control in the sphere of distributing charitable payments, see Stéphane Dudoignon, "Status, Strategies and Discourses of a Muslim 'Clergy' under a Christian Law: Polemics about the Collection of the *Zakat* in Late Imperial Russia," in *Islam in Politics in Russia and Central Asia* (*Early 18th–late 20th Centuries*), ed. Stéphane Dudoignon and Hisao Komatsu (London and New York: Kegan Paul, 2001), 52–54.

2 Conclusion

Although the reader may gain the impression that the stories examined in this chapter contradict one another, this is not really the case. First of all, flexibility of thought must be considered. The religious elite did not pose the issue of preserving authority within the colonial situation in a single way – either self-isolation with respect to the empire or, on the contrary, trust. OMSA, especially in the example of the first case, tried to use imperial law and administrative resources to strengthen its influence in the Kazakh steppe, stressing that the colonial transformation of *sharīʿa* might bring mutual advantage. Clearly, flexibility also characterized many colonial officials, who, given the peculiarities of the context, were obliged to ignore certain imperial reforms concerning Islam and the *biy*s' court. All these actions bolstered legal diversity, which encompassed not only the parallel existence of various legal systems (*sharīʿa, ʿādat* , and Russian law), but also the particulars of the thinking of the representatives of legal culture. Accordingly, appealing to one legal establishment or another was based not only on a certain mentality (or tradition), i.e. a conviction that the *biy*s' court or a *qāżī* would be more competent than the magistrates' (Russian) court, but also on the awareness of the broad procedural potential of the colonial situation.

This argument leads to the second important conclusion of this article. At issue is the time and the expansion of experience within the imperial context. I have considered, in fact, a wide range of events, spanning the period from the 19th to early 20th centuries. The actions of the people and institutions that participated in these events are impossible to comprehend simply by employing linear models (i.e., everything changed following some predictable scenario) or the logic of binary oppositions, according to which every new reform produced a new degree of separation between the Muslims and the empire. I believe that the *biy*s and the mullahs of the first half of the 19th century differed from the *biy*s and the mullahs of the early 20th century. While mastering the system of colonial knowledge, they also were acquiring additional opportunities for interacting with their fellow believers and friends (based on Islamic discourse) within a broader spatial framework[130] – for example, due to the annexation of the new eastern territories to the Russian empire, and the development of education and the press. For this reason, both Nawan

130 Mustafa Tuna, *Imperial Russia's Muslims: Islam, Empire, and European Modernity, 1788–1914* (Cambridge: Cambridge University Press, 2015), 11–14.

Ḥażrat and Ghŭmar Qarash – who mastered the Russian language, gained access to the public word (the press), and studied Russian laws – obtained new resources in order to fight more effectively against their Muslim opponents and against hostile-minded imperial officials for authority and power in local Islamic communities.

Bibliography

Abashin, Sergei. "Kalym i makhr v Srednei Azii: Pravo ili ritual?" *Otechestvennye zapiski*, 5 (2003), 34–48. https://strana-oz.ru/2003/5/kalym-i-mazr-v-sredney-azii-pravo-ili-ritual (*sic*, accessed February 15, 2021).

Äbuev, Qadirzhan. *Nauan Khazïret. Kökshe Aristari*. Astana, 2001.

Aqan Serï Qoramsaŭli. "Kökshetauda Nauan Molda men Khamidolla Noghay Moldasi Baqas Bolghanda, Khamidolla Aqan Serïnïng Aytqani." In *Aqan Serï Qoramsaŭli, Ükïlï Ibiray Sandibayŭli, Baluan Sholaq Baymirzaŭli. Shigharmalari* (Almaty: Nŭrli Press.kz, 2014), 97–99.

Atash, Berïk, and Quanish Ölzhan. *Ghŭmar Qarash*. Almaty: QR BĞM ĞK Filosofiya, Sayasattanu jäne Dïn Tanu Instituti, 2014.

Azamatov, Danil'. *Orenburgskoe magometanskoe dukhovnoe sobranie v kontse 18–19 vekakh*. Ufa: Gilem, 1999.

"Bāb al-Fatāwī." *Mäg'lümat*, 9 (1908), 177–178.

"Bāb al-Fatāwī." *Mäg'lümat*, 11 (1908), 223–225.

"Bāb al-Fatāwī." *Mäg'lümat*, 12 (1908), 253–257.

"Bāb al-Fatāwī." *Mäg'lümat*, 13 (1908), 273–275.

"Bāb al-Fatāwī." *Mäg'lümat*, 14 (1908), 296–299.

"Bāb al-Fatāwī." *Mäg'lümat*, 15 (1908), 315–317.

"Bāb al-Fatāwī." *Mäg'lümat*, 16 (1908), 343–348.

"Bāb al-Fatāwī." *Mäg'lümat*, 44 (1910), 1086–1087.

"Bāb al-Fatāwī." *Mäg'lümat*, 52 (1910), 1352–1353.

Babadzhanov, B.M. *Kokandskoe khanstvo: Vlast', politika, religiia*. Tashkent, Tokio: Yangi nashr, 2010.

Bikkulov, Kasim. *Bädälche*. Kazan, 1909.

Boranbaeva, Baqtili. *Ghŭmar Qarashtiň Ömïrï men Qoghamdiq-Sayasi Qizmetï (1875–1921)*. Tarikh Ghilimi Kandidatï Aftoreferatï. Oral: Batis Qazaqstan Memlekettï Universitettï, 2009.

Central State Archive of the Republic of Kazakhstan (TsGARK). F. 345, op. 1, dd. 337, 1600; F. 369, op. 1, dd. 780, 3728, 3822.

Crews, Robert. *For Prophet and Tsar: Islam and Empire in Russia and Central Asia*. Cambridge: Harvard University Press, 2006.

DeWeese, Devin. "It was a Dark and Stagnant Night ('til the Jadids Brought the Light): Cliches, Biases, and False Dichotomies in the Intellectual History of Central Asia." *Journal of the Economic and Social History of the Orient*, 59 (2016), 37–92.

Dudoignon, Stéphane. "Status, Strategies and Discourses of a Muslim 'Clergy' under a Christian Law: Polemics about the Collection of the Zakat in Late Imperial Russia." In *Islam in Politics in Russia and Central Asia (Early 18th–late 20th Centuries)*, ed. Stéphane Dudoignon and Hisao Komatsu (London and New York: Kegan Paul, 2001), 43–73.

Dzhampeisova, Zhanar. *Kazakhskoe obschestvo i pravo v poreformennoi stepi*. Astana: ENU imeni L.N. Gumileva, 2006.

Erofeeva, Irina V. "Kak kazakhi stali kirgizami. K istorii odnoi terminologicheskoi putanitsi." *Astana*, 5 (2005), 23–27.

Farkhshatov, Marsil' ed. *"Delo" bashkirskogo sheikha Zainulli Rasuleva (1872–1917): Vlast' i sufizm v poreformennoi Bashkirii. Sbornik Dokumentov*. Ufa: Institut Istorii, Iazyka i Literatury UNZ RAN, 2009.

"Fidya dur Khakinda." *Mäg'lümat*, 17 (1908), 372–373.

Frank, Allen J., and Mirkasyim Usmanov, ed. and trans. *Materials for the Islamic History of Semipalatinsk: Two Manuscripts by Aḥmad-Walī al-Qazānī and Qurbānʿalī Khālidī*. *ANOR*, 11. Halle/Berlin, 2001.

Frank, Allen J. *Muslim Religious Institutions in Imperial Russia: The Islamic World of Novouzensk District and the Kazakh Inner Horde, 1780–1910*. Leiden-Boston-Köln: Brill, 2001.

Frank, Allen J. *Bukhara and the Muslims of Russia: Sufism, Education, and Paradox of Islamic Prestige*. Leiden & Boston: Brill, 2012.

Frank, Allen J. "Islamic Transformation on the Kazakh Steppe, 1742–1917: Toward an Islamic History of Kazakhstan under Russian Rule." In *The Construction and Deconstruction of National Histories in Slavic Eurasia*, ed. Tadayuki Hayashi (Sapporo: Slavic Research Center, 2003), 261–289.

Giliazov, G. and Akhmet'ianova, G., trans. *Sbornik statei, posviaschennykh stoletiyu Shikhab ad-Din Mardzhani, izdannyi v Kazani v 1915 godu*. Kazan: Tatarskoe Knizhnoe Izdatel'stvo, 2015.

Ghilmani, Säduaqas. *Zamanmizda bolghan ghŭlamalardiň tarikhtari*. Tom 1, ed. and trans. Ashirbek Muminov and Allen Frank. Almaty: Daik-Press, 2013.

Ishankulov, Khadzhikurban. *Brak i svad'ba u naseleniia Khodzhenta v novoe vremia*. Dushanbe: Donish', 1972.

Kappeler, Andreas. "Dve traditsii v otnosheniiakh Rossii k musul'manskim narodam Rossiiskoi imperii." *Otechestvennaia istoriia*, 2 (2003), 129–135.

Kemper, Michael. *Sufii i uchenye v Tatarstane i Bashkortostane: Islamskii diskurs pod imperskim upravleniem*, trans. Iskander Giliazov. Kazan: Rossiiskii Islamskii Universitet, 2008.

Khālidī, Qurbān-ʿAlī. *An Islamic Biographical Dictionary of the Eastern Kazakh Steppe (1770–1912)*, trans. Allen J. Frank and Mirkasyim A. Usmanov. Leiden-Boston: Brill. 2005.

Khālidī, Qurbān-ʿAlī. *Tawārīkh-i Khamsa-yi sharqī*. Kazan: Tipografiia Kazakova, 1910.

Kisliakov, Nikolai. *Ocherki po istorii sem'i i braka u narodov Srednei Azii i Kazakhstana*. Leningrad: Nauka, 1969.

Kraft, Ivan. *Sudebnaia chast' v Turkestanskom krae i stepnykh oblastiakh*. Orenburg: Tipo-Litografiia P.N. Zharinova, 1898.

Lobacheva, Nadezhda. "Makhr." In *Islam na territorii byvshei Rossiiskoi imperii*, Sostavitel' Stanislav Prozorov. Tom 1. Moscow: Vostochnaia Literatura, 2006.

Mäg'lümat, 7–8 (1916), 33–34.

Makhmutov, Zufar. *Istoriia Tatar Astany: pervaia polovina 19–nachalo 21 vekov*. Kazan: Tatarskoe Knizhnoe Izdatel'stvo, 2017.

Martin, Virginia. *Law and Custom in the Steppe: The Kazakhs of the Middle Horde and Russian Colonialism in the Nineteenth Century*. London and New York: Routledge, 2001.

Martin, Virginia. "Kazakh Oath-Taking in Colonial Courtrooms Legal Culture and Russian Empire-Building." In *Orientalism and Empire in Russia*, ed. Michael David-Fox, Peter Holquist, and Alexander Martin (Bloomington: Indiana University Press, 2006; Kritika Historical Studies 3), 323–354.

"Mäs'älä." *Dīn va maʿīshat*, 13 (1910), 194–195.

Masevich, Margarita, ed. *Materialy po istorii politicheskogo stroia Kazakhstana*. Tom 1. Alma-Ata: Izdatel'stvo Akademii Nauk Kazakhskoi SSR, 1961.

Mäshïmbaev, Serïk. *Qos Özen Aralighindaghi Kaztalov audanininň tarikhi*. Almati: Nurpress, 2016.

Meshal, Reem A. *Sharīʿa and the Making of the Modern Egyptian: Islamic Law and Custom in the Courts of Ottoman Cairo*. Cairo and New York: The American University in Cairo Press, 2014.

Meyer, James H. "Speaking Sharia to the State: Muslim Protesters, Tsarist Officials, and the Islamic Discourses of Late Imperial Russia," *Kritika: Explorations in Russian and Eurasian History 14.3* (2013): 485–505.

Muminov, Ashirbek. *Khanafitskii mazkhab v istorii Tsentral'noi Azii*. Almaty: Qazaq Entsiklopediyasi, 2015.

National Archive of the Republic of Bashkortostan (NA RB). F. I-295, op. 3, dd. 5111, 5487; op. 4, d. 2978; op. 6, d. 3248.

Osmanov, Magomet, trans. *Koran*. Sankt-Petersburg: Dilia, 2009.

"Polozhenie ob upravlenii Turkestanskogo kraia." In *Svod zakonov Rossiiskoi imperii*. Tom 2 (Sankt-Petersburg, 1912), 318–346.

Privratsky, Bruce G. *Muslim Turkistan: Kazak Religion and Collective Memory*. Richmond, Surrey: Routledge, 2001.

Qapkaev, Ghinayatullah. "Mäkhkämäi Shärgiyädän." *Mäg'lümat*, 15 (1908), 314.

Qapkaev, Ghinayatullah. "Röeyäte Khilyäle Khosusinda." *Mäg'lümat*, 6 (1916), 10.

Qapkaev, Ghinayatullah. "Vakiflardan Khisabnamäkär." *Mäg'lümat*, 55 (1910), 1452.

Qapkaev, Ghinayatullah. "Täwarikh vä anlarning mälbäeläre khakinda täkhkiykat'." *Mäg'lümat*, 23 (1909), 521.

Qapkaev, Ghinayatullah. "Bägze söällärgä Cävab Urininda." *Dianat*, 1 (1926), 8.

Qapkaev, Ghinayatullah. "Ghibadät vä mönajat." *Dianat*, 3 (1926), 48–49.

Qarash, Ākhūnd Ghŭmar. "Zan mäselesï (Shariği mäsele)." *Qazaq*, 50 (1914), 2–3.

Qarash, Ghŭmar. *Bädel-Khazhi*. Kazan: Elektro-Tipografiia "Umid," 1913.

Qarash, Ghŭmar. *Bala Tŭlpar: Ölen zhinaghi*. Upï, 1911.

Qarash, Ghŭmar. "Mäzlumälär khakinda." *Shura*, 9 (1911), 260–261.

Qarash, Ghŭmar. *Örnek*. Upï, 1911.

Qarash, Ghŭmar. *Oygha kelgen pïkïrlerïm*. Orinbor, 1910.

Qarash, Ghŭmar. *Zamana*. Almaty: Ghilim, 2000.

Riżā al-Dīn b. Fakhr al-Dīn. *Dini vä izhtimagiy mäs'äläläг*. Kazan: Rukhiyät, 2001.

Riżā al-Dīn b. Fakhr al-Dīn. *Asar. 3–4 tomnar*. Kazan: Rukhiyät, 2010.

Russian State Historical Archive (RGIA). F. 821, op. 8, dd. 602, 1021; op. 10, d. 29; F. 853, op. 2, d. 65.

Sartori, Paolo, and Shablei, Pavel. "Sud'ba imperskikh kodifikatsionnykh proektov: Adat i Shariat v Kazakhskoi stepi." *Ab Imperio*, 2 (2015): 63–105.

Sartori, Paolo. "Authorized Lies: Colonial Agency and Legal Hybrids in Tashkent, c. 1881–1893." *Journal of the Economic and Social History of the Orient*, 55 (2012), 688–717.

Sartori, Paolo. *Visions of Justice: Sharīʿa and Cultural Change in Russian Central Asia*. Leiden: Brill, 2016.

Sartori, Paolo. "What We Talk about When We Talk about Taqlīd in Russian Central Asia." In *Shariʿa in the Russian Empire: The Reach and Limits of Islamic Law in Central Eurasia, 1550–1917*, ed. Paolo Sartori and Danielle Ross (Edinburgh: Edinburgh University Press, 2020), 299–327.

State Archive of Orenburg Region (GAOO). F. 6, op. 6, d. 12681.

Svod zakonov Rossiiskoi imperii. Grazhdanskii polozheniia. Tom 10. Chast' 1. Stat'ia 63. Sankt-Petersburg, 1887.

Tagantzev, Nikolai, ed. *Ulozheniia o nakazaniiakh ugolovnykh i ispravitel'nykh*. Sankt-Petersburg, 1898.

Täzh-Mŭrat, Maqsat. "Tŭrlausiz Tŭlgha, Tauqimettï Taghdir." In *Käbisa Zhil: Zertteuler, Esseler, Ädebi Tolghamdar*. Astana: Khŭsnikhat, 2009.

Täzh-Mŭrat, Maqsat. *Ghŭmar Qarash: Ömirï men Shiğarmashiliği*. Aktöbe: Poligrafiia, 2004.

Tuna, Mustafa. *Imperial Russia's Muslims: Islam, Empire, and European Modernity, 1788–1914*. Cambridge: Cambridge University Press, 2015.

"Vedomost' lit. A. o naselenii Akmolinskoi oblasti za 1882 god." In *Obzor Akmolinskoi oblasti za 1882 god* (Omsk: Tipografiia Akmolinskogo Oblastnogo Pravleniia).

Wensinck, Arent Jan. "Nāfila." In *The Encyclopaedia of Islam. New Edition*, ed. C.E. Bosworth, E. van Donzel, W.P. Heinrichs and Ch. Pellat, vol. 7 (Leiden/New York: Brill, 1993): 878–879.

Werth, Paul. *The Tsar's Foreign Faiths. Toleration and the Fate of Religious Freedom in Imperial Russia*. Oxford: Oxford University Press, 2014.

Zagidullin, Il'dus, ed. *Osoboe soveschianie po musul'manskim delam 1914 goda*. Kazan: Ikhlas, 2011.

Zhanaev, Bolat, Viacheslav Inochkin, and Saniia Sagnaeva, eds. *Istoriia Bukeevskogo khanstva. 1801–1852*. Almaty: Daik-Press, 2002.

Continuities and Complexities of the Islamic Discourse in Daghestan from the 1920s to the 1980s

What the Soviets Did Not Know about Their Own Islam

Shamil Shikhaliev

Over the last decades Russian journalists and scholars of religious, political, and Islamic studies have been discussing what makes "good" and "bad" Islam, what kind of Islam is useful, correct and "traditional" for Russia, and what Islam is harmful, wrong and "not traditional." Government officials, religious functionaries, and the leaders of the Islamic communities in the Russian Federation participate in this debate. The various contributors to this debate often ignore the heterogeneity of Islam, including the multitude of Islamic trends and movements that developed in the various regions of Russia. Equally ignored are the historical conditions under which these trends emerged and developed, as well as the historical polemics and debates among various Muslim elites themselves.

In the North Caucasus, debates about "right" and "wrong" forms of Islam have been unfolding from the late Russian imperial period and throughout the Soviet era. Already during the long *jihād* in Daghestan and Chechnya (ca. 1828–1859), Muslim scholars engaged in heated discussions and polemics about the legitimacy, from the point of view of *sharīʿa*, of Imam Shamil's Islamic state project, of his *jihād* against Russia, as well as of his call to *hijra*, meaning his demand that Muslims living under non-Islamic rule should move to the regions he controlled to support the *jihād*.[1] Equally heated were debates about the relationship between Sufism and *jihād*, that is, whether the Naqshbandiyya Sufi brotherhood indeed served as an instrument, or even as an ideology, of Shamil's struggle against Russian rule. In Daghestan, these discussions continued after the end of the Great Caucasus War in 1864 in the polemical writings of pre-revolutionary Muslim scholars.

The aim of this chapter is not to give a survey of these historical and contemporary debates; neither is it an attempt to answer the question of which Islam is "right" and which is "wrong." Rather, this chapter will study the Soviet pre-history of the current Islamic discourse in the region by focusing on Daghestani writings from the 1920s to the 1980s. I am specifically interested in

1 Michael Kemper, "The Daghestani Legal Discourse on the Imamate," *Central Asian Survey*, 21/3 (2002), 161–174.

 | DOI:10.1163/9789004527096_012

how the discourse about "traditional" Islam functioned in this period, and how different fractions of the religious elite presented their various positions on this issue after it had been legalized (with important limitations) in the USSR in the mid-1940s.

1 The Return of Islam to Soviet Daghestan

In the late imperial and early Soviet periods, Muslims in the Caucasus rarely participated in debates among Tsarist and Bolshevik administrators of the region about Islam. In the late Tsarist era, Islam was largely "ignored" by the administration. The government did not support Islamic scholars and their institutions; it also refrained from confronting it or from reorganizing the Islamic infrastructure of mosques and madrasas (Islamic schools). Yet after the Bolshevik revolution and the devastating Civil War in the Caucasus, the Soviet administration increased pressure on Islamic scholars. By the late 1920s, Soviet policy became more hostile to Islam supporting outright repressions, executing and exiling thousands of imams and Islamic intellectuals, and closing down all Islamic schools and mosques. This was a major break with previous policies in Daghestan and had disastrous effects on Muslim communities, and on Islamic civilization in the North Caucasus.

In the late 1920s, knowledge of Russian had not yet spread widely in Daghestan. It was only after the opening of new Soviet educational institutions, by the middle of the twentieth century, and especialy 1950s and 1970s that Russian became the main language of inter-ethnic communication in the Daghestan Autonomous Soviet Socialist Republic. By the 1960s and 1970s Russian replaced earlier literary languages that had served as lingua francas for the various nationalities of Daghestan, such as the North Caucasian variants of Turki (in Daghestan, forms close to contemporary Kumyk and Azerbaijani), and Arabic as the major language for writing about Islam.

During the Second World War, the Soviet leadership incorporated a part of the religious elite of the North Caucasus into its state structures and created a new Soviet Islamic spiritual personnel. At that time, however, neither the Soviet ruling elites (*nomenklatura*) of Daghestan nor the Party organs in remote Moscow had any knowledge about the religious language of Islam. This knowledge was interrupted when the madrasas were closed. Even local Party officials could not read Arabic or the local languages (like Avar, Kumyk, Dargin, Lak) that had been written in the Arabic script before the Soviet alphabet changes of the 1920s and 1930s. Arabic and the Caucasus vernaculars written in Arabic script, however, continued to be used by the Islamic students and scholars that survived the repression or that had been born in later decades until the collapse of the USSR.

For these reasons we see that in the period under consideration here, many translations were produced. Texts about Islam written in national languages in Arabic script needed to be translated into Russian, in order to be legible to the new republican and Union authorities. But many original Arabic and vernacular texts in Arabic script of the second half of the 20th century remained untranslated, and only few of them have been made available to a broader public in recent years.[2]

After WWII, discussions about Islam in the USSR took place in centralized organizations for Muslims established in the various regions of the Soviet Union. In 1943 and 1944, Spiritual Administrations (that is, state-controlled Muftiates) had been set up in Tashkent (for the Muslims of Central Asia and Kazakhstan) and in Baku (for the Muslims of the South Caucasus). In May 1944, a congress of representatives from various Muslim communities of the North Caucasus proclaimed the establishment of a Spiritual Administration for the Muslims of the North Caucasus (*Dukhovnoe upravlenie musul'man Severnogo Kavkaza* – DUMSK). The congress also elaborated the internal regulations for DUMSK, and decided upon its structure and responsibilities.

In the following decades the work of DUMSK was controlled by the Council for Religious Cults (*Sovet po delam religioznykh kul'tov*, SDRK [after 1965: *Sovet po delam religii*, SDR]). The SDRK/SDR was set up under the Council of Ministers, the state organ responsible for religious activity and organizations in the USSR. It was based in Moscow, but had a representative (*upolnomochennyi*) in each of the Soviet autonomous republics and areas. In the North Caucasus the representatives were equally attached to the respective local governments.

The function of the Council for Religious Cults (SDRK) was to oversee the centralized religious organizations of all confessions in the USSR, to check whether they conformed to Soviet legislation on religious affairs in the respective areas, and to suggest improvements in these regulations.[3] In practice, the function of the SDRK/SDR was to limit the visibility of religion in the

---

2 Michael Kemper and Shamil Shikhaliev, "Administrative Islam: Two Soviet Fatwas from the North Caucasus," *Islamic Authority and the Russian Language: Studies on Texts from European Russia, the North Caucasus and West Siberia*, ed. Alfrid K. Bustanov and Michale Kemper (Amsterdam: Pegasus, 2012), 55–102.

3 Between 1944 and 1965 the Russian Orthodox Church was controlled by a special Council for Affairs of the ROC; in 1965 this council was merged with SDRK into SDR.

public sphere.[4] The council and its local representatives were always closely linked to the organs of state security; indeed all Daghestani representatives (I. Zakar'iaev, 1944–1958; M.-S. Gadzhiev, 1958–1977; S.A. Dervishbekov, 1977–1989) had worked in the Interior Ministry (MVD) or in the security service (NKVD-MGB-KGB) before being appointed to the SDRK/SDR.

2 Sufism and Russian Rule

One of the tasks of the SDRK/SDR was to fight against that subset of the Islamic spiritual elite that remained outside or beyond the control of their respective Muftiate and therefore of the Soviet organs that directed and monitored these Spiritual Administrations. It is therefore not surprising that it is in the documents of the SDRK/SDR, and of the Muftiates themselves, that we come across references to such Muslim scholars as "unofficial servants of the cult" (*neofitsial'nye sluzhiteli kul'ta*) and "unofficial clergy" (*neofitsial'noe dukhovenstvo*). Such terms could be applied in particular to Sufi shaykhs and their followers, which defied control of the Soviet Muftiates, and consequently of the Soviet party-state. These Soviet documents also distinguish between "official" Islam – understood as state-conforming or "correct," and "parallel" Islam – which is by definition "wrong." This division, which we still encounter today, is thus a Soviet construction.

Sufism and the associated practices such as veneration of Muslim saints (Ar., *awliyā'*) were constructed as "enemies" and attacked in the Soviet press, both in Russian and in Daghestan's national languages. Large numbers of brochures against Sufism, as well as against Islam as a whole, were widely distributed. Most of these were written by Soviet social scientists who worked in research institutes; in 1954, when the Central Committee reinvigorated atheist propaganda, many of these specialists obtained chairs of scientific atheism in the Soviet universities. These scholars presented followers of Sufism as "obscurantists" (*mrakobesy*), reactionaries, and enemies of Soviet power and Soviet society. Their accusations against Islam and Sufism were of a general nature and lumped the various groups together. These critics made no effort to understand what Sufis had to say about Islam. They also lacked the education and willingness to engage Sufi writings in Arabic, Turkic or Persian languages.

---

4 For Soviet Islam see the documents collected and analyzed in Dmitrii Iu. Arapov, *Islam i sovetskoe gosudarstvo (1944–1990): Sbornik dokumentov*, vol. 3 (Moscow: Mardzhani, 2011); Yaacov Ro'i, *Islam in the Soviet Union: From the Second World War to Gorbachev* (London: Hurst, 2000).

Often what they wrote against contemporary Islamic practices was shaped by outdated ideas from the Tsarist or early Soviet periods.

To be sure, the Daghestani Sufis of the late Tsarist period were almost united in their rejection of Russian rule over the Muslims of the North Caucasus, even if not all of them called for an armed struggle against the "damned *ʿurūs*." For example, in the late 19th century the well-known Naqshbandiyya shaykh Shuʿayb al-Bāginī (from the Avar village of Baginub, died in 1912) deplored non-Muslim rule over the believers in Daghestan in the following terms:

> We ask Allah the Almighty to preserve, in His mercy and with His sympathy, Istanbul [that is, the Ottoman Empire] and our Daghestani lands, and to protect it from all calamities and misfortunes that emanate from the government of the Russian state, and also from the devilish British state and other states of unbelievers. May Allah the Almighty revert the machinations and evil actions that come from these states, as well as the evil treachery in their hearts, against them, and may He leave them without His mercy. (...)[5]
>
> Imam Shamil was taken captive in the fortress of Gunib [in 1859], and the Daghestani lands fell into the hands of the unbelievers. May Allah the Almighty leave them without support. The pure *sharīʿa* was destroyed by the hands of the impure, and the *sharīʿa* laws were left [without application] like an orphan without a father. (...) The people are hard pressed by the Russian state, and by the growing number of unbelievers, hypocrites (*munāfiqūn*) and liars (*fujjār*).[6]

Yet it would also be wrong to accept Soviet social scientists' claims about Sufism, and all Sufis in the Caucasus and in Daghestan, as the eternal enemy of Russian authority. In the late imperial period the relations between Sufis and the state were more complex. Following the end of the Great Caucasus War in 1859 (in the North East Caucasus) and 1864 (in its western part), some Sufi masters performed the emigration (*hijra*) to the Ottoman Empire, and called upon their followers and fellow Muslims to do the same. Others adapted to the new situation, and some accepted positions in the Russian administration. Within the new system of the so-called "military-popular administration" (*voenno-narodnoe upravlenie*) some became *qāżīs* on village, regional, and

5 Shuʿayb ibn Idrīs al-Bāginī, *Ṭabaqāt al-khwājagān al-naqshbandiyya wa sādāt al-mashāʾikh al-khālidiyya al-maḥmūdiyya*, ed. ʿAbd al-Qādir ʿAṭā al-Bakrī (Damascus: Dār al-Nuʿmān li l-ʿulūm, 1996), 395.

6 al-Bāginī, *Ṭabaqāt al-khwājagān*, 364.

even all-Daghestani levels; others served in the "verbal" (*slovesnyi*) and "people's" courts, where a mix of customary law (*ʿādat*) and *sharīʿa* was applied.

The Russian administration took a cautious approach to Sufis. Fearing popular unrest and having understood the Sufis' influence on the population, they permitted the publication of some Sufi works.[7] By contrast, in the Soviet Union any public appearance of Sufism, and of Islam as a religion, was banned already in the late 1920s.

3 Soviet *fatwās* against Sufism

From their imperial predecessors, Soviet critics of Sufism inherited a range of sceptical and apprehensive attitudes towards Sufism. Pre-revolutionary terms such as "*muridism*" (R. *miuridizm*) denoted the idea of a militant Sufism that opposes Russian rule in the area.[8] Due to colonial phobias in Soviet era, Sufism was regarded as one of Islam's "sects" that was dangerous to society and to the state; in this formulation the historical development of Sufism, and the diversity of its groups and practices, were completely overlooked. It should be noted that in the nineteenth-century North Eastern Caucasus, Sufism spread in the form of three brotherhoods (*ṭarīqas*): the Naqshbandiyya, the Qādiriyya, and the Shādhiliyya. Each one had various wings (Ar., *wirds*). Even within one brotherhood, the shaykhs' political positions on Soviet power differed dramatically.[9] Attitudes towards the state as well as ritual practices continue to be diverse until today.[10]

---

7 More than ten Daghestani works on Sufism were published in the Islamic publishing houses of Port-Petrovsk (the later Makhachkala), Temir-Khan Shura (Buinaksk) and Kazan, in Arabic, Avar, Kumyk, and Chechen; all of these passed imperial censorship in St. Petersburg. The overall number of works on Sufism from the mid-nineteenth to the mid-twentieth century, including those that remained unpublished, amounts to sixty. See Shamil Sh. Shikhaliev, "Dagestanskaia sufiiskaia literatura 19–20 veka," in *Dukhovnaia literatura: aspekty izucheniia*, ed. M.A. Guseinov (Makhachkala: IIaLI, 2011), 299–324.

8 See M. Kemper, V.O. Bobrovnikov, "Miuridizm," *Islam na territorii byvshei Rossiiskoi imperii: entsiklopedicheskii slovar'*, ed. Stanislav M. Prozorov, fascicle 5 (Moscow: Vostochnaia literatura, 2012), 98–99.

9 For Sufis' relations to Soviet power see M. Kemper, "Khalidiyya Networks in Dagestan and the Question of Jihad," *Die Welt des Islams* 42/1 (2002), 41–71.

10 Shamil Shikhaliev, "Sufi Practices and Muslim Identities in Naqshibandi and Shadhili Lodges in Northern Daghestan," in *Islam and Sufism in Daghestan*, ed. Moshe Gammer (Helsinki, 2009), 43–56; idem, "Sufiiskii sheikh segodnia," *Ètnograficheskoe obozrenie* 2006, No. 2, 24–34.

These internal divisions were ignored both by Soviet critics of Sufism and by Cold War Western "Sovietologists" specializing in Soviet Islam, whose assessments of "the Islamic threat to the Soviet state" relied largely on Soviet anti-Islamic publications.[11] Soviet anti-Islamic writers often claimed that all Muslim believers of the North Caucasus belonged to some Sufi order. In reality, not all of those whom the Soviets regarded as "unofficial clergy" were Sufis. Our fieldwork of the last decade demonstrates that in the second half of the 20th century, the region had only few active Sufi branches (*wirds*).[12]

In addition to spreading anti-Sufi propaganda in the press and in schools, SDRK records demonstrate that the Soviet struggle against Sufism also made direct use of local organs of power. To take an example, on 9 February 1953 the representative for affairs of religious cults at the Daghestani Council of Ministers was invited to Moscow to report about how, in Daghestan, "the orders of the SDRK are carried out, and how the pilgrimage to 'holy sites' is being stopped."[13] The chairmen of the regional executive committees (that is, of the village authorities) also regularly received letters with orders from the Presidium of the Central Committee of the Communist Party to enforce prohibitions against visits to shrines.[14]

At the forefront of the Soviet struggle against Sufism was the North Caucasus Muftiate (DUMSK). From the mid-1940s until the second half of the 1980s, DUMSK issued a series of *fatwās* (religious legal opinions) against Sufism and the veneration of local saints and shrines (Ar., *ziyārat*). Initiatives for these *fatwās* usually came from the Soviet organs and in particular from the SDRK/SDR and its authorized representatives in the regions. The style and the terminology used in these texts strongly suggests that they were edited by Party functionaries.[15] The earliest of these *fatwās* that we know about were published by DUMSK in 1953. They were produced in four Daghestani languages –

11 Alexandre Bennigsen and S.Enders Wimbush, *Mystics and Commissars: Sufism in the Soviet Union* (London, Berkeley, 1985).

12 I conducted field work in seven rayons (districts) of the Republic Daghestan, within the framework of the project *From Kolkhoz to Jamaat. The Politicisation of Islam in the Rural Communities of the Former USSR: An Interregional Comparative Study, 1950s–2000s*, supported by the Volkswagen Foundation (2009–2011).

13 "Perepiska s partiinymi organami, rai(gorispolkomami) i drugimi mestnymi organizatsiami po voprosam religioznykh kul'tov za 1958–1959 gg.," Tsentral'nyi Gosudarstvennyi Arkhiv Respubliki Dagestan (in the following: TsGA RD), fond r-1234, opis'4, delo 12, fol. 20.

14 "Tsirkuliar Soveta Ministrov DASSR predsedateliam raiispolkomov Karabudakhkentskogo, Buinakskogo, Sergokalinskogo, Kakhibskogo raionov ot 25 dekabria 1958 g.," TsGA RD, fond r-1234, op. 4, delo 16, fol. 35.

15 For an initial analysis see Kemper and Shikhaliev, "Administrative Islam," 55–102.

Kumyk, Avar, Dargin and Lak – all written in Arabic script and printed in a lithographic style that was used in the Muslim printing houses before 1917.[16]

One of these *fatwās* from 1953 – here in a Kumyk variant – discusses the difference between true Sufi masters and false shaykhs:

> In former times Daghestan had no shaykhs who would independently issue a *wird* [here: a specific prayer litany characteristic for the Sufi group in question]. (…) Never were there any persons who followed the *ṭarīqa*, neither men nor women; everybody just followed the *sharīʿa*. Neither Abu Muslim, who once was shaykh in Daghestan, nor Asilder,[17] who became a shaykh in later times, nor anybody else ever called upon any other Muslim to join *muridism*.[18] When shaykhhood and *muridism* later spread among the population, the Muslims began to believe in [the shaykhs] and to regard this [veneration] as a blessed activity. They felt they had to bow before them, and people started to become shaykhs by themselves. Therefore some Muslims, who had obtained an education and who thought of themselves as well-educated scholars, started to present themselves as shaykhs and to gather *murīds*. Accordingly, many self-proclaimed shaykhs started to appear. (…) People who want to be shaykh had to have the necessary document testifying to their status (*ijāza*). Nevertheless, the self-proclaimed shaykhs arranged such papers for themselves by illicit means, and began to use them. (…)
>
> The self-proclaimed shaykhs that appear in our days spread discord and strife (*fitna*) among the Muslims. We do not claim that all shaykhs that lived in Daghestan were self-proclaimed, but we do say that many of them were. (…) For to be a real shaykh, several conditions must be met. First, a person who intends to become shaykh has to learn from a [senior] shaykh who already has the necessary level of knowledge. From

---

16 "Resheniia, prokazy, protokoly soveta po delam religii pri SM DASSR za 1966 g.," TsGA RD, fond r-1234, op. 4, delo 35, fol. 120.

17 For the mythical figure of Abu Muslim in Daghestan see V.O. Bobrovnikov, "Abu Muslim," *Islam na territorii byvshei Rossiiskoi imperii: entsiklopedicheskii slovar'*, vol. 1, ed. by Stanislav M. Prozorov (Moscow: Vostochnaia literatura, 2006), 15–19. On the (fifteenth-century) saint Asilder al-Harkasī see *Die Islamgelehrten Daghestans und ihre arabischen Werke. Naḏīr ad-Durgilīs (st. 1935) Nuzhat al-aḏhān fī tarāǧim ʿulamāʾ Dāǧistān*, ed. and transl. Michael Kemper and Amri R. Šixsaidov (*Muslim Culture in Russia and Central Asia*, vol. 4) (Berlin: Klaus Schwarz, 2004), 43–44.

18 In the Kumyk version of this *fatwā* the term *muridchilīq* is used, obviously a translation from Russian *muridism*; the term does not exist in the Kumyk language.

> this shaykh he needs to get the respective paper that would allow him to give a *wird* [in the sense of litany] to his followers. Second, such a person needs to be male.[19]

The Muftiate's position on Sufism is also clear from a speech given by the DUMSK Mufti Mukhammad-Hajji Kurbanov in 1966. In what follows we try to preserve the original style of the document, which is a Russian-language report of the speech:

> All of these actions [of shrine veneration] are not in accordance with Islam, but somehow men are visiting the *ziiarat*s [i.e., Sufi sites, Ar. sg. *ziyārat*] together with women, [which is] not allowed. Those self-proclaimed shaykhs, they use the backwardness (*otstalost'*) of the believing citizens (*grazhdane veruiushchie*), take their valuable donations. [Therefore] the Spiritual Administration decided to withhold all imposters from their bad doings and to put an end to this, and it explained to the believers which *ziiarat*s may be visited and which may not, according to the Quran and the hadith. (…). We all know that in the beginning of the month Rajab and in mid-Shaʿban, men and women jointly go to visit *ziiarat*s. These visits are not permitted in the Qur'an. On the contrary, they are forbidden. All of these actions were carried out by false shaykhs, and only for their personal benefit. Such visits were also rejected by famous scholars of the *sharīʿa*, and also by the scholarly masters of the '*Tarikat*.' (…) The wife of the Prophet Magomed, Allah bless him, Aishat (Allah be content with her) said that the prophet Magomed said that those are cursed who turned the graves of their prophets into praying houses, and she added that I forbid [anyone] to turn my grave into a praying house.[20]

In this speech, the Mufti does not speak out against Sufism per se; nor does he say that Sufism in general violates the norms of the *sharīʿa*. Rather, his attack concentrates on what he calls the "self-proclaimed shaykhs" (*sheikhi-samozvantsy*) who misuse donations of believers for their personal interests.

---

19 *Shimali Qavqaz muslimanlarï dini idarasïnnan 'Murajaʿat-name'* ["Address of the North Caucasus Muslim Administration," in the Kumyk language, lithographical print] (Buinaksk, 1953), 14–16.

20 "Vystuplenie muftiia musul'man Severnogo Kavkaza o 'ziiaratakh,'" TsGA RD, fond r-1234, op. 4, delo 35, fol. 122.

His other critique focuses on the mixing of genders during shrine visits. *Ziyārats* (shrine pilgrimages) are furthermore a problem because when people perform these rituals the shrines take on the functions of a mosque, an interpretation that seems preposterous from the perspective of a state organization in charge of controlling the few existing "official" mosques in the country. The Mufti therefore used Islamic sources to argue that the mixing of men and women, as well as the construction of praying facilities at tombs, violates Islamic law.

In other parts of this speech, as well as in other DUMSK documents, Mufti Kurbanov also draws on the Shāfiʿī legal tradition, quoting from works of *fiqh* (Islamic law) that have been used in Daghestan since the 17th century.[21]

These arguments demonstrate that the Mufti's position on Sufism was more complex than the crude anti-Islamic stance of Soviet academic scholars. It indicated that Sufism had a place in Islamic history, and perhaps even in Daghestan, but that it had to be regulated. Anybody claiming to be a Sufi needed to have met certain requirements. He needed to have learned from a senior Sufi master and to have obtained a written license to teach. It is on these grounds that Kurbanov rejected the claims of contemporary "pretenders." One might say that this might have implied that there was no "real" Sufism left in the country.

These *fatwās* and speeches emanating from DUMSK echo the rhetoric developed earlier by a number of prominent Daghestani Muslim reformers who called for a modernization of Muslim education, and several of them also for a reform of Islamic law. In the late 1920s some important reformers published articles in the Arabic-language Daghestani journal *Bayān al-ḥaqā'iq* in which they argued that Sufism in Daghestan had been degraded and deformed.[22] Mufti Kurbanov borrowed concepts and terminology from these earlier critics of contemporary Sufi practice. But Kurbanov's statements even go back to the local Sufi tradition that he criticizes: in fact his concept of "self-proclaimed shaykhs" (*shaikhi-samozvantsy*) is a Russian translation of the Arabic term *mutashayyikhūn* ("would-be shaykhs") which was quite common in polemics of Sufis against each other; thus the aforementioned shaykh Shuʿayb al-Bāginī had already used the Arabic term in his late nineteenth-century writings when challenging his rivals' claims to shaykhhood.[23]

21 Works that are referred to include Fakhr al-Dīn Rāzī's *al-Tafsīr al-kabīr* (a Qur'an commentary), Ibn Ḥajar al-Haytamī's *al-Fatāwā al-kubrā* (jurisprudence), and several others.

22 Amir R. Navruzov, "Baian al-khaka'ik – pechatnyi organ uchenykh-arabistov Dagestana pervoi treti XX veka," *Pax Islamica* (2011), no. 2, 18–27.

23 al-Bāginī, *Ṭabaqāt al-khwājagān*, 397, 419–421.

4 Islamic Reformism in Daghestan: Education and Islamic Legal Reform

When exploring continuities between Soviet and Islamic reformist arguments we must keep in mind that reformism appeared in Daghestan in two variants. The first approach focused on modernization in the field of Islamic education; it emphasized the need to establish regular school classes and curricula, adopt modern methodologies of teaching, and introduce secular subjects. The second approach went further and demanded the modernization of Islamic law (*fiqh*). These two groups – which can both be seen as the constituents of a Daghestani variant of reformism[24] – both polemicized against the adherents of what they called the "old system" (Kumyk: *esgi qaida*), that is, the traditional madrasa system that strictly followed the Shāfiʿī school tradition. This "old system" focused on the learning of Arabic according to methods that had been used in the medieval Middle East and that were maintained in Daghestan over the centuries until the arrival of reformism (and, we may add, that is still in use today).

The debates over changes in the field of Islamic law centred on several theoretical issues. The first was a question about the degree of permissibility of *ijtihād*, or individual reasoning on the basis of a strict methodology of how to interpret the foundational texts of Islam in order to develop answers to new questions, or new answers to old questions.[25] The idea of *ijtihād* challenged what was often perceived as the "blind" following (*taqlīd*) of one's own legal tradition.[26] Those reformists who called for a rethinking of the Islamic legal practice argued for a re-evaluation of the relationship between the four accepted legal school (*madhhab*s) of Sunni Islam. This amounted to the possibility that a highly trained scholar could use solutions proposed by all four

24 In the present contribution I avoid the use of the overall term Jadidism, in order to nuance the differences among the Daghestani reformers, and also to emphasize the Middle Eastern influences on their more radical wing (which is easily downplayed when using the term Jadidism, which implies that the Daghestanis participated above all in a Russian/Tatar cultural and educational reform movement). See, however, our positioning of Daghestani Reformism in Shamil Shikhaliev, "Musul'manskoe reformatorstvo v Dagestane (1900–1930)," in *Gosudarstvo, religiia, tserkov' v Rossii i za rubezhom* (Moskow: RANKHiGS, 2017), 134–169; See also Michael Kemper and Shamil Shikhaliev, "Qadimism and Jadidism in Twentieth-Century Daghestan," *Asiatische Studien – Études Asiatiques*, 69/3 (2015), 593–624.

25 On *ijtihād* see J. Schacht, "Idjtihad," *The Encyclopaedia of Islam* – New Edition, ed. P.J. Bearman et al., vol. 3 (Leiden – London, 1986), 1026–1027.

26 N. Calder, "Taḳlīd," *The Encyclopaedia of Islam* – New Edition, ed. P.J. Bearman et al., vol. 10 (Leiden – London, 1986), 137–138.

*madhhab*s if his individual legal reasoning was sound; in extreme situations, he could even go beyond all four.

The adherents of the more moderate ("educational") trend of Daghestani reformism included well-known scholars such as Abū Sufyān Akaev (1872–1931), the Kumyk editor of *Bayān al-ḥaqā'iq* (1925–1928),[27] publicists/intellectuals such as Muḥammad-Mirza Mavraev (1878–1964), the Avar founder and director of the first and only Islamic typographical house in Daghestan; and Sufis such as Sayf Allah-Qadi Bashlarov (1852–1919),[28] a Lak who took the Naqshbandiyya Mahmūdiyya from Tatar Sufis and became known for introducing Shādhiliyya elements into the teaching of the Mahmūdiyya. Other Jadids interested primarily in the more narrowly "educational" types of reforms also included the historians Muḥammad-Qadi Dibirov (1875–1929, an ethnic Avar) and Jamāl al-Dīn-ḥājjī from Karabudakhkent (1858–1947, a Kumyk).

This moderate group of reformers called only for a reform of the Muslim system of education, and remained loyal followers of the Daghestani Shāfiʿī tradition; they opposed the more radical reformers' claims to independent *ijtihād*. Also, they held that Sufism as such was fully legitimate and attacked only those whom they regarded as "false shaykhs," who did not have an *ijāza* (license) to teach Sufism and whom they regarded as violating the principles of Sufi ritual practice. It is this tradition of moderate reformism that Soviet Mufti Kurbanov followed when he criticized the "false shaykhs" without, however, rejecting Sufism in general.

5 The Issue of *ijtihād* and *taqlīd*

The more radical trend of Islamic reformism was represented by ʿAli Kaiaev (ʿAlī al-Ghumūqī, 1878–1943, from the Lak town of Kumukh), a well-known Muslim journalist, teacher, and scholar. ʿAli Kaiev and his disciples called for the application of full, independent *ijtihād* (or "absolute" *ijtihād*, *ijtihād muṭlaq*) that would, if necessary, also transcend the boundaries of any existing *madhhab*.[29] He did so in his published works, including newspaper articles,

27 On Akaev see Gasan M.-R. Orazaev, "Osnovnye vekhi v zhizni i tvorchestve Abusuf'iana Akaeva," in *Literaturnoe i nauchnoe nasledie Abusuf'iana Akaeva*, ed. by G.M.-R. Orazaev (Makhachkala, 1992), 106–116; *Abu Suf'ian Akaev: Epokha, zhizn', deiatel'nost'*, edited by G. Orazaev (Makhachkala: Dagestanskoe knizhnoe izdatel'stvo, 2012).

28 Shamil Sh. Shikhaliev, "Saipulla-kadi," *Islam na territorii byvshei Rossiiskoi imperii*, ed. by Stanislav M. Prozorov, fascicle 4 (Moscow: Vostochnaia literatura, 2003), 72–73.

29 Amir R. Navruzov, *"Dzharidat Dagistan" – araboiazychnaia gazeta kavkazskikh dzhadidov* (Moscow: Mardzhani, 2012), 162.

but also in a significant amount of works that remained in manuscript form. As a popular writer in the Arabic, Turkic and Lak languages, Kaiaev left an enormous impact on debates about a whole variety of educational, historical and Islamic topics.

Kaiaev was embedded in a larger network and conversation among reformers during this period. From 1913 to 1918 Kaiaev was the chief editor of the Arabic-language newspaper *Jarīdat Dāghistān*, which was published in Temir-Khan Shura (today Buinaksk), an administrative center of Daghestan. This newspaper was inspired by the famous journal *al-Manār* ("The Lighthouse"), published in Cairo by the Egyptian reformist Rashīd Riḍā (1865–1935).[30] Kaiaev had studied at al-Azhar in the early 20th century, and reportedly collaborated with Riḍā during this period. Kaiaev's views on *ijtihād* were shared by Muḥammad ʿAbd al-Rashīd al-Harakānī (from the Avar village of Arakani, 1900–1927), Muḥammad ʿUmarī al-Uḥlī (from the Avar village of Okhli, b. 1895, d. in the 1940s), Masʿūd al-Muhūkhī (from the Avar Mogokh, 1893–1941), ʿAbd al-Raḥīm al-ʿAymakī (d. in the 1980s), as well as the Avars Muḥammad-Saiid Saidov (1902–1985) and Muḥammad G. Nurmagomedov (1909–1995). Next to educational modernization, this more radical group also called for *ijtihād*, and it went beyond the critique of individual Sufis by arguing that Sufism as such is a "harmful innovation" (*bidʿa*) in Islam.

The discussions among these reformist groups in the 1920s about what was to be taught, how, and in which languages, became obsolete when the Soviet government decided to eliminate Islamic education and to replace it with secular mass education in both Russian and the major Daghestani national languages.[31] All Islamic schools were closed down in the late 1920s. For this reason, many of the reformists started to work in Soviet schools, but when the government did not need them anymore they were replaced by a new generation of Soviet-educated teachers. Many reformists were executed during the Great Terror of the late 1930s, and many more died in the early 1940s in the GULag prison camps or in exile. Yet when the Soviets eventually introduced a new system of Muftiates in the years 1943–1944, they also had to open at least one madrasa that would produce the new imams of the Soviet Union; this would be the "Mir-i Arab" madrasa in Bukhara (re-est. 1946). Ten years later, they also opened the Barak-Khan madrasa in Tashkent (1956–1961, then in 1971 transformed into the Tashkent Islamic Institute). And with the new establishment of a Soviet Islamic elite, also the debates of the 1920s and 1930s on issues of Islamic legal methodologies and the legitimacy of Sufism became central

30 Navruzov, "*Dzharidat Dagistan*," 180–181.

31 Navruzov, "*Dzharidat Dagistan*," 57–67.

again. In the 1980s and 1990s, finally, these debates regained a prominent place also in the public sphere.

Kaiaev was certainly the most productive and most radical writer on *ijtihād* in Daghestan.[32] The question of *ijtihād* is also dealt with in manuscripts preserved from Nadhīr al-Durgilī (from Dorgeli, 1891–1935),[33] Yūsuf al-Jungūtī (from Dzhengutai, 1869–1929),[34] Masʿūd al-Muhūkhī,[35] Ghazanav al-Gubdānī (from Gubden, died in the late 1940s),[36] and in writings of other scholars. It should be noted, however, that *ijtihād* is not synonymous with any kind of "free speculation about Islam;" to the contrary, the classical legal literature describes rigid conditions that a *mujtahid* (a scholar performing *ijtihād*) must fulfill in order to legitimately engage in *ijtihād*. These demands (in terms of authority, erudition, skills as well as the methodology to be employed) were so high that most Daghestani scholars believed that there was no chance to reform the system of Islamic law outside of the dominant Shāfiʿī *madhhab*; *ijtihād* within a given legal school might still be possible, but "absolute *ijtihād*" independent of the existing schools was regarded as too daring, and as impossible.[37]

Like many of their contemporaries in other countries, the Daghestani reformers interpreted the "backwardness" and the "colonial subjugation" of their own society as consequences of social ossification and of *taqlīd*, that is, of the practice of blindly following the tradition of customs and customary law (*ʿādat*). Intellectually, they saw it as a consequence of traditional scholarship being stuck in religious scholasticism (understood as the mindless engagement in commentaries upon commentaries), without any innovation. This state of religious and intellectual weakness was what allowed the great colonial powers Britain and France to surpass and dominate the Muslim world. This topos occurred already in the writings of the late nineteenth-century Sufi shaykh Shuʿayb al-Bāginī, as seen above; it would later recur in speeches and

---

32 ʿAlī ibn ʿAbd al-Hamīd al-Ghumūqī, *Risāla fi-l-taqlīd wa jawāz al-talfīq*, ms Institut Istorii, Arkheologii i etnografii Dagestanskogo nauchnogo tsentra RAN (in the following: IIAE), fond M.-S. Saidov, op. 1, no. 37, fols 101a–106b.

33 Nadhīr al-Durgilī, *al-Ijtihād wa-l-taqlīd*, ms IIAE, fond M.-S. Saidov, op. 1, no. 35, fols 1a–29b; idem, *al-Taʿlīq al-ḥamīd ʿalā'l-qawl al-sadīd*, IIAE, fond M.-S. Saidov, op. 1, no. 35, fols 68a–103b.

34 Yūsuf al-Jungūtī, *al-Qawl al-sadid fī ḥasm māddat al-ijtihād wa wujūb al-taqlīd*, IIAE, fond M.-S. Saidov, op. 1, no. 35, fols 32a–103b.

35 Masʿūd ibn Muḥammad al-Muhūkhī, *Kharq al-asdād ʿan abwāb al-ijtihād*, ms., 63 fols. Private collection Abubakr Saidbekov (b. 1976), Khasaviurt.

36 Ghazanaw al-Gubdānī, *Risāla fī radd ʿalā risāla ʿAlī al-Ghumūqī*, IIAE, fond M.-S. Saidov, op. 1, no. 37, fols 107b–111b.

37 For the conditions for *ijtihād*, see ʿAbd al-Wahhāb Tāj al-Dīn al-Subkī, *Jamʿ al-jawāmiʿ fī usūl al-fiqh* (Beirut: Dār al-kutub al-ʿilmiyya, 2003), 120–122.

fatwās of Soviet Muftis, and is still alive in the public discourse today, with the United States often regarded as the source of all problems in the Muslim world.

Masʿūd al-Muhūkhī saw the way out of this darkness in the study of natural sciences, in the rejection of the blind imitation of tradition, and in the development of the Muslim world according to modern standards.[38] Also Jamāl al-Dīn-ḥājjī from Karabudakhkent believed in the power of modern knowledge, and called upon his contemporaries to embrace the achievements of modern Western sciences.[39]

The radical representatives of Daghestani reformism also understood the importance of modernizing education and familiarizing Daghestan with modern secular sciences. In addition, however, they encouraged that Daghestan's Muslims apply *ijtihād* in all spheres of Islam (that is, in the *furūʿ*), leaving untouched only the fundaments of belief (*uṣūl*) from which the *furūʿ* must be derived.

These radical reformers thus had a lasting impact on the formulation of official Soviet Islam in the post-WWII period in terms of their anti-colonial pathos (which was easily brought into harmony with Soviet declarations of support for the liberation of the Muslim world from Western oppression), their critical reformulation of Islam (against *taqlīd*), and their rejection of "false shaykhs" and practices of shrine veneration.

The theoretical issues of *taqlīd* and *ijtihād* in the legal sphere were also discussed in terms of specific practical application. One of these issues was the Islamic procedure for divorce. The proponents of *ijtihād* maintained that divorce was only finalized when the husband pronounced the *ṭalāq* formula three times at various occasions, not at once in conjunction; in contrast, the more moderate reformists, as well as the adherents of traditional Daghestani Shafiʿism, held that the divorce was already valid if the three pronouncements were made in direct succession.[40] They also disagreed about the question of how to perform the noon prayer on Fridays. The radical group of reformers

38 Masʿūd ibn Muḥammad al-Muhūkhī, "Nahnu wa'l-ʿulūm al-ʿaṣriyya," *Bayān al-ḥaqā'iq* (1926) no. 5, 2–3.

39 Jamāl al-Dīn al-Gharabudāghi, *Tārīkh Qawqāz wa qarya Gharabudaghkent*, ms. IIAE, fond 1, opis' 1, delo 414, fol. 1a. This treatise was written between 1922 and 1926. See: Gasan M.-R. Orazaev, *Istoriia Kavkaza i seleniia Karabudakhkent Dzhamalutdina-khadzhi Karabudakhkentskogo* (Makhachkala, 2001), 12. Most probably he was influenced by Ottoman as well as by Arabic literature, as well as by works of al-Afghānī. For the Daghestani reception of the latter, see Jamāl al-Dīn al-Afghānī, *Radd ʿalā'l-dahriyyin*, IIAE, fond M.-S. Saidov, op. 1, no. 90b, fols 95a–132a.

40 ʿAbd al-Ḥafiẓ al-Uḥlī, *al-Jawāb al-ṣaḥīḥ li'l-akh al-muṣlih*, ms., fol. 12. From the collection of Abduragim Abdurakhmanov, Nizhnii Dzhengutai. Cf. ʿAlī ibn ʿAbd al-Ḥamīd al-Ghumūqī, *Ṭalāq*, ms. IIAE, fond M.-S. Saidov, op. 1, no. 50, fol. 7a.

argued that to perform an extra noon prayer after the Friday prayer was a harmful innovation (*bidʿa*).[41] Their opponents regarded the independent noon prayer as obligatory under certain conditions.[42] Both these discussions continued throughout the Soviet period and are still alive today.

6 Critiques of Sufism

Equally important for the Soviet and post-Soviet Islamic discourse in Daghestan were the reformers' writings about Sufism written in first third of the 20th century. Most criticism focused on the Sufi concepts of *tawaṣṣul* (according to which the Sufi master or a saint of the past can act as a mediator between the individual and Allah), *dhikr* (the collective remembering of Allah, often by repeating His names, and connected to breathing techniques), and *rābiṭa* (the spiritual connection between master and disciple by way of concentration). For establishing the *rābiṭa*, the Mahmūdiyya Sufi brotherhood encouraged the use of photographs of the master to help the student create an image of the latter in his mind. ʿAli Kaiaev's disciples saw these techniques as a blatant departure from the basic regulations of Islam. In one case, the young Muḥammad-Saiid Saidov (who would later become a well-known Orientalist in a Soviet research institute in Makhachkala) accused Sufis in one of his letters (dated 29 March 1924) of ignorance, violating the *sharīʿa* norms, unbelief (*kufr*), and of simply pursuing monetary goals.[43]

A more moderate critic of Sufism, Abū Sufyān Akaev, attacked individual shaykhs of his time (first third of the 20th century) for what he saw as a violation of the principles of their own *ṭarīqa*s and for misusing their influence over *murīd*s (Sufi disciples) for material gains. At the same time he wrote a number of articles in *Bayān al-ḥaqāʾiq* in which he sympathized with Sufism. For example, he wrote:

> While it is true that Sufism is not mentioned in the Qurʾan and the hadith, this trend should not be rejected as long as it [here: the particular *ṭarīqa* or group to which the Sufi in question belongs] is in accordance with the Qurʾan and Sunna.[44]

41 Navruzov, "*Dzharidat Dagistan*," 134.

42 Navruzov, "*Dzharidat Dagistan*," 129–135.

43 Arabic-language letter Muḥammad-Saiid Saidov to Masʿūd al-Muhūkhī, 29 March 1924, IIAE, fond M.-S. Saidov, op. 5, no. 30.

44 Abū Sufyān ibn Akay, "Al-Tashayyukh fi-l-sharīʿa," *Bayān al-ḥaqāʾīq* (1925), no. 1, p. 11.

Akaev also wrote a whole book (in the Kumyk language) about Sufi ethics and the ritual practices of the Naqshbandiyya brotherhood,[45] in which he criticized shaykhs who exploited their disciples; the true shaykh, he wrote, does not accept gifts but makes a living through normal work. Akaev also displayed his respect for the Sufi tradition by publishing fragments of texts composed by Middle Eastern and Daghestani Sufis. To give another example, the Naqshbandiyya and Shādhiliyya shaykh Sayf Allah Bashlarov, who was a supporter of educational reformism, often polemicized against other Sufis of his era.[46] Bashlarov's disciple and successor, the Avar shaykh Ḥasan Ḥilmī al-Qahī (from the village of Kakhib, 1856–1937) wrote a whole Arabic-language work against "pseudo-shaykhs," whom he identified above all in a rival Naqshbandiyya line, the Khālidiyya.[47]

These debates about real and fraudulent shaykhs among the Naqshbandiyya and Shādhiliyya groups of Daghestan continued throughout the Soviet era. Daghestani Sufi masters described what they envisioned to be the real or "perfect" shaykh (*al-murshid al-kāmil*). They emphasized possession of an authentic written license (*ijāza*) from the shaykh's master and the uninterrupted chain of transmission (*silsila*) from master to student. At the same time, Daghestani Sufis also had to defend their teachings and practices from attacks by above mentioned reformists, who were, and are, often referred to as "Wahhabis" by Sufi scholars. Several of these defences against "Wahhabism" date from the early Soviet years; among these we found one Arabic-language work by Muḥammad al-Yaʿsūbī ("Response of al-Yaʿsūbī against the Lies of the Wahhābī al-Harakānī"), written in 1924 against the above-mentioned radical reformer ʿAbd al-Rashīd al-Harakānī (d. 1927).[48] Note that al-Harakānī was a local reformist of the more radical trend, but by no means a follower of the Wahhabi school from Saudi Arabia; rather, already in those years defenders of Sufism began to call every critic of Sufism a "Wahhabi," with "Wahhabism" then becoming equivalent to a bad innovation entering the Caucasus from the Middle East. This "Wahhabism" discourse is still dominant in post-Soviet Daghestan.[49]

---

45 Abū Sufyān ibn Akay, *Wasīlat al-najāt* (Temir-Khan Shura: Mavraev, 1908) (in Kumyk).

46 Sayf Allāh al-Nitsubkrī, *Maktūbāt Khālid Sayf Allāh ilā fuqarāʾ ahl Allāh*, ed. ʿAbd al-Qādir ʿAṭā al-Bakrī (Damascus: Dār al-Nuʿmān li-l-ʿulūm, 1998), 21.

47 Ḥasan ibn Muḥammad Ḥilmī al-Qahī, *Tanbīh al-sālikīn ilā ghurūr al-mutashayyikhīn*, ed. ʿAbd al-Qādir ʿAṭā al-Bakrī (Damascus: Dār al-Nuʿmān li l-ʿulūm, 1996).

48 Muḥammad al-Yaʿsūbī al-Asawī, *Ajwibat al-ʿAsalī al-Yaʿsūbī ʿalā turahāt al-Wahhābī al-Harakānī*, ms (copied 12 Dhu-l-Ḥijja 1381 /17 May 1962), 35 fols. From the private collection of of Shamsuddin Magomedov (b. 1983), village of Datuna.

49 Michael Kemper and Shamil Shikhaliev, "Islam and Political Violence in Post-Soviet Daghestan: Discursive Strategies of the Sufi Masters," in *Constellations of the Caucasus:*

7 The Soviet Islamic Elite between Reformism and Sufism, 1944–1978

We already saw that the two trends of Daghestani reformism had a significant influence on the formation of the new Soviet discourse on Islam that emerged in the mid-1940s. However, we should also not overestimate the DUMSK personnel's sympathies with reformism. If we look at the biographies of those who worked in the Soviet Muftiate for the North Caucasus we find that several of them were in fact connected to Sufism; and so were some of the imams who served in the few official ("legal") mosques in Daghestan. In fact, three of the four Soviet Muftis of the Spiritual Administration of the Muslims of the North Caucasus, as well as a majority of the DUMSK staff (which underwent little structural transformation between 1944 and 1978) came from Daghestan, and more precisely from Daghestan's Muslim elite whose identity had since the 19th century been closely linked to Sufism. These functionaries had obtained a traditional Islamic education in the pre-revolutionary period or in the early Soviet years, which means that their teachers had often been shaykhs or disciples (*murīd*s) of the Naqshbandiyya-Khālidiyya, the Naqshbandiyya-Maḥmūdiyya, or the Shādhiliyya. From DUMSK documents we know, for example, that the "workers in the mosque of Makhachkala, Abdullakh Gadzhiev, Zainuddin Shugaibov, and Abdulvagap Akhmedov, were followers of the Sufi line of shaykh Ali-Hajji Akushinskii."[50] This Akushinskii (1847–1930) was a much revered Dargin shaykh of the Khālidiyya. In other words, a Khālidiyya affiliation did not preclude Islamic specialists from finding jobs in the DUMSK administration and its mosques. Until 1978, when the Balkar Maḥmūd-ḥājjī Gekkiev became Mufti of DUMSK (on him more below), there were only two members of DUMSK who were active opponents of Sufism: the deputy of Mufti Shamsuddin Abdullaev (died in 1984) and member of DUMSK Fakhr al-Dīn Magomedov (died in 1962) who was a *qāżī* of the mosque in Arakani village and in the early Soviet period studied with the above-mentioned reformists – ʿAbd al-Rashīd al-Harakānī and Masʿūd al-Muhūkhī.[51]

As these examples demonstrate, post-World War II Soviet Islamic elites in Daghestan had a complex relationship with these different groups of reformists and Sufi shaykhs. This is demonstrated by one Arabic manuscript that I discovered, the polemical treatise "The Right Answer to the Honorable Brother" (*al-Jawāb al-ṣaḥīḥ li'l-akh al-muṣliḥ*), composed by ʿAbd al-Ḥafīẓ-ḥājjī al-Uḥlī

Empires. Peoples and Faiths, ed. Michael Reynolds and Hirotake Maeda (*Interdisciplinary Journal of Middle Eastern Studies*, 17 [2016]), 117–154.

50 "Zhaloby i otkloneniia khodataistva ob otkrytii molitvennykh domov veruiushchikh musul'man za 1953–1957 gg.," TsGA RD, fond r-1234, op. 4, delo 7, fols 39–40.

51 Interview with Ali Omarov (b. 1956), the son of ʿAbd al-Ḥafīẓ-ḥājjī al-Uḥlī (May 2016).

(Umarov/Okhlinskii) in 1949.[52] ʿAbd al-Ḥafīẓ-ḥājjī was the Chairman of a DUMSK control commission (a financial structure that documents donations from the population, and is accountable to the authorized representative of the SDR) and served as DUMSK Chairman/Mufti in 1975–1978.

The author, ʿAbd al-Ḥafīẓ-ḥājjī, was the uncle of the above-mentioned Muḥammad ʿUmarī al-Uḥlī, who as a disciple of Kaiaev belonged to the radical critics of Sufism; but ʿAbd al-Ḥafīẓ-ḥājjī's 1949 treatise is a harsh polemic against the views of pre-revolutionary and early Soviet reformists from Daghestan, as well as against "Wahhabis" from what had become Saudi Arabia. Dressing his arguments in the form of an advice to a certain "brother in faith Sakhrat Allah al-Anṣalṭī (Mirzoev, d. 1970s)," ʿAbd al-Ḥafīẓ-ḥājjī al-Uḥlī criticizes the radical reformers (whom he addresses as Jadids) and, again, the "Wahhabis" from the position of Shāfiʿī law and Ashʿarī theology, which he sees as the only true schools. The author thus defends the traditional Daghestani *taqlīd*.

ʿAbd al-Ḥafīẓ-ḥājjī al-Uḥlī regards both Wahhabism and radical reformism as dangerous for Muslims. The first part of his work is a short history of the Wahhabi movement in the Najd, starting with its founder, Muḥammad ibn ʿAbd al-Wahhāb (d. 1792). The second part is a refutation of Jamāl al-Dīn al-Afghānī, Muḥammad ʿAbduh, and Rashīd Riḍā, the famous Muslim reformists active in Egypt and the larger Muslim world; ʿAbd al-Ḥafīẓ-ḥājjī al-Uḥlī obviously regarded them as outside factors that shaped radical reformism in Daghestan. Interestingly, ʿAbd al-Ḥafīẓ-ḥājjī distinguished two groups of the reformers and named the first the "Wahhabi movement" and the second the "Jadidi movement," which in his opinion was "more harmful than Wahhabism." The third part of ʿAbd al-Ḥafīẓ-ḥājjī al-Uḥlī's *Jawāb* is a critique of the Daghestani reformists themselves, in particular of the aforementioned Ali Kaiaev, Muḥammad al-ʿUmarī al-Uḥlī, ʿAbd al-Rashīd al-Harakānī, and Masʿūd al-Muhūkhī.

ʿAbd al-Ḥafīẓ-ḥājjī al-Uḥlī presents himself as a defender of Sufism, and he draws on the works of several Daghestani Sufis, including anti-reformist statements by Sufi shaykh Sharaf al-Dīn al-Kikūnī (d. 1936) from the Naqshbandiyya-Khālidiyya, and from works by Ḥasan Ḥilmī al-Qahī (d. 1937) from the Naqshbandiyya-Maḥmūdiyya and Shādhiliyya.

Interestingly, the appendix of ʿAbd al-Ḥafīẓ-ḥājjī al-Uḥlī's manuscript contains a number of "peer-reviews" written by other Daghestani scholars, which praise the value of ʿAbd al-Ḥafīẓ-ḥājjī's *Jawāb*. This feature, a kind of PR in

52 Shamil Sh. Shikhaliev, "Al-Dzhavab as-salikh li-l-akh al-muslikh' ʿAbd al-Khafiz Okhlinskogo," in *Dagestan i musul'manskii Vostok: Sbornik statei*, ed. Alikber K. Alikberov and Vladimir O. Bobrovnikov (Moscow: Mardzhani, 2010), 324–340.

manuscript form, was not uncommon in early twentieth-century manuscript works; they were meant to give the book and its author credibility and to widen its circulation.[53] What is striking about these reviews is that they were composed by people who in that period worked, like ʿAbd al-Ḥafīẓ-ḥājjī al-Uḥlī himself, in the administration of DUMSK, or who held important positions as *imams* in the registered mosques of Daghestan. In other words, ʿAbd al-Ḥafīẓ-ḥājjī al-Uḥlī's pro-Sufi and anti-reformist arguments are here supported by the very scholars who also signed the aforementioned DUMSK anti-Sufi *fatwā* of 1953 that drew heavily from Daghestani reformist discourse! These reviews include Muḥammad-ḥājjī Kurbanov (who became Mufti a year later, in 1950); Sakhrat Allah Mirzoev, the imam of the mosque in Botlikh and member of DUMSK (and also the personal addressee of ʿAbd al-Ḥafīẓ-ḥājjī al-Uḥlī's *Jawāb*); Tatam Karabudagov, a member of DUMSK from 1947 to well into the 1970s; and other *imāms* of the registered mosques in Daghestan.

While attacking the reformists who advocated *ijtihād*, ʿAbd al-Ḥafīẓ-ḥājjī al-Uḥlī neglects to mention those who called only for a modernization of Islamic education. The omission of "educational reformism" suggests that ʿAbd al-Ḥafīẓ-ḥājjī al-Uḥlī and his reviewers were not against those modernizers who did not attack Sufism and *taqlīd* in legal issues. Moreover, ʿAbd al-Ḥafīẓ-ḥājjī al-Uḥlī, in this work, does not discuss the political positions of the reformists, and their relations to the secular authorities. In other words, while the *fatwās* were written on state demand, from political positions, with a minimal amount of Islamic sources and Islamic methodology, works like ʿAbd al-Ḥafīẓ-ḥājjī al-Uḥlī's *Jawāb* represent a different type of writing by the same DUMSK functionaries, but completely within the Islamic discourse of the 1920s and 1930s, with no references to Soviet power – as if it was not there.

ʿAbd al-Ḥafīẓ-ḥājjī al-Uḥlī's work shows us that the members of the DUMSK apparatus, although they joined the Soviet *nomenklatura*, had ideas about Sufism that differed from those of the Council for Religious Cults (SDRK/SDR), who guided their DUMSK work on behalf of the Soviet government. In other words, the members of DUMSK under pressure and on the request of the Council for Religious Cults had to publish the *fatwās* against Sufism. However, at the same time, the members of DUMSK were Sufis themselves and therefore they wrote the positive review on ʿAbd al-Ḥafīẓ-ḥājjī's work.

The repeated anti-Sufi *fatwās* of DUMSK can therefore only be interpreted as a result of direct pressure from representatives of SDR in Daghestan. The link to Sufism of DUMSK members also explains why DUMSK *fatwās* did not condemn Sufism as a whole, at least not until 1978, but only condemned the "false

53 ʿAbd al-Ḥafīẓ-ḥājjī al-Uḥlī, *al-Jawāb al-ṣaḥīḥ li-l-akh al-muṣlih*, fols 23b–26b.

shaykhs," leaving open the possibility that "real" shaykhs did exist (though perhaps not in contemporary Daghestan). The critique of shrine veneration in these *fatwās* was partly also shared by Sufis themselves.

These DUMSK critiques of "false" shaykhs and certain Sufi practices that were grounded in Islamic law were therefore not new in Daghestan. Such debates had been central to Daghestani Islamic discourse since before the Bolshevik revolution and continued into the early years of Soviet rule. These nuances, however, were ignored by the SDRK/SDR officers who were unprepared to analyze these Islamic discourses. There were no specialists in the SDRK able and willing to distinguish between specific and general critiques of Sufism.

8 Mufti Gekkiev: The Turn to Radical Anti-Sufism

After 1978, a newly appointed Mufti, Maḥmūd-ḥājjī Gekkiev (1935–2007, Mufti 1978–1989), changed the course of the official policy on Sufism. With Gekkiev, the directorship of the Spiritual Administration of Muslims of the North Caucasus was for the first time given not to a Daghestani but to a representative of another nationality of the region, namely to an ethnic Balkar (from the autonomous republic of Kabardino-Balkariia). Gekkiev was therefore not educated in the Daghestani tradition; he obtained his Islamic education at the official Soviet "Mir-i Arab" madrasa in Bukhara. He had no sympathies for Sufism, and his *fatwās* issued in the 1980s did not only condemn individual aspects of Sufism but were rather directed against Sufism in general.

In one of Gekkiev's later *fatwās* (from 1986) we find the following argument:

> Allah the Almighty teaches the Orthodox Muslims in His Holy Scripture that in their prayers they should address Him directly, and they should not use the mediation of individual persons, even if these are regarded as saintly. (…) Neither during the lifetime of the prophet, nor during the rightly-guided caliphs were there any mystical trends – there was no Sufism, there were no *murīds* [Sufi disciples], and accordingly there were none of their features. This means that when the believer carries out the religious rituals he has to follow only the pillars of the Islamic dogmas, namely the Qur'an and the Sunna. Everything else is a new invention.[54]

---

54 "Fetva Dukhovnogo sobraniia musul'man Severnogo Kavkaza o nesovmestimosti 'Miuridizma' s osnovnymi dogmami islamskogo shariata ot 20 iiunia 1986 g.," pp. 4–5. Copies are in possession of the author.

In another *fatwā* against the veneration of holy sites, Gekkiev notes:

> If you ask [in a prayer] that your problems be resolved in a good way, and if you are convinced that these wishes will be resolved by those who are buried in the *mazārs* (holy places) [where you pray], or by Allah but through their mediation – then this makes you falling away from the true religion, that is, turning to paganism.[55]

Gekkiev avoids Arabic terminology in this Russian-language *fatwā*, but it is clear that he struggles against *tawaṣṣul*, one of the major tenets of Sufism: the mediating role of shaykhs between Allah and the individual believer. His rejection of Sufism as illicit innovation (Ar. *bidʿa*) that results in apostasy and paganism could not be harsher.

Gekkiev did not touch upon the question of *ijtihād* in his *fatwās*, but as far as the question of Sufism is concerned we can safely say that this last North Caucasus Mufti of the Soviet period returned to the ideas of the more radical reformists who rejected Sufism in its entirety. The Soviets finally had a Mufti whose Salafi views corresponded to the crude anti-Sufi propaganda of their social scientists; and while after the end of the USSR the Muftiate returned into the hands of Sufis, the condemnation of Sufism continued, now by "unofficial" Salafis like the well-known Muḥammad Bagauddin from Sasitl' (b. 1946).

Gekkiev's policy also included a change of staff of DUMSK; he replaced persons with a local educational background by Daghestanis who had, just like himself, studied at the "Mir-i Arab" madrasa. During the ten years that Gekkiev remained in office, DUMSK more clearly represented the interests of the Soviet government than those of the Muslim believers.[56] This resulted in the Muftiate's loss of authority among the population already by the mid-1980s; and Gekkiev's common North Caucasus Spiritual Administration eventually fell apart into "national" units in 1989, that is, two years before the dissolution of the USSR.

---

55 "Fetva Dukhovnogo sobraniia musul'man Severnogo Kavkaza o nesovmestimosti 'Miuridizma' s osnovnymi dogmami islamskogo shariata ot 20 iiunia 1986 g.," p. 6.

56 Interviews with some persons who served as imams in Daghestani mosques in the 1980s, or had relations to DUMSK: Murtazali Iakupov (b. 1954); Il'ias-hajji Il'iasov (1947–2012), Ali-hajji Umarov (b. 1956) (June–July, 2011).

9 Conclusion

These cases demonstrate that Islam in Daghestan defied easy binary oppositions. Sufism was divided into various brotherhoods whose representatives attacked and defied each other. The reformists were united in their advocacy for educational reform but split over issues of *ijtihād* and *taqlīd*, and in their critique of Sufism. The Soviets first promoted the reformists (including the more radicals like Kaiaev) to Soviet schools but then killed or exiled them (but not all, since Kaiaev's disciple Saidov continued his career at the Soviet Institute of History, Language and Literature). After the massive repression of Islam and its representatives, but still under Stalin, the state set up an Islamic administration – DUMSK – that drew on the very social groups whom the Soviet organs had so cruelly decimated. Its *fatwās* from the early 1950s through the 1980s used Islamic sources to support Soviet agendas. Equally dysfunctional is the distinction between "official" and "unofficial" Islam set up by DUMSK: "officials" could produce very "non-official" (namely, positive) interpretations of Sufism in their closed circle while accommodating state demand for anti-Sufi propaganda in their public *fatwās*. Yet, such behaviour did not make them "oppositional" or "illegal" – and even the anti-Sufi *fatwās* are after all not what the Soviet organs might have seen in them. Until 1978 those who worked in the Soviet DUMSK, and those against whom they had to produce *fatwās*, all originated from the same educational system of madrasas of the early Soviet period. Their personal relations continued to cross the artificial lines created by the Soviets. What we observe today in Daghestan is no less complex.

Acknowledgments

I am grateful to Dr. Masha Kirasirova (New York University Abu Dhabi), Prof. Michael Kemper (Amsterdam University) and Dr. Vladimir Bobrovnikov (Instutute of Oriental Studies, Moscow) who helped me with translation and made important suggestions and corrections to a previous draft.

Bibliography

Sources

ʿAbd al-Ḥafīẓ al-Uḥlī. al-Jawāb al-ṣaḥīḥ li'l-akh al-muṣlih. Ms., fol. 12. From the collection of Abduragim Abdurakhmanov, Nizhnii Dzhengutai.

ʿAbd al-Wahhāb Tāj al-Dīn al-Subkī. *Jamʿ al-jawāmiʿ fī usūl al-fiqh*. Beirut: Dār al-kutub al-ʿilmiyya, 2003.

Abū Sufyān ibn Akay. "Al-Tashayyukh fi-l-sharīʿa." *Bayān al-ḥaqāʾiq*, 1925, no. 1, 11–12.

Abū Sufyān ibn Akay, *Wasīlat al-najāt*. Temir-Khan Shura: Mavraev, 1908.

ʿAlī ibn ʿAbd al-Ḥamīd al-Ghumūqī. *Risāla fi'l-taqlīd wa-jawāz al-talfīq*. Ms Institut Istorii, Arkheologii i etnografii Dagestanskogo nauchnogo tsentra RAN (IIAE), fond M.-S. Saidov, op. 1, no. 37, fols. 101a–106b.

ʿAlī ibn ʿAbd al-Ḥamīd al-Ghumūqī. *Ṭalāq*. Ms. IIAE, fond M.-S. Saidov, op. 1, no. 50.

Arabic-language letter Muḥammad-Saiid Saidov to Masʿūd al-Muhūkhī, 29 March 1924, IIAE, fond M.-S. Saidov, op. 5, no. 30.

"Fetva Dukhovnogo sobraniia musul'man Severnogo Kavkaza o nesovmestimosti 'Miuridizma' s osnovnymi dogmami islamskogo shariata ot 20 iiunia 1986 g." Copies are in possession of the author.

Ghazanaw al-Gubdānī. *Risāla fī radd ʿalā risāla ʿAlī al-Ghumūqī*. IIAE, fond M.-S. Saidov, op. 1, no. 37, fols 107b–111b.

Ḥasan ibn Muḥammad Ḥilmī al-Qahī. *Tanbīh al-sālikīn ilā ghurūr al-mutashayyikhīn*, ed. ʿAbd al-Qādir ʿAṭā al-Bakrī. Damascus: Dār al-Nuʿmān li-l-ʿulūm, 1996.

Jamāl al-Dīn al-Afghānī. *Radd ʿala-l-dahriyyin*. IIAE, fond M.-S. Saidov, op. 1, no. 90b, fols 95a–132a.

Jamāl al-Dīn al-Gharabudāghī. *Tarīkh Qawqāz wa qarya Gharabudaghkent*. Ms. IIAE, fond 1, opis' 1, delo 414.

Masʿūd ibn Muḥammad al-Muhūkhī. *Kharq al-asdād ʿan abwāb al-ijtihād*. Ms., 63 fols.

Masʿūd ibn Muḥammad al-Muhūkhī. "Nahnu wa'l-ʿulūm al-ʿasriyya." *Bayān al-ḥaqāʾiq*, 1926, no. 5, 2–3.

Muḥammad al-Yaʿsūbī al-ʿAsawī. *Ajwibat al-ʿAsalī al-Yaʿsūbī ʿalā turahāt al-Wahhābī al-Harakānī*. Ms (copied 12 Dhū'l-Ḥijja 1381 /17 May 1962), 35 fols. From the private collection of Shamsuddin Magomedov (b.1983), village of Datuna.

Nadhīr al-Durgilī. *al-Ijtihād wa-l-taqlīd*. Ms IIAE, fond M.-S. Saidov, op. 1, no. 35, fols 1a–29b.

Nadhīr al-Durgilī. *al-Taʿlīq al-ḥamīd ʿalā'l-qawl al-sadīd*. IIAE, fond M.-S. Saidov, op. 1, no. 35, fols 68a–103b.

"Perepiska s partiinymi organami, rai(gorispolkomami) i drugimi mestnymi organizatsiami po voprosam religioznykh kul'tov za 1958–1959 gg." Tsentral'nyi Gosudarstvennyi Arkhiv Respubliki Dagestan (TsGA RD), fond r-1234, opis'4, delo 12.

"Resheniia, prokazy, protokoly soveta po delam religii pri SM DASSR za 1966 g." TsGA RD, fond r-1234, op. 4, delo 35.

Sayf Allāh al-Nitsubkrī. *Maktūbāt Khālid Sayf Allāh ilā fuqarāʾ ahl Allāh*, ed. ʿAbd al-Qādir ʿAṭā al-Bakrī. Damascus: Dār al-Nuʿmān li-l-ʿulūm, 1998.

Shimali Qavqaz muslimanlarï dini idarasïnnan ʿMurajaʿat-nameʾ ["Address of the North Caucasus Muslim Administration," in the Kumyk language, lithographical print]. Buinaksk, 1953.

Shuʿayb ibn Idrīs al-Bāginī. *Ṭabaqāt al-khwājagān al-naqshbandiyya wa-sādāt al-mashā'ikh al-khālidiyya al-maḥmūdiyya*, ed. ʿAbd al-Qādir ʿAṭā al-Bakrī. Damascus: Dār al-Nuʿmān li'l-ʿulūm, 1996.

"Tsirkuliar Soveta Ministrov DASSR predsedateliam raiispolkomov Karabudakhkentskogo, Buinakskogo, Sergokalinskogo, Kakhibskogo raionov ot 25 dekabria 1958 g." TsGA RD, fond r-1234, op. 4, delo 16.

"Vystuplenie muftiia musul'man Severnogo Kavkaza o 'ziiaratakh'." TsGA RD, fond r-1234, op. 4, delo 35.

Yūsuf al-Jungūtī. *al-Qawl al-sadid fī ḥasm māddat al-ijtihād wa wujūb al-taqlīd*. IIAE, fond M.-S. Saidov, op. 1, no. 35, fols 32a–103b.

"Zhaloby i otkloneniia khodataistva ob otkrytii molitvennykh domov veruiushchikh musul'man za 1953–1957 gg." TsGA RD, fond r-1234, op. 4, delo 7.

Literature

Abu Suf''ian Akaev: Epokha, zhizn', deiatel'nost', ed. Gasan Orazaev. Makhachkala: Dagestanskoe knizhnoe izdatel'stvo, 2012.

Arapov, Dmitrii Iu. *Islam i sovetskoe gosudarstvo (1944–1990): Sbornik dokumentov*, vol. 3 (Moscow: Mardzhani, 2011).

Bennigsen, Alexandre, and S. Enders Wimbush. *Mystics and Commissars: Sufism in the Soviet Union*. Berkeley/Los Angeles: University of California Press, 1985.

Bobrovnikov, Vladimir O. "Abu Muslim." *Islam na territorii byvshei Rossiiskoi imperii: entsiklopedicheskii slovar'*, vol. 1, ed. by Stanislav M. Prozorov (Moscow: Vostochnaia literatura, 2006), 15–19.

Calder, N. "Taḳlīd." *The Encyclopaedia of Islam*, New Edition, ed. P.J. Bearman *et al.*, vol. 10 (Leiden–London, 1986), 137–138.

al-Durgilī, Nadhīr. *Die Islamgelehrten Daghestans und ihre arabischen Werke. Naḏīr ad-Durgilīs (st. 1935) Nuzhat al-adhān fī tarāǧim ʿulamā' Dāġistān*, ed. and transl. Michael Kemper and Amri R. Šixsaidov. Berlin: Klaus Schwarz, 2004; *Muslim Culture in Russia and Central Asia*, vol. 4.

Kemper, Michael. "The Daghestani Legal Discourse on the Imamate." *Central Asian Survey*, 21/3 (2002), 161–174.

Kemper, Michael. "Khalidiyya Networks in Dagestan and the Question of Jihad." *Die Welt des Islams*, 42/1 (2002), 41–71.

Kemper, Michael, and Vladimir Bobrovnikov. "Miuridizm." *Islam na territorii byvshei Rossiiskoi imperii: entsiklopedicheskii slovar'*, ed. Stanislav M. Prozorov, fascicle 5 (Moscow: Vostochnaia literatura, 2012), 98–99.

Kemper, Michael, and Shamil Shikhaliev. "Administrative Islam: Two Soviet Fatwas from the North Caucasus." In *Islamic Authority and the Russian Language: Studies on Texts from European Russia, the North Caucasus and West Siberia*, ed. Alfrid K. Bustanov and Michael Kemper (Amsterdam: Pegasus, 2012), 55–102.

Kemper, Michael, and Shamil Shikhaliev. "Islam and Political Violence in Post-Soviet Daghestan: Discursive Strategies of the Sufi Masters." In *Constellations of the Caucasus: Empires. Peoples and Faiths*, ed. Michael Reynolds and Hirotake Maeda (*Interdisciplinary Journal of Middle Eastern Studies*, 17 [2016]), 117–154.

Kemper, Michael, and Shamil Shikhaliev. "Qadimism and Jadidism in Twentieth-Century Daghestan." *Asiatische Studien – Études Asiatiques*, 69/3 (2015), 593–624.

Navruzov, Amir R. "Baian al-khaka'ik – pechatnyi organ uchenykh-arabistov Dagestana pervoi treti XX veka." *Pax Islamica*, 2011, no. 2, 18–27.

Navruzov, Amir R. *"Dzharidat Dagistan" – araboiazychnaia gazeta kavkazskikh dzhadidov*. Moscow: Mardzhani, 2012.

Orazaev, Gasan M.-R. *Istoriia Kavkaza i seleniia Karabudakhkent Dzhamalutdina-khadzhi Karabudakhkentskogo*. Makhachkala, 2001.

Orazaev, Gasan M.-R. "Osnovnye vekhi v zhizni i tvorchestve Abusuf"iana Akaeva." In *Literaturnoe i nauchnoe nasledie Abusuf"iana Akaeva*, ed. by G.M.-R. Orazaev (Makhachkala, 1992), 106–116.

Ro'i, Yaacov. *Islam in the Soviet Union: From the Second World War to Gorbachev*. London: Hurst, 2000.

Schacht, J. "Idjtihād." *The Encyclopaedia of Islam*, New Edition, ed. P.J. Bearman *et al.*, vol. 3 (Leiden–London, 1986), 1026–1027.

Shikhaliev, Shamil Sh. "Dagestanskaia sufiiskaia literatura 19–20 veka." In *Dukhovnaia literatura: aspekty izucheniia*, ed. M.A. Guseinov (Makhachkala: IIaLI, 2011), 299–324.

Shikhaliev, Shamil Sh. "'Al-Dzhavab as-salikh li-l-akh al-muslikh' 'Abd al-Khafiz Okhlinskogo." In *Dagestan i musul'manskii Vostok: Sbornik statei*, ed. Alikber K. Alikberov and Vladimir O. Bobrovnikov (Moscow: Mardzhani, 2010), 324–340.

Shikhaliev, Shamil. "Musul'manskoe reformatorstvo v Dagestane (1900–1930)." In *Gosudarstvo, religiia, tserkov' v Rossii i za rubezhom* (Moskow: RANKHiGS, 2017), 134–169.

Shikhaliev, Shamil' Sh. "Saipulla-kadi." *Islam na territorii byvshei Rossiiskoi imperii*, ed. Stanislav M. Prozorov, fascicle 4 (Moscow: Vostochnaia literatura, 2003), 72–73.

Shikhaliev, Shamil. "Sufi Practices and Muslim Identities in Naqshibandi and Shadhili Lodges in Northern Daghestan." In *Islam and Sufism in Daghestan*, ed. Moshe Gammer (Helsinki, 2009), 43–56.

Shikhaliev, Shamil. "Sufiiskii sheikh segodnia." *Ètnograficheskoe obozrenie*, 2006, No. 2, 24–34.

Tell the Mufti

Looking for Spiritual Guidance in Soviet Uzbekistan (1960s–1980s)

Paolo Sartori and Bakhtiyar Babajanov

1 Introduction[1]

Who embodied religious authority in Central Asia after the Second World War, and how did Muslims regard such figures of authority? This is a major question in the history of Islam in Soviet Central Asia and one that hitherto has been left mostly unaddressed.

Historians of Central Asia noted long ago that the establishment of the Spiritual Board of the Muslims of Central Asia and Kazakhstan (known by the Russian acronym SADUM) represented a substantial change in the history of Islamic authority. Established in 1943 in Tashkent to normalize Muslim-state relations, to stir a feeling of patriotism among the Central Asian population,[2] and to mobilize indigenous forces in the war against Nazi Germany,[3] SADUM was a centralized, hierarchical, and heavily bureaucratized institution designed to control religious personnel across the region: it was headed by a mufti who was flanked by a cohort of scholars who assisted him in various tasks ranging from the writing of fatwas to collecting sensitive data for the Council for the Affairs of Religious Cults (see below). The institution had national branches in each of the five Central Asian Soviet republics, Kazakhstan, Kyrgyzstan, Tajikistan, Turkmenistan, Uzbekistan, as well as in the Karakalpak Autonomous SSR. Each national branch was termed a *qāżīyat* after its main representative, i.e., a *qāżī* (Cyr., *qozi*). At the regional level the Tashkent office

1 This chapter was written within the framework of the project "Seeing Like an Archive: Documents and Forms of Governance in Islamic Central Asia" (START – Y704) and the Thematic Platform "Religion, Society and State in Eurasia: Past and Present." We are grateful to the FWF (Austrian Science Fund) and the Austrian Academy of Sciences for financial support. Thanks are due also to Abdulaziz Mansur (Deputy Chief Mufti of Uzbekistan) and Sharifjon Islamov (Institute of Oriental Studies of the Academy of Sciences of Uzbekistan) for facilitating access to records in Tashkent.

2 Eren Tasar, "Islamically Informed Soviet Patriotism in postwar Kyrgyzstan," *Cahiers du Monde Russe*, 52/2–3 (2011), pp. 387–404.

3 Jeff Eden, "A Soviet Jihad against Hitler: Ishan Babakhan calls Central Asian Muslims to War." *Journal of the Economic and Social History of the Orient*, 59/1–2 (2016), pp. 237–264.

 | DOI:10.1163/9789004527096_013

of SADUM was at the center of a web of officially-registered mosques, shrines, and two madrasas,[4] which were administered by the office of the *muḥtasib*.[5]

SADUM also served to establish a liaison between Central Asian Muslims and the Council for the Affairs of Religious Cults (CARC), whose main objective was to spread anti-religious propaganda and eradicate all forms of religiosity, which had "survived" the Bolshevik Revolution, the Cultural Revolution (1928–32) and the Great Terror (1937–38). Seen from the state's perspective, SADUM was a tool in the hands of the Communist Party to make Islam subject to the episteme of the secular state.

A recent study by Eren Tasar has looked insightfully at the ways in which SADUM's *ʿulamā* played a meaningful role as cultural brokers. Their mediating activity was two-pronged: on the one hand they helped the Soviet state reach into what was regarded by Central Asians as an "Islamic sphere," and on the other they provided Muslims with a reliable and authoritative interlocutor when seeking spiritual guidance. More specifically, by excavating the archives of the national branches of SADUM and reading the historical detritus left

4 We say here *officially* because in Central Asia after the Second World War there also existed mosques and shrines that were not registered and that therefore operated illegally or semi-illegally, though this does not mean that the state did not know about their existence. The works of Ya'acov Ro'i and Eren Tasar provide a wealth of archival material showing that especially in the 1950s, the state attempted to register such institutions in order to target Islamic practice more effectively. See Ya'acov Ro'i, *Islam in the Soviet Union: from the Second World War to Gorbachev* (London: Hurst and Company, 2000); Eren Tasar, *Soviet and Muslim: The Institutionalization of Islam in Central Asia, 1943–1991* (Oxford: Oxford University Press, 2017), especially chap. 2.

5 While SADUM employed a seemingly *traditional* Islamic terminology for administrative purposes (*muftī, qāżī, muḥtasib*), a terminology projecting an idea of indigeneity and institutional continuity with the pre-Soviet (and pre-colonial) past, it is equally clear that most such terms underwent major semantic change and began to denote *new* institutions. Soviet *qāżīs* did not adjudicate disputes, nor did their offices issue deeds in respect of the generic conventions of Islamic law. They could and did of course collaborate with the mufti in the crafting of a fatwa. However, Soviet fatwas departed considerably from established compositional practices that are known from earlier periods. We shall come back to this aspect of SADUM in the course of this chapter. The term *muḥtasib* too had little to do with the way in which it was used in the past. Usually deployed to denote a market superintendent, the word *muḥtasib* acquired in the Soviet period a different meaning, that of regional representative, devoid, that is, of specific legalistic nuances. When referring to Islamic terminology in the context of the Soviet Islamic sphere, we have here privileged transliteration from the Arabic-script, for SADUM's members used to craft records (including their private correspondence) either according to the orthographic rules of Chaghatay/Eastern Turkic (*turkī*) or the reformed Arabic alphabet of the 1920s. The documentation we offer here in translation was written in Cyrillic Uzbek, however, and when transliterating its most significant terms, we follow the conventions first introduced in Uzbekistan in the 1990s.

behind by such an institution, Tasar's work opens new vistas on how *ʿulamā* representing the Board navigated between "hard-liners" and "moderates," the USSR's changing policies toward the Middle East and Muslim countries, and the 'input' coming from Soviet Central Asian citizens in general.

Little has been done so far, however, to map the contours of SADUM's authority among Central Asian Muslims. The first generation of *ʿulamā* working for the Spiritual Board most certainly enjoyed recognized authority over local communities and across devotional and initiatic networks. Born between the end of the 19th- and the turn of the 20th century, most of the *ʿulamā* holding official positions immediately after the Second World War embodied a type of Islamic scholarship and specialized knowledge that in the 1940s and 1950s began to be regarded as *uncommon*. In the interwar period the Soviet state took various measures to do away with key traditional institutions, and these measures foregrounded Islamic education. Not only were institutes of Islamic higher learning (*madrasas*) shut down, but also charitable endowments (sing. *waqf*, pl. *awqāf*), which had financed institutes of Islamic learning (including Sufi convents, *khānaqāhs*), became targets of reforms and were ultimately disbanded in 1928.[6] These measures struck a lethal blow to the corporate dimension of Islamic scholarship by curtailing the resources needed for its transmission and perpetuation. In addition, while at the beginning of the 1920s local *ʿulamā* could still hope for cooptation by the state, starting from 1929 Muslim scholars began to suffer from marginalization. The situation worsened at the end of the 1930s when, during the Red Terror, a sizable (though unknown to this day) number of scholars was exiled and sentenced either to forced labor or to death;[7] those who could elude the surveillance of the Soviet secret police (NKVD) simply went abroad, often to Afghanistan, China, Egypt, India, or Saudi Arabia. Given the challenges that they had endured in the interwar period and during the Second World War, the authority of *ʿulamā* who survived the 1940s, including those who entered SADUM, did not diminish in the eyes of Central Asians, even though Muslim scholars operated under the rule of a government advocating for the eradication of religion.

6 Niccolò Pianciola and Paolo Sartori, "Waqf in Turkestan: The Colonial Legacy and the Fate of an Islamic Institution in Early Soviet Central Asia, 1917–1924," *Central Asian Survey*, 26/4 (2007), pp. 475–498; Beatrice Penati, "On the Local Origins of the Soviet Attack on 'Religious' Waqf in the Uzbek SSR (1927)," *Acta Slavica Iaponica*, 36 (2015), pp. 39–72.

7 Shoshana Keller argues that in Uzbekistan alone "more than 14,000 Muslim clergy were arrested, killed, exiled from their homes, or driven out of the USSR" during the Cultural Revolution and Great Terror; see her *To Moscow, Not Mecca: The Soviet Campaign against Islam in Central Asia, 1917–1941* (Westport, Connecticut: Praeger, 2001), p. 241.

2 Challenging SADUM's Authority

While the authority of the *ʿulamā* representing SADUM did not wane, it did not remain unchallenged. And there were different forces eroding the authority of SADUM's scholarship. The first one was CARC, which often pushed SADUM to take positions vis-á-vis Islamic religiosity in Central Asia, and which made SADUM unpopular before "Muslim believers."[8] CARC pushed SADUM to issue fatwas that supported Soviet state-sanctioned forms of conduct among Muslims. Such fatwas were designed to push Central Asians to embrace an ostensibly modern life-style and submit to a secular notion of "religion," which was premised on the understanding that the state alone could define the space for Islam. In practice, fatwas reflected the policy of the state to regulate ritual observance and confine it either to the mosque or to gatherings requiring permission from authorities.[9] Such fatwas necessarily aimed at changing most Muslims' behavioral patterns in public. They therefore targeted believers' garb, which amounted, for example, to forbidding women in 1947 to wear the headscarf covering their face (Uzb. *paranji*).[10] More generally, they

8 We employ the terms "Muslim believers" to refer to Central Asians and Soviet citizens of various walks of life, who either manifested or claimed attachment to Islamically-informed religiosity. Far from projecting Muslimness where none in fact existed, such a label translates the Uzbek expression *mu"min musulmonlar*, which, as it transpires from our documentation, was often used in local parlance among Muslim communities in Uzbekistan after the Second World War.

9 Z. Babakhanov, "Imam-khatibam i chlenam ispol'nitelnogo organa mechetei," undated, TsGARUz, f. R-2456, op. 1, d. 540, ll. 70–73.

10 Tasar, *Soviet and Muslim*, pp. 149–151. See also I. Sattiev, "Dopol'nitelnoe raz'iasnienie o noshenii parandzhi," TsGARUz, f. R-2456, op. 1, d. 477, ll. 140–141. Sattiev, who at that time was deputy of the mufti Ishan Boboxonov, argued that the Qur'an and the Sunna do not say anything at all about the need for women to cover their face and that the use of the *paranji* reflected merely a customary practice among the peoples of Central Asia. In addition, he claimed that the fatwa was received enthusiastically by women and that many of them "began to be involved in public life and embraced contemporary science and culture" (*èta fetva byla pravil'no vospriniata mnogimi veruiushchimi, blagodaria chemu bol'shinstvo zhenshchin s udovol'stviem navsegda brosili parandzhu. Mnogie iz nykh aktivno prikliuchilis' v obshchestvennuiu zhizn' i za ovladenie sovremennoi naukoi i kul'tury.*). Another SADUM member who actively initiated Soviet forms of women's emancipation was Yusufxon Shokirov, son of Olimxon To'ra Shokirxo'jayev, who served as *qāżī* of the Kyrgyz SSR (see below, note 47). He prepared for publication an article entitled "Problems of Equality of Women and Their Resolution," in which he argued that the status of women in Islam is misrepresented by both conservative theologians and atheists. His argumentation is clearly influenced by Egyptian reformers of the late 19th and early 20th centuries. Yusufkhan Shakirov got acquainted with their works while studying at al-Azhar University (1949–1953). See Bakhtiyar M. Babadjanov, "'Paradise at the Feet of

attempted to constrain the space for expressions of devotion, spirituality, and Islamically-informed ethics. For this reason we encounter fatwas allowing for the breaking of the fast during Ramadan[11] or avoiding praying altogether for working purposes or fatwas that prohibited communal prayers and rituals outside of the mosque.[12] Needless to say, such fatwas were disregarded by many, treated on a par with Party resolutions, i.e., the bureaucratic output of Soviet policies of secularization designed to undermine Muslim religiosity.[13] It does not take a great leap of imagination to suppose that many Central Asians must have perceived SADUM as yet another institution conducting activities that were entangled with state policies of forced secularization.

It is important, however, to clarify that during the nearly five decades of its existence, SADUM cultivated an ambivalent relationship toward CARC and its various representatives. At times SADUM's records seem to suggest that state *ʿulamā* resented the pressure exerted by CARC to issue certain fatwas. One can equally observe a purposeful alliance between CARC and SADUM to attack religious practices (which we may term "Sufi") and which enjoyed great popularity in the region.[14] We shall come back to this over the course of the chapter.

Second, starting from the second half of the 1970s members of a younger generation of Muslim scholars (usually referred to in the sources as "young mullahs," Uzb. *mullo-bachchalar*) began to challenge specific doctrinal positions as well as the political quietism represented typically by older scholars (including members of SADUM). They applied various instruments to distinguish themselves, to gain the attention of local Muslim constituencies, and thus to lay their claim on spiritual authority. "Young mullahs" disputed the Islamic licitness of ritual practices such as the visitation of shrines, cast as a manifestation of "polytheism" (Uzb. *shirk*), and they did so by claiming that such practices represented an "unlawful innovation" (Uzb. *bidʿat*). Their critique was predicated upon the assumption that Ḥanafīsm, the school of law which for

---

Mothers and Women:' Soviet and Post-Soviet Discourses of the Emancipation Forms of Muslim Women," in *Islam and Gender in Central Asia: Soviet Modernization and Today's Society*, ed. Ch. Obiya (Kyoto: CIAS, Kyoto University, 2016), pp. 19–33.

11 Ziautdin Khan ibn Ishan Babakhan, "O poste Ramadana," TsGARUz, f. R-2456, op. 1, d. 637, ll. 67–68.

12 These are just a few examples taken from what is a very substantial body of fatwas issued by SADUM. The documentation which we offer here in translation reflects the outreach and reactions to many such fatwas designed to regulate and constrain ritual practices in public.

13 On this point, see below.

14 See Paolo Sartori and Bakhtiyar Babajanov, "Being Soviet, Muslim, Modernist, and Fundamentalist in 1950s Central Asia," *Journal of the Economic and Social History of the Orient*, 62/1 (2019), pp. 108–163 and Tasar, *Soviet and Muslim*, chap. 4.

centuries had been dominant in Central Asia, was a superfluous accessory to the Qur'ān and the Sunna and that, as such, the ideological edifice of Ḥanafīsm required to be dismantled. They therefore concentrated their efforts on eroding the notion of "customs" (Uzb. *urf-odat*), which was central to the mainstream Uzbek discourse on Ḥanafī identity. In addition, they became vocal opponents of political disengagement, openly criticized Muslim scholars who, willingly or not, cooperated with the state, and went so far as to theorize the need to wage a holy war (Uzb. *jihod/ghazavot*) against the USSR. In addition, they embodied a new ritual conduct at the mosque, and did so ostentatiously, especially during the Friday prayer. For example, they urged mosque-goers to keep their arms in front of the chest when standing during the prayer rather than letting them fall by their sides, or to answer the imam's prayer with a loud "amen" (Uzb. *omin*) rather than with a whisper (see infra). Their behavior gained them the label of "Wahhabis" (Uzb. *Vahhobiylar*), a term which in local parlance in fact meant different things, ranging from "ignorant innovators" to "fundamentalist" and "anti-mazhab."[15] Though they always occupied a minority position in Central Asia, the anti-Ḥanafī critique of the so-called "young mullahs" contributed to the deterioration of SADUM's authority.

Third, there existed in Central Asia after the Second World War figures of Islamic authority whom believers perceived as *alternative* to the staff of SADUM based in Tashkent and its representatives on the spot, i.e., the imams and the members of national *qāżīyat*s as well as regional *muḥtasibat*s. Such alternative figures of authority were individuals who exemplified an understanding of Islam far removed *ideologically* from the sermons and the fatwas issued by SADUM. Indeed, as we sift through unpublished Soviet ethnography,[16] which

15 Bakhtiyar Babadjanov, "Debates over Islam in Contemporary Uzbekistan: A View from Within," in *Devout Societies vs. Impious States? Transmitting Islamic Learning in Russia, Central Asia and China, through the Twentieth Century* (Proceedings of an International Colloquium Held in the Carré des Sciences, French Ministry of Research, Paris, November 12–13, 2001), ed. Stéphane Dudoignon (Berlin: Schwarz, 2004), pp. 39–60; Bakhtiyar M. Babadzhanov, Ashirbek K. Muminov, and A. von Kügelgen (eds.), *Disputy musul'manskikh religioznykh avtoritetov v Tsentral'noi Azii v XX veke* (*Almaty*: Daik Press, 2007); Stéphane A. Dudoignon and Sayyid Ahmad Qalandar, "'They Were All from the Country:' The Revival and Politicisation of Islam in the Lower Wakhsh River Valley of the Tajik SSR (1947–1997)," in *Allah's Kolkhozes: Migration, De-Stalinisation, Privatisation and the New Muslim Congregations in the Soviet Realm (1950s–2000s)*, ed. Stéphane A. Dudoignon and Christian Noack (Berlin: Klaus Schwarz, 2014), pp. 47–122, especially pp. 52–53.

16 Soviet ethnography represents a genre of historical documentation of manifestations of Muslim religiosity in Soviet Central Asia, which has remained to this day surprisingly and

illuminates aspects of communal life mostly in rural areas of Central Asia, we can observe manifestations of a distinct kind of religiosity, closer to the sensibilities of demographics with vested interests in the preservation of certain Islamically-informed traditions, other than what was propounded by board members. Embodiments of this type of Muslim religiosity could be found across the entire social and institutional gamut of rural Central Asia. Alternative figures could be individuals such as shrine-keepers (*shaykhs/ishans*), i.e., people who were "registered" as employees of SADUM and thus operated legally.[17] But there were also individuals whose religious services were not sanctioned by SADUM and thus operated illegally and nevertheless enjoyed authority within local constituencies. This was a natural outcome of SADUM's championing the process of centralization and control of state-approved Muslim religious personnel.

This group of unregistered religious authorities expanded far and wide. It included, for example, mullahs whose mosques had been taken over by SADUM, which then imposed members of its own network upon the mosques.[18] But the group also included scholars who never sought the sanction of the state, "fell silent," and found a job in or moved across collective farms,[19] for example, a fact that did not prevent them from offering religious services and, at times, manifesting their critique against SADUM. One is also reminded of "female

undeservedly underused. For examples of what can be achieved by mining this genre, see Devin DeWeese, "Shamanization in Central Asia," *Journal of the Economic and Social History of the Orient*, 57/2 (2014), pp. 326–363, and Paolo Sartori, "Of Saints, Shrines, and Tractors: Untangling the Meaning of Islam in Soviet Central Asia," *Journal of Islamic Studies*, 30/3 (2019), pp. 367–405.

17 The growing gap between SADUM, which developed a vision of religiosity premised on scripturalism and puritanism (as reflected by fatwas and imams' sermons), and the system of religious meaning steeped in Sufi practices and hagiographic traditions (which we find alive and well mostly, though not exclusively, in rural areas) is discussed in Sartori, "Of Saints, Shrines, and Tractors: : Untangling the Meaning of Islam in Soviet Central Asia," pp. 389–392, and in Stéphane A. Dudoignon, "Holy Virgin Lands? Demographic Engineering, Heritage Management and the Sanctification of Territories in ex-Soviet Central Asia, since WWII," in *From the Khan's Oven: Studies in the History of Central Asian Religions in Honor of Devin DeWeese*, ed. Eren Tasar, Allen J. Frank and Jeff Eden (Leiden: Brill, 2022), pp. 358–408.

18 This point has been eloquently articulated in Eren Tasar, "Sufism on the Soviet Stage: Holy People and Places in Central Asia's Socio-Political Landscape After World War II," in *Sufism in Central Asia: New Perspectives on Sufi Traditions, 15th–21st Centuries*, ed. Devin DeWeese and Jo-Ann Gross (Leiden: Brill, 2018), pp. 267–270.

19 S.A. Dudoignon, "From Revival to Mutation: The Religious Personnel of Islam in Tajikistan, from de-Stalinization to Independence (1955–91)," *Central Asian Survey*, 30 (2011), pp. 53–80.

mullahs" (Uzb. *otin-oy/otincha*),[20] healers (Uzb. *parixon/porxon*),[21] and other individuals who supplied religious services to communities of believers in specific circumstances. Such individuals carried out, for example, funerary rituals called *sadr*, prayers for rain, the practice of *fidya*, etc. We shall come to such figures during the course of this chapter.

A fourth and final force that did much to put SADUM's authority into crisis was Islamic scripturalism, and it came directly from the ranks of the Spiritual Board. Scripturalist and explicit fundamentalist tendencies manifested themselves among state-sanctioned *ʿulamā* at least from the early 1950s and became even more prominent in the following decades. In a recent study we showed that SADUM included scholars who prior to the October Revolution propounded a reformist vision of Islam, which was premised upon the eradication of "customary practices" (and especially the whole set of rituals attached to the cult of saints and shrine visitation) from Muslims' religious practice. It is now plain that the fatwas designed to make shrine visitation in Central Asia illegal from the point of view of *sharīʿa* reflected an initiative of SADUM's *ʿulamā* and, more specifically, it can be attributed to the *qāżī* of the Kyrgyz SSR, Olimxon To'ra Shokirxo'jayev (Rus. Alim-Khan Tiura Shakirkhodzhaev) (1881–1966).[22] In issuing such fatwas, SADUM in fact instrumentalized CARC's concern about manifestations of devotion to the saints performed at the main shrines in the region. If regarded from this point of view, SADUM's fatwas against shrine visitation, and its scripturalism in general, represent a point of contact first with CARC and secondly with the so-called "young mullahs" we discussed above, who first appeared in the late 1970s.[23]

20 Sigrid Kleinmichel, *Ḫalpa in Choresm (Ḫwārazm) und Ātin Āyi im Ferghanatal. Zur Geschichte des Lesens in Usbekistan im 20. Jahrhundert* (Berlin: Klaus Schwarz, 2000); Annette Krämer, *Geistliche Autorität und islamische Gesellschaft im Wandel: Studien über Frauenälteste (otin und xalfa) im unabhängigen Usbekistan* (Berlin: Klaus Schwarz, 2002).

21 See Iu. V. Knorozov, "Mazar Shamun-nabi," *Sovetskaia ètnografiia*, 1949, No. 2, pp. 86–97; Iu.V. Knorozov, "Shamanskii zikr v podzemel'e Mazlumkhan-sulu," *Ètnograficheskoe obozrenie*, 1994, No. 6, pp. 91–96.

22 Sartori and Babajanov, "Being Soviet, Muslim, Modernist, and Fundamentalist in 1950s Central Asia."

23 It should be noted, however, that although it championed an aggressive policy against *specific* religious practices associated with the cult of saints, SADUM did not attempt to disrupt shrine visitation altogether. In fact, SADUM's critique of pilgrims' religious behavior was accompanied by equally assertive measures to appoint its own members to the various posts of shrine keepers. At the same time, SADUM sought to undermine the moral status of individuals who commanded authority over a given shrine community, not only *shaykhs*, that is, but also those who worked as bursars. By claiming that the new appointees would ensure that shrine visitation be performed in accordance with the *sharīʿa*, SADUM effectively attempted to gain control of all the donations to the shrines.

The goal of this chapter is twofold. We want to supply material to illuminate the complex relationship between the various sources of Islamic authority in Central Asia after the Second World War, which we have just reviewed. Our second objective is to exemplify the lucid as well as challenging responses of Soviet Muslims toward SADUM's initiatives to regulate religiosity, especially in the sphere of rituals. We shall do so by introducing here material, which has so far escaped the attention of historians of the region, i.e., missives that Central Asians sent by regular mail to the Spiritual Board, some of which are addressed directly to the mufti. We hope to draw a picture of Central Asian Muslims not as passive recipients of Soviet policies on Islam, but one of active participation in the definition of what Eren Tasar has termed the "Islamic sphere" of Soviet Central Asia.

***Pattalar* – Notes on "Small Pieces of Paper."** In 2015 we came across a collection of records referred to as *pattalar* (Uzb., "small pieces of paper") among the private possessions of Sheikh Abdulaziz Mansur, an Uzbek *ʿālim* who worked at SADUM's Fatwa Department (*Fatvolar bo'limi*) between the years 1982 and 1991 and has served intermittently the Muslim Spiritual Board of Uzbekistan from the demise of the USSR to this day in various capacities.[24] Such letters vary in generic composition ranging from questions of Islamic jurisprudence and issues of ethics to complaints about specific fatwas issued by SADUM and conflicts among various religious groups in Uzbekistan. Interestingly, some of them include answers (Uzb. *javob*), often formulated in Soviet Uzbek bureaucratese and thus in an exceedingly laconic fashion, which the Spiritual Board issued to its appellants. However, most of such missives are left without any answer. We were able to examine approximately one hundred specimens of this compositional "genre" (though one may cast some doubt at our use of the latter term), for we enjoyed only intermittent access to the collection.

At first glance Sheikh Abdulaziz Mansur's collection of *pattalar* looks like a random assemblage of letters awaiting systematization. They are not grouped by thematic subject, nor by chronology, and they are just distributed gracelessly across four folders (Rus. *papka*). In fact, we learned during our first encounter with this documentation that such missives entered SADUM's archives accidentally, and that we must thank Sheikh Abdulaziz Mansur for taking measures to preserve them from destruction in the early 1990s, when

See Sartori, "Of Saints, Shrines, and Tractors: Untangling the Meaning of Islam in Soviet Central Asia," p. 395 and Tasar, *Soviet and Muslim*, pp. 227–240.

24 Haydarkhon Yo'ldoshkho'jaev and Irodakhon Qayumova, *O'zbekiston ulamolari* (Tashkent: Movarrounnahr nashriyoti, 2015), pp. 110–112.

mufti Shaykh Muhammad Sodiq Muhammad Yusuf attempted to dismantle SADUM's documentation.

Though cursory, our acquaintance with these records proved nevertheless sufficient to appreciate their enormous historical significance. The *pattalar* shed light on many aspects of believers' understanding of Islam in post-Stalin Central Asia. More specifically, they illuminate many Uzbeks' dissatisfaction with the narrow, puritanical, and overtly normative approach of Soviet Islamic authorities toward religious practices that were perceived and conceptualized as deep-seated in local systems of signification. Most of the missives addressed to the office of the Soviet mufti from the early 1960s to the 1980s show that a substantial number of Central Asian Muslims openly disputed SADUM's policy of banning rituals such as shrine visitation, acts of collective remembrance, and *zikr* (among many others) by declaring them inadmissible from the point of view of *sharīʿa*. SADUM's most effective instrument to implement such policy was to issue fatwas (Uzb. *fatvo*; Rus. *fetva*), which had little resemblance, however, to the legal opinions issued by muftis prior to Sovietization. Indeed, under the rule of the khans and throughout the tsarist period, the term fatwa designated legal opinions given on a specific point of law. Usually they were produced at the request of a party to a dispute in order to confer additional legal force to a claim during a litigation heard by *qāżīs*. Even though such opinions embodied the authority of the jurists who appended their seals thereupon, they were not binding and therefore they could be ignored at court or by other institutions of recognized legal authority (the royal court and other muftis).[25] In the post-Stalin period, however, the meaning of the term underwent a process of change whereby it came to denote an Islamic legal "ruling" (Uzb. *buyruq*), or at least this is the way in which Uzbeks referred to SADUM's fatwas between the 1960s and the 1980s. This was an important lexical shift and one which indicates that Central Asian Muslims began to regard Soviet muftis' fatwas on a par with the resolutions of the Communist Party. This change in meaning should not come as a surprise, for, as early as the 1940s, CARC itself began to refer to fatwas as *shariatskie ukazy* (Rus. "sharia-based resolutions"),[26] and one should not rule out the possibility that such bureaucratic expression percolated through the meanders of Soviet institutions and eventually informed Central Asians' understanding of the term fatwa.

---

25 Paolo Sartori, *Visions of Justice: Sharīʿa and Cultural Change in Russian Central Asia* (Leiden: Brill, 2016), chap. 5.

26 I. Polianskii (secretary of CARC, Moscow) to Iskanderov (Plenipotentiary of CARC, Tashkent), chap. 5.08.12.1947, Central State Archive of Uzbekistan (Tashkent, henceforth TsGARUz), f. R-2456, op. 1, d. 61, l. 15.

The documentation that we offer here in translation shows that SADUM's fatwas could and did reach communities living in collective farms and in rural areas, thereby projecting their policies upon a substantial portion of the Central Asian population. Indeed, believers were exposed to such policies during Friday sermons, when, by acting effectively as spokespersons of SADUM, imams conveyed to parishes the contents of the fatwas issued in Tashkent. It is striking that, in addressing their concerns for the prohibition of certain rituals, local Muslims requested from the muftis additional explanation. So far removed were the fatwas from local conceptualizations of Islam that we often find that Uzbeks turned to the mufti to ascertain themselves whether what they had heard from imams was indeed true (*shu gap rostmi?/bularni gapi rostmi?*). That there existed an ideological and cultural gap between SADUM and Central Asian Muslims is confirmed by the disappointingly formulaic answers, which we read at the bottom of the *patta*s. The mufti's reactions (or the reactions of the personnel of his office, for that matter) to Muslims' glaring frustration and requests for further clarification proved inadequate. Indeed, it often amounted to dispatching members of the *raikom*, the same imams, or the representatives of neighbourhood communities (*mahalla*) to the localities, to explain once again the contents of the fatwas to local people – the same fatwas that had caused so much distress among believers in the first place. Thus, SADUM's officials often behaved in the same fashion as the *agitprop*.

In the face of the challenges posed by SADUM's policies, our documentation exemplifies the resourcefulness of Soviet subjects in pursuit of Islamic ethical guidance. The *patta*s clearly indicate that Muslims often turned to female mullahs for advice and that such individuals were intimately familiar with Islamic creeds (*ʿaqāʾid*), could cite the scriptures (the Qurʾān and the Sunna), and as such, were regarded as figures embodying knowledge of Islamic ethics and normativity. It is not rare to encounter questions addressed to the mufti in which appellants refer to *otin-oyi*s as figures of Islamic authority who articulated different, indeed alternative views on matters of worship than what was prescribed by SADUM's personnel. In the eyes of Muslims in search of spiritual support, *otin-oyi*s represented individuals who could, if need be, access Islamic book culture. It is important to remind ourselves that in no way did Central Asians consider *otin-oyi*s to be lacking in the kind of specialized knowledge that one might attribute exclusively to the *ʿulamā*.[27]

27 This was noted first by Stéphane A. Dudoignon in his review of "Habiba Fathi, *Femmes d'autorité dans l'Asie centrale contemporaine. Quête des ancêtres et recompositions identitaires dans l'islam postsoviétique*." *Cahiers du Monde russe* 47.4 (2006), pp. 951–957.

When read in this light, the *patta*s supply material to redefine the epistemic contours of Islam in the USSR. Indeed, the small stories enshrined in the missives addressed to the mufti do suggest that the Soviet Union offered not only space for semantic ambiguity,[28] but also space for epistemic diversity in which the definition of notions such as *sharīʿa* and Muslimness (*musulmonchilik*) mattered greatly to the everyday life of communities of Soviet citizens.[29]

In June 2019, we were finally able to secure a copy of a substantial number of such documents, which we had first examined in 2015. At our disposal are records written in Cyrillic, in the Uzbek language. Most of them were authored by elderly people who must have taken advantage of the help of younger relatives. While showing at times traces of regional dialects, our *pattalar* nevertheless reflect more the conventions of modern Uzbek, than the creativity of their authors.

In the following section we provide in translation a selection of ten *pattalar*. We divided them chronologically in three sections to cover the 1960s, 1970s, and 1980s. Our systematization thus follows the periodization offered in Tasar's *Soviet and Muslim*, which views the Khruschev's period as a decade of attack against devotional practices associated with the cult of saints; it regards the 1970s as an epoch of containment of public manifestations of religiosity; and it portrays the 1980s as an era of relaxation marked by the emergence of a new cohort of religious figures (referred to in disparaging terms as "Wahhabis," Uzb. *Vahhobiylar*, "young mullahs," Uzb. *mullo-bachchalar*, and "Wahhabi young mullahs," see below), who openly disputed the authority of Ḥanafī traditionalists. While the last section shows that by the end of the 1980s, in public Muslim perception, SADUM was drifting away from the spiritual needs and religious sensibilities of the constituencies it purported to represent, our material equally illuminates the fact that people began to recognize a similarity between SADUM's puritanical drive and the so-called Wahhabis of the Ferghana Valley. This complicates further the narrative propounded by the last Soviet Mufti and one of the most influential ʿ*ulamā* of independent Uzbekistan, the late Shaykh Muhammad Sodiq Muhammad Yusuf, who claimed that in late Soviet Uzbekistan, Muslim scholars were divided into

---

28 On the notion of "semantic ambiguity" when observing manifestations of Islamic religiosity in late Soviet Central Asia, see Sergei Abashin, "A Prayer for Rain: Practising Being Soviet and Muslim," *Journal of Islamic Studies*, 25/2 (2014), pp. 178–200.

29 The Islamic sphere of Soviet Central Asia has been conceptualised as an episteme in Sartori, "Of Saints, Shrines, and Tractors." For a discussion about the interpretive opportunities opened by such conceptualization, see Eren Tasar, "*Mantra*: A Review Essay on Islam in Soviet Central Asia," *Journal of the Economic and Social History of the Orient*, 63 (2020), pp. 389–433.

three different groups: the Ḥanafī traditionalists, the so-called "young mullahs" ("Wahhabis"), and the state mullahs (members of SADUM).[30] It now transpires from the *pattas* in our possession that when regarded from the perspective of local communities of believers from the Ferghana Valley, in the 1980s the constituency of Uzbek *ʿulamā* at the republican level was split mainly into two. On the one hand, Muslims regarded as "traditionalists" those scholars who preserved the integrity of the Ḥanafī school of law, especially with regard to rituals of worship. On the other, there were scholars, mostly puritanical and fundamentalist in inspiration, who equated such practices with manifestations of polytheism and thus urged believers to abandon them. Our documentation suggests that puritanical sensibilities cut across a wide spectrum of the Uzbek *ʿulamā* in the Soviet period and were embodied both by SADUM members as well as the so-called "young mullahs" ("Wahhabis"); hence the accusation of Wahhabism addressed to the SADUM in one of the *pattas* translated here below.

Manifestations of the doctrinal conflicts among *ʿulamā* leading to such a split (otherwise known as the "Great Schism")[31] were recorded in the Ferghana Valley at the end of the 1970s. The documentation is relatively well known and has been commented upon several times.[32] What requires further reflection and study, however, is the fact that such a split appears to have occurred in fact much earlier in Central Asia, and that it acquired particular social significance once puritanical and fundamentalist sensibilities began to inform SADUM's policies,[33] significance which one can appreciate down to the present.[34]

---

30 Babadjanov, "Debates over Islam in Contemporary Uzbekistan;" Tasar, *Soviet and Muslim*, p. 357.

31 B. Babadjanov and M. Kamilov, "Muhammadjan Hindustani (1892–1989) and the Beginning of the 'Great Schism' among the Muslims of Uzbekistan," in *Islam in Politics in Russia and Central Asia* (*Early Eighteenth to Late Twentieth Centuries*), ed. S.A. Dudoignon and H. Komatsu (London: Kegan Paul, 2001), pp. 195–219.

32 The latest synopsis of such conflicts is Vera Exnerova, "Radical Islam from Below: The Mujaddidiya and Hizb-ut-Tahrir in the Ferghana Valley," in *Islam Society, and Politics in Central Asia*, ed. Pauline Jones (Pittsburgh: Pittsburgh University Press, 2017), pp. 55–76.

33 See our "Being Soviet, Muslim, Modernist, and Fundamentalist in 1950s Central Asia," and Bakhtiyar Babadzhanov and Paolo Sartori, "U istokov sovetskogo diskursa o 'khoroshem islame' sovetskoi Tsentral'noi Azii," *Ab Imperio* 12/3 (2018), pp. 219–255.

34 Johan Rasanayagam, *Islam in Post-Soviet Uzbekistan: The Morality of Experience* (Cambridge: Cambridge University Press, 2011), esp. 144–153; Allen Frank and Jahangir Mamatov, *Uzbek Islamic Debates: Texts, Translations, and Commentary* (Loisdale, C.T: Dunwoody Press, 2006), esp. Abduvoli Qori Mirzoyev's lectures 30 and 55 on polytheism (*shirk*).

Texts in Translation

1960s

Example 1

Bukhara, 1964.
Akmal Qurbonov, barber (*sartarosh*), 69 years.

To the [Spiritual] Board, the muftis.

Question: In our noble Bukhara since time immemorial people perform visitation (*ziyorat*) to the shrine of Bahovuddin Balogardon [Bahāʾ al-Dīn Naqshband] and spend time there during the saint-day festivals (*sayil*),[35] and during the celebration for the end of the Ramadan (*hayit*).[36] For several years now, the imams have been telling us to do away with this customary practice (*bu odatni to'xtatinglar deb*); also all the scholars of the Mir-i Arab [madrasa] are against it.[37] In their Friday sermons they [imams] refer to the fatwas of so and so from the Spiritual Board and read them [to the believers]. We are at a loss because they said that pilgrimage is forbidden (*harom*), alms-giving (*nazrga sadaqalarga*) is forbidden, and also saint-day festivals are forbidden. We do not know, maybe they put on black glasses. What is left to [us] Muslims? What happened to our great scholars (*olimoni kalon*)? What kind of times do we live in? After the war, no one touched our shrines (*ziyoratgohlarimiz*): [the shrine] of Bahovuddin Balogardon was [open] for Muslims, and it belonged to the [Spiritual] Board. Pilgrimage to shrines could be performed without any restriction. At that time [they said that shrine visitation] was [a practice] consistent with *sharīʿa* (*ba-shari'at edi*); what now? Is it no more in accordance with *sharīʿa*? [If so], was *sharīʿa* different at that time? It seems a new *sharīʿa* has now been released. The population of Bukhara the Noble is not pleased [with this]. Please understand all these things. Why did we fall into such conditions? And peace be with you!

---

35 *Sayil* (Ar. *sayl*, lit. 'flowing') is a term used to denote a complex of celebrations, devotional rites, and fairs held during Muslim saint-day festivals in the vicinity of Muslim shrines. They were usually held in spring, after Nowruz (the New Year according to the Iranian calendar) and in autumn. In the Soviet period, during *sayil*s Muslims traveled across republican borders to perform the ritual visitation to a shrine and live there in communities, also for several weeks. See Gleb P. Snesarev, *Khorezmskie legendy kak istochnik po istorii religioznykh kul'tov Srednei Azii* (Moscow: Nauka, 1983), pp. 49, 55, 74, 115–120.

36 Here the author refers to *ʿīd al-Fiṭr*.

37 This suggests that the *ʿulamā* of the Mir-i Arab madrasa had contacts with the community of believers in Bukhara.

Example 2
Qarshi district, collective farm named Hamza, 1962
Sayida Sobitboy qizi

To the *qazi*s of the Spiritual Board.

Since time immemorial we have performed the *sadr*[38] during the ritual prayer (*janoza*) at funerals. After such prayer we hold mourning feasts [called] "three," "seven," and "forty."[39] Now our elders together with the party committee claim that our doings are not at all in accordance with *sharīʿa*. They explain to us that such a command (*buyruq*) has come down to us from his Excellency the mufti; they shout at us, and threaten us! Why is it that what used to be in the *sharīʿa* has disappeared today? Please, explain. The appellant – [*signature*].

Answer: Let the responsible person from the Spiritual Board look for this locality and, together with the people from the local community (*mahalla*),

38 The *sadr* is a funerary rite known through several ethnographic descriptions: Z. Tadzhikova, "Pesni pokhoronnogo obriada tadzhikov (po materialam zeravshanskikh èkspeditsii)," in *Problemy muzykal'nogo fol'klora narodov SSSR: Stat'i i materialy* (Moscow: Muzyka, 1973), pp. 95–100; G.P. Snesarev, *Relikty domusul'manskikh verovanii i obriadov u uzbekov Khorezma* (Moscow: Nauka, 1969), p. 155. For a discussion of this body of literature from a historical perspective, see DeWeese, "Shamanization in Central Asia," pp. 348–349. This ritual is usually performed in the house of the deceased. Women (and less often men) usually stand in a circle, dance, beat themselves on the chest, and repeat religious formulas as if they were singing. The most experienced woman leads the ritual (*sadr-ona*/*sadr-boshi*) often by singing the *hikmat*s attributed to Khoja Ahmad Yasavi. The other participants stand in a circle and repeat the same formulas and move rhythmically to the center of the circle and back. The ritual of *sadr* can be accompanied by the loud *zikr* (*zikr-i jahr*), which is usually regarded as the hallmark of a particular brand of Sufism, and thus associated with other funerary rites of Sufi origin bearing different names such as *zikr*, *jahr*, *samāʿ*, *pā*; see A. Mardonova, *Traditsionnye pokhoronno-pominal'nye obriady tadzhikov gissarskoi doliny* (*kontsa XIX–nachala XX* w.) (Dushanbe: Donish, 1998), pp. 83–92 and È.G. Gafferberg, "Perezhitki religioznykh predstvalenii u beludzhei," in G.P. Snesarev and V.N. Basilov (eds.), *Domusul'manskie verovaniia i obriady v Srednei Azii* (Moscow: Nauka, 1975), p. 246, footnote 51. Such ritual can be now observed as performed precisely in this fashion in some areas of Qashqadaryo (southern Uzbekistan). In the region (*viloyat*) of Tashkent, the *sadr* has morphed into a slightly different ritual complex. Prior to the removal of the corpse, the closest relatives of the deceased take improvised sticks and walk around the yard by shouting *voy jigarim!* ("O my dear"). Women gather in a circle, cover their heads with black scarves, beat themselves on the chest, repeat the formulas mentioned above, and cry loudly.

39 This is a ritual to remember the deceased on the third, seventh and fortieth day after his/her death. SADUM's *ʿulamā* deemed such ritual inadmissible from the point of view of *sharīʿa* and issued a number of fatwas to this effect, TsGARUz, f. R-2456, op. 1, d. 622, ll. 39–42.

visit the collective farm and clarify [the issues to the people]. Let them read the required fatwas.[40]

Example 3
Tashkent district, Qishlaq Hasan-tepa, Marx Collective Farm, 1967.
Zumrat Polvon-ota qizi[41]

To the Imam of the Kukcha Mosque. Question: Our customary practices (*odatlarimiz*), which we performed since time immemorial (*eskidan*) at weddings, or during funerals and mourning prayers (*janaza-yu a'zalarimizda*), have provoked troubles (*janjal*) among the elders of our *mahalla*. Some of them say that all these [customs] contradict our *sharīʿa*, while others say they do not. Who is right? Why do all our customary practices (*odatlarimiz*), which we have long been performing, now contradict [*sharīʿa*]? If all this is done in the way of Allah, what is wrong with them? They [the elders] scolded us [for performing such rituals] under the rule of the Tsar (*poshsho*), but we performed them under Lenin and Stalin. Regards (signature).[42]

Answer: All necessary measures were taken. We involved a representative of the District Committee (*Raikom*) and the deputy of the *qozi* in [Tashkent].

Example 4
Zangi Ota, 1969
Qumrokhon Otakhon qizi
To his Excellency the Mufti.

Question: Every year during the celebration of Nowruz the women of our neighbourhood community (*mahalla*) perform shrine visitations (*ziyorat*). We begin by visiting [the shrine of] Zangi-bobo,[43] then we make pilgrimage [to

40 It is clear from this and similar answers that either the mufti or the officials of the Spiritual Board working at the Fatwa Department believed that to read out a fatwa and explain its contents to the people would be enough to persuade the latter to do away with certain religious practices. On the back of the record we read the expression *bajarildi* (Uzb. "executed"), a calque from the Russian *vypolnenno*, a formulaic term often deployed in Soviet bureaucratese.

41 The original record written in Uzbek shows phonetic features of the dialect of the Tashkent region. In some places punctuation marks are put in accordance with the meaning of the sentences.

42 The signature is written in the Latin script.

43 On this shrine and the Sufi narrative connected to the holy persona of Zangi Ata, see Sergei Abashin, "Zangi-ata," in *Islam v territorii byvshei Rossiiskoi imperii: èntsiklopedicheskii slovar'*, ed. S.M. Prozorov, vol. 3 (Moscow: Vostochnaia Literatura RAN, 2006), pp. 40–41.

the shrine of] Sultan-bobo and the saints of Turkestan,[44] and then we come back. We make donations (*nazr*) [to the shrines] from what we [were able to] put aside. We perform a small *zikr*, and [sometimes] we perform *sadr*. These are customary ritual practices that came down to us from our grandmothers (*ènalarimizdan qolgan odatlarimiz*).[45] Now we have heard that according to the imams, such shrine visitations and our donations, which come from our pure heart, are useless, and that they are not written in the [books of] *sharīʿa*. Are these words true? And what is the harm of all this? My older sister was an *otin-oyi*[46] and she knew *sharīʿa*, but she never said anything to this effect. Now I hope to receive an answer from You. This [*patta*] was written by my granddaughter and I signed it [signature].

Answer: Let the *Qozi* of Tashkent and the imam of the Zangi-Ota mosque contact [the representatives of] the *mahalla* and clarify [the issues to the people]. Let them take copies of the fatwas issued by his Excellence the Mufti[47] and distribute them to the aforementioned people. Let them clarify [the issues]

44 The author here refers to the shrine complex of Khoja Ahmad Yasavi in the city of Turkestan, southern Kazakhstan. The shrine complex in question has been the subject of veneration since at least the Timurid period. Communities claiming genealogical and initiatic connections to Khoja Ahmad Yasavi have enjoyed recognized spiritual authority, administered the shrine complex in various capacities, and thus enjoyed fiscal privileges until Sovietization. For more on this, see Devin DeWeese, "The Politics of Sacred Lineages in 19th-Century Central Asia: Descent Groups Linked to Khwaja Ahmad Yasavi in Shrine Documents and Genealogical Charters," *International Journal of Middle East Studies*, 31 (1999), pp. 507–530.

45 The usual formula is *èna-bobolarimizdan* ("From our forefathers"; see below). The author of the letter emphasizes (perhaps unwillingly) that she perceived this ritual as typical of a female religious milieu.

46 Uzb. "Female mullah."

47 The text here refers to fatwas most probably issued by the Mufti Ziyouddin Boboxonov, in office from 1957 to 1983. From the context it is not quite clear which fatwas are meant, though the author most probably referred to the legal opinions that condemned the practices of shrine visitation and making donations to the benefit of the shrines, their keepers, and the shrine communities. Two of them were issued between 1958 and 1959 and were signed by Ziyouddin, SADUM's deputy representative Ismail Sattiev, the *qāżī* of the Kyrgyz SSR Olimxon To'ra Shokirxo'jayev, and Fozil-Xo'ja Sodiqxo'jayev, head of the Fatwa Department. While they are premised upon arguments derived from Islamic jurisprudence, specifically extracted from recognized authorities of the Ḥanafī school of law, they equally include many citations from the Qur'ān and the Sunna and, in so doing, they exemplify a scripturalist treatment of practices connected to shrine visitation. In fact, these two fatwas embody parts of previous texts prepared in 1952 and in 1954 by Shokirxo'jayev and should be viewed in continuity with, and as a further evolution of, a type of Islamic reformist thinking that manifested itself in the region prior to the October Revolution (see our "Being Soviet, Muslim, Modernist, and Fundamentalist in 1950s Central Asia").

at the level of the *mahalla* both with reference to [Soviet] legislation (*qonun*) and in accordance with the *sharīʿa*.

1970s

Example 5

Zafar District (*rayun*), 1971.
Bunisa Majid qizi
To the attention of the *Qozi* and the leadership of Imams

I, Bunisa, daughter of Majid, retired three years ago. Recently my eldest daughter died. With whom should I share my grief? On whose shoulder should I cry? Now, for the sake of my daughter's memory, and to secure a reward in the afterlife (*savob*), we began to perform rituals (*marosimlar*) that came down to us from our ancestors (*èna-bobolarimizdan*). We [organized commemorations] on the third and seventh day [after her death]. When [we held a commemoration] after forty days, the imam came to our house and said: "All that you're doing, you do in vain (*bekor*). All your rituals (*rusumlaringiz*) will not count as *savob* for your daughter." Our *otin-oyi*, instead, claims that it will, because the Qur'an is read during such commemorations. All this will secure *savob*. What shall we do? If the practices of our ancestors disappear in an instant, and if they say that the rituals we performed [for the benefit of] our departed do not count as *savob*, all of this adds more sorrow to our grief. Whom shall we listen to, if one says this, and the other says that? I felt profoundly distressed at the words of our imam. Give me an answer to all this! I beg you: do not disregard my request. Bunisa Majid qizi.

No answer.

Example 6

Verkhne-Chirchik district, Kaltepa village, 1974.
Samandar Kholiqov, 56 years old, mechanic in a collective farm.
To the Imams and muftis of our [Spiritual] Board

In earlier times we used to celebrate Nowruz at the seasonal camp (*shiypon*) of our brigade[48] and performed the ritual prayer (*namoz*) as we could. Those who were literate among us performed the duties of imam. We did [this] without attracting too much attention. Five, six years ago we heard from our imam in

48 This refers to the practice whereby during the summer, collective farms supplied workers (divided into "brigades") with temporary constructions including dormitories, kitchens, and a Lenin room.

Chirchik that we should not perform the prayer during Nowruz. [And so] we stopped, despite the fact that our forefathers (*ota-bobolarimiz*) used to pray [on such an occasion] and it was customary practice (*odat*). Then came the order (*buyruq*) that the prayer to celebrate the end of the Ramadan (*hayit*) should be performed only in the mosque. But according to the hadith,[49] the prayer should be read under the open sky, and you know about it (*o'zlaringa ma'lumdur bu narsa*). "Let it be," we said, also to this. Even if the mosque was far away, we made an effort to perform [the ritual] and there we went. We went to the mosque to pray after the breaking of the fasting (*ro'za*), but once there we found that the police and kolkhoz's party organizers (*parturglar*)[50] were standing at the door and compiling a list of all those who came [to pray]. Then they confused us, threatening to fire us all from work. In the end we could not understand [what was happening]! You, too, represent a state office (*davlat kanturi*)! If you issued the order (*buyruq*) for us to perform the ritual prayer only in mosques, then why do party organizers and police prevent us from doing so? People are at a loss. Those who perform the *namoz* among us are few, but they too are in distress. Therefore, we turn to you with the request to solve this issue. After all, there is no harm from us if we worship (*ibodat*) the way we can. We do not do anything against the state: we fulfil the working plan (*ish piloni*) with surplus; they give us prizes [for it], and we carry out everything they tell us. What else do you need [from us] (*nema kerak yana*)? Looking forward [to receiving] your answer.

No answer given.

Example 7
Tashkent, *mahalla* "Samarqand Darvoz," 1978
Robiya Rafiq-Kho'ja qizi
To the Spiritual Board

My name is Robiya, daughter of Rafiqkho'ja, and I came several times to the [Spiritual] Board and requested it to consider the issue of my pilgrimage to Mecca (*hajj*). For years have I suffered because of this. I even dared to submit applications, but the answer I received was that women are not allowed there. But our *otin-oyi* said that this is not true and that women too [in fact] go on

49 This hadith is taken from al-Bukhari's *Sahih*.

50 On the complex, often contradictory relations between the echelons of collective farms (chair/*rais*, party organizers, bursars, etc.) and Muslim believers, see Sergei Abashin, "Stalin's Rais: Governance Practices in a Central Asian kolkhoz," *Central Asian Survey*, 36/1 (2017), pp. 131–147.

hajj. She even cited several examples from the world of Islam. She also read [examples] from old books about how our mother 'A'isha performed the hajj, about how the wives of the companions (*sahobalar*) also fulfilled this obligation (*farz*). Please consider my request again, I beg you. I dream about the saint Khizr-bobo[51] who tells me to fulfill this duty. I never missed a single prayer, I pay the *zakot* even with my little pension, and I never broke fasting. According to the order (*buyruq*) of the Spiritual Board, I also stopped performing shrine visitations (*ziyoratlargayam bormiy qo'ydim*). And I never uttered a single word against the state. My children are ready to pay whatever sum is needed [for the hajj]. At this point I feel reassured that my children will bear the costs. Please solve my question positively. Robiya Rafiq-Kho'ja qizi, from "Samarqand Darvaza." I beg you! Peace be upon you, the mercy and blessings of Allah!

The [same] answer is given again (*javobi qayta berildi*).

1980s

Example 8
Jizzakh, Zaamin district, 1981.
The elders of the Duoba village (4 people)
To his Excellence Mufti Ziyouddin Qori

We, who appended our signatures [to this letter], live in the village of Duoba, in the Zomin district, region of Jizzakh. For a long time, we have been expressing the desire to go on the hajj and visit the shrines in Mecca. At first we were nine people. Now, five of our friends have died and they were not destined to perform the hajj. We ask you once again to allow at least one of us to go to Mecca.[52] He would fulfill the obligation (*farz*) for all of us. Whatever issue one takes a look at, one notices that the journal *Musulmonlar* always prints the

51 The author here refers to Khiżr, a saintly figure widely venerated in Central Asia and alternatively identified as a saint among the friends of God (*awliyā'*), a prophet, or an angel. "Regarded as a source of esoteric wisdom and supernatural abilities, Khiżr is often depicted in Sufi lore as an old man who offers guidance in times of crisis. Khiżr is believed by most Sufis to be the unnamed figure in the Qur'ān who guides Moses (Q 18:65–82)" (Jeff Eden, *Warrior Saints of the Silk Road: Legends of the Qarakhanids* [Leiden: Brill, 2018], p. 91); see also Jo-Ann Gross, "The Biographical Tradition of Muḥammad Bashārā: Sanctification and Legitimation in Tajikistan," in *Sufism in Central Asia: New Perspectives on Sufi Traditions, 15th–21st Centuries*, ed. Devin DeWeese and Jo-Ann Gross (Leiden: Brill, 2018), pp. 310–314.

52 In Soviet Central Asia, the hajj was strictly regimented and its performance was allowed only to a rather limited number of people; see Tasar, *Soviet and Muslim*, 262–277.

same list of pilgrims (*hojilari qatorida bir khil kishilar ro'ykhati*) coming from our region (*o'lka*). Is it just (*insofdanmi*) when the same people perform the hajj five-six or even ten times? [And if so], according to which Hadith? After all, there are so many believers (*mu''min insonlar*) who are looking forward to [going to Mecca]. Let them go: in the end, it will count as a reward in the afterlife (*bularga yo'l ochish oxir savob bo'lardiku*).[53] We are ordinary Muslims (*oddiy musulmonlar*) and [thus] cannot understand the affairs of the Spiritual Board. We always comply with state policies, and we quietly perform all our acts of worship (*ibodatlar*) and [fulfill all our] obligations. What have we done not to be considered worthy [for the hajj]? To sum up, if you do not want to solve our issue, we then defer to your good conscience, and entrust everything to Allah. May the peace and the mercy of Allah be upon you. Amen!

No answer.

Example 9

Qoqand, 1983
Abdulhakim qori Salimjon qori o'ghli
To the Spiritual Board

May the peace and blessings of Allah be upon you! Glory to Allah, the Creator of the Two Worlds! We repeat our praise to our great Messenger Muhammad, the Seal of the Prophets – may the peace and blessings of Allah be upon him! – and to his descendants and relatives! We open our hands for prayer and ask Allah the Almighty to assign to his Excellence [the late] Mufti Eshon Bobokhon and his son Ziyovuddin Qori a suitable place in the Garden of Eden, according to their good deeds and status. Dear Mufti [Shamsuddin Bobokhonov]! You have been given [the post of] Mufti, and therefore we hope that in this position you will continue to shed light on the path of the true *sharīʿa* to protect Islam, which is our sacred religion, for our Muslim brothers and sisters, and our younger sisters, like your father and grandfather [did before you]. [My name is] Abdulhokim Qori Solimjon Qori and I was born in Qoqand 67 years ago and I've seen a lot in my life. For four years I served as the Imam at the Friday Mosque in Asaka,[54] but my health failed, and I left [that post]. I do continue to participate [, however,] in the affairs of the neighbourhood (*mahalla*) and Muslim believers (*mu''min musulmonlar*). However, as stated in the hadith of

53 In the original the sentence is not complete.

54 District in the southeast of the Ferghana Valley, located in the territory of Kyrgyzstan (Osh region).

the Great Messenger, [...][55] the explanations should be short. So let me go to the main content of [my letter].

The unpleasant events and disputes that have occurred [recently] have thrown the Muslims of Qoqand and the [community of believers] of the [Ferghana] Valley as a whole into a state of anxiety and fear; and they have led our faithful brothers astray from the true path of Islam. Therefore, I resolved to write this letter. You are well aware that these discords (*fitnalar*) were initiated by young mullahs (*mullaw̱achchalar*), who fashioned themselves with the attire of Wahhabis. We, the elders (*qariyalar*), believe that to prevent this [state of anarchy from coming into being] is the duty of the [Spiritual] Board. The elders of other areas share the same opinion: I travel a lot and therefore I know [the situation quite] well. And yet, in matters of acts of worship (*ibodat*) or in other matters of religious practice many discords manifest themselves (*fitnalar*) among Muslims, which deserve to be discussed in a special meeting (*qurultoy*) [of SADUM]. Let me give you an example. With an example [after all, even] a child will understand, so spoke Mashrab-Bobo.[56] [Let me start from] the ablutions: discord presented itself as to how one should wash his legs (*makhs tortish*).[57] For this reason, young mullahs (*mullaḇachchalar*) enter the mosques without having completed their ablutions (*tahorati tu'la bo'lmagan*), that is only by sprinkling water on their boots (*patinkalar* < *batinki*). But how can they proceed by analogy with the practice of sprinkling water on their boots, when they should not be wearing either boots or galoshes![58]

Let me draw your esteemed attention to other questions that are well known to you. [There are] female-mullahs (*otinoy*), street prayer-reciters (*duoxonlar*), beggars (*tilamchilar*), who ask for alms (*nazr va sadaqa*) by claiming

---

55 The original shows some blank space, which most probably the author planned to fill in with a quotation from the Arabic.

56 Bābā-Raḥīm Mashrab (1657–1711?) was a mystic poet who wrote in Turkic. The information about him is mostly legendary, but it is known that he tried to become a student of the famous Naqshbandī Sufi from Kashghar, Āfāq-Khwāja (d. 1694).

57 This passage refers to the ritual of washing the feet during the ablutions (*tahorat*). More specifically, here the author is signalling the habit of performing only incomplete ablutions, which caused major conflicts within various mosque communities in Namangan in the 1980s. In winter believers often wore leather boots (*patinki*), and also put galoshes (*kafsh/kowush*) upon them. In such cases Muslims who went to the mosque performed their ablutions by sprinkling water on their boots, thereby avoiding to laboriously take off their shoes.

58 Abdulhakim-Qori here means that the so-called young mullahs considered it licit from a normative point of view to sprinkle water on their shoes, because they saw an analogy between such an action and the established ritual practice of wiping their legs with a wet hand (*maxs tortish*). The author suggests that many frowned upon such a new habit.

[that they operate] 'on the way of Allah' and [for such purposes] visit [private] homes, bazaars and especially the holy shrines. Their number is increasing day by day in ways unseen [so far]. How can we stop this? [I ask] because our women, out of ignorance, run after female mullahs (*otincha*) and leave a lot of money at the shrines, while their children and grandchildren go around in rags. And all [this occurs when] the activists of the neighbourhood (*mahalla posponlari*) and the imams of the [local] mosques get together, visit the *mahallas* and tell [people] to stop visiting shrines, thereby leading them astray from the true path; [thus] they renewed the discord that already existed. The poor believers fell between the hammer and the anvil. On the one hand, [we have] the Wahhabis, who, narrow-minded as they are and lacking deep knowledge of our *sharīʿa* and customs, taint the good name of Islam, deceive the people who have taken their bait, and intensify their actions. On the other hand, [we have the] representatives of [the Spiritual] Board [, SADUM,] and the imams, who [go around] and yell [at everyone] to stop visiting shrines, as if the performance of the latter was contrary to the *sharīʿa*. But we know well that long ago, these words have come from people who caused a terrible [state of] anarchy [among Muslims]. Yes, if you say that people have been indulging in this custom, this is true. But if we do away completely with shrine visitations, will this not be contrary to the *sharīʿa* [in itself]? Now it is appropriate to recall the hadith: ... How can we move away from the prescription of our Prophet about shrine visitation, which reminds us today about Judgment Day? Then what will become of our Muslimness (*musulmonchilik*)?

Shrine visitation falls within the rubric of acts of worship (*ziyorat ibodat masalalari qatorida*), as you well know; and today for many of our Muslims, especially women, shrine visitation is a devotional practice (*ibodat amali*). [We know that] many people do not perform acts [of worship] completely, and [what do we do about it?] Instead of bringing order to shrine visitation, we abandon it completely! Then what will come out of it? That is, if we do away even with such practices, then what will be of Islam? Won't this damage the faith of people who do not practice even further? Can't you just show them the true rules of conduct[59] so that they [the people] do not fall into polytheism (*shirk*). Or is it a sensible move to cut the branch on which we sit, like Nasreddin Efendi did? I have spent time with your grandfather Eshon Boboxon. How many times have I received his blessings! This man did a lot to regulate

59 Abdulhakim-Qori is here most probably suggesting that it would be enough for SADUM to introduce restrictions to the ritual complex identified with shrine visitation, which consisted of prohibiting certain practices such as pilgrims' rubbing the "holy dust" on the face, lighting candles, crying out loud, etc.

shrine visitation, but he knew the Hadith well and did not reject it altogether! After him, for some reason, [SADUM's] initiatives have evolved in such a way that they completely contradicted the Hadith. All because of the intrigues of those seditious [members] of the [Spiritual] Board (*idoradagi fitnachi*).

They issue fatwas, in which, they say, this act is out of the norm, this one is contrary to the *sharīʿa*, and that one is another disgrace. Whatever they ask, they talk about the deeds of the ancients, and they even instigate believers to fanaticism. But the majority does not pay attention to such things. That is, [the majority] proceeds along its own path, while the [Spiritual] Board and the Wahhabis are pulling [people] each in their own direction. This is to be found in the stories of Saadi Shirazi.[60] Everyone pulls the cart along the way he knows, by ignoring the Hadith. What kind of situation is this? Is this not the beginning of anarchy? And other troublemakers further muddle the waters by claiming that [Spiritual] Board [in fact] became a nest of Wahhabis (*idora vohhobiylashti*).

For this reason, if in the near future, you don't follow the tradition of your eminent grandfather, and don't convene a big conference, disagreement, anarchy, and disregard for the authorities will increase among the believers. [We shall encounter] a situation like on Judgment Day. We, the elders, have high hopes in you, we hope that you feel responsible. I shall stop my statement here, and I will write again if need be.

Peace be upon you! (further a brief well-meaning prayer).

Example 10
Namangan, Kosonsoy district, December 1989
Elders of the *Tutzor* mahalla (22 people)
To the Mufti and the officials of the Spiritual Board

We support the policy of freedom in religious affairs, which followed the announcement of Perestroika in our country.[61] After the opening of mosques in some *mahallas*, a lot of funds were collected for their upkeep, people came out together, gathered in groups and carried out a number of voluntary works (*hasharlar*). We repaired our mosques, brought their courtyards back to life;

60 Here is a reference to the well-known 13th-century poet Musharrif al-Dīn Abū Muḥammad Muṣliḥ ibn ʿAbdullah Shīrāzī, known by his literary nickname Saʿdī. His *Gulistān* ("The Rose Garden") was compulsory reading in the madrasa curriculum, and it clearly remained an important component of underground Islamic teaching in Central Asia after the Second World War.

61 *Biz davlatimizda qayta qurish siyosatu è"lon qiligach, diniy masalalarda ham èrkinlik siyosatini qullab quvatlaymiz.*

we laid inside walkways and carpets, which we brought there from home. Then came the young Wahhabis (*vahhobiy bachchalar*) when everything was made ready and took our mosque. They do not acknowledge us. [Instead,] they make fun of us when we come [to the mosque] to pray (*namozga kelganlarimizda*). They climbed onto the pulpit (*minbar*) [of the mosque], without having participated in its repair, without having spent a penny on it. And they took our mats for prayers (*joyi-namozlarimizni o'zlashtirishopti*). They even ceased to pay respect to their parents. They don't have respect for the elders, they perform the prayer in a strange way (*namozlarini begonacha o'qib*); even the ablutions they can't do properly. These unfortunate things happened to us; it was a catastrophe (*balo*). The Imam[62] appointed by our *qoziyat* took their side. He did not trust our words. We wrote to Umar-Khon Qori,[63] *qozi* of Namangan, but to no avail. They are overwhelmed by their own conflicts in Namangan.[64] Now, our request to the Spiritual Board is not to spare efforts to help us take possession of our own mosques. If needed, we shall organize a demonstration (*yurish*). Peace be upon you! The elders of the Tutzor *mahalla*.

3 Conclusion

The documentation we have offered here in translation corroborates the idea that the USSR may be more usefully regarded as a "religious space," as suggested

62 In the record the name of the imam in question has been smeared to prevent its deciphering.

63 Umar-Khon Qori (b. 1950) is a controversial figure in the religious landscape of Namangan and Uzbekistan in the 1980s and 1990s. Having been trained in unofficial Islamic study-groups in the Ferghana Valley, he commanded authority over various constituencies in Namangan to the extent that Shaykh Muhammad Sodiq Muhammad Yusuf appointed him to the post of *qāżī* in 1989. While he openly disputed the authority of the so-called "Wahhabis," he equally gathered Islamic radicals around himself. For more on him, see Martha Brill Olcott, "Roots of Radical Islam in Central Asia," *Carnegie Papers*, 77 (2007), pp. 20–22.

64 The author here gestures only in passing at the various conflicts among mosque communities, which occurred in the region of Namangan in the second half of the 1980s after the so-called "Waḥhabis" rose to prominence. By the period in which this letter was written, the label *vahhobiy* had already morphed into a catch-all term, which encompassed *ʿulamā* with puritanical credentials and a cast of religiously enthused, though often aggressive characters. For more on this subject, see Bakhtiyar M. Babadjanov, "The Economic and Religious History of a Kolkhoz Village: Khojawot from Soviet Modernisation to the Aftermath of the Islamic Revival," in *Allah's Kolkhozes: Migration, De-Stalinisation, Privatisation and the New Muslim Congregations in the Soviet realm (1950s–2000s)*, ed. S.A. Dudoignon and C. Noack (Berlin: Klaus Schwarz, 2014), pp. 202–263.

in the introduction to this volume. More specifically, if read together, our *pattalar* invite us to conceptualize manifestations of Muslim religiosity in Soviet Central Asia as part and parcel of a broader cultural field that Eren Tasar has persuasively termed the "Islamic sphere." We welcome the adoption of such conceptualization, for it facilitates our imagining Muslimness beyond the constraints placed by the Soviet state through its bureaucratic apparatus, instruments of surveillance, and policing organs. The Islamic sphere was instead shaped by forms of knowledge, notions of moral authority, and models of ethical edification that defied the measures of containment designed and adopted by the Soviet state. It is of course true that Islamic knowledge, morality, and ethics suffered from a severe process of erosion and underwent major transformations throughout the Soviet period (and the meaning of those transformations remains to be studied properly). At the same time, however, the missives sent to SADUM show clearly that Muslims filtered Soviet reality through an Islamic cosmogony that served as a powerful resource to confer meaning on their lives. Having recognised how the Islamic sphere in fact permeated this and other documentation coming from the Soviet archives of Muslim religiosity, we should make a further move and reject as entirely unconvincing the notion that manifestations of Muslimness in the USSR reflected either the "resilience" of religion or "resistance" to Sovietization.[65]

To fully appreciate the force of our argument, let us consider references to *sharīʿa* that one encounters in the records we have presented in this chapter. They no doubt suggest that *sharīʿa* was still regarded, in Central Asia after the Second World War, as an apparatus of knowledge usable to define Muslim orthopraxy and to measure behavior. One may object that such references are merely aspirational, for the Soviet Union did not recognise *sharīʿa* as an official source of law. In fact, we learn from the documentation at our disposal as well from the records produced by SADUM that *sharīʿa* enjoyed a rather ambiguous status in Soviet Central Asia. First, the crafting of fatwas issued by SADUM (including those commissioned directly by CARC), to be read before mosque communities, was clearly premised upon notions of Islamic jurisprudence. And our sources make abundantly clear that Soviet Muslims accorded such legal opinions a highly prescriptive status.[66] Second, *sharīʿa* played a meaningful role in the definition of tasks among SADUM's employees. Not only was the mufti expected to "shed light on the path of the true *sharīʿa* to protect

65 This move has been also eloquently advocated in Eren Tasar, "Institutions: A Lens on Soviet Islam," *Central Asian Affairs*, 7 (2020), p. 373.

66 See, also, J. Eden, *God Save the USSR: Soviet and Muslims in the Second World War* (Oxford: Oxford University Press, 2021), p. 163.

Islam" (see Document 9), but also "ordinary" imams were required to sign a contract stipulating that their behavior should follow the precepts of *sharīʿa*.[67] Third, Islamic law, more broadly conceived, continued to influence behavior among Soviet Central Asians who believed in the importance of Islamic orthopraxis and therefore embraced a type of habitus which they perceived as in accordance with *sharīʿa*. Examples of such habitus are several: the preference among Soviet Muslims for religious marriages (*nikoh*) at the expense of civil weddings;[68] the practice of polygamy which "was not uncommon in the rural parts of Central Asia," indeed openly tolerated, and at times even encouraged;[69] and the payment of Islamically-mandated charity such as *zakāt* and *ʿushr* to finance communal activities and the upkeep of mosques.[70]

At the same time, the records we have offered here in translation show a certain degree of absorption of specific messages conveyed by both SADUM and the government. Indeed, some Central Asians showed deference and compliance with the regulations coming from SADUM, for they regarded the mufti an undisputed source of authority. At the same time, however, one should also consider that there was much that did *not* percolate through the meanders of Soviet institutions, and hence failed to shape Central Asians' Muslimness. In fact, many openly criticized SADUM's attacks against devotional practices associated with shrine visitation as disrespectful of established religious traditions and harmful to the integrity of Muslims' identity. It is therefore unsurprising to find one Abdulhokim Qori, clearly an experienced observer of things Muslim in the Ferghana Valley, warning the mufti Shamsuddin Boboxonov of the dangers coming with the attacks against shrine visitations. In so doing, Abdulhokim Qori argued, SADUM had brought anarchy into the community of believers and pushed Muslims to view its representatives as being as divisive as the "Wahhabis."

Clearly, Abdulhokim Qori represented a critical point of view. However, he still regarded Shamsuddin Boboxonov a source of *moral* authority. This transpires from the fact that Abdulhokim Qori attributed authorship of the fatwas against shrine visitation not to the mufti himself, but to other members of SADUM. This was a sleight of hand, of course; in fact, moral status mattered before the community of believers. And being a member of the Boboxonov family, Shamsuddin enjoyed a certain degree of moral standing. It is for this

67 M. Buttino, *Samarcanda: storie in una città dal 1945 a oggi* (Napoli: Viella, 2015), pp. 124–126.

68 Y. Ro'i, *Islam in the Soviet Union: From the Second World War to Gorbachev*, pp. 83, 346, 363, 531–534.

69 Ro'i, *Islam in the Soviet Union: From the Second World War to Gorbachev*, pp. 538–539, 580.

70 Ro'i, *Islam in the Soviet Union: From the Second World War to Gorbachev*, pp. 126, 141 n. 159, 234.

reason that Abdulhokim Qori invited Shamsuddin to follow the role model of his grandfather, Eshon Boboxonov, who had championed a conciliatory approach towards the cult of the saints in the 1940s and the 1950s.[71]

While appreciating the degree to which Central Asians critically reflected on the messages coming from SADUM, it is equally important to note that they could and did turn to other individuals of recognised authority while seeking for spiritual guidance. Repeated references to the recognised authority of "female-mullahs" (*otin-oyi*), which we have encountered in our *pattalar*, point to Central Asians' resourcefulness in religious matters. But they also refer to the capaciousness of the Islamic sphere in Soviet Central Asia, a cultural field inhabited by a plurality of religious figures whose social significance we have yet to appreciate in full.

Collecting and reflecting upon documentation such as the records we have presented here becomes essential if one wants to overcome the obtuseness of the dominant frameworks available for analysing manifestations of Muslimness in the USSR. More importantly, to pay sustained attention to ego sources is key to historicising the vitality of the Islamic episteme, i.e., a knowledge field encompassing notions of ethics, morality, and aesthetics, which was constitutive of what Central Asians perceived as their being Muslim.[72] Such imperative stems precisely from the neglect of the mundane, the quotidian, the sort of "everyday-life" accounts that historians of Soviet Central Asia have been so stubbornly avoiding armed solely with a scepticism that looks almost fideistic.[73]

When we begin to hypothesize that such a thing as "Soviet Islam" existed and represented a distinctive lived reality emerging from a unique convergence of circumstances, then our next task must be filling in the vast gaps in our knowledge with all the texture, details, and nuance of lived life. The petitions which ordinary Uzbeks submitted to SADUM after the Second World War point to the existence of a vibrant world of religiosity which we may term "Islamic" where many cultivated their Muslimness in ways that were at odds with visions of orthopraxis championed by the Spiritual Board. While often

---

71 Tasar, "Sufism on the Soviet Stage," pp. 275–80.

72 Sartori, "Of Saints, Shrines, and Tractors: Untangling the Meaning of Islam in Soviet Central Asia."

73 For a critique of this approach, see P. Sartori, "'On the Importance of Having a Method': Reading Atheistic Documents on Islamic Revival in 1950s Central Asia," in E. Tasar, A.J. Frank, J. Eden (eds), *From the Khans' Oven. Studies on the History of Central Asian Religions in Honor of Devin DeWeese*, (Leiden: Brill, 2021), pp. 284–322.

criticised for their devotional excesses and spiritual exuberance, however, the communities of pious and observant Uzbeks who inhabited that world were extremely sensitive to the activities and the pronouncements of the SADUM. Evidently, notwithstanding alternative sources of religious authority, the words of the Soviet mufti mattered to the faithful in Uzbekistan.[74]

Bibliography

Abashin, Sergei. "A Prayer for Rain: Practising Being Soviet and Muslim." *Journal of Islamic Studies*, 25/2 (2014), 178–200.

Abashin, Sergei. "Stalin's Rais: Governance Practices in a Central Asian kolkhoz." *Central Asian Survey* 36/1 (2017), pp. 131–147.

Abashin, Sergei. "Zangi-ata." In *Islam v territorii byvshei Rossiiskoi imperii: èntsiklopedicheskii slovar'*, ed. S.M. Prozorov, vol. 3. Moscow: Vostochnaia Literatura RAN, 2006, pp. 40–41.

Babadjanov, Bakhtiyar. "Debates over Islam in Contemporary Uzbekistan: A View from Within." In *Devout Societies vs. Impious States? Transmitting Islamic Learning in Russia, Central Asia and China, through the Twentieth Century* (Proceedings of an International Colloquium Held in the Carré des Sciences, French Ministry of Research, Paris, November 12–13, 2001), ed. Stéphane Dudoignon. Berlin: Schwarz, 2004, pp. 39–60.

Babadjanov, Bakhtiyar M. "The Economic and Religious History of a Kolkhoz Village: Khojawot from Soviet Modernisation to the Aftermath of the Islamic Revival." In *Allah's Kolkhozes: Migration, De-Stalinisation, Privatisation and the New Muslim Congregations in the Soviet realm (1950s–2000s)*, ed. Stéphane A. Dudoignon and Christian Noack. Berlin: Klaus Schwarz, 2014, pp. 202–263.

Babadjanov, Bakhtiyar M. "'Paradise at the Feet of Mothers and Women:' Soviet and Post-Soviet Discourses of the Emancipation Forms of Muslim Women." In *Islam and Gender in Central Asia: Soviet Modernization and Today's Society*, ed. Ch. Obiya. Kyoto: CIAS, Kyoto University, 2016, pp. 19–33.

Babadjanov, B., and M. Kamilov. "Muhammadjan Hindustani (1892–1989) and the Beginning of the 'Great Schism' among the Muslims of Uzbekistan." In *Islam in*

74 This is a point worth emphasizing given the remarkable tenacity with which the argument that SADUM mattered little to Soviet Muslims has been marshalled in recent years in spite of its being empirically unsubstantiated. See, for example, A. Khalid, "Review of Soviet and Muslim: The Institutionalization of Islam in Central Asia by Eren Tasar," *Slavic Review* 77 (2018), pp. 1035–1037.

Politics in Russia and Central Asia (Early Eighteenth to Late Twentieth Centuries), ed. S.A. Dudoignon and H. Komatsu. London: Kegan Paul, 2001, pp. 195–219.

Babadzhanov, Bakhtiyar M., Ashirbek K. Muminov, and A. von Kügelgen, eds. *Disputy musul'manskikh religioznykh avtoritetov v Tsentral'noi Azii v XX veke*. Almaty: Daik Press, 2007.

Babadzhanov, Bakhtiyar, and Paolo Sartori. "U istokov sovetskogo diskursa o 'khoroshem islame' sovetskoi Tsentral'noi Azii." *Ab Imperio*, 12/3 (2018), pp. 219–255.

Buttino, Marco. *Samarcanda: storie in una città dal 1945 a oggi*. Naples: Viella, 2015.

DeWeese, Devin. "The Politics of Sacred Lineages in 19th-Century Central Asia: Descent Groups Linked to Khwaja Ahmad Yasavi in Shrine Documents and Genealogical Charters." *International Journal of Middle East Studies*, 31 (1999), pp. 507–530.

DeWeese, Devin. "Shamanization in Central Asia." *Journal of the Economic and Social History of the Orient*, 57/2 (2014), pp. 326–363.

Dudoignon, S.A. "From Revival to Mutation: The Religious Personnel of Islam in Tajikistan, from de-Stalinization to Independence (1955–91)." *Central Asian Survey*, 30 (2011), pp. 53–80.

Dudoignon, Stéphane A. "Holy Virgin Lands? Demographic Engineering, Heritage Management and the Sanctification of Territories in ex-Soviet Central Asia, since WWII." In *From the Khan's Oven: Studies on the History of Central Asian Religions in Honor of Devin DeWeese*, ed. Eren Tasar, Allen J. Frank and Jeff Eden. Leiden: Brill, 2021, pp. 358–408.

Dudoignon, Stéphane A. Review of Habiba Fathi, *Femmes d'autorité dans l'Asie centrale contemporaine. Quête des ancêtres et recompositions identitaires dans l'islam post-soviétique*. Paris: Maisonneuve & Larose, n.d. [2004]. *Cahiers du Monde russe*, 47/4 (2006), pp. 951–957.

Dudoignon, Stéphane A., and Sayyid Ahmad Qalandar. "'They Were All from the Country:' The Revival and Politicisation of Islam in the Lower Wakhsh River Valley of the Tajik SSR (1947–1997)." In *Allah's Kolkhozes: Migration, De-Stalinisation, Privatisation and the New Muslim Congregations in the Soviet Realm (1950s–2000s)*, ed. Stéphane A. Dudoignon and Christian Noack. Berlin: Klaus Schwarz, 2014, pp. 47–122.

Eden, Jeff. "A Soviet Jihad against Hitler: Ishan Babakhan calls Central Asian Muslims to War." *Journal of the Economic and Social History of the Orient*, 59/1–2 (2016), pp. 237–264.

Eden, Jeff, tr. *Warrior Saints of the Silk Road: Legends of the Qarakhanids*. Leiden: Brill, 2018.

Eden, Jeff. *God Save the USSR: Soviet and Muslims in the Second World War*. Oxford: Oxford University Press, 2021.

Exnerova, Vera. "Radical Islam from Below: The Mujaddidiya and Hizb-ut-Tahrir in the Ferghana Valley." In *Islam Society, and Politics in Central Asia*, ed. Pauline Jones. Pittsburgh: Pittsburgh University Press, 2017, pp. 55–76.

Frank, Allen J., with Jahangir Mamatov. *Uzbek Islamic Debates: Texts, Translations, and Commentary*. Springfield, Virginia: Dunwoody Press, 2006.

Gafferberg, È.G. "Perezhitki religioznykh predstvalenii u beludzhei." In *Domusul'manskie verovaniia i obriady v Srednei Azii*, ed. G.P. Snesarev and V.N. Basilov. Moscow: Nauka, 1975, pp. 224–247.

Gross, Jo-Ann. "The Biographical Tradition of Muḥammad Bashārā: Sanctification and Legitimation in Tajikistan." In *Sufism in Central Asia: New Perspectives on Sufi Traditions, 15th–21st Centuries*, ed. Devin DeWeese and Jo-Ann Gross. Leiden: Brill, 2018, pp. 299–331.

Keller, Shoshana. *To Moscow, Not Mecca: the Soviet Campaign against Islam in Central Asia, 1917–1941*. Westport, Connecticut: Praeger, 2001.

Khalid, Adeeb. "Review of Soviet and Muslim: The Institutionalization of Islam in Central Asia by Eren Tasar," *Slavic Review* 77 (2018), pp. 1035–1037.

Kleinmichel, Sigrid. *Ḫalpa in Choresm (Ḫwārazm) und Ātin Āyi im Ferghanatal. Zur Geschichte des Lesens in Usbekistan im 20. Jahrhundert*. Anor, No. 4. Berlin: Das Arabische Buch, 2000.

Knorozov, Iu. V. "Mazar Shamun-nabi." *Sovetskaia ètnograjiia*, 1949, No. 2, pp. 86–97.

Knorozov, Iu. V. "Shamanskii zikr v podzenrel'e Mazlumkhan-sulu." *Ètnograficheskoe obozrenie*, 1994, No. 6, pp. 91–96.

Krämer, Annette. *Geistliche Autorität und islamische Gesellschaft im Wandel: Studien über Frauenälteste (otin und xalfa) im unabhängigen Usbekistan*. Berlin: Klaus Schwarz, 2002.

Mardonova, A. *Traditsionnye pokhoronno-pominal'nye obriady tadzhikov gissarskoi doliny (kontsa XIX-nachala XX vv.)*. Dushanbe: Donish, 1998.

Olcott, Martha Brill. "Roots of Radical Islam in Central Asia." *Carnegie Papers* 77 (2007), 20–22.

Penati, Beatrice. "On the Local Origins of the Soviet Attack on 'Religious' Waqf in the Uzbek SSR (1927)." *Acta Slavica Iaponica*, 36 (2015), pp. 39–72.

Pianciola, Niccolò, and Paolo Sartori. "Waqf in Turkestan: The Colonial Legacy and the Fate of an Islamic Institution in Early Soviet Central Asia, 1917–1924." *Central Asian Survey*, 26/4 (2007), pp. 475–498.

Rasanayagam, Johan. *Islam in Post-Soviet Uzbekistan: The Morality of Experience*. Cambridge: Cambridge University Press, 2011.

Ro'i, Ya'acov. *Islam in the Soviet Union: from the Second World War to Gorbachev*. London: Hurst and Company, 2000.

Sartori, Paolo. "Of Saints, Shrines, and Tractors: Untangling the Meaning of Islam in Soviet Central Asia." *Journal of Islamic Studies*, 30/3 (2019), pp. 367–405.

Sartori, Paolo. "'On the Importance of Having a Method': Reading Atheistic Documents on Islamic Revival in 1950s Central Asia." In *From the Khan's Oven: Studies on the History of Central Asian Religions in Honor of Devin DeWeese*, ed. Eren Tasar, Allen J. Frank and Jeff Eden. Leiden: Brill, 2021, pp. 284–322.

Sartori, Paolo. *Visions of Justice: Sharīʿa and Cultural Change in Russian Central Asia.* Leiden: Brill, 2016.

Sartori, Paolo, and Bakhtiyar Babajanov. "Being Soviet, Muslim, Modernist, and Fundamentalist in 1950s Central Asia." *Journal of the Economic and Social History of the Orient*, 62/1 (2019), pp. 108–163.

Snesarev, G.P. *Khorezmskie legendy kak istochnik po istorii religioznykh kul'tov Srednei Azii.* Moscow: Nauka, 1983.

Snesarev, G.P. *Relikty domusul'manskikh verovanii i obriadov u uzbekov Khorezma.* Moscow: Nauka, 1969.

Tadzhikova, Z. "Pesni pokhoronnogo obriada tadzhikov (po materialam zeravshanskikh èkspeditsii)." In *Problemy muzykal'nogo fol'klora narodov SSSR: Stat'i i materialy.* Moscow: Muzyka, 1973, pp. 95–100.

Tasar, Eren. "Institutions: A Lens on Soviet Islam" [Book Discussion on *Soviet and Muslim: The Institutionalization of Islam in Central Asia*, by Eren Tasar]. *Central Asian Affairs*, 7 (2020), pp. 370–375.

Tasar, Eren. "Islamically Informed Soviet Patriotism in Postwar Kyrgyzstan." *Cahiers du Monde Russe*, 52/2–3 (2011), pp. 387–404.

Tasar, Eren. "Mantra: A Review Essay on Islam in Soviet Central Asia." *Journal of the Economic and Social History of the Orient*, 63 (2020), pp. 389–433.

Tasar, Eren. *Soviet and Muslim: The Institutionalization of Islam in Central Asia, 1943–1991.* Oxford: Oxford University Press, 2017.

Tasar, Eren. "Sufism on the Soviet Stage: Holy People and Places in Central Asia's Socio-Political Landscape After World War II." In *Sufism in Central Asia: New Perspectives on Sufi Traditions, 15th–21st Centuries*, ed. Devin DeWeese and Jo-Ann Gross. Leiden: Brill, 2018, pp. 256–283.

Yo'ldoshkho'jaev, Haydarkhon, and Irodakhon Qayumova. *O'zbekiston ulamolari.* Tashkent: Movarrounnahr nashriyoti, 2015.

Index

Note: f indicates figure; n indicates note; t indicates table

Printed in the United States
by Baker & Taylor Publisher Services